Washington Criminal Procedure 2018

MW00896622

CHAPTER 10.01 RCW GENERAL PROVISIONS

10.01.030 Pleadings—Forms abolished.

Table of Contents

CHAPTER 10.58 RCW EVIDENCE

CHAPTER 10.61 RCW VERDICTS

CHAPTER 10.64 RCW JUDGMENTS AND SENTENCES

CHAPTER 10.77 RCW CRIMINALLY INSANE—PROCEDURES

CHAPTER 10.79 RCW SEARCHES AND SEIZURES

CHAPTER 10.95 RCW CAPITAL PUNISHMENT—AGGRAVATED FIRST DEGREE MURDER

CHAPTER 10.96 RCW CRIMINAL PROCESS RECORDS

CHAPTER 10.97 RCW WASHINGTON STATE CRIMINAL RECORDS PRIVACY ACT

CHAPTER 10.98 RCW CRIMINAL JUSTICE INFORMATION ACT

CHAPTER 10.99 RCW DOMESTIC VIOLENCE—OFFICIAL RESPONSE

CHAPTER 10.101 RCW INDIGENT DEFENSE SERVICES

Chapter 10.01 RCW GENERAL PROVISIONS

10.01.030
Pleadings—Forms abolished.

All the forms of pleading in criminal actions heretofore existing, are abolished; and hereafter, the forms of pleading, and the rules by which the sufficiency of pleadings is to be determined, are those prescribed herein.

[Code 1881 § 1002; **1873 p 224 § 185; 1869 p 240 § 180;** RRS § 2022.]

10.01.040
Statutes—Repeal or amendment—Saving clause presumed.

No offense committed and no penalty or forfeiture incurred previous to the time when any statutory provision shall be repealed, whether such repeal be express or implied, shall be affected by such repeal, unless a contrary intention is expressly declared in the repealing act, and no prosecution for any offense, or for the recovery of any penalty or forfeiture, pending at the time any statutory provision shall be repealed, whether such repeal be express or implied, shall be affected by such repeal, but the same shall proceed in all respects, as if such provision had not been repealed, unless a contrary intention is expressly declared in the repealing act. Whenever any criminal or penal statute shall be amended or repealed, all offenses committed or penalties or forfeitures incurred while it was in force shall be punished or enforced as if it were in force, notwithstanding such amendment or repeal, unless a contrary intention is expressly declared in the amendatory or repealing act, and every such amendatory or repealing statute shall be so construed as to save all criminal and penal proceedings, and proceedings to recover forfeitures, pending at the time of its enactment, unless a contrary intention is expressly declared therein.

[**1901 ex.s. c 6 § 1;** RRS § 2006.]

10.01.050

Convictions—Necessary before punishment.

No person charged with any offense against the law shall be punished for such offense, unless he or she shall have been duly and legally convicted thereof in a court having competent jurisdiction of the case and of the person.

[**2010 c 8 § 1001;** Code 1881 § 770; **1854 p 76 § 6;** RRS § 2118.]

10.01.060

Conviction—Requisites—Waiver of jury trial.

No person informed against or indicted for a crime shall be convicted thereof, unless by admitting the truth of the charge in his or her plea, by confession in open court, or by the verdict of a jury, accepted and recorded by the court: PROVIDED HOWEVER, That except in capital cases, where the person informed against or indicted for a crime is represented by counsel, such person may, with the assent of the court, waive trial by jury and submit to trial by the court.

[**2010 c 8 § 1002; 1951 c 52 § 1; 1909 c 249 § 57; 1891 c 28 § 91;** Code 1881 § 767; **1873 p 180 § 3; 1869 p 198 § 3; 1859 p 105 § 3; 1854 p 76 § 3;**RRS § 2309.]

NOTES:

Self-incriminating testimony: State Constitution Art. 1 § 9.

10.01.070

Corporations—Amenable to criminal process—How.

Whenever an indictment or information shall be filed in any superior court against a corporation charging it with the commission of a crime, a summons shall be issued by the clerk of such court, signed by one of the judges thereof, commanding the sheriff forthwith to notify the accused thereof, and commanding it to appear before such court at such time as shall be specified in said summons. Such summons and a copy of the indictment or information shall be at once delivered by such clerk to said sheriff and by the sheriff forthwith served and returned in the manner provided for service of summons upon such corporation in a civil action. Whenever a complaint against a corporation, charging it with the commission of a crime, shall be made before any district or municipal judge, a like summons, signed by such judge, shall be issued, which, together with a copy of said complaint, shall be delivered to the sheriff at once and by the sheriff forthwith served as herein provided.

[**1987 c 202 § 147; 1911 c 29 § 1;** RRS § 2011-1.]

NOTES:

> **Intent—1987 c 202:** See note following RCW **2.04.190**.

10.01.090

Corporations—Judgment against.

If the corporation shall be found guilty and a fine imposed, it shall be entered and docketed by the clerk, or district or municipal court as a judgment against the corporation, and it shall be of the same force and effect and be enforced against such corporation in the same manner as a judgment in a civil action.

[**1987 c 202 § 148; 1911 c 29 § 3;** RRS § 2011-3.]

NOTES:

> **Intent—1987 c 202:** See note following RCW **2.04.190**.

10.01.100

Corporations—Penalties—Fines in lieu of other punishments.

Every corporation guilty of a violation of any law of the state of Washington, where the prescribed penalty is, for any reason, incapable of execution or enforcement against such corporation, shall be punished by a fine of not more than ten thousand dollars, if such offense is a felony; or, by a fine of not more than one thousand dollars if such offense is a gross misdemeanor; or, by a fine of not more than five hundred dollars if such offense is a misdemeanor.

[**1925 ex.s. c 101 § 1;** RRS § 2011-4.]

10.01.120

Pardons—Reprieves—Commutations.

Whenever a prisoner has been sentenced to death, the governor shall have power to commute such sentence to imprisonment for life at hard labor; and in all cases in which the governor is authorized to grant pardons or commute sentence of death, he or she may, upon the petition of the person convicted, commute a sentence or grant a pardon, upon such conditions, and with such restrictions, and under such limitations as he or she may think proper; and he or she may issue his or her warrant to all proper officers to carry into effect such pardon or commutation, which warrant shall be obeyed and executed, instead of the sentence, if any, which was originally given. The governor may also, on good cause shown, grant respites or reprieves from time to time as he or she may think proper.

[**2010 c 8 § 1003;** Code 1881 § 1136; **1854 p 128 § 174;** RRS § 2223.]

NOTES:

Governor's powers: State Constitution Art. 3 §§ 9, 11.

Record of pardons, etc., governor to keep: RCW **43.06.020**.

10.01.130
Witnesses' fees.

No fees shall be allowed to witnesses in criminal causes unless they shall have reported their attendance at the close of each day's session to the clerk in attendance thereon.

[**1895 c 10 § 1;** RRS § 498, part. FORMER PART OF SECTION: **1895 c 10 § 2;** RRS § 498, part, now codified as RCW **10.01.140**.]

NOTES:

Rules of court: Cf. CrR 6.12.

Witness fees: Chapters **2.40**, **12.16** RCW.

10.01.140
Mileage allowance—Jurors—Witnesses.

No allowance of mileage shall be made to a juror or witness who has not verified his or her claim of mileage under oath before the clerk of the court on which he or she is in attendance.

[**2010 c 8 § 1004; 1895 c 10 § 2;** RRS § 498, part. Formerly RCW **10.01.130**, part.]

10.01.150

Charges arising from official acts of state officers or employees— Defense by attorney general.

Whenever a state officer or employee is charged with a criminal offense arising out of the performance of an official act which was fully in conformity with established written rules, policies, and guidelines of the state or state agency, the employing agency may request the attorney general to defend the officer or employee. If the agency finds, and the attorney general concurs, that the officer's or employee's conduct was fully in accordance with established written rules, policies, and guidelines of the state or a state agency and the act performed was within the scope of employment, then the request shall be granted and the costs of defense shall be paid by the requesting agency: PROVIDED, HOWEVER, If the agency head is the person charged, then approval must be obtained from both the attorney general and the state auditor. If the court finds that the officer or employee was performing an official act, or was within the scope of employment, and that his or her actions were in conformity with the established rules, regulations, policies, and guidelines of the state and the state agency, the cost of any monetary fine assessed shall be paid from the liability account.

[**2010 c 8 § 1005; 1999 c 163 § 6; 1975 1st ex.s. c 144 § 1.**]
NOTES:

> **Effective date—1999 c 163:** See note following RCW **4.92.130**.

10.01.160

Costs—What constitutes—Payment by defendant—Procedure— Remission—Medical or mental health treatment or services.

*** CHANGE IN 2018 *** (SEE **1783-S2.SL**) ***

(1) The court may require a defendant to pay costs. Costs may be imposed only upon a convicted defendant, except for costs imposed upon a defendant's entry into a deferred prosecution program, costs imposed upon a defendant for pretrial supervision, or costs imposed upon a defendant for preparing and serving a warrant for failure to appear.

(2) Costs shall be limited to expenses specially incurred by the state in prosecuting the defendant or in administering the deferred prosecution program under chapter **10.05** RCW or pretrial supervision. They cannot include expenses inherent in providing a constitutionally guaranteed jury trial or expenditures in connection with the maintenance and operation of government agencies that must be made by the public irrespective of specific violations of law. Expenses incurred for serving of warrants for failure to appear and jury fees under RCW**10.46.190** may be included in costs the court may require a defendant to pay. Costs for administering a deferred prosecution may not exceed two hundred fifty dollars. Costs for administering a pretrial supervision other than a pretrial electronic alcohol monitoring program, drug monitoring program, or 24/7 sobriety program may not exceed one hundred fifty dollars. Costs for preparing and serving a warrant for failure to appear may not exceed one hundred dollars. Costs of incarceration imposed on a defendant convicted of a misdemeanor or a gross misdemeanor may not exceed the actual cost of incarceration. In no case may the court require the offender to pay more than one hundred dollars per day for the cost of incarceration. Payment of other court-ordered financial obligations, including all legal financial obligations and costs of supervision take precedence over the payment of the cost of incarceration ordered by the court. All funds received from defendants for the cost of incarceration in the county or city jail must be remitted for criminal justice purposes to the county or city that is responsible for the defendant's jail costs. Costs imposed constitute a judgment against a defendant and survive a dismissal of the underlying action against the defendant. However, if the defendant is acquitted on the underlying action, the costs for preparing and serving a warrant for failure to appear do not survive the acquittal, and the judgment that such costs would otherwise constitute shall be vacated.

(3) The court shall not order a defendant to pay costs unless the defendant is or will be able to pay them. In determining the amount and method of payment of costs, the court shall take account of the financial resources of the defendant and the nature of the burden that payment of costs will impose.

(4) A defendant who has been ordered to pay costs and who is not in contumacious default in the payment thereof may at any time petition the sentencing court for remission of the payment of costs or of any unpaid portion thereof. If it appears to the satisfaction of the court that payment of the amount due will impose manifest hardship on the defendant or the defendant's immediate family, the court may remit all or part of the amount due in costs, or modify the method of payment under RCW **10.01.170**.

(5) Except for direct costs relating to evaluating and reporting to the court, prosecutor, or defense counsel regarding a defendant's competency to stand trial as provided in RCW **10.77.060**, this section shall not apply to costs related to medical or mental health treatment or services a defendant receives while in custody of the secretary of the department of social and health services or other governmental units. This section shall not prevent the secretary of the department of social and health services or other governmental units from imposing liability and seeking reimbursement from a defendant committed to an appropriate facility as provided in RCW **10.77.084** while criminal proceedings are stayed. This section shall also not prevent governmental units from imposing liability on defendants for costs related to providing medical or mental health treatment while the defendant is in the governmental unit's custody. Medical or mental health treatment and services a defendant receives at a state hospital or other facility are not a cost of prosecution and shall be recoverable under RCW **10.77.250** and**70.48.130**, chapter **43.20B** RCW, and any other applicable statute.

[**2015 3rd sp.s. c 35 § 1; 2010 c 54 § 1; 2008 c 318 § 2; 2007 c 367 § 3; 2005 c 263 § 2; 1995 c 221 § 1; 1994 c 192 § 1; 1991 c 247 § 4; 1987 c 363 § 1; 1985 c 389 § 1;** 1975-'76 2nd ex.s. c 96 § 1.]

NOTES:

Findings—Intent—2008 c 318: "The legislature finds that because of the decision in Utter v. DSHS, 165 P.3d 399 (Wash. 2007), there is unintended ambiguity about the authority of the secretary of the department of social and health services under the criminal procedure act to seek reimbursement from defendants under RCW **10.77.250** who are committed for competency evaluation and mental health treatment under RCW **10.77.060** and **10.77.084**, and the general provision prohibiting a criminal defendant from being charged for prosecution related costs prior to conviction provided in RCW **10.01.160**. Mental health evaluation and treatment, and other medical treatment relate entirely to the medically necessary care that defendants receive at state hospitals and other facilities. The legislature intended for treatment costs to be the responsibility of the defendant's insurers and ultimately the defendant based on their ability to pay, and it is permissible under chapters **10.77**, 70.48, and **43.20B** RCW for the state and other governmental units to assess financial liability on defendants who become patients and receive medical and mental health care. The legislature further finds that it intended that a court order staying criminal proceedings under RCW **10.77.084**, and committing a defendant to the custody of the secretary of the department of social and health services for placement in an appropriate facility involve costs payable by the defendant, because the commitment primarily and directly benefits the defendant through treatment of their medical and mental health conditions. The legislature did not intend for medical and mental health services provided to a defendant in the custody of a governmental unit, and the associated costs, to be costs related to the prosecution of the defendant. Thus, if a court orders a stay of the criminal proceeding under RCW **10.77.084** and orders commitment to the custody of the secretary, or if at any time a defendant receives other medical care while in custody of a governmental unit, but prior to conviction, the costs associated with such care shall be the responsibility of the defendant and the defendant's insurers as provided in chapters **10.77**, 70.48, and **43.20B** RCW. The intent of the legislature is to clarify this reimbursement requirement, and the purpose of this act is to make retroactive, remedial, curative, and technical amendments in order to resolve any ambiguity about the legislature's intent in enacting these chapters." [**2008 c 318 § 1.**]

Effective date—2008 c 318: "This act is necessary for the immediate preservation of the public peace, health, or safety, or support of the state government and its existing public institutions, and takes effect immediately [April 1, 2008]." [**2008 c 318 § 3.**]

Commitment for failure to pay fine and costs: RCW **10.70.010**, **10.82.030**.

Defendant liable for costs: RCW **10.64.015**.

Fine and costs—Collection and disposition: Chapter **10.82** RCW.

10.01.170
Fine or costs—Payment within specified time or installments.

*** CHANGE IN 2018 *** (SEE **1783-S2.SL**) ***

When a defendant is sentenced to pay a fine or costs, the court may grant permission for payment to be made within a specified period of time or in specified installments. If no such permission is included in the sentence the fine or costs shall be payable forthwith.

[1975-'76 2nd ex.s. c 96 § 2.]

NOTES:

Payment of fine and costs in installments: RCW **9.92.070**.

10.01.180
Fine or costs—Default in payment—Contempt of court—Enforcement, collection procedures.

*** CHANGE IN 2018 *** (SEE **1783-S2.SL**) ***

(1) A defendant sentenced to pay a fine or costs who defaults in the payment thereof or of any installment is in contempt of court as provided in chapter **7.21** RCW. The court may issue a warrant of arrest for his or her appearance.

(2) When a fine or assessment of costs is imposed on a corporation or unincorporated association, it is the duty of the person authorized to make disbursement from the assets of the corporation or association to pay the fine or costs from those assets, and his or her failure to do so may be held to be contempt.

(3) If a term of imprisonment for contempt for nonpayment of a fine or costs is ordered, the term of imprisonment shall be set forth in the commitment order, and shall not exceed one day for each twenty-five dollars of the fine or costs, thirty days if the fine or assessment of costs was imposed upon conviction of a violation or misdemeanor, or one year in any other case, whichever is the shorter period. A person committed for nonpayment of a fine or costs shall be given credit toward payment for each day of imprisonment at the rate specified in the commitment order.

(4) If it appears to the satisfaction of the court that the default in the payment of a fine or costs is not contempt, the court may enter an order allowing the defendant additional time for payment, reducing the amount thereof or of each installment or revoking the fine or costs or the unpaid portion thereof in whole or in part.

(5) A default in the payment of a fine or costs or any installment thereof may be collected by any means authorized by law for the enforcement of a judgment. The levy of execution for the collection of a fine or costs shall not discharge a defendant committed to imprisonment for contempt until the amount of the fine or costs has actually been collected.

[**2010 c 8 § 1006; 1989 c 373 § 13;** 1975-'76 2nd ex.s. c 96 § 3.]

NOTES:

Fine and costs—Collection procedure, commitment for failure to pay, execution against defendant's property: Chapter **10.82** RCW.

10.01.190

Prosecutorial powers of attorney general.

In any criminal proceeding instituted or conducted by the attorney general, the attorney general and assistants are deemed to be prosecuting attorneys and have all prosecutorial powers vested in prosecuting attorneys of the state of Washington by statute or court rule.

[**1981 c 335 § 4.**]

NOTES:

> **Purpose—1981 c 335:** See RCW **43.10.230**.

10.01.200

Registration of sex offenders and kidnapping offenders—Notice to defendants.

The court shall provide written notification to any defendant charged with a sex offense or kidnapping offense of the registration requirements of RCW **9A.44.130**. Such notice shall be included on any guilty plea forms and judgment and sentence forms provided to the defendant.

[**1997 c 113 § 5; 1990 c 3 § 404.**]

NOTES:

> **Reviser's note:** The definitions in RCW **9A.44.128** apply to this section.
>
> **Findings—1997 c 113:** See note following RCW **4.24.550**.
>
> **Index, part headings not law—Severability—Effective dates—Application—**

1990 c 3: See RCW **18.155.900** through **18.155.902**.

Sex offense and kidnapping offense defined: RCW **9A.44.128**.

10.01.210

Offender notification and warning.

Any and all law enforcement agencies and personnel, criminal justice attorneys, sentencing judges, and state and local correctional facilities and personnel may, but are not required to, give any and all offenders either written or oral notice, or both, of the sanctions imposed and criminal justice changes regarding armed offenders, including but not limited to the subjects of:

(1) Felony crimes involving any deadly weapon special verdict under *RCW **9.94A.602**;

(2) Any and all deadly weapon enhancements under RCW **9.94A.533** (3) or (4), or both, as well as any federal firearm, ammunition, or other deadly weapon enhancements;

(3) Any and all felony crimes requiring the possession, display, or use of any deadly weapon as well as the many increased penalties for these crimes including the creation of theft of a firearm and possessing a stolen firearm;

(4) New prosecuting standards established for filing charges for all crimes involving any deadly weapons;

(5) Removal of good time for any and all deadly weapon enhancements; and

(6) Providing the death penalty for those who commit first degree murder: (a) To join, maintain, or advance membership in an identifiable group; (b) as part of a drive-by shooting; or (c) to avoid prosecution as a persistent offender as defined in RCW **9.94A.030**.

[**2002 c 290 § 23;** 1995 c 129 § 18 (Initiative Measure No. 159).]

NOTES:

*Reviser's note: RCW **9.94A.602** was recodified as RCW **9.94A.825** pursuant to **2009 c 28 § 41.**

Effective date—2002 c 290 §§ 7-11 and 14-23: See note following RCW **9.94A.515**.

Intent—2002 c 290: See note following RCW **9.94A.517**.

Findings and intent—Short title—Severability—Captions not law—1995 c 129: See notes following RCW **9.94A.510**.

10.01.220

City attorney, county prosecutor, or other prosecuting authority—Filing a criminal charge—Contribution, donation, payment.

A city attorney, county prosecutor, or other prosecuting authority may not dismiss, amend, or agree not to file a criminal charge in exchange for a contribution, donation, or payment to any person, corporation, or organization. This does not prohibit:

(1) Contribution, donation, or payment to any specific fund authorized by state statute;

(2) The collection of costs associated with actual supervision, treatment, or collection of restitution under agreements to defer or divert; or

(3) Dismissal following payment that is authorized by any other statute.

[**2007 c 367 § 1.**]

10.01.230
Victim impact panel registry—Panel minimum standards.

(1) The Washington traffic safety commission may develop and maintain a registry of qualified victim impact panels. When imposing a requirement that an offender attend a victim impact panel under RCW **46.61.5152**, the court may refer the offender to a victim impact panel that is listed in the registry. The Washington traffic safety commission may consult with victim impact panel organizations to develop and maintain a registry.

(2) To be listed on the registry, the victim impact panel must meet the following minimum standards:

(a) The victim impact panel must address the effects of driving while impaired on individuals and families and address alternatives to drinking and driving and drug use and driving;

(b) The victim impact panel shall have at least two different speakers, one of whom is a victim survivor of an impaired driving crash, to present their stories in person. A victim survivor may be the panel facilitator. The victim impact panel should be a minimum of sixty minutes of presentation, not including registration and administration time;

(c) The victim impact panel shall have policies and procedures to recruit, screen, train, and provide feedback and ongoing support to the panelists. The panel shall take reasonable steps to verify the authenticity of each panelist's story;

(d) Pursuant to (b) of this subsection, the victim impact panel shall use in-person speakers for each presentation for a minimum of sixty minutes of presentation. The victim impact panel may supplement the in-person presentations with prerecorded videos, but in no case shall the videos shown exceed fifteen minutes of presentation;

(e) The victim impact panel shall charge a reasonable fee to all persons required to attend, unless otherwise ordered by the court;

(f) The victim impact panel shall have a policy to prohibit admittance of anyone under the influence of alcohol or drugs, or anyone whose actions or behavior are otherwise inappropriate. The victim impact panel may institute additional admission requirements;

(g) The victim impact panel shall maintain attendance records for at least five years;

(h) The victim impact panel shall make reasonable efforts to use a facility that meets standards established by the Americans with disabilities act;

(i) The victim impact panel may provide referral information to other community services; and

(j) The victim impact panel shall have a designated facilitator who is responsible for the compliance with these minimum standards and who is responsible for maintaining appropriate records and communication with the referring courts and probationary departments regarding attendance or nonattendance.

[**2016 c 203 § 10; 2011 c 293 § 15.**]

Chapter 10.04 RCW DISTRICT COURT PROCEDURE—GENERALLY

NOTES:

Rules of court: See Criminal Rules for Courts of Limited Jurisdiction (CrRLJ).

10.04.020
Arrest—Offense committed in view of district judge.

When any offense is committed in view of any district judge, the judge may, by verbal direction to any deputy, or if no deputy is present, to any citizen, cause such deputy or citizen to arrest such offender, and keep such offender in custody for the space of one hour, unless such offender shall sooner be taken from such custody by virtue of a warrant issued on complaint on oath. But such person so arrested, shall not be confined in jail, nor put upon any trial, until arrested by virtue of such warrant.

[**1987 c 202 § 149;** Code 1881 § 1888; Code 1881 § 1889, part; **1873 p 382 § 186; 1854 p 260 § 173;** RRS § 1926, part.]

NOTES:

      Intent—1987 c 202: See note following RCW **2.04.190**.

10.04.040

Cash bail in lieu of recognizance.

    District courts or committing magistrates may accept money as bail from persons charged with bailable offenses, and for the appearance of witnesses in all cases provided by law for the recognizance of witnesses. The amount of such bail or recognizance in each case shall be determined by the court in its discretion, and may from time to time be increased or decreased as circumstances may justify. The money to be received and accounted for in the same manner as provided by law for the superior courts.

[**1987 c 202 § 150; 1919 c 76 § 1;** RRS § 1957 1/2.]

NOTES:

      Intent—1987 c 202: See note following RCW **2.04.190**.

Excessive bail or fines, cruel punishment prohibited: State Constitution Art. 1 § 14.

10.04.050

Jury—If demanded.

    In all trials for offenses within the jurisdiction of a district judge, the defendant or the state may demand a jury, which shall consist of six, or a less number, agreed upon by the state and accused, to be impaneled and sworn as in civil cases; or the trial may be by the judge. When the complaint is for a crime or misdemeanor in the exclusive jurisdiction of the superior court, the justice hears the case as a committing magistrate, and no jury shall be allowed.

[**1987 c 202 § 151; 1891 c 11 § 1;** Code 1881 § 1890; **1875 p 51 § 2; 1873 p 382 § 188;** 1854 p 260 § 174, part; RRS § 1927.]

NOTES:

　　　　Intent—1987 c 202: See note following RCW **2.04.190**.

Charging juries: State Constitution Art. 4 § 16.

Convicted persons liable for costs and jury fees: RCW **10.46.190**.

Right to trial by jury: State Constitution Art. 1 § 21.

10.04.070

Plea of guilty.

The defendant may plead guilty to any offense charged.

[Code 1881 § 1892; **1873 p 383 § 190;** 1854 p 260 § 174, part; RRS § 1929.]

10.04.100

Verdict of guilty—Proceedings upon.

The judge, if the prisoner is found guilty, shall assess the prisoner's punishment; or if, in the judge's opinion, the punishment the judge is authorized to assess is not adequate to the offense, he or she may so find, and in such case the judge shall order such defendant to enter recognizance to appear in the superior court of the county, and shall also recognize the witnesses, and proceed as in proceedings by a committing magistrate.

[**1987 c 202 § 152; 1891 c 11 § 2;** Code 1881 § 1891; **1873 p 382 § 189;** 1854 p 260 § 174; RRS § 1928.]

NOTES:

　　　　Intent—1987 c 202: See note following RCW **2.04.190**.

10.04.101

Assessment of punishment by courts organized under 1961 justice of the peace act.

See RCW **3.66.065**.

10.04.110

Judgment—Entry—Execution—Remittance of district court fines, etc.

In all cases of conviction, unless otherwise provided in this chapter, the judge shall enter judgment for the fine and costs against the defendant, and may commit him or her to jail until the amount of such fine and costs owing are paid, or the payment thereof be secured as provided by RCW **10.04.120**. The amount of such fine and costs owing shall be computed as provided for superior court cases in RCW**10.82.030** and **10.82.040**. Further proceedings therein shall be had as in like cases in the superior court: PROVIDED, That all fees, fines, forfeitures and penalties collected or assessed by a district court because of the violation of a state law shall be remitted as provided in chapter**3.62** RCW as now exists or is later amended.

[**2010 c 8 § 1007; 1987 c 202 § 153; 1969 ex.s. c 199 § 10; 1967 c 200 § 6; 1891 c 11 § 6;** Code 1881 § 1896; **1873 p 383 § 194; 1854 p 261 § 176;**RRS § 1933.]

NOTES:

Intent—**1987 c 202:** See note following RCW **2.04.190**.

Convicted persons liable for jury fees: RCW **10.46.190**.

10.04.120

Stay of execution.

Every defendant may stay the execution for the fine and costs for thirty days, by procuring sufficient sureties, to be approved by the district judge, to enter into recognizance before the district judge for the payment of the fine and costs; the entry of such recognizance shall be made on the docket of the district judge, and signed by the sureties, and shall have the same effect as a judgment, and if the same be not paid in thirty days, the district judge shall proceed as in like cases in the superior court.

[**1987 c 202 § 154;** Code 1881 § 1897; **1873 p 383 § 195; 1854 p 261 § 176;** RRS §
1934.]
NOTES:

> Intent—**1987 c 202:** See note following RCW **2.04.190**.

10.04.800
Proposed forms for criminal actions.

The district and municipal court judges' association may propose to the supreme
court suggested forms for criminal actions for inclusion in the justice court criminal rules.

[**1994 c 32 § 6; 1987 c 202 § 155.**]
NOTES:
Rules of court: CrRLJ 2.1, 4.2.

> Intent—**1987 c 202:** See note following RCW **2.04.190**.

Chapter 10.05 RCW DEFERRED

PROSECUTION—COURTS OF LIMITED

JURISDICTION

10.05.010
Petition—Eligibility.

(1) In a court of limited jurisdiction a person charged with a misdemeanor or gross
misdemeanor may petition the court to be considered for a deferred prosecution
program. The petition shall be filed with the court at least seven days before the date
set for trial but, upon a written motion and affidavit establishing good cause for the delay

and failure to comply with this section, the court may waive this requirement subject to the defendant's reimbursement to the court of the witness fees and expenses due for subpoenaed witnesses who have appeared on the date set for trial.

(2) A person charged with a traffic infraction, misdemeanor, or gross misdemeanor under Title **46** RCW shall not be eligible for a deferred prosecution program unless the court makes specific findings pursuant to RCW **10.05.020** or *section 18 of this act. Such person shall not be eligible for a deferred prosecution program more than once; and cannot receive a deferred prosecution under both RCW **10.05.020** and *section 18 of this act. Separate offenses committed more than seven days apart may not be consolidated in a single program.

(3) A person charged with a misdemeanor or a gross misdemeanor under chapter **9A.42** RCW shall not be eligible for a deferred prosecution program unless the court makes specific findings pursuant to RCW **10.05.020**. Such person shall not be eligible for a deferred prosecution program more than once.

[**2008 c 282 § 15; 2002 c 219 § 6; 1998 c 208 § 1; 1985 c 352 § 4; 1982 1st ex.s. c 47 § 26; 1975 1st ex.s. c 244 § 1.**]

NOTES:

*Reviser's note: Section 18 of this act was vetoed by the governor.

Intent—Finding—2002 c 219: See note following RCW **9A.42.037**.

Effective date—1998 c 208: "This act takes effect January 1, 1999." [**1998 c 208 § 7.**]

Legislative finding—1985 c 352: "The legislature finds that the deferred prosecution program is an alternative to punishment for persons who will benefit from a treatment program if the treatment program is provided under circumstances that do not unreasonably endanger public safety or the traditional goals of the criminal justice system. This alternative to punishment is dependent for success upon appropriate treatment and the willingness and ability of the person receiving treatment to cooperate fully with the treatment program. The legislature finds that some persons have sought deferred prosecution but have been unable or unwilling to cooperate with treatment requirements and escaped punishment because of the difficulties in resuming prosecution after significant delay due to the absence of witnesses at a later date and the congestion in courts at a later date. The legislature further finds that the deferred prosecution statutes require clarification. The purpose of sections 4 through 19 of this act is to provide specific standards and procedures for judges and prosecutors to use in carrying out the original intent of the deferred prosecution statutes." [**1985 c 352 § 3.**]

   Severability—1985 c 352: "If any provision of this act or its application to any person or circumstance is held invalid, the remainder of the act or the application of the provision to other persons or circumstances is not affected." [**1985 c 352 § 22.**]

   Severability—1982 1st ex.s. c 47: See note following RCW **9.41.190**.

10.05.015
Statement of availability.

   At the time of arraignment a person charged with a violation of RCW **46.61.502** or **46.61.504** may be given a statement by the court that explains the availability, operation, and effects of the deferred prosecution program.
[**1985 c 352 § 5.**]
NOTES:
   Legislative finding—Severability—1985 c 352: See notes following RCW **10.05.010**.

10.05.020
Requirements of petition—Rights of petitioner—Court findings.
   (1) Except as provided in subsection (2) of this section, the petitioner shall allege under oath in the petition that the wrongful conduct charged is the result of or caused by substance use disorders or mental problems for which the person is in need of treatment and unless treated the probability of future recurrence is great, along with a statement that the person agrees to pay the cost of a diagnosis and treatment of the alleged problem or problems if financially able to do so. The petition shall also contain a case history and written assessment prepared by an approved substance use disorder treatment program as designated in chapter **71.24** RCW if the petition alleges a

substance use disorder or by an approved mental health center if the petition alleges a mental problem.

(2) In the case of a petitioner charged with a misdemeanor or gross misdemeanor under chapter **9A.42** RCW, the petitioner shall allege under oath in the petition that the petitioner is the natural or adoptive parent of the alleged victim; that the wrongful conduct charged is the result of parenting problems for which the petitioner is in need of services; that the petitioner is in need of child welfare services under chapter**74.13** RCW to improve his or her parenting skills in order to better provide his or her child or children with the basic necessities of life; that the petitioner wants to correct his or her conduct to reduce the likelihood of harm to his or her minor children; that in the absence of child welfare services the petitioner may be unable to reduce the likelihood of harm to his or her minor children; and that the petitioner has cooperated with the department of social and health services to develop a plan to receive appropriate child welfare services; along with a statement that the person agrees to pay the cost of the services if he or she is financially able to do so. The petition shall also contain a case history and a written service plan from the department of social and health services.

(3) Before entry of an order deferring prosecution, a petitioner shall be advised of his or her rights as an accused and execute, as a condition of receiving treatment, a statement that contains: (a) An acknowledgment of his or her rights; (b) an acknowledgment and waiver of the right to testify, the right to a speedy trial, the right to call witnesses to testify, the right to present evidence in his or her defense, and the right to a jury trial; (c) a stipulation to the admissibility and sufficiency of the facts contained in the written police report; and (d) an acknowledgment that the statement will be entered and used to support a finding of guilty if the court finds cause to revoke the order granting deferred prosecution. The petitioner shall also be advised that he or she may, if he or she proceeds to trial and is found guilty, be allowed to seek suspension of some or all of the fines and incarceration that may be ordered upon the condition that he or she seek treatment and, further, that he or she may seek treatment from public and private agencies at any time without regard to whether or not he or she is found guilty of

the offense charged. He or she shall also be advised that the court will not accept a petition for deferred prosecution from a person who: (i) Sincerely believes that he or she is innocent of the charges; (ii) sincerely believes that he or she does not, in fact, suffer from alcoholism, drug addiction, or mental problems; or (iii) in the case of a petitioner charged under chapter **9A.42** RCW, sincerely believes that he or she does not need child welfare services.

(4) Before entering an order deferring prosecution, the court shall make specific findings that: (a) The petitioner has stipulated to the admissibility and sufficiency of the facts as contained in the written police report; (b) the petitioner has acknowledged the admissibility of the stipulated facts in any criminal hearing on the underlying offense or offenses held subsequent to revocation of the order granting deferred prosecution; (c) the petitioner has acknowledged and waived the right to testify, the right to a speedy trial, the right to call witnesses to testify, the right to present evidence in his or her defense, and the right to a jury trial; and (d) the petitioner's statements were made knowingly and voluntarily. Such findings shall be included in the order granting deferred prosecution.

[**2016 sp.s. c 29 § 525; 2010 c 269 § 9; 2008 c 282 § 16; 2002 c 219 § 7; 1996 c 24 § 1; 1985 c 352 § 6; 1975 1st ex.s. c 244 § 2.**]

NOTES:

> **Effective dates—2016 sp.s. c 29:** See note following RCW **71.05.760**.

> **Short title—Right of action—2016 sp.s. c 29:** See notes following RCW **71.05.010**.

> **Effective date—2010 c 269:** See note following RCW **46.20.385**.

> **Intent—Finding—2002 c 219:** See note following RCW **9A.42.037**.

> **Legislative finding—Severability—1985 c 352:** See notes following RCW **10.05.010**.

Criminal history and driving record: RCW **46.61.513**.

10.05.030
Arraignment continued—Treatment referral.

The arraigning judge upon consideration of the petition and with the concurrence of the prosecuting attorney may continue the arraignment and refer such person for a diagnostic investigation and evaluation to an approved substance use disorder treatment program as designated in chapter **71.24** RCW, if the petition alleges a substance use disorder, to an approved mental health center, if the petition alleges a mental problem, or the department of social and health services if the petition is brought under RCW **10.05.020**(2).

[**2016 sp.s. c 29 § 526; 2002 c 219 § 8; 1999 c 143 § 42; 1975 1st ex.s. c 244 § 3.**]
NOTES:

Reviser's note: As to the constitutionality of the language "and with the concurrence of the prosecuting attorney," see State ex rel. Schillberg v. Cascade Dist. Court, 94 Wn.2d 772, 621 P.2d 115 (1980).

Effective dates—2016 sp.s. c 29: See note following RCW **71.05.760**.

Short title—Right of action—2016 sp.s. c 29: See notes following RCW **71.05.010**.

Intent—Finding—2002 c 219: See note following RCW **9A.42.037**.

10.05.040
Investigation and examination.

*** CHANGE IN 2018 *** (SEE **1388-S.SL**) ***

The *facility to which such person is referred, or the department of social and health services if the petition is brought under RCW**10.05.020**(2), shall conduct an investigation and examination to determine:

(1) Whether the person suffers from the problem described;

(2) Whether the problem is such that if not treated, or if no child welfare services are provided, there is a probability that similar misconduct will occur in the future;

(3) Whether extensive and long term treatment is required;

(4) Whether effective treatment or child welfare services for the person's problem are available; and

(5) Whether the person is amenable to treatment or willing to cooperate with child welfare services.

[**2002 c 219 § 9; 1985 c 352 § 7; 1975 1st ex.s. c 244 § 4.**]

NOTES:

 *Reviser's note: Chapter **70.96A** RCW was amended by 1990 c 151, changing "treatment facility" to "treatment program." Chapter**70.96A** RCW was subsequently repealed and/or recodified in its entirety pursuant to 2016 sp.s. c 29 §§ 301, effective April 1, 2018, 601, and 701.

 Intent—Finding—2002 c 219: See note following RCW **9A.42.037**.

 Legislative finding—Severability—1985 c 352: See notes following RCW **10.05.010**.

10.05.050
Report to court—Recommended treatment plan—Commitment to provide treatment.

 *** CHANGE IN 2018 *** (SEE **1388-S.SL**) ***

 (1) The *facility, or the department of social and health services if the petition is brought under RCW **10.05.020**(2), shall make a written report to the court stating its findings and recommendations after the examination required by RCW **10.05.040**. If its findings and recommendations support treatment or the implementation of a child welfare service plan, it shall also recommend a treatment or service plan setting out:

 (a) The type;

 (b) Nature;

 (c) Length;

 (d) A treatment or service time schedule; and

 (e) Approximate cost of the treatment or child welfare services.

 (2) In the case of a child welfare service plan, the plan shall be designed in a manner so that a parent who successfully completes the plan will not be likely to withhold the basic necessities of life from his or her child.

(3) The report with the treatment or service plan shall be filed with the court and a copy given to the petitioner and petitioner's counsel. A copy of the treatment or service plan shall be given to the prosecutor by petitioner's counsel at the request of the prosecutor. The evaluation facility, or the department of social and health services if the petition is brought under RCW **10.05.020**(2), making the written report shall append to the report a commitment by the *treatment facility or the department of social and health services that it will provide the treatment or child welfare services in accordance with this chapter. The facility or the service provider shall agree to provide the court with a statement every three months for the first year and every six months for the second year regarding (a) the petitioner's cooperation with the treatment or child welfare service plan proposed and (b) the petitioner's progress or failure in treatment or child welfare services. These statements shall be made as a declaration by the person who is personally responsible for providing the treatment or services.

[**2002 c 219 § 10; 1985 c 352 § 8; 1975 1st ex.s. c 244 § 5.**]

NOTES:

*Reviser's note: Chapter **70.96A** RCW was amended by 1990 c 151, changing "treatment facility" to "treatment program." Chapter**70.96A** RCW was subsequently repealed and/or recodified in its entirety pursuant to 2016 sp.s. c 29 §§ 301, effective April 1, 2018, 601, and 701.

Intent—Finding—2002 c 219: See note following RCW **9A.42.037**.

Legislative finding—Severability—1985 c 352: See notes following RCW **10.05.010**.

10.05.055
Child welfare services.

Child welfare services provided under chapter **74.13** RCW pursuant to a deferred prosecution ordered under RCW **10.05.060** may not be construed to prohibit the department from providing services or undertaking proceedings pursuant to chapter **13.34** or **26.44** RCW.

[**2002 c 219 § 12.**]

NOTES:

Intent—Finding—2002 c 219: See note following RCW **9A.42.037**.

10.05.060
Procedure upon approval of plan.

If the report recommends treatment, the court shall examine the treatment plan. If it approves the plan and the petitioner agrees to comply with its terms and conditions and agrees to pay the cost thereof, if able to do so, or arrange for the treatment, an entry shall be made upon the person's court docket showing that the person has been accepted for deferred prosecution. A copy of the treatment plan shall be filed with the court. If the charge be one that an abstract of the docket showing the charge, the date of the violation for which the charge was made, and the date of petitioner's acceptance is required to be sent to the department of licensing, an abstract shall be sent, and the department of licensing shall make an entry of the charge and of the petitioner's acceptance for deferred prosecution on the department's driving record of the petitioner. The entry is not a conviction for purposes of Title **46** RCW. Upon receipt of the abstract of the docket, the department shall issue the petitioner a probationary license in accordance with RCW **46.20.355**, and the petitioner's driver's license shall be on probationary status for five years from the date of the violation that gave rise to the charge. The department shall maintain the record for ten years from date of entry of the order granting deferred prosecution.
[**2009 c 135 § 1; 1994 c 275 § 17; 1990 c 250 § 13; 1985 c 352 § 9; 1979 c 158 § 4; 1975 1st ex.s. c 244 § 6.**]

NOTES:

Short title—Effective date—1994 c 275: See notes following RCW **46.04.015**.

Effective dates—1990 c 250 §§ 1-13: See note following RCW **46.18.215**.

Severability—1990 c 250: See note following RCW **46.18.215**.

Legislative finding—Severability—1985 c 352: See notes following RCW **10.05.010**.

10.05.070

Arraignment when treatment rejected.

When treatment is either not recommended or not approved by the judge, or the petitioner declines to accept the treatment plan, the petitioner shall be arraigned on the charge.

[**1985 c 352 § 10; 1975 1st ex.s. c 244 § 7.**]

NOTES:

Legislative finding—Severability—1985 c 352: See notes following RCW **10.05.010**.

10.05.080

Evidence, uses and admissibility.

If the petition is not approved or is withdrawn before approval, evidence pertaining to or resulting from the petition and/or investigation is inadmissible in any trial on the charges, but shall be available for use after a conviction in determining a sentence.

[**1985 c 352 § 11; 1975 1st ex.s. c 244 § 8.**]

NOTES:

Legislative finding—Severability—1985 c 352: See notes following RCW **10.05.010**.

10.05.090

Procedure upon breach of treatment plan.

If a petitioner, who has been accepted for a deferred prosecution, fails or neglects to carry out and fulfill any term or condition of the petitioner's treatment plan or any term or condition imposed in connection with the installation of an interlock or other device under RCW**46.20.720**, the facility, center, institution, or agency administering the treatment or the entity administering the use of the device, shall immediately report such breach to the court, the prosecutor, and the petitioner or petitioner's attorney of record, together with its recommendation. The court upon receiving such a report shall hold a hearing to determine whether the petitioner should be removed from the deferred prosecution program. At the hearing, evidence shall be taken of the petitioner's alleged failure to comply with the treatment plan or device installation and the petitioner shall have the right to present evidence on his or her own behalf. The court shall either order that the petitioner continue on the treatment plan or be removed from deferred prosecution. If removed from deferred prosecution, the court shall enter judgment pursuant to RCW **10.05.020** and, if the charge for which the deferred prosecution was granted was a misdemeanor or gross misdemeanor under Title **46** RCW, shall notify the department of licensing of the removal and entry of judgment.

[**2010 c 269 § 10; 2008 c 282 § 17; 1997 c 229 § 1; 1994 c 275 § 18; 1985 c 352 § 12; 1975 1st ex.s. c 244 § 9.**]

NOTES:

> **Effective date—2010 c 269:** See note following RCW **46.20.385**.
>
> **Effective date—1997 c 229:** "This act takes effect January 1, 1998." [**1997 c 229 § 15.**]
>
> **Short title—Effective date—1994 c 275:** See notes following RCW **46.04.015**.
>
> **Legislative finding—Severability—1985 c 352:** See notes following RCW **10.05.010**.

10.05.100

Conviction of similar offense.

If a petitioner is subsequently convicted of a similar offense that was committed while the petitioner was in a deferred prosecution program, upon notice the court shall remove the petitioner's docket from the deferred prosecution file and the court shall enter judgment pursuant to RCW **10.05.020**.

[**1998 c 208 § 2; 1985 c 352 § 13; 1975 1st ex.s. c 244 § 10.**]

NOTES:

> **Effective date—1998 c 208:** See note following RCW **10.05.010**.
>
> **Legislative finding—Severability—1985 c 352:** See notes following RCW **10.05.010**.

10.05.110

Trial delay not grounds for dismissal.

Delay in bringing a case to trial caused by a petitioner requesting deferred prosecution as provided for in this chapter shall not be grounds for dismissal.

[**1985 c 352 § 14; 1975 1st ex.s. c 244 § 11.**]

NOTES:

Legislative finding—Severability—1985 c 352: See notes following RCW **10.05.010**.

10.05.120

Dismissal of charges.

(1) Three years after receiving proof of successful completion of the two-year treatment program, and following proof to the court that the petitioner has complied with the conditions imposed by the court following successful completion of the two-year treatment program, but not before five years following entry of the order of deferred prosecution pursuant to a petition brought under RCW **10.05.020**(1), the court shall dismiss the charges pending against the petitioner.

(2) When a deferred prosecution is ordered pursuant to a petition brought under RCW **10.05.020**(2) and the court has received proof that the petitioner has successfully completed the child welfare service plan, or the plan has been terminated because the alleged victim has reached his or her majority and there are no other minor children in the home, the court shall dismiss the charges pending against the petitioner: PROVIDED, That in any case where the petitioner's parental rights have been terminated with regard to the alleged victim due to abuse or neglect that occurred during the pendency of the deferred prosecution, the termination shall be per se evidence that the petitioner did not successfully complete the child welfare service plan.

[**2003 c 220 § 1; 2002 c 219 § 14; 1998 c 208 § 3; 1994 c 275 § 19; 1985 c 352 § 15; 1983 c 165 § 45; 1975 1st ex.s. c 244 § 12.**]

NOTES:

Intent—Finding—2002 c 219: See note following RCW **9A.42.037**.

Effective date—1998 c 208: See note following RCW **10.05.010**.

Short title—Effective date—1994 c 275: See notes following RCW **46.04.015**.

Legislative finding—Severability—1985 c 352: See notes following RCW **10.05.010**.

Legislative finding, intent—Effective dates—Severability—1983 c 165: See notes following RCW **46.20.308**.

10.05.130
Services provided for indigent defendants.

Funds shall be appropriated from the fines and forfeitures of the court to provide investigation, examination, report and treatment plan for any indigent person who is unable to pay the cost of any program of treatment.
[**1975 1st ex.s. c 244 § 13.**]

10.05.140
Conditions of granting.

As a condition of granting a deferred prosecution petition, the court shall order that the petitioner shall not operate a motor vehicle upon the public highways without a valid operator's license and proof of liability insurance. The amount of liability insurance shall be established by the court at not less than that established by RCW **46.29.490**. As a condition of granting a deferred prosecution petition on any alcohol-dependency based case, the court shall also order the installation of an ignition interlock under RCW **46.20.720**. The required periods of use of the interlock shall be not less than the periods provided for in RCW **46.20.720**. As a condition of granting a deferred prosecution petition, the court may order the petitioner to make restitution and to pay costs as defined in RCW **10.01.160**. To help ensure continued sobriety and reduce the likelihood of reoffense, the court may order reasonable conditions during the period of the deferred prosecution including, but not limited to, attendance at self-help recovery support groups for alcoholism or drugs, complete abstinence from alcohol and all nonprescribed mind-altering drugs, periodic urinalysis or breath analysis, and maintaining law-abiding behavior. The court may terminate the deferred prosecution program upon violation of the deferred prosecution order.

[**2016 c 203 § 11; 2013 2nd sp.s. c 35 § 21; 2011 c 293 § 8; 2004 c 95 § 1; 2003 c 220 § 2; 1999 c 331 § 4; 1997 c 229 § 2; 1991 c 247 § 1; 1985 c 352 § 16.**]

NOTES:

> **Effective date—2011 c 293 §§ 1-9:** See note following RCW **46.20.385**.
>
> **Effective date—1999 c 331:** See note following RCW **9.94A.525**.
>
> **Effective date—1997 c 229:** See note following RCW **10.05.090**.
>
> **Legislative finding—Severability—1985 c 352:** See notes following

RCW **10.05.010**.

10.05.150

Alcoholism program requirements.

A deferred prosecution program for alcoholism shall be for a two-year period and shall include, but not be limited to, the following requirements:

(1) Total abstinence from alcohol and all other nonprescribed mind-altering drugs;

(2) Participation in an intensive inpatient or intensive outpatient program in a state-approved substance use disorder treatment program;

(3) Participation in a minimum of two meetings per week of an alcoholism self-help recovery support group, as determined by the assessing agency, for the duration of the treatment program;

(4) Participation in an alcoholism self-help recovery support group, as determined by the assessing agency, from the date of court approval of the plan to entry into intensive treatment;

(5) Not less than weekly approved outpatient counseling, group or individual, for a minimum of six months following the intensive phase of treatment;

(6) Not less than monthly outpatient contact, group or individual, for the remainder of the two-year deferred prosecution period;

(7) The decision to include the use of prescribed drugs, including disulfiram, as a condition of treatment shall be reserved to the treating facility and the petitioner's physician;

(8) All treatment within the purview of this section shall occur within or be approved by a state-approved substance use disorder treatment program as described in *chapter **70.96A** RCW;

(9) Signature of the petitioner agreeing to the terms and conditions of the treatment program.

[**2016 sp.s. c 29 § 527; 1999 c 143 § 43; 1985 c 352 § 17.**]

NOTES:

> ***Reviser's note:** Chapter **70.96A** RCW was entirely repealed or recodified as sections in chapter **71.24** RCW by 2016 sp.s. c 29, effective April 1, 2018.

> **Effective dates—2016 sp.s. c 29:** See note following RCW **71.05.760**.

> **Short title—Right of action—2016 sp.s. c 29:** See notes following RCW **71.05.010**.

> **Legislative finding—Severability—1985 c 352:** See notes following RCW **10.05.010**.

10.05.160

Appeal of deferred prosecution order.

The prosecutor may appeal an order granting deferred prosecution on any or all of the following grounds:

(1) Prior deferred prosecution has been granted to the defendant;

(2) Failure of the court to obtain proof of insurance or a treatment plan conforming to the requirements of this chapter;

(3) Failure of the court to comply with the requirements of RCW **10.05.100**;

(4) Failure of the evaluation facility to provide the information required in RCW **10.05.040** and **10.05.050**, if the defendant has been referred to the facility for treatment. If an appeal on such basis is successful, the trial court may consider the use of another treatment program;

(5) Failure of the court to order the installation of an ignition interlock or other device under RCW **10.05.140**.

[**2010 c 269 § 11; 2008 c 282 § 19; 1999 c 143 § 44; 1998 c 208 § 4; 1985 c 352 § 18.**]

NOTES:

> **Effective date—2010 c 269:** See note following RCW **46.20.385**.

> **Effective date—1998 c 208:** See note following RCW **10.05.010**.

> **Legislative finding—Severability—1985 c 352:** See notes following RCW **10.05.010**.

10.05.170
Supervision as condition—Levy of assessment.

As a condition of granting deferred prosecution, the court may order supervision of the petitioner during the period of deferral and may levy a monthly assessment upon the petitioner as provided in RCW **10.64.120**. In a jurisdiction with a probation department, the court may appoint the probation department to supervise the petitioner. In a jurisdiction without a probation department, the court may appoint an appropriate person or agency to supervise the petitioner. A supervisor appointed under this section shall be required to do at least the following:

(1) If the charge for which deferral is granted relates to operation of a motor vehicle, at least once every six months request from the department of licensing an abstract of the petitioner's driving record; and

(2) At least once every month make contact with the petitioner or with any agency to which the petitioner has been directed for treatment as a part of the deferral.

[**1991 c 247 § 2; 1985 c 352 § 19.**]

NOTES:

> **Legislative finding—Severability—1985 c 352:** See notes following RCW **10.05.010**.

Chapter 10.10 RCW CRIMINAL APPEALS FROM DISTRICT COURTS

NOTES:

Rules of court: Rules for Appeal of Decisions of Courts of Limited Jurisdiction (RALJ).

10.10.010
Court rules.

Every person convicted before a district judge of any offense may appeal from the judgment as provided by court rules.

[**1987 c 202 § 156;** 1891 c 29 § 6, part; RRS § 1919, part. Prior: Code 1881 § 1898, part; 1877 p 203 § 7, part; 1873 p 384 § 196, part; **1854 p 261 § 177.** Formerly RCW **10.10.010, 10.10.020,** and **10.10.030.**]

NOTES:

Intent—1987 c 202: See note following RCW **2.04.190.**

10.10.060
Appeal—Costs—Default.

The appellant in a criminal action shall not be required to advance any fees in claiming his or her appeal nor in prosecuting the same; but if convicted in the appellate court, or if sentenced for failing to prosecute his or her appeal, he or she may be required as a part of the sentence to pay the costs of the prosecution. If the appellant shall fail to enter and prosecute his or her appeal he or she shall be defaulted of his or her recognizance, if any was taken, and the superior court may award sentence against him or her for the offense whereof he or she was convicted in like manner as if he or she had been convicted thereof in that court; and if he or she be not then in custody process may be issued to bring him or her into court to receive sentence.

[**2010 c 8 § 1008; 1891 c 29 § 7;** RRS § 1920. Prior: Code 1881 § 1900; 1873 p 384 § 198, part; **1854 p 261 § 179.** Formerly RCW **10.10.060** and **10.10.080.**]

Chapter 10.14 RCW HARASSMENT

10.14.010
Legislative finding, intent.

The legislature finds that serious, personal harassment through repeated invasions of a person's privacy by acts and words showing a pattern of harassment designed to coerce, intimidate, or humiliate the victim is increasing. The legislature further finds that the prevention of such harassment is an important governmental objective. This chapter is intended to provide victims with a speedy and inexpensive method of obtaining civil antiharassment protection orders preventing all further unwanted contact between the victim and the perpetrator.

[**1987 c 280 § 1.**]

10.14.020
Definitions.

Unless the context clearly requires otherwise, the definitions in this section apply throughout this chapter.

(1) "Course of conduct" means a pattern of conduct composed of a series of acts over a period of time, however short, evidencing a continuity of purpose. "Course of conduct" includes, in addition to any other form of communication, contact, or conduct, the sending of an electronic communication, but does not include constitutionally protected free speech. Constitutionally protected activity is not included within the meaning of "course of conduct."

(2) "Unlawful harassment" means a knowing and willful course of conduct directed at a specific person which seriously alarms, annoys, harasses, or is detrimental to such person, and which serves no legitimate or lawful purpose. The course of conduct shall be such as would cause a reasonable person to suffer substantial emotional distress, and shall actually cause substantial emotional distress to the petitioner, or, when the course of conduct would cause a reasonable parent to fear for the well-being of their child.

[**2011 c 307 § 2; 2001 c 260 § 2; 1999 c 27 § 4; 1995 c 127 § 1; 1987 c 280 § 2.**]

NOTES:

Reviser's note: The definitions in this section have been alphabetized pursuant to RCW **1.08.015**(2)(k).

Findings—Intent—2001 c 260: "The legislature finds that unlawful harassment directed at a child by a person under the age of eighteen is not acceptable and can have serious consequences. The legislature further finds that some interactions between minors, such as "schoolyard scuffles," though not to be condoned, may not rise to the level of unlawful harassment. It is the intent of the legislature that a protection order sought by the parent or guardian of a child as provided for in this chapter be available only when the alleged behavior of the person under the age of eighteen to be restrained rises to the level set forth in chapter **10.14** RCW." [**2001 c 260 § 1.**]

Intent—1999 c 27: See note following RCW **9A.46.020**.

10.14.030

Course of conduct—Determination of purpose.

In determining whether the course of conduct serves any legitimate or lawful purpose, the court should consider whether:

(1) Any current contact between the parties was initiated by the respondent only or was initiated by both parties;

(2) The respondent has been given clear notice that all further contact with the petitioner is unwanted;

(3) The respondent's course of conduct appears designed to alarm, annoy, or harass the petitioner;

(4) The respondent is acting pursuant to any statutory authority, including but not limited to acts which are reasonably necessary to:

(a) Protect property or liberty interests;

(b) Enforce the law; or

(c) Meet specific statutory duties or requirements;

(5) The respondent's course of conduct has the purpose or effect of unreasonably interfering with the petitioner's privacy or the purpose or effect of creating an intimidating, hostile, or offensive living environment for the petitioner;

(6) Contact by the respondent with the petitioner or the petitioner's family has been limited in any manner by any previous court order.

[**1987 c 280 § 3.**]

10.14.040

Protection order—Petition.

There shall exist an action known as a petition for an order for protection in cases of unlawful harassment.

(1) A petition for relief shall allege the existence of harassment and shall be accompanied by an affidavit made under oath stating the specific facts and circumstances from which relief is sought.

(2) A petition for relief may be made regardless of whether or not there is a pending lawsuit, complaint, petition, or other action between the parties.

(3) All court clerks' offices shall make available simplified forms and instructional brochures. Any assistance or information provided by clerks under this section does not constitute the practice of law and clerks are not responsible for incorrect information contained in a petition.

(4) Filing fees are set in RCW **36.18.020**, but no filing fee may be charged for a petition filed in an existing action or under an existing cause number brought under this

chapter in the jurisdiction where the relief is sought or as provided in RCW **10.14.055**. Forms and instructional brochures shall be provided free of charge.

(5) A person is not required to post a bond to obtain relief in any proceeding under this section.

(6) The parent or guardian of a child under age eighteen may petition for an order of protection to restrain a person age eighteen years or over from contact with that child upon a showing that contact with the person to be enjoined is detrimental to the welfare of the child.

(7) The parent or guardian of a child under the age of eighteen may petition in superior court for an order of protection to restrain a person under the age of eighteen years from contact with that child only in cases where the person to be restrained has been adjudicated of an offense against the child protected by the order, or is under investigation or has been investigated for such an offense. In issuing a protection order under this subsection, the court shall consider, among the other facts of the case, the severity of the alleged offense, any continuing physical danger or emotional distress to the alleged victim, and the expense, difficulty, and educational disruption that would be caused by a transfer of the alleged offender to another school. The court may order that the person restrained in the order not attend the public or approved private elementary, middle, or high school attended by the person under the age of eighteen years protected by the order. In the event that the court orders a transfer of the restrained person to another school, the parents or legal guardians of the person restrained in the order are responsible for transportation and other costs associated with the change of school by the person restrained in the order. The court shall send notice of the restriction on attending the same school as the person protected by the order to the public or approved private school the person restrained by the order will attend and to the school the person protected by the order attends.

[**2002 c 117 § 1; 2001 c 260 § 3.** Prior: **1995 c 292 § 2; 1995 c 127 § 2; 1987 c 280 § 4.**]

NOTES:

> **Findings—Intent—2001 c 260:** See note following RCW **10.14.020**.

10.14.045

Protection order commissioners—Appointment authorized.

In each county, the superior court may appoint one or more attorneys to act as protection order commissioners pursuant to this chapter to exercise all powers and perform all duties of a court commissioner appointed pursuant to RCW **2.24.010** provided that such positions may not be created without prior consent of the county legislative authority. A person appointed as a protection order commissioner under this chapter may also be appointed to any other commissioner position authorized by law.

[**2013 c 84 § 20.**]

10.14.050

Administrator for courts—Forms, information.

The administrator for the courts shall develop and prepare, in consultation with interested persons, model forms and instructional brochures required under RCW **10.14.040**(3).

[**1987 c 280 § 5.**]

10.14.055

Fees excused, when.

No fees for filing or service of process may be charged by a public agency to petitioners seeking relief under this chapter from a person who has stalked them as that term is defined in RCW **9A.46.110**, or from a person who has engaged in conduct that would constitute a sex offense as defined in *RCW **9A.44.130**, or from a person who is a family or household member as defined in **RCW **26.50.010**(2) who has engaged in conduct that would constitute domestic violence as defined in **RCW **26.50.010**(1).

[**2002 c 117 § 2.**]

NOTES:

Reviser's note: *(1) RCW **9A.44.130** was amended by 2010 c 267 § 2, removing the definition of "sex offense" and "kidnapping offense." Those terms are now defined in RCW **9A.44.128**.

(2) RCW **26.50.010 was alphabetized pursuant to RCW **1.08.015**(2)(k), changing subsections (2) and (1) to subsections (6) and (3), respectively.

10.14.060
Proceeding in forma pauperis.

Persons seeking relief under this chapter may file an application for leave to proceed in forma pauperis on forms supplied by the court. If the court determines that a petitioner lacks the funds to pay the costs of filing, the petitioner shall be granted leave to proceed in forma pauperis and no filing fee or any other court related fees shall be charged by the court to the petitioner for relief sought under this chapter. If the petitioner is granted leave to proceed in forma pauperis, then no fees for service may be charged to the petitioner.

[**1987 c 280 § 6.**]

10.14.065
Orders—Judicial information system to be consulted.

Before granting an order under this chapter, the court may consult the judicial information system, if available, to determine criminal history or the pendency of other proceedings involving the parties.

[**2011 c 307 § 6.**]

10.14.070
Hearing—Service.

Upon receipt of the petition alleging a prima facie case of harassment, other than a petition alleging a sex offense as defined in chapter**9A.44** RCW or a petition for a stalking protection order under chapter **7.92** RCW, the court shall order a hearing which shall be held not later than fourteen days from the date of the order. If the petition alleges a sex offense as defined in chapter **9A.44** RCW, the court shall order a hearing which shall be held not later than fourteen days from the date of the order. Except as provided in RCW **10.14.085**, personal service shall be made upon the respondent not less than five court days before the hearing. If timely personal service cannot be made, the court shall set a new hearing date and shall either require additional attempts at obtaining personal service or permit service by publication as provided by RCW **10.14.085**. If the court permits service by publication, the court shall set the hearing date not later than twenty-four days from the date of the order. The court may issue an ex parte order for protection pending the hearing as provided in RCW **10.14.080** and **10.14.085**.

[**2013 c 84 § 30; 2005 c 144 § 1; 1992 c 143 § 10; 1987 c 280 § 7.**]

10.14.080
Antiharassment protection orders—Ex parte temporary—Hearing—Longer term, renewal—Acts not prohibited.

(1) Upon filing a petition for a civil antiharassment protection order under this chapter, the petitioner may obtain an ex parte temporary antiharassment protection order. An ex parte temporary antiharassment protection order may be granted with or without notice upon the filing of an affidavit which, to the satisfaction of the court, shows reasonable proof of unlawful harassment of the petitioner by the respondent and that great or irreparable harm will result to the petitioner if the temporary antiharassment protection order is not granted.

(2) An ex parte temporary antiharassment protection order shall be effective for a fixed period not to exceed fourteen days or twenty-four days if the court has permitted service by publication under RCW **10.14.085**. The ex parte order may be reissued. A full hearing, as provided in this chapter, shall be set for not later than fourteen days from the issuance of the temporary order or not later than twenty-four days if service by publication is permitted. Except as provided in RCW **10.14.070** and **10.14.085**, the respondent shall be personally served with a copy of the ex parte order along with a copy of the petition and notice of the date set for the hearing. The ex parte order and

notice of hearing shall include at a minimum the date and time of the hearing set by the court to determine if the temporary order should be made effective for one year or more, and notice that if the respondent should fail to appear or otherwise not respond, an order for protection will be issued against the respondent pursuant to the provisions of this chapter, for a minimum of one year from the date of the hearing. The notice shall also include a brief statement of the provisions of the ex parte order and notify the respondent that a copy of the ex parte order and notice of hearing has been filed with the clerk of the court.

(3) At the hearing, if the court finds by a preponderance of the evidence that unlawful harassment exists, a civil antiharassment protection order shall issue prohibiting such unlawful harassment.

(4) An order issued under this chapter shall be effective for not more than one year unless the court finds that the respondent is likely to resume unlawful harassment of the petitioner when the order expires. If so, the court may enter an order for a fixed time exceeding one year or may enter a permanent antiharassment protection order. The court shall not enter an order that is effective for more than one year if the order restrains the respondent from contacting the respondent's minor children. This limitation is not applicable to civil antiharassment protection orders issued under chapter **26.09**, 26.10, or **26.26** RCW. If the petitioner seeks relief for a period longer than one year on behalf of the respondent's minor children, the court shall advise the petitioner that the petitioner may apply for renewal of the order as provided in this chapter or if appropriate may seek relief pursuant to chapter **26.09** or **26.10** RCW.

(5) At any time within the three months before the expiration of the order, the petitioner may apply for a renewal of the order by filing a petition for renewal. The petition for renewal shall state the reasons why the petitioner seeks to renew the protection order. Upon receipt of the petition for renewal, the court shall order a hearing which shall be not later than fourteen days from the date of the order. Except as provided in RCW **10.14.085**, personal service shall be made upon the respondent not less than five days before the hearing. If timely service cannot be made the court shall set a new hearing date and shall either require additional attempts at obtaining personal

service or permit service by publication as provided by RCW **10.14.085**. If the court permits service by publication, the court shall set the new hearing date not later than twenty-four days from the date of the order. If the order expires because timely service cannot be made the court shall grant an ex parte order of protection as provided in this section. The court shall grant the petition for renewal unless the respondent proves by a preponderance of the evidence that the respondent will not resume harassment of the petitioner when the order expires. The court may renew the protection order for another fixed time period or may enter a permanent order as provided in subsection (4) of this section.

(6) The court, in granting an ex parte temporary antiharassment protection order or a civil antiharassment protection order, shall have broad discretion to grant such relief as the court deems proper, including an order:

(a) Restraining the respondent from making any attempts to contact the petitioner;

(b) Restraining the respondent from making any attempts to keep the petitioner under surveillance;

(c) Requiring the respondent to stay a stated distance from the petitioner's residence and workplace; and

(d) Considering the provisions of RCW **9.41.800**.

(7) The court in granting an ex parte temporary antiharassment protection order or a civil antiharassment protection order, shall not prohibit the respondent from exercising constitutionally protected free speech. Nothing in this section prohibits the petitioner from utilizing other civil or criminal remedies to restrain conduct or communications not otherwise constitutionally protected.

(8) The court in granting an ex parte temporary antiharassment protection order or a civil antiharassment protection order, shall not prohibit the respondent from the use or enjoyment of real property to which the respondent has a cognizable claim unless that order is issued under chapter **26.09** RCW or under a separate action commenced with a summons and complaint to determine title or possession of real property.

(9) The court in granting an ex parte temporary antiharassment protection order or a civil antiharassment protection order, shall not limit the respondent's right to care,

control, or custody of the respondent's minor child, unless that order is issued under chapter **13.32A**, 26.09, 26.10, or **26.26** RCW.

(10) A petitioner may not obtain an ex parte temporary antiharassment protection order against a respondent if the petitioner has previously obtained two such ex parte orders against the same respondent but has failed to obtain the issuance of a civil antiharassment protection order unless good cause for such failure can be shown.

(11) The court order shall specify the date an order issued pursuant to subsections (4) and (5) of this section expires if any. The court order shall also state whether the court issued the protection order following personal service or service by publication and whether the court has approved service by publication of an order issued under this section.

[**2011 c 307 § 3; 2001 c 311 § 1; 1995 c 246 § 36; 1994 sp.s. c 7 § 448; 1992 c 143 § 11; 1987 c 280 § 8.**]

NOTES:

Severability—1995 c 246: See note following RCW **26.50.010**.

Finding—Intent—Severability—1994 sp.s. c 7: See notes following RCW **43.70.540**.

Effective date—1994 sp.s. c 7 §§ 401-410, 413-416, 418-437, and 439-460: See note following RCW **9.41.010**.

10.14.085

Hearing reset after ex parte order—Service by publication— Circumstances.

(1) If the respondent was not personally served with the petition, notice of hearing, and ex parte order before the hearing, the court shall reset the hearing for twenty-four days from the date of entry of the order and may order service by publication instead of personal service under the following circumstances:

(a) The sheriff or municipal officer files an affidavit stating that the officer was unable to complete personal service upon the respondent. The affidavit must describe the number and types of attempts the officer made to complete service;

(b) The petitioner files an affidavit stating that the petitioner believes that the respondent is hiding from the server to avoid service. The petitioner's affidavit must state the reasons for the belief that the respondent is avoiding service;

(c) The server has deposited a copy of the summons, in substantially the form prescribed in subsection (3) of this section, notice of hearing, and the ex parte order of protection in the post office, directed to the respondent at the respondent's last known address, unless the server states that the server does not know the respondent's address; and

(d) The court finds reasonable grounds exist to believe that the respondent is concealing himself or herself to avoid service, and that further attempts to personally serve the respondent would be futile or unduly burdensome.

(2) The court shall reissue the temporary order of protection not to exceed another twenty-four days from the date of reissuing the ex parte protection order and order to provide service by publication.

(3) The publication shall be made in a newspaper of general circulation in the county where the petition was brought and in the county of the last known address of the respondent once a week for three consecutive weeks. The newspaper selected must be one of the three most widely circulated papers in the county. The publication of summons shall not be made until the court orders service by publication under this section. Service of the summons shall be considered complete when the publication has been made for three consecutive weeks. The summons must be signed by the petitioner. The summons shall contain the date of the first publication, and shall require the respondent upon whom service by publication is desired, to appear and answer the petition on the date set for the hearing. The summons shall also contain a brief statement of the reason for the petition and a summary of the provisions under the ex parte order. The summons shall be essentially in the following form:

In the . . . . court of the state of Washington for the county of . . . .

. . . ., Petitioner

vs.   No. . . . . . .

. . . ., Respondent

The state of Washington to . . . . (respondent):

You are hereby summoned to appear on the . . . . day of . . . . . ., (year) . . . ., at . . . . a.m./p.m., and respond to the petition. If you fail to respond, an order of protection will be issued against you pursuant to the provisions of chapter **10.14** RCW, for a minimum of one year from the date you are required to appear. A temporary order of protection has been issued against you, restraining you from the following: (Insert a brief statement of the provisions of the ex parte order). A copy of the petition, notice of hearing, and ex parte order has been filed with the clerk of this court.

. . . .

Petitioner . . . .

[**2016 c 202 § 4; 1992 c 143 § 12.**]

10.14.090
Representation or appearance.

(1) Nothing in this chapter shall preclude either party from representation by private counsel or from appearing on his or her own behalf.

(2) The court may require the respondent to pay the filing fee and court costs, including service fees, and to reimburse the petitioner for costs incurred in bringing the action, including a reasonable attorney's fee. If the petitioner has been granted leave to proceed in forma pauperis, the court may require the respondent to pay the filing fee and costs, including services fees, to the county or municipality incurring the expense. [**1992 c 143 § 14; 1987 c 280 § 9.**]

10.14.100
Service of order.

(1) An order issued under this chapter shall be personally served upon the respondent, except as provided in subsections (5) and (7) of this section.

(2) The sheriff of the county or the peace officers of the municipality in which the respondent resides shall serve the respondent personally unless the petitioner elects to have the respondent served by a private party.

(3) If the sheriff or municipal peace officer cannot complete service upon the respondent within ten days, the sheriff or municipal peace officer shall notify the petitioner.

(4) Returns of service under this chapter shall be made in accordance with the applicable court rules.

(5) If an order entered by the court recites that the respondent appeared in person before the court, the necessity for further service is waived and proof of service of that order is not necessary. The court's order, entered after a hearing, need not be served on a respondent who fails to appear before the court, if material terms of the order have not changed from those contained in the temporary order, and it is shown to the court's satisfaction that the respondent has previously been personally served with the temporary order.

(6) Except in cases where the petitioner has fees waived under RCW **10.14.055** or is granted leave to proceed in forma pauperis, municipal police departments serving documents as required under this chapter may collect the same fees for service and mileage authorized by RCW**36.18.040** to be collected by sheriffs.

(7) If the court previously entered an order allowing service by publication of the notice of hearing and temporary order of protection pursuant to RCW **10.14.085**, the court may permit service by publication of the order of protection issued under RCW **10.14.080**. Service by publication must comply with the requirements of RCW **10.14.085**.

[**2002 c 117 § 3**; **2001 c 311 § 2**; **1992 c 143 § 15**; **1987 c 280 § 10.**]

10.14.105

Order following service by publication.

Following completion of service by publication as provided in RCW **10.14.085**, if the respondent fails to appear at the hearing, the court may issue an order of protection as provided in RCW **10.14.080**. That order must be served pursuant to RCW **10.14.100**, and forwarded to the appropriate law enforcement agency pursuant to RCW **10.14.110**.

[**1992 c 143 § 13.**]

10.14.110

Notice to law enforcement agencies—Enforceability.

(1) A copy of an antiharassment protection order granted under this chapter shall be forwarded by the clerk of the court on or before the next judicial day to the appropriate law enforcement agency specified in the order.

Upon receipt of the order, the law enforcement agency shall forthwith enter the order into any computer-based criminal intelligence information system available in this state used by law enforcement agencies to list outstanding warrants. The law enforcement agency shall expunge expired orders from the computer system. Entry into the law enforcement information system constitutes notice to all law enforcement agencies of the existence of the order. The order is fully enforceable in any county in the state.

(2) The information entered into the computer-based system shall include notice to law enforcement whether the order was personally served or served by publication.
[**1992 c 143 § 16; 1987 c 280 § 11.**]

10.14.115

Enforcement of order—Knowledge prerequisite to penalties— Reasonable efforts to serve copy of order.

(1) When the court issues an order of protection pursuant to RCW **10.14.080**, the court shall advise the petitioner that the respondent may not be subjected to the penalties set forth in RCW **10.14.120** and **10.14.170** for a violation of the order unless the respondent knows of the order.

(2) When a peace officer investigates a report of an alleged violation of an order for protection issued under this chapter the officer shall attempt to determine whether the respondent knew of the existence of the protection order. If the officer determines that the respondent did not or probably did not know about the protection order, the officer shall make reasonable efforts to obtain a copy of the protection order and serve it on the respondent during the investigation.

[**1992 c 143 § 17.**]

10.14.120
Disobedience of order—Penalties.

Any willful disobedience by a respondent age eighteen years or over of any temporary antiharassment protection order or civil antiharassment protection order issued under this chapter subjects the respondent to criminal penalties under this chapter. Any respondent age eighteen years or over who willfully disobeys the terms of any order issued under this chapter may also, in the court's discretion, be found in contempt of court and subject to penalties under chapter **7.21** RCW. Any respondent under the age of eighteen years who willfully disobeys the terms of an order issued under this chapter may, in the court's discretion, be found in contempt of court and subject to the sanction specified in RCW **7.21.030**(4).

[**2001 c 260 § 4; 1989 c 373 § 14; 1987 c 280 § 12.**]

NOTES:

Findings—Intent—2001 c 260: See note following RCW **10.14.020**.

10.14.125
Service by publication—Costs.

The court may permit service by publication under this chapter only if the petitioner pays the cost of publication or if the petitioner's costs have been waived pursuant to RCW **10.14.055**, unless the county legislative authority allocates funds for service of process by publication for petitioners who are granted leave to proceed in forma pauperis.

[**2002 c 117 § 4; 1992 c 143 § 18.**]

10.14.130
Exclusion of certain actions.

Protection orders authorized under this chapter shall not be issued for any action specifically covered by chapter **7.90**, 10.99, or **26.50** RCW.

[**2006 c 138 § 22; 1987 c 280 § 13.**]
NOTES:

Short title—2006 c 138: See RCW **7.90.900**.

10.14.140
Other remedies.

Nothing in this chapter shall preclude a petitioner's right to utilize other existing civil remedies.

[**1987 c 280 § 14.**]

10.14.150
Jurisdiction.

(1) The district courts shall have original jurisdiction and cognizance of any civil actions and proceedings brought under this chapter, except the district court shall transfer such actions and proceedings to the superior court when it is shown that (a) the respondent to the petition is under eighteen years of age; (b) the action involves title or possession of real property; (c) a superior court has exercised or is exercising jurisdiction over a proceeding involving the parties; or (d) the action would have the effect of interfering with a respondent's care, control, or custody of the respondent's minor child.

(2) Municipal courts may exercise jurisdiction and cognizance of any civil actions and proceedings brought under this chapter by adoption of local court rule, except the municipal court shall transfer such actions and proceedings to the superior court when it is shown that (a) the respondent to the petition is under eighteen years of age; (b) the action involves title or possession of real property; (c) a superior court has exercised or is exercising jurisdiction over a proceeding involving the parties; or (d) the action would have the effect of interfering with a respondent's care, control, or custody of the respondent's minor child.

(3) Superior courts shall have concurrent jurisdiction to receive transfer of antiharassment petitions in cases where a district or municipal court judge makes

findings of fact and conclusions of law showing that meritorious reasons exist for the transfer. The municipal and district courts shall have jurisdiction and cognizance of any criminal actions brought under RCW **10.14.120** and **10.14.170**.

[**2011 c 307 § 1; 2005 c 196 § 1; 1999 c 170 § 1; 1991 c 33 § 2; 1987 c 280 § 15.**]

NOTES:

Effective date—1991 c 33: See note following RCW **3.66.020**.

10.14.155

Personal jurisdiction—Nonresident individual.

(1) In a proceeding in which a petition for an order for protection under this chapter is sought, a court of this state may exercise personal jurisdiction over a nonresident individual if:

(a) The individual is personally served with a petition within this state;

(b) The individual submits to the jurisdiction of this state by consent, entering a general appearance, or filing a responsive document having the effect of waiving any objection to consent to personal jurisdiction;

(c) The act or acts of the individual or the individual's agent giving rise to the petition or enforcement of an order for protection occurred within this state;

(d)(i) The act or acts of the individual or the individual's agent giving rise to the petition or enforcement of an order for protection occurred outside this state and are part of an ongoing pattern of harassment that has an adverse effect on the petitioner or a member of the petitioner's family or household and the petitioner resides in this state; or

(ii) As a result of acts of harassment, the petitioner or a member of the petitioner's family or household has sought safety or protection in this state and currently resides in this state; or

(e) There is any other basis consistent with RCW **4.28.185** or with the constitutions of this state and the United States.

(2) For jurisdiction to be exercised under subsection (1)(d)(i) or (ii) of this section, the individual must have communicated with the petitioner or a member of the petitioner's

family, directly or indirectly, or made known a threat to the safety of the petitioner or member of the petitioner's family while the petitioner or family member resides in this state. For the purposes of subsection (1)(d)(i) or (ii) of this section, "communicated or made known" includes, but is not limited to, through the mail, telephonically, or a posting on an electronic communication site or medium. Communication on any electronic medium that is generally available to any individual residing in the state shall be sufficient to exercise jurisdiction under subsection (1)(d)(i) or (ii) of this section.

(3) For the purposes of this section, an act or acts that "occurred within this state" includes, but is not limited to, an oral or written statement made or published by a person outside of this state to any person in this state by means of the mail, interstate commerce, or foreign commerce. Oral or written statements sent by electronic mail or the internet are deemed to have "occurred within this state."

[**2010 c 274 § 308.**]

NOTES:

      Intent—**2010 c 274:** See note following RCW **10.31.100**.

10.14.160

Where action may be brought.

For the purposes of this chapter an action may be brought in:

(1) The judicial district of the county in which the alleged acts of unlawful harassment occurred;

(2) The judicial district of the county where any respondent resides at the time the petition is filed;

(3) The judicial district of the county where a respondent may be served if it is the same county or judicial district where a respondent resides;

(4) The municipality in which the alleged acts of unlawful harassment occurred;

(5) The municipality where any respondent resides at the time the petition is filed; or

(6) The municipality where a respondent may be served if it is the same county or judicial district where a respondent resides.

[**2005 c 196 § 2; 1992 c 127 § 1; 1987 c 280 § 16.**]

10.14.170

Criminal penalty.

Any respondent age eighteen years or over who willfully disobeys any civil antiharassment protection order issued pursuant to this chapter shall be guilty of a gross misdemeanor.

[**2001 c 260 § 5; 1987 c 280 § 17.**]

NOTES:

> **Findings—Intent—2001 c 260:** See note following RCW **10.14.020**.

10.14.180

Modification of order.

Upon application with notice to all parties and after a hearing, the court may modify the terms of an existing order under this chapter. In any situation where an order is terminated or modified before its expiration date, the clerk of the court shall forward on or before the next judicial day a true copy of the modified order or the termination order to the appropriate law enforcement agency specified in the modified order or termination order. Upon receipt of the order, the law enforcement agency shall promptly enter it in the law enforcement information system.

[**1987 c 280 § 18.**]

10.14.190

Constitutional rights.

Nothing in this chapter shall be construed to infringe upon any constitutionally protected rights including, but not limited to, freedom of speech and freedom of assembly.

[**1987 c 280 § 19.**]

10.14.200

Availability of orders in family law proceedings.

Any order available under this chapter may be issued in actions under chapter **13.32A**, 26.09, 26.10, or **26.26** RCW. An order available under this chapter that is issued under those chapters shall be fully enforceable and shall be enforced pursuant to the provisions of this chapter.

[**1999 c 397 § 4; 1995 c 246 § 35.**]

NOTES:

   Severability—1995 c 246: See note following RCW **26.50.010**.

10.14.210

Court appearance after violation.

(1) A defendant arrested for violating any civil antiharassment protection order issued pursuant to this chapter is required to appear in person before a magistrate within one judicial day after the arrest. At the time of the appearance, the court shall determine the necessity of imposing a no-contact order or other conditions of pretrial release in accordance with RCW **9A.46.050**.

(2) A defendant who is charged by citation, complaint, or information with violating any civil antiharassment protection order issued pursuant to this chapter and not arrested shall appear in court for arraignment in accordance with RCW **9A.46.050**.

(3) Appearances required pursuant to this section are mandatory and cannot be waived.

[**2012 c 223 § 4.**]

10.14.800

Master petition pattern form to be developed—Recommendations to legislature.

The legislature respectfully requests that:

(1) By January 1, 2014, the administrative office of the courts shall develop a single master petition pattern form for all antiharassment and stalking protection orders issued under chapter **7.92** RCW and this chapter. The master petition must prompt petitioners to disclose on the form whether the petitioner who is seeking an ex parte order has

experienced stalking conduct as defined in RCW **7.92.020**. An antiharassment order and stalking protection order issued under chapter **7.92** RCW and this chapter must substantially comply with the pattern form developed by the administrative office of the courts.

(2) The Washington state supreme court gender and justice commission, to the extent it is able, in consultation with Washington coalition of sexual assault programs, Washington state coalition against domestic violence, Washington association of prosecuting attorneys, Washington association of criminal defense lawyers, and Washington association of sheriffs and police chiefs, consider other potential solutions to reduce confusion about which type of protection order a petitioner should seek and to provide any recommendations to the legislature by January 1, 2014.

[**2013 c 84 § 21.**]

Chapter 10.16 RCW PRELIMINARY HEARINGS

NOTES:

Magistrates: Chapter **2.20** RCW.

Municipal judges as magistrates: RCW **35.20.020**, **35.20.250**.

10.16.080
Discharge of defendant—Frivolous complaints.

If it should appear upon the whole examination that no offense has been committed, or that there is not probable cause for charging the defendant with an offense, he or she shall be discharged, and if in the opinion of the magistrate, the complaint was malicious, or without probable cause, and there was no reasonable ground therefor, the costs shall be taxed against the party making the complaint.

[**2010 c 8 § 1009;** Code 1881 § 1925; **1873 p 395 § 223; 1854 p 107 § 31;** RRS § 1954.]

10.16.100
Abstract of costs forwarded with transcript.

In all cases where any magistrate shall order a defendant to recognize for his or her appearance before a district or superior court, the magistrate shall forward with the papers in the case, an abstract of the costs that have accrued in the case, and such costs shall be subject to the final determination of the case.

[**1987 c 202 § 163;** Code 1881 § 1937; **1873 p 397 § 236; 1854 p 109 § 44;** RRS § 1966.]

NOTES:

Intent—**1987 c 202:** See note following RCW **2.04.190**.

10.16.110
Statement of prosecuting attorney if no information filed—Court action.

It shall be the duty of the prosecuting attorney of the proper county to inquire into and make full examination of all the facts and circumstances connected with any case of preliminary examination, as provided by law, touching the commission of any offense wherein the offender shall be committed to jail, or become recognized or held to bail; and if the prosecuting attorney shall determine in any such case that an information ought not to be filed, he or she shall make, subscribe, and file with the clerk of the court a statement in writing containing his or her reasons, in fact and in law, for not filing an information in such case, and such statement shall be filed at and during the session of court at which the offender shall be held for his or her appearance: PROVIDED, That in such case such court may examine such statement, together with the evidence filed in the case, and if upon such examination the court shall not be satisfied with such statement, the prosecuting attorney shall be directed by the court to file the proper information and bring the case to trial.

[**2010 c 8 § 1010; 1890 p 102 § 6;** RRS § 2053. Formerly RCW **10.16.110** and **10.16.120.**]

10.16.145
Witnesses—Recognizances with sureties.

If the magistrate shall be satisfied that there is good cause to believe that any such witness will not perform the condition of his or her recognizance unless other security be given, such magistrate may order the witness to enter into recognizance with such sureties as may be deemed necessary for his or her appearance at court.

[**2010 c 8 § 1011;** Code 1881 § 1930; **1873 p 396 § 229; 1854 p 108 § 37;** RRS § 1960. Formerly codified in RCW **10.16.140**, part.]

NOTES:

Rules of court: This section probably superseded by CrR 6.13. See comment after CrR 6.13.

10.16.150
Recognizances for minors.

When any minor is a material witness, any other person may be allowed to recognize for the appearance of such witness, or the magistrate may, in his or her discretion, take the recognizance of such minor in a sum not exceeding fifty dollars which shall be valid and binding in law, notwithstanding the disability of minority.

[**2010 c 8 § 1012; 1973 1st ex.s. c 154 § 19;** Code 1881 § 1931; **1873 p 396 § 230; 1854 p 108 § 38;** RRS § 1961.]

NOTES:

Rules of court: This section probably superseded by CrR 6.13. See comment after CrR 6.13.

Severability—1973 1st ex.s. c 154: See note following RCW **2.12.030.**

10.16.160

Witnesses—Failure to furnish recognizance—Commitment— Deposition—Discharge.

All witnesses required to recognize with or without sureties shall, if they refuse, be committed to the county jail by the magistrate, there to remain until they comply with such orders or be otherwise discharged according to law: PROVIDED, That when the magistrate is satisfied that any witness required to recognize with sureties is unable to comply with such order, the magistrate shall immediately take the deposition of such witness and discharge the witness from custody upon the witness' own recognizance. The testimony of the witness shall be reduced to writing by a district judge or some competent person under the judge's direction, and only the exact words of the witness shall be taken; the deposition, except the cross-examination, shall be in the narrative form, and upon the cross-examination the questions and answers shall be taken in full. The defendant must be present in person when the deposition is taken, and shall have an opportunity to cross-examine the witnesses; the defendant may make any objections to the admission of any part of the testimony, and all objections shall be noted by the district judge; but the district judge shall not decide as to the admissibility of the evidence, but shall take all the testimony offered by the witness. The deposition must be carefully read to the witness, and any corrections the witness may desire to make thereto shall be made in presence of the defendant by adding the same to the deposition as first taken; it must be signed by the witness, certified by the district judge, and transmitted to the clerk of the superior court, in the same manner as depositions in civil actions. And if the witness is not present when required to testify in the case, either before the grand jury or upon the trial in the superior court, the deposition shall be submitted to the judge of such superior court, upon the objections noted by the district judge, and such judge shall suppress so much of said deposition as such judge shall find to be inadmissible, and the remainder of the deposition may be read as evidence in the case, either before the grand jury or upon the trial in the court.

[**1987 c 202 § 164; 1891 c 11 § 15;** Code 1881 § 1932; **1877 p 203 § 8; 1873 p 396 § 232; 1854 p 108 § 39;** RRS § 1962. Formerly RCW **10.16.160,10.16.170,** and **10.16.180.**]

NOTES:

Rules of court: This section modified if not superseded by CrR 6.13. See comment after CrR 6.13.

Intent—1987 c 202: See note following RCW **2.04.190.**

Chapter 10.19 RCW BAIL AND APPEARANCE BONDS

NOTES:

Bail

arresting officer's duties regarding: RCW **10.31.030.**

pending appeal to supreme court: RCW **10.73.040.**

traffic offenses, nonresidents: RCW **46.64.035.**

Fugitives, bail: Chapter **10.88** RCW.

Recognizance

for stay of execution: RCW **10.82.020, 10.82.025.**

to keep the peace as incidence of conviction of crime: RCW **10.64.070, 10.64.075.**

Recognizances relative to preliminary hearings: Chapter **10.16** RCW.

10.19.040

Officers authorized to take recognizance and approve bail.

Any officer authorized to execute a warrant in a criminal action, may take the recognizance and justify and approve the bail; he or she may administer an oath and examine the bail as to its sufficiency.

[**2010 c 8 § 1013;** Code 1881 § 1034; **1873 p 229 § 214; 1854 p 114 § 78;** RRS § 2087. FORMER PART OF SECTION: **1891 c 11 § 13;** Code 1881 § 1927; **1873 p 395 § 225; 1854 p 108 § 33;** RRS § 1957, now codified in RCW **10.16.070.**]

10.19.055
Class A or B felony offenses—Bail for release determined by judicial officer.

Bail for the release of a person arrested and detained for a class A or B felony offense must be determined on an individualized basis by a judicial officer.

[**2012 c 6 § 1; 2010 c 254 § 2.**]

10.19.060
Certification and filing of recognizances.

Every recognizance taken by any peace officer must be certified by him or her forthwith to the clerk of the court to which the defendant is recognized. The clerk must thereupon record the recognizance in the order book, and, from the time of filing, it has the same effect as if taken in open court.

[**2010 c 8 § 1014;** Code 1881 § 1035; **1873 p 230 § 215; 1854 p 114 § 79;** RRS § 2088.]

10.19.065
Taking and entering recognizances.

Recognizances in criminal proceedings may be taken in open court and entered on the order book.

[Code 1881 § 1033; **1854 p 114 § 77;** RRS § 2086.]

10.19.090

Forfeiture, exoneration of recognizances—Judgment—Execution.

In criminal cases where a recognizance for the appearance of any person, either as a witness or to appear and answer, shall have been taken and a default entered, the recognizance shall be declared forfeited by the court, and at the time of adjudging such forfeiture said court shall enter judgment against the principal and sureties named in such recognizance for the sum therein mentioned, and execution may issue thereon the same as upon other judgments. If the surety is not notified by the court in writing of the unexplained failure of the defendant to appear within thirty days of the date for appearance, then the forfeiture shall be null and void and the recognizance exonerated.
[**1986 c 322 § 2;** Code 1881 § 1137; **1873 p 230 § 217; 1867 p 103 § 1;** RRS § 2231.]
NOTES:

Severability—1986 c 322: "If any provision of this act or its application to any person or circumstance is held invalid, the remainder of the act or the application of the provision to other persons or circumstances is not affected." [**1986 c 322 § 6.**]

10.19.100

Stay of execution of forfeiture judgment—Bond.

The parties, or either of them, against whom such judgment may be entered in the superior or supreme courts, may stay said execution for sixty days by giving a bond with two or more sureties, to be approved by the clerk, conditioned for the payment of such judgment at the expiration of sixty days, unless the same shall be vacated before the expiration of that time.
[**1891 c 28 § 86;** Code 1881 § 1138; **1873 p 242 § 281; 1867 p 103 § 2;** RRS § 2232. FORMER PART OF SECTION: **1891 c 28 § 87;** Code 1881 § 1139; **1867 p 103 § 3;** RRS § 2233, now codified as RCW **10.19.105.**]

10.19.105

Forfeiture judgment vacated on defendant's production—When.

If a bond be given and execution stayed, as provided in RCW **10.19.100**, and the person for whose appearance such recognizance was given shall be produced in court before the expiration of said period of sixty days, the judge may vacate such judgment upon such terms as may be just and equitable, otherwise execution shall forthwith issue as well against the sureties in the new bond as against the judgment debtors.

[**1891 c 28 § 87;** Code 1881 § 1139; **1867 p 103 § 3;** RRS § 2233. Formerly RCW **10.19.100**, part.]

10.19.110

Recognizances before district judge or magistrate—Forfeiture—Action.

All recognizances taken and forfeited before any district judge or magistrate, shall be forthwith certified to the clerk of the superior court of the county; and it shall be the duty of the prosecuting attorney to proceed at once by action against all the persons bound in such recognizances, and in all forfeited recognizances whatever, or such of them as the prosecuting attorney may elect to proceed against.

[**1987 c 202 § 165;** Code 1881 § 1166; **1873 p 230 § 215; 1854 p 128 § 175;** RRS § 2234. FORMER PART OF SECTION: Code 1881 § 1936; **1873 p 397 § 235; 1863 p 390 § 216; 1859 p 141 § 185; 1854 p 109 § 43;** RRS § 1965, now codified as RCW **10.16.190**.]

NOTES:

Intent—1987 c 202: See note following RCW **2.04.190**.

10.19.120

Actions not barred by defect of form or formality.

No action brought on any recognizance, bail, or appearance bond given in any criminal proceeding whatever shall be barred or defeated, nor shall judgment be arrested thereon, by reason of any neglect or omission to note or record the default of any principal or surety at the time when such default shall happen, or by reason of any defect in the form of the recognizance, if it sufficiently appear from the tenor thereof at what court or before what district judge the party or witness was bound to appear, and that the court or magistrate before whom it was taken was authorized by law to require and take such recognizance; and a recognizance may be recorded after execution awarded.

[**1987 c 202 § 166; 1891 c 28 § 88;** Code 1881 § 1167; **1854 p 129 § 176;** RRS § 2235. FORMER PART OF SECTION: Code 1881 § 749; **1854 p 219 § 489;** RRS § 777, now codified as RCW **19.72.170.**]

NOTES:

       Intent—1987 c 202: See note following RCW **2.04.190.**

10.19.140

Return of bond to surety, when.

If a forfeiture has been entered against a person in a criminal case and the person is returned to custody or produced in court within twelve months from the forfeiture, then the full amount of the bond, less any and all costs determined by the court to have been incurred by law enforcement in transporting, locating, apprehending, or processing the return of the person to the jurisdiction of the court, shall be remitted to the surety if the surety was directly responsible for producing the person in court or directly responsible for apprehension of the person by law enforcement.

[**1986 c 322 § 3.**]

NOTES:

       Severability—1986 c 322: See note following RCW **10.19.090.**

10.19.150

Liability of surety, limitation.

The liability of the surety is limited to the amount of the bond when acting within the scope of the surety's duties in issuing the bond.

[**1986 c 322 § 4.**]

NOTES:

10.19.160

Surrender of person under surety's bond.

The surety on the bond may return to custody a person in a criminal case under the surety's bond if the surrender is accompanied by a notice of forfeiture or a notarized affidavit specifying the reasons for the surrender. The surrender shall be made to the county or city jail affiliated with the jurisdiction issuing the warrant resulting in bail. Upon surrender, a person must be held until the next judicial day or until another bond is posted.

[**2017 c 78 § 1; 1986 c 322 § 5.**]

NOTES:

10.19.170

Violent offenders—Reasons for release without bail.

Notwithstanding CrR 3.2, a court who releases a defendant arrested or charged with a violent offense as defined in RCW **9.94A.030** on the offender's personal recognizance or personal recognizance with conditions must state on the record the reasons why the court did not require the defendant to post bail.

[**1996 c 181 § 1.**]

Chapter 10.21 RCW BAIL DETERMINATIONS UNDER ARTICLE I, SECTION 20— CONDITIONS OF RELEASE

10.21.010
Intent.

It is the intent of the legislature to enact a law for the purpose of reasonably assuring public safety in bail determination hearings and hearings pursuant to the proposed amendment to Article I, section 20 of the state Constitution set forth in House Joint Resolution No. 4220. Other provisions of law address matters relating to assuring the appearance of the defendant at trial and preventing interference with the administration of justice.

[**2010 c 254 § 3.**]

NOTES:

Intent—2010 c 254: "The legislature intends by this act to require an individualized determination by a judicial officer of conditions of release for persons in custody for felony. This requirement is consistent with constitutional requirements and court rules regarding the right of a detained person to a prompt determination of probable cause and judicial review of the conditions of release and the requirement that judicial determinations of bail or release be made no later than the preliminary appearance stage." [**2010 c 254 § 1.**]

Contingent effective date—2010 c 254: "Sections 1 and 2 of this act take effect January 1, 2011. Sections 3 through 10 of this act take effect January 1, 2011, only if the proposed amendment to Article I, section 20 of the state Constitution proposed in House Joint Resolution No. 4220 is validly submitted to and is approved and ratified by the voters at the next general election. If the proposed amendment is not approved and ratified, sections 3 through 11 of this act are null and void in their entirety." [**2010 c 254 § 14.**] House Joint Resolution No. 4220 was approved and ratified by the voters November 2, 2010.

10.21.015
Pretrial release program.

*** CHANGE IN 2018 *** (SEE **5987.SL**) ***

(1) Under this chapter, "pretrial release program" is any program, either run directly by a county or city, or by a private or public entity through contract with a county or city, into whose custody an offender is released prior to trial and which agrees to supervise the offender. As used in this section, "supervision" includes, but is not limited to, work release, day monitoring, electronic monitoring, or participation in a 24/7 sobriety program.

(2) A pretrial release program may not agree to supervise, or accept into its custody, an offender who is currently awaiting trial for a violent offense or sex offense, as defined in RCW **9.94A.030**, who has been convicted of one or more violent offenses or sex offenses in the ten years before the date of the current offense, unless the offender's release before trial was secured with a payment of bail.

[**2015 2nd sp.s. c 3 § 20; 2014 c 24 § 1.**]
NOTES:
   Finding—Intent—2015 2nd sp.s. c 3: See note following RCW **10.21.055**.

10.21.017
Home detention.

*** CHANGE IN 2018 *** (SEE **5987.SL**) ***

Under this chapter, "home detention" means any program meeting the definition of home detention in RCW **9.94A.030**, and complying with the requirements of RCW **9.94A.736**.

[**2015 c 287 § 6.**]

10.21.020

Appearance before judicial officer—Issuance of order.

Upon the appearance before a judicial officer of a person charged with an offense, the judicial officer must issue an order that, pending trial, the person be:

(1) Released on personal recognizance;

(2) Released on a condition or combination of conditions ordered under RCW **10.21.030** or other provision of law;

(3) Temporarily detained as allowed by law; or

(4) Detained as provided under chapter 254, Laws of 2010.

[**2010 c 254 § 4.**]

NOTES:

Intent—Contingent effective date—2010 c 254: See notes following RCW **10.21.010**.

10.21.030

Conditions of release—Judicial officer may amend order.

*** CHANGE IN 2018 *** (SEE **5987.SL**) ***

(1) The judicial officer may at any time amend the order to impose additional or different conditions of release. The conditions imposed under this chapter supplement but do not supplant provisions of law allowing the imposition of conditions to assure the appearance of the defendant at trial or to prevent interference with the administration of justice.

(2) Appropriate conditions of release under this chapter include, but are not limited to, the following:

(a) The defendant may be placed in the custody of a pretrial release program;

(b) The defendant may have restrictions placed upon travel, association, or place of abode during the period of release;

(c) The defendant may be required to comply with a specified curfew;

(d) The defendant may be required to return to custody during specified hours or to be placed on electronic monitoring, as defined in RCW**9.94A.030**, if available. The defendant, if convicted, may not have the period of incarceration reduced by the number of days spent on electronic monitoring;

(e) The defendant may be required to comply with a program of home detention, as defined in RCW **9.94A.030**;

(f) The defendant may be prohibited from approaching or communicating in any manner with particular persons or classes of persons;

(g) The defendant may be prohibited from going to certain geographical areas or premises;

(h) The defendant may be prohibited from possessing any dangerous weapons or firearms;

(i) The defendant may be prohibited from possessing or consuming any intoxicating liquors or drugs not prescribed to the defendant. The defendant may be required to submit to testing to determine the defendant's compliance with this condition;

(j) The defendant may be prohibited from operating a motor vehicle that is not equipped with an ignition interlock device;

(k) The defendant may be required to report regularly to and remain under the supervision of an officer of the court or other person or agency; and

(l) The defendant may be prohibited from committing any violations of criminal law.
[**2015 c 287 § 5; 2014 c 24 § 2; 2010 c 254 § 5.**]
NOTES:

      Intent—Contingent effective date—2010 c 254: See notes following RCW **10.21.010**.

10.21.040

Detention order—Hearing—Expedited review.

If, after a hearing on offenses prescribed in Article I, section 20 of the state Constitution, the judicial officer finds, by clear and convincing evidence, that a person shows a propensity for violence that creates a substantial likelihood of danger to the community or any persons, and finds that no condition or combination of conditions will reasonably assure the safety of any other person and the community, such judicial officer must order the detention of the person before trial. The detainee is entitled to expedited review of the detention order by the court of appeals under the writ provided in RCW **7.36.160**.

[**2010 c 254 § 6.**]

NOTES:

       Intent—Contingent effective date—2010 c 254: See notes following RCW **10.21.010**.

10.21.050

Conditions of release—Judicial officer to consider available information.

*** CHANGE IN 2018 *** (SEE **5987.SL**) ***

The judicial officer must, in determining whether there are conditions of release that will reasonably assure the safety of any other person and the community, take into account the available information concerning:

(1) The nature and circumstances of the offense charged, including whether the offense is a crime of violence;

(2) The weight of the evidence against the defendant; and

(3) The history and characteristics of the defendant, including:

(a) The person's character, physical and mental condition, family ties, employment, financial resources, length of residence in the community, community ties, past conduct, history relating to drug or alcohol abuse, criminal history, and record concerning appearance at court proceedings;

(b) Whether, at the time of the current offense or arrest, the defendant was on community supervision, probation, parole, or on other release pending trial, sentencing, appeal, or completion of sentence for an offense under federal, state, or local law; and

(c) The nature and seriousness of the danger to any person or the community that would be posed by the defendant's release.

[2010 c 254 § 7.]

NOTES:

> **Intent—Contingent effective date—2010 c 254:** See notes following RCW **10.21.010**.

10.21.055

Conditions of release—Requirements—Ignition interlock device—24/7 sobriety program monitoring—Notice by court, when—Release order.

(1)(a) When any person charged with a violation of RCW **46.61.502**, **46.61.504**, **46.61.520**, or **46.61.522**, in which the person has a prior offense as defined in RCW **46.61.5055** and the current offense involves alcohol, is released from custody at arraignment or trial on bail or personal recognizance, the court authorizing the release shall require, as a condition of release that person comply with one of the following four requirements:

(i) Have a functioning ignition interlock device installed on all motor vehicles operated by the person, with proof of installation filed with the court by the person or the certified interlock provider within five business days of the date of release from custody or as soon thereafter as determined by the court based on availability within the jurisdiction; or

(ii) Comply with 24/7 sobriety program monitoring, as defined in RCW **36.28A.330**; or

(iii) Have an ignition interlock device on all motor vehicles operated by the person pursuant to (a)(i) of this subsection and submit to 24/7 sobriety program monitoring pursuant to (a)(ii) of this subsection, if available, or alcohol monitoring, at the expense of the person, as provided in RCW **46.61.5055**(5) (b) and (c); or

(iv) Have an ignition interlock device on all motor vehicles operated by the person and that such person agrees not to operate any motor vehicle without an ignition interlock device as required by the court. Under this subsection (1)(a)(iv), the person must file a sworn statement with the court upon release at arraignment that states the person will not operate any motor vehicle without an ignition interlock device while the ignition interlock restriction is imposed by the court. Such person must also submit to 24/7 sobriety program monitoring pursuant to (a)(ii) of this subsection, if available, or alcohol monitoring, at the expense of the person, as provided in RCW **46.61.5055**(5) (b) and (c).

(b) The court shall immediately notify the department of licensing when an ignition interlock restriction is imposed: (i) As a condition of release pursuant to (a) of this subsection; or (ii) in instances where a person is charged with, or convicted of, a violation of RCW **46.61.502**,**46.61.504**, **46.61.520**, or **46.61.522**, and the offense involves alcohol. If the court imposes an ignition interlock restriction, the department of licensing shall attach or imprint a notation on the driving record of any person restricted under this section stating that the person may operate only a motor vehicle equipped with a functioning ignition interlock device.

(2)(a) Upon acquittal or dismissal of all pending or current charges relating to a violation of RCW **46.61.502**, **46.61.504**, **46.61.520**, or**46.61.522**, or equivalent local ordinance, the court shall authorize removal of the ignition interlock device and lift any requirement to comply with electronic alcohol/drug monitoring imposed under subsection (1) of this section. Nothing in this section limits the authority of the court or department under RCW **46.20.720**.

(b) If the court authorizes removal of an ignition interlock device imposed under this section, the court shall immediately notify the department of licensing regarding the lifting of the ignition interlock restriction and the department of licensing shall release any attachment, imprint, or notation on such person's driving record relating to the ignition interlock requirement imposed under this section.

(3) When an ignition interlock restriction imposed as a condition of release is canceled, the court shall provide a defendant with a written order confirming release of

the restriction. The written order shall serve as proof of release of the restriction until which time the department of licensing updates the driving record.

[**2016 c 203 § 16; 2015 2nd sp.s. c 3 § 2; 2013 2nd sp.s. c 35 § 1.**]

NOTES:

        Finding—Intent—2015 2nd sp.s. c 3: "The legislature finds that impaired driving continues to be a significant cause of motor vehicle crashes and that additional measures need to be taken to identify people who are driving under the influence, provide appropriate sanctions, and ensure compliance with court-ordered restrictions. The legislature intends to increase the availability of forensic phlebotomists so that offenders can be appropriately and efficiently identified. The legislature further intends to require consecutive sentencing in certain cases to increase punishment and supervision of offenders. The legislature intends to clarify ignition interlock processes and requirements to ensure that those offenders ordered to have ignition interlock devices do not drive vehicles without the required devices." [**2015 2nd sp.s. c 3 § 1.**]

10.21.060
Hearing—Appearance—Defendant's right to representation—Detention of defendant.

(1) The judicial officer must hold a hearing in cases involving offenses prescribed in Article I, section 20, to determine whether any condition or combination of conditions will reasonably assure the safety of any other person and the community upon motion of the attorney for the government.

(2) The hearing must be held immediately upon the defendant's first appearance before the judicial officer unless the defendant, or the attorney for the government, seeks a continuance. Except for good cause, a continuance on motion of such person may not exceed five days (not including any intermediate Saturday, Sunday, or legal holiday), and a continuance on motion of the attorney for the government may not exceed three days (not including any intermediate Saturday, Sunday, or legal holiday). During a continuance, such person must be detained.

(3) At the hearing, such defendant has the right to be represented by counsel, and, if financially unable to obtain representation, to have counsel appointed. The defendant must be afforded an opportunity to testify, to present witnesses, to cross-examine witnesses who appear at the hearing, and to present information by proffer or otherwise. The rules concerning admissibility of evidence in criminal trials do not apply to the presentation and consideration of information at the hearing. The facts the judicial officer uses to support a finding that no condition or combination of conditions will reasonably assure the safety of any other person and the community must be supported by clear and convincing evidence of a propensity for violence that creates a substantial likelihood of danger to the community or any persons.

(4) The defendant may be detained pending completion of the hearing. The hearing may be reopened, before or after a determination by the judicial officer, at any time before trial if the judicial officer finds that information exists that was not known to the movant at the time of the hearing and that has a material bearing on the issue whether there are conditions of release that will reasonably assure the safety of any other person and the community.

[**2010 c 254 § 8.**]

NOTES:

Intent—Contingent effective date—2010 c 254: See notes following RCW **10.21.010**.

10.21.070

Release order—Requirements.

In a release order issued under RCW **10.21.030** the judicial officer must:

(1) Include a written statement that sets forth all the conditions to which the release is subject, in a manner sufficiently clear and specific to serve as a guide for the defendant's conduct; and

(2) Advise the defendant of:

(a) The penalties for violating a condition of release, including the penalties for committing an offense while on pretrial release; and

(b) The consequences of violating a condition of release, including the immediate issuance of a warrant for the defendant's arrest.

[**2010 c 254 § 9.**]

NOTES:

    Intent—Contingent effective date—2010 c 254: See notes following RCW **10.21.010**.

10.21.080

Detention order—Requirements—Temporary release.

(1) In a detention order issued under RCW **10.21.040**, the judicial officer must:

(a) Include written findings of fact and a written statement of the reasons for the detention;

(b) Direct that the person be committed to the custody of the appropriate correctional authorities for confinement separate, to the extent practicable, from persons awaiting or serving sentences or being held in custody pending appeal; and

(c) Direct that the person be afforded reasonable opportunity for private consultation with counsel.

(2) The judicial officer may, by subsequent order, permit the temporary release of the person, in the custody of an appropriate law enforcement officer or other appropriate person, to the extent that the judicial officer determines such release to be necessary for preparation of the person's defense or for another compelling reason.

[**2010 c 254 § 10.**]

NOTES:

    Intent—Contingent effective date—2010 c 254: See notes following RCW **10.21.010**.

10.21.090

Home detention or electronic monitoring—Conditions.

A monitoring agency, as defined in RCW **9.94A.736**, may not agree to monitor pursuant to home detention or electronic monitoring an offender who is currently awaiting trial for a violent or sex offense, as defined in RCW **9.94A.030**, unless the defendant's release before trial is secured with a payment of bail. If bail is revoked by the court or the bail bond agency, the court shall note the reason for the revocation in the court file.

[**2015 c 287 § 12.**]

10.21.900
Construction of chapter.

Nothing in this chapter may be construed as modifying or limiting the presumption of innocence.

[**2010 c 254 § 11.**]

NOTES:

Intent—Contingent effective date—2010 c 254: See notes following RCW **10.21.010**.

Chapter 10.22 RCW COMPROMISE OF MISDEMEANORS

10.22.010
When permitted—Exceptions.

When a defendant is prosecuted in a criminal action for a misdemeanor, other than a violation of RCW **9A.48.105**, for which the person injured by the act constituting the offense has a remedy by a civil action, the offense may be compromised as provided in RCW **10.22.020**, except when it was committed:

(1) By or upon an officer while in the execution of the duties of his or her office;

(2) Riotously;

(3) With an intent to commit a felony; or

(4) By one family or household member against another as defined in RCW **10.99.020** and was a crime of domestic violence as defined in RCW **10.99.020**.
[**2010 c 8 § 1015; 2008 c 276 § 308; 1999 c 143 § 45; 1989 c 411 § 3;** Code 1881 § 1040; **1854 p 115 § 84;** RRS § 2126. FORMER PART OF SECTION: Code 1881 § 1935; **1873 p 397 § 234; 1854 p 109 § 42;** RRS § 1964, now codified as RCW **10.16.135**.]

NOTES:

Severability—Part headings, subheadings not law—2008 c 276: See notes following RCW **36.28A.200**.

10.22.020
Procedure—Costs.

In such case, if the party injured appear in the court in which the cause is pending at any time before the final judgment therein, and acknowledge, in writing, that he or she has received satisfaction for the injury, the court may, in its discretion, on payment of the costs incurred, order all proceedings to be discontinued and the defendant to be discharged. The reasons for making the order must be set forth therein and entered in the minutes. Such order is a bar to another prosecution for the same offense.
[**2010 c 8 § 1016; 1891 c 28 § 63;** Code 1881 §§ 1041, 1042; **1873 p 230 § 220; 1854 p 115 § 84;** RRS § 2127.]

10.22.030
Compromise in all other cases forbidden.

No offense can be compromised, nor can any proceedings for the prosecution or punishment thereof be stayed upon a compromise, except as provided in this chapter.
[**1891 c 28 § 64;** Code 1881 § 1043; RRS § 2128.]

Chapter 10.25 RCW JURISDICTION AND VENUE

10.25.065
Perjury outside the state.

Perjury committed outside of the state of Washington in a statement, declaration, verification, or certificate authorized by RCW **9A.72.085** is punishable in the county in this state in which occurs the act, transaction, matter, action, or proceeding, in relation to which the statement, declaration, verification, or certification was given or made.
[**1981 c 187 § 4.**]

10.25.070
Change of venue—Procedure.

The defendant may show to the court, by affidavit, that he or she believes he or she cannot receive a fair trial in the county where the action is pending, owing to the prejudice of the judge, or to excitement or prejudice against the defendant in the county or some part thereof, and may thereupon demand to be tried in another county. The application shall not be granted on the ground of excitement or prejudice other than prejudice of the judge, unless the affidavit of the defendant be supported by other evidence, nor in any case unless the judge is satisfied the ground upon which the application is made does exist.
[**2010 c 8 § 1017; 1891 c 28 § 7;** Code 1881 § 1072; **1854 p 117 § 98;** RRS § 2018.]

10.25.130
Costs.

When a criminal case is transferred to another county pursuant to this chapter the county from which such case is transferred shall pay to the county in which the case is tried all costs accrued for per diem and mileage for jurors and witnesses and all other costs properly charged to a convicted defendant.

[**1961 c 303 § 2.**]

10.25.140
Change of venue by outside jury.

When a change of venue is ordered and the court, upon motion to transfer a jury or in the absence of such motion, determines that it would be more economical to move the jury than to move the pending action and that justice will be served, a change of venue shall be accomplished by the selection of a jury in the county to which the venue would otherwise have been transferred and the selected jury moved to the county where the indictment or information was filed.

[**1981 c 205 § 1.**]

Chapter 10.27 RCW GRAND JURIES— CRIMINAL INVESTIGATIONS

NOTES:

Interpreters—Legal proceedings: Chapter **2.42** RCW.

Juries: Chapter **2.36** RCW.

10.27.010
Short title—Purpose.

This chapter shall be known as the criminal investigatory act of 1971 and is enacted on behalf of the people of the state of Washington to serve law enforcement in combating crime and corruption.

[1971 ex.s. c 67 § 1.]

10.27.020
Definitions.

For the purposes of this chapter:

(1) The term "court" shall mean any superior court in the state of Washington.

(2) The term "public attorney" shall mean the prosecuting attorney of the county in which a grand jury or special grand jury is impaneled; the attorney general of the state of Washington when acting pursuant to RCW **10.27.070**(9) and, the special prosecutor appointed by the governor, pursuant to RCW **10.27.070**(10), and their deputies or special deputies.

(3) The term "indictment" shall mean a written accusation found by a grand jury.

(4) The term "principal" shall mean any person whose conduct is being investigated by a grand jury or special inquiry judge.

(5) The term "witness" shall mean any person summoned to appear before a grand jury or special inquiry judge to answer questions or produce evidence.

(6) A "grand jury" consists of twelve persons, is impaneled by a superior court and constitutes a part of such court. The functions of a grand jury are to hear, examine and investigate evidence concerning criminal activity and corruption and to take action with respect to such evidence. The grand jury shall operate as a whole and not by committee.

(7) A "special inquiry judge" is a superior court judge designated by a majority of the superior court judges of a county to hear and receive evidence of crime and corruption.

[1988 c 188 § 16; 1971 ex.s. c 67 § 2.]
NOTES:

Legislative findings—Severability—Effective date—1988 c 188: See notes following RCW **2.36.010**.

10.27.030
Summoning grand jury.

No grand jury shall be summoned to attend at the superior court of any county except upon an order signed by a majority of the judges thereof. A grand jury shall be summoned by the court, where the public interest so demands, whenever in its opinion there is sufficient evidence of criminal activity or corruption within the county or whenever so requested by a public attorney, corporation counsel or city attorney upon showing of good cause.

[**1971 ex.s. c 67 § 3.**]

10.27.040

Selection of grand jury members.

Members of the grand jury shall be selected in the manner provided in chapter **2.36** RCW.

[**1988 c 188 § 17; 1971 ex.s. c 67 § 4.**]

NOTES:

Legislative findings—Severability—Effective date—1988 c 188: See notes following RCW **2.36.010**.

10.27.050

Special inquiry judge—Selection.

In every county a superior court judge as designated by a majority of the judges shall be available to serve as a special inquiry judge to hear evidence concerning criminal activity and corruption.

[**1971 ex.s. c 67 § 5.**]

10.27.060

Discharge of panel, juror—Grounds.

Neither the grand jury panel nor any individual grand juror may be challenged, but the court may:

(1) At any time before a grand jury is sworn discharge the panel and summon another if it finds that the original panel does not substantially conform to the requirements of chapter **2.36** RCW; or

(2) At any time after a grand juror is drawn, refuse to swear him or her, or discharge him or her after he or she has been sworn, upon a finding that he or she is disqualified from service pursuant to chapter **2.36** RCW, or incapable of performing his or her duties because of bias or prejudice, or guilty of misconduct in the performance of his or her duties such as to impair the proper functioning of the grand jury.

[**2010 c 8 § 1018; 1971 ex.s. c 67 § 6.**]

10.27.070
Oath—Officers—Witnesses.

(1) When the grand jury is impaneled, the court shall appoint one of the jurors to be foreperson, and also another of the jurors to act as foreperson in case of the absence of the foreperson.

(2) The grand jurors must be sworn pursuant to the following oath: "You, as grand jurors for the county of . . . . . ., do solemnly swear (or affirm) that you will diligently inquire into and true presentment make of all such matters and things as shall come to your knowledge and you will submit things truly as they come to your knowledge, according to your charge the laws of this state and your understanding; you shall indict no person through envy, hatred, malice or political consideration; neither will you leave any person unindicted through fear, favor, affection, reward or the hope thereof or political consideration. The counsel of the state, his or her advice, and that of your fellows you shall keep secret."

(3) After a grand jury has been sworn, the court must deliver or cause to be delivered to each grand juror a printed copy of all the provisions of this chapter, and the court may give the grand jurors any oral or written instructions, or both, relating to the proper performance of their duties at any time it deems necessary or appropriate.

(4) The court shall appoint a reporter to record the proceedings before the grand jury or special inquiry judge, and shall swear him or her not to disclose any testimony or the

name of any witness except as provided in RCW **10.27.090**. In addition, the foreperson of the grand jury may, in his or her discretion, select one of the grand jurors to act as secretary to keep records of the grand jury's business.

(5) The court, whenever necessary, shall appoint an interpreter, and shall swear him or her not to disclose any testimony or the name of any witness except as provided in RCW **10.27.090**.

(6) When a person held in official custody is a witness before a grand jury or special inquiry judge, a public servant, assigned to guard him or her during his or her appearance may accompany him or her. The court shall swear such public servant not to disclose any testimony or the name of any witness except as provided in RCW **10.27.090**.

(7) Proceedings of a grand jury shall not be valid unless at least twelve of its members are present. The foreperson or acting foreperson of the grand jury shall conduct proceedings in an orderly manner and shall administer an oath or affirmation in the manner prescribed by law to any witness who shall testify before the grand jury.

(8) The legal advisers of a grand jury are the court and public attorneys, and a grand jury may not seek or receive legal advice from any other source. When necessary or appropriate, the court or public attorneys or both must instruct the grand jury concerning the law with respect to its duties or any matter before it, and such instructions shall be recorded by the reporter.

(9)(a) Upon request of the prosecuting attorney of the county in which a grand jury or special inquiry judge is impaneled, the attorney general shall assist such prosecuting attorney in attending such grand jury or special inquiry judge.

(b) Whenever directed by the court, the attorney general shall supersede the prosecuting attorney in attending the grand jury and in which event the attorney general shall be responsible for the prosecution of any indictment returned by the grand jury.

(c) When the attorney general is conducting a criminal investigation pursuant to powers otherwise granted to him or her, he or she shall attend all grand juries or special inquiry judges in relation thereto and shall prosecute any indictments returned by a grand jury.

(10) After consulting with the court and receiving its approval, the grand jury may request the governor to appoint a special prosecutor to attend the grand jury. The grand jury shall in the request nominate three persons approved by the court. From those nominated, the governor shall appoint a special prosecutor, who shall supersede the prosecuting attorney and the attorney general and who shall be responsible for the prosecution of any indictments returned by the grand jury attended by him or her.

(11) A public attorney shall attend the grand jurors when requested by them, and he or she may do so on his or her own motion within the limitations of RCW **10.27.020**(2), **10.27.070**(9) and **10.27.070**(10) hereof, for the purpose of examining witnesses in their presence, or of giving the grand jurors legal advice regarding any matter cognizable by them. He or she shall also, when requested by them, draft indictments and issue process for the attendance of witnesses.

(12) Subject to the approval of the court, the corporation counsel or city attorney for any city or town in the county where any grand jury has been convened may appear as a witness before the grand jury to advise the grand jury of any criminal activity or corruption within his or her jurisdiction.

[**2010 c 8 § 1019; 1971 ex.s. c 67 § 7.**]

10.27.080

Persons authorized to attend—Restrictions on attorneys.

No person shall be present at sessions of the grand jury or special inquiry judge except the witness under examination and his or her attorney, public attorneys, the reporter, an interpreter, a public servant guarding a witness who has been held in custody, if any, and, for the purposes provided for in RCW **10.27.170**, any corporation counsel or city attorney. The attorney advising the witness shall only advise such witness concerning his or her right to answer or not answer any questions and the form of his or her answer and shall not otherwise engage in the proceedings. No person other than grand jurors shall be present while the grand jurors are deliberating or voting. Any person violating either of the above provisions may be held in contempt of court.

[**2010 c 8 § 1020; 1971 ex.s. c 67 § 8.**]

10.27.090

Secrecy enjoined—Exceptions—Use and availability of evidence.

(1) Every member of the grand jury shall keep secret whatever he, she, or any other grand juror has said, and how he, she, or any other grand juror has voted, except for disclosure of indictments, if any, as provided in RCW **10.27.150**.

(2) No grand juror shall be permitted to state or testify in any court how he, she, or any other grand juror voted on any question before them or what opinion was expressed by himself, herself, or any other grand juror regarding such question.

(3) No grand juror, public or private attorney, city attorney or corporation counsel, reporter, interpreter or public servant who held a witness in custody before a grand jury or special inquiry judge, or witness, principal or other person shall disclose the testimony of a witness examined before the grand jury or special inquiry judge or other evidence received by it, except when required by the court to disclose the testimony of the witness examined before the grand jury or special inquiry judge for the purpose of ascertaining whether it is consistent with that of the witness given before the court, or to disclose his or her testimony given before the grand jury or special inquiry judge by any person upon a charge against such person for perjury in giving his or her testimony or upon trial therefor, or when permitted by the court in furtherance of justice.

(4) The public attorney shall have access to all grand jury and special inquiry judge evidence and may introduce such evidence before any other grand jury or any trial in which the same may be relevant.

(5) The court upon a showing of good cause may make any or all grand jury or special inquiry judge evidence available to any other public attorney, prosecuting attorney, city attorney or corporation counsel upon proper application and with the concurrence of the public attorney attending such grand jury. Any witness' testimony, given before a grand jury or a special inquiry judge and relevant to any subsequent proceeding against the witness, shall be made available to the witness upon proper application to the court. The court may also, upon proper application and upon a

showing of good cause, make available to a defendant in a subsequent criminal proceeding other testimony or evidence:

(a) When given or presented before a special inquiry judge, if doing so is in the furtherance of justice; or

(b) When given or presented before a grand jury, if the court finds that doing so is necessary to prevent an injustice and that there is no reason to believe that doing so would endanger the life or safety of any witness or his or her family. The cost of any such transcript made available shall be borne by the applicant.

[**2010 c 8 § 1021; 1971 ex.s. c 67 § 9.**]

10.27.100
Inquiry as to offenses—Duties—Investigation.

The grand jurors shall inquire into every offense triable within the county for which any person has been held to answer, if an indictment has not been found or an information filed in such case, and all other indictable offenses within the county which are presented to them by a public attorney or otherwise come to their knowledge. If a grand juror knows or has reason to believe that an indictable offense, triable within the county, has been committed, he or she shall declare such a fact to his or her fellow jurors who may begin an investigation. In such investigation the grand juror may be sworn as a witness.

[**2010 c 8 § 1022; 1971 ex.s. c 67 § 10.**]

10.27.110
Duration of sessions—Extensions.

The length of time which a grand jury may sit after being convened shall not exceed sixty days. Before expiration of the sixty day period and any extensions, and upon showing of good cause, the court may order the grand jury panel extended for a period not to exceed sixty days.

[1971 ex.s. c 67 § 11.]

10.27.120

Self-incrimination—Right to counsel.

Any individual called to testify before a grand jury or special inquiry judge, whether as a witness or principal, if not represented by an attorney appearing with the witness before the grand jury or special inquiry judge, must be told of his or her privilege against self-incrimination. Such an individual has a right to representation by an attorney to advise him or her as to his or her rights, obligations, and duties before the grand jury or special inquiry judge, and must be informed of this right. The attorney may be present during all proceedings attended by his or her client unless immunity has been granted pursuant to RCW **10.27.130**. After immunity has been granted, such an individual may leave the grand jury room to confer with his or her attorney.

[**2010 c 8 § 1023; 1971 ex.s. c 67 § 12.**]

10.27.130

Self-incrimination—Refusal to testify or give evidence—Procedure.

If in any proceedings before a grand jury or special inquiry judge, a person refuses, or indicates in advance a refusal, to testify or provide evidence of any other kind on the ground that he or she may be incriminated thereby, and if a public attorney requests the court to order that person to testify or provide the evidence, the court shall then hold a hearing and shall so order unless it finds that to do so would be clearly contrary to the public interest, and that person shall comply with the order. The hearing shall be subject to the provisions of RCW **10.27.080**and **10.27.090**, unless the witness shall request that the hearing be public.

If, but for this section, he or she would have been privileged to withhold the answer given or the evidence produced by him or her, the witness may not refuse to comply with the order on the basis of his or her privilege against self-incrimination; but he or she shall not be prosecuted or subjected to criminal penalty or forfeiture for or on account of any transaction, matter, or fact concerning which he or she has been ordered to testify pursuant to this section. He or she may nevertheless be prosecuted for failing to comply with the order to answer, or for perjury or for offering false evidence to the grand jury.

[**2010 c 8 § 1024; 1971 ex.s. c 67 § 13.**]

10.27.140
Witnesses—Attendance.

(1) Except as provided in this section, no person has the right to appear as a witness in a grand jury or special inquiry judge proceeding.

(2) A public attorney may call as a witness in a grand jury or special inquiry judge proceeding any person believed by him or her to possess information or knowledge relevant thereto and may issue legal process and subpoena to compel his or her attendance and the production of evidence.

(3) The grand jury or special inquiry judge may cause to be called as a witness any person believed by it to possess relevant information or knowledge. If the grand jury or special inquiry judge desires to hear any such witness who was not called by a public attorney, it may direct a public attorney to issue and serve a subpoena upon such witness and the public attorney must comply with such direction. At any time after service of such subpoena and before the return date thereof, however, the public attorney may apply to the court which impaneled the grand jury for an order vacating or modifying the subpoena on the grounds that such is in the public interest. Upon such application, the court may in its discretion vacate the subpoena, extend its return date, attach reasonable conditions to directions, or make such other qualification thereof as is appropriate.

(4) The proceedings to summon a person and compel him or her to testify or provide evidence shall as far as possible be the same as proceedings to summon witnesses and compel their attendance. Such persons shall receive only those fees paid witnesses in superior court criminal trials.

[**2010 c 8 § 1025; 1971 ex.s. c 67 § 14.**]

10.27.150

Indictments—Issuance.

After hearing, examining, and investigating the evidence before it, a grand jury may, in its discretion, issue an indictment against a principal. A grand jury shall find an indictment only when from all the evidence at least three-fourths of the jurors are convinced that there is probable cause to believe a principal is guilty of a criminal offense. When an indictment is found by a grand jury the foreperson or acting foreperson shall present it to the court.

[**2010 c 8 § 1026;** 1971 ex.s. c 67 § 15.]

10.27.160

Grand jury report.

The grand jury may prepare its conclusions, recommendations and suggestions in the form of a grand jury report. Such report shall be released to the public only upon a determination by a majority of the judges of the superior court of the county court that (1) the findings in the report deal with matters of broad public policy affecting the public interest and do not identify or criticize any individual; (2) the release of the report would be consistent with the public interest and further the ends of justice; and (3) release of the report would not prejudice any pending criminal investigation or trial.

[**1971 ex.s. c 67 § 16.**]

10.27.170

Special inquiry judge—Petition for order—Investigation of sexual exploitation of children.

(1) When any public attorney, corporation counsel or city attorney has reason to suspect crime or corruption, within the jurisdiction of such attorney, and there is reason to believe that there are persons who may be able to give material testimony or provide material evidence concerning such suspected crime or corruption, such attorney may petition the judge designated as a special inquiry judge pursuant to RCW**10.27.050** for

an order directed to such persons commanding them to appear at a designated time and place in said county and to then and there answer such questions concerning the suspected crime or corruption as the special inquiry judge may approve, or provide evidence as directed by the special inquiry judge.

(2) Upon petition of a prosecuting attorney for the establishment of a special inquiry judge proceeding in an investigation of sexual exploitation of children under RCW **10.112.010**, the court shall establish the special inquiry judge proceeding, if appropriate, as soon as practicable but no later than seventy-two hours after the filing of the petition.

[**2017 c 114 § 3; 1971 ex.s. c 67 § 17.**]

NOTES:

Findings—2017 c 114: See note following RCW **10.112.010**.

10.27.180

Special inquiry judge—Disqualification from subsequent proceedings.

The judge serving as a special inquiry judge shall be disqualified from acting as a magistrate or judge in any subsequent court proceeding arising from such inquiry except alleged contempt for neglect or refusal to appear, testify or provide evidence at such inquiry in response to an order, summons or subpoena.

[**1971 ex.s. c 67 § 18.**]

10.27.190

Special inquiry judge—Direction to public attorney for proceedings in another county—Procedure.

Upon petition of a public attorney to the special inquiry judge that there is reason to suspect that there exists evidence of crime and corruption in another county, and with the concurrence of the special inquiry judge and prosecuting attorney of the other county, the special inquiry judge may direct the public attorney to attend and participate in special inquiry judge proceedings in the other county held to inquire into crime and corruption which relates to crime or corruption under investigation in the initiating county.

The proceedings of such special inquiry judge may be transcribed, certified and filed in the county of the public attorney's jurisdiction at the expense of that county.

[**1971 ex.s. c 67 § 19.**]

Chapter 10.29 RCW STATEWIDE SPECIAL INQUIRY JUDGE ACT

NOTES:

Special inquiry judge: RCW **10.27.050**, **10.27.170** through **10.27.190**.

10.29.010
Short title.

This chapter shall be known and may be cited as the Statewide Special Inquiry Judge Act.

[**1980 c 146 § 1.**]

10.29.020
Intent.

It is the intent of the legislature in enacting this chapter to strengthen and enhance the ability of the state to detect and eliminate organized criminal activity.

[**1980 c 146 § 2.**]

10.29.050
Powers and duties of statewide special inquiry judge.

A statewide special inquiry judge shall have the following powers and duties:

(1) To hear and receive evidence of crime and corruption.

(2) To appoint a reporter to record the proceedings; and to swear the reporter not to disclose any testimony or the name of any witness except as provided in RCW **10.27.090**.

(3) Whenever necessary, to appoint an interpreter, and to swear him or her not to disclose any testimony or the name of any witness except as provided in RCW **10.27.090**.

(4) When a person held in official custody is a witness before a statewide special inquiry judge, a public servant, assigned to guard him or her during his or her appearance may accompany him or her. The statewide special inquiry judge shall swear such public servant not to disclose any testimony or the name of any witness except as provided in RCW **10.27.090**.

(5) To cause to be called as a witness any person believed by him or her to possess relevant information or knowledge. If the statewide special inquiry judge desires to hear any such witness who was not called by the special prosecutor, it may direct the special prosecutor to issue and serve a subpoena upon such witness and the special prosecutor must comply with such direction. At any time after service of such subpoena and before the return date thereof, however, the special prosecutor may apply to the statewide special inquiry judge for an order vacating or modifying the subpoena on the grounds that such is in the public interest. Upon such application, the statewide special inquiry judge may in its discretion vacate the subpoena, extend its return date, attach reasonable conditions to directions, or make such other qualification thereof as is appropriate.

(6) Upon a showing of good cause may make available any or all evidence obtained to any other public attorney, prosecuting attorney, city attorney, or corporation counsel upon proper application and with the concurrence of the special prosecutor. Any witness' testimony, given before a statewide special inquiry judge and relevant to any subsequent proceeding against the witness, shall be made available to the witness upon proper application to the statewide special inquiry judge. The statewide special

inquiry judge may also, upon proper application and upon a showing of good cause, make available to a defendant in a subsequent criminal proceeding other testimony or evidence when given or presented before a special inquiry judge, if doing so is in the furtherance of justice.

(7) Have authority to perform such other duties as may be required to effectively implement this chapter, in accord with rules adopted by the supreme court relating to these proceedings.

(8) Have authority to hold in contempt of court any person who shall disclose the name or testimony of a witness examined before a statewide special inquiry judge except when required by a court to disclose the testimony given before such statewide special inquiry judge in a subsequent criminal proceeding.

[**2010 c 8 § 1027; 1980 c 146 § 5.**]

10.29.060
Disclosures by witness—Penalty.

Any witness who shall disclose the fact that he or she has been called as a witness before a statewide special inquiry judge or who shall disclose the nature of the testimony given shall be guilty of a misdemeanor.

[**1980 c 146 § 6.**]

10.29.070
Rules.

The supreme court shall develop and adopt rules to govern the procedures of a statewide special inquiry judge proceeding including rules assuring the confidentiality of all proceedings, testimony, and the identity of persons called as witnesses. The adoption of such rules shall be subject to the approval of such rules by the senate and house judiciary committees.

[**1980 c 146 § 7.**]

10.29.100
Vacancy in office.

Whenever a statewide special inquiry judge or special prosecutor appointed under this chapter dies or in any other way is rendered incapable of continuing the duties of his or her office, a successor shall be appointed to serve for the remainder of the judge's or prosecutor's term in the manner provided for by *RCW **10.29.030** and **10.29.080** for the appointment of statewide special inquiry judges and special prosecutors.

[**1980 c 146 § 10.**]

NOTES:

*Reviser's note: RCW **10.29.030** and **10.29.080** were repealed by **2009 c 560 § 24.**

10.29.110
Duties of special prosecutor or designee.

The special prosecutor or his or her designee shall:

(1) Attend all proceedings of the statewide special inquiry judge;

(2) Have the authority to issue subpoenas for witnesses statewide;

(3) Examine witnesses, present evidence, draft reports as directed by the statewide special inquiry judge, and draft and file informations under RCW **10.29.120**.

[**2010 c 8 § 1028; 1980 c 146 § 11.**]

10.29.120
Advising county prosecuting attorney—Filing and prosecution of informations—Expenses of prosecutions.

(1) The special prosecutor shall advise the county prosecuting attorney in any affected county of the nature of the statewide special inquiry judge investigation and of any informations arising from such proceedings unless such disclosures will create a substantial likelihood of a conflict of interest for the county prosecuting attorney.

(2) The special prosecutor may file and prosecute an information in the county where proper venue lies, after having advised the county prosecuting attorney as provided in this section and determined that such prosecuting attorney does not intend to do so, or pursuant to an agreement between them that the special prosecutor shall do so.

(3) Informations filed and prosecuted pursuant to this chapter shall meet the requirements of chapter **10.37** RCW.

(4) The expenses of prosecutions initiated and maintained by the special prosecutor shall be paid as part of the statewide special inquiry judge program as provided in *RCW **10.29.090**.

[**1980 c 146 § 12.**]

NOTES:

Reviser's note: RCW **10.29.090** was repealed by **2009 c 560 § 24.**

10.29.130
Disqualification of judge from subsequent proceedings.

The judge serving as a special inquiry judge shall be disqualified from acting as a magistrate or judge in any subsequent court proceeding arising from such inquiry except alleged contempt for neglect or refusal to appear, testify, or provide evidence at such inquiry in response to an order, summons, or subpoena.

[**1980 c 146 § 13.**]

Chapter 10.31 RCW WARRANTS AND ARRESTS

NOTES:

Rules of court: Warrant upon indictment or information—CrR 2.2.

Search and seizure: Chapter **10.79** RCW.

10.31.030
Service—How—Warrant not in possession, procedure—Bail.

The officer making an arrest must inform the defendant that he or she acts under authority of a warrant, and must also show the warrant: PROVIDED, That if the officer does not have the warrant in his or her possession at the time of arrest he or she shall declare that the warrant does presently exist and will be shown to the defendant as soon as possible on arrival at the place of intended confinement: PROVIDED, FURTHER, That any officer making an arrest under this section shall, if the person arrested wishes to deposit bail, take such person directly and without delay before a judge or before an officer authorized to take the recognizance and justify and approve the bail, including the deposit of a sum of money equal to bail. Bail shall be the amount fixed by the warrant. Such judge or authorized officer shall hold bail for the legal authority within this state which issued such warrant if other than such arresting authority.

[**2010 c 8 § 1029; 1970 ex.s. c 49 § 3; 1891 c 28 § 43;** Code 1881 § 1030; **1873 p 229 § 210; 1854 p 114 § 74;** RRS § 2083.]

NOTES:

        Severability—1970 ex.s. c 49: See note following RCW **9.69.100**.

Bail: Chapter **10.19** RCW.

10.31.040
Officer may break and enter.

To make an arrest in criminal actions, the officer may break open any outer or inner door, or windows of a dwelling house or other building, or any other inclosure, if, after notice of his or her office and purpose, he or she be refused admittance.

[**2010 c 8 § 1030;** Code 1881 § 1170; **1854 p 129 § 179;** RRS § 2082.]

10.31.050
Officer may use force.

If after notice of the intention to arrest the defendant, he or she either flee or forcibly resist, the officer may use all necessary means to effect the arrest.
[**2010 c 8 § 1031;** Code 1881 § 1031; **1873 p 229 § 211; 1854 p 114 § 75;** RRS § 2084.]

10.31.060
Arrest by telegraph or teletype.

Whenever any person or persons shall have been indicted or accused on oath of any public offense, or thereof convicted, and a warrant of arrest shall have been issued, the magistrate issuing such warrant, or any justice of the supreme court, or any judge of either the court of appeals or superior court may indorse thereon an order signed by him or her and authorizing the service thereof by telegraph or teletype, and thereupon such warrant and order may be sent by telegraph or teletype to any marshal, sheriff, constable or police officer, and on the receipt of the telegraphic or teletype copy thereof by any such officer, he or she shall have the same authority and be under the same obligations to arrest, take into custody and detain the said person or persons, as if the said original warrant of arrest, with the proper direction for the service thereof, duly indorsed thereon, had been placed in his or her hands, and the said telegraphic or teletype copy shall be entitled to full faith and credit, and have the same force and effect in all courts and places as the original; but prior to indictment and conviction, no such order shall be made by any officer, unless in his or her judgment there is probable cause to believe the said accused person or persons guilty of the offense charged: PROVIDED, That the making of such order by any officer aforesaid, shall be prima facie evidence of the regularity thereof, and of all the proceedings prior thereto. The original warrant and order, or a copy thereof, certified by the officer making the order, shall be preserved in the telegraph office or police agency from which the same is sent, and in telegraphing or teletyping the same, the original or the said certified copy may be used.

[**2010 c 8 § 1032; 1971 c 81 § 48; 1967 c 91 § 1;** Code 1881 § 2357; **1865 p 75 § 16;** RRS § 2081. Formerly RCW **10.31.060** through **10.31.090**.]

10.31.100

Arrest without warrant.

A police officer having probable cause to believe that a person has committed or is committing a felony shall have the authority to arrest the person without a warrant. A police officer may arrest a person without a warrant for committing a misdemeanor or gross misdemeanor only when the offense is committed in the presence of an officer, except as provided in subsections (1) through (11) of this section.

(1) Any police officer having probable cause to believe that a person has committed or is committing a misdemeanor or gross misdemeanor, involving physical harm or threats of harm to any person or property or the unlawful taking of property or involving the use or possession of cannabis, or involving the acquisition, possession, or consumption of alcohol by a person under the age of twenty-one years under RCW **66.44.270**, or involving criminal trespass under RCW **9A.52.070** or **9A.52.080**, shall have the authority to arrest the person.

(2) A police officer shall arrest and take into custody, pending release on bail, personal recognizance, or court order, a person without a warrant when the officer has probable cause to believe that:

(a) An order has been issued of which the person has knowledge under RCW **26.44.063**, or chapter **7.92**, 7.90, 9A.46, 10.99, 26.09, 26.10, 26.26, 26.50, or **74.34** RCW restraining the person and the person has violated the terms of the order restraining the person from acts or threats of violence, or restraining the person from going onto the grounds of or entering a residence, workplace, school, or day care, or prohibiting the person from knowingly coming within, or knowingly remaining within, a specified distance of a location or, in the case of an order issued under RCW **26.44.063**, imposing any other restrictions or conditions upon the person; or

(b) A foreign protection order, as defined in RCW **26.52.010**, has been issued of which the person under restraint has knowledge and the person under restraint has violated a provision of the foreign protection order prohibiting the person under restraint from contacting or communicating with another person, or excluding the person under restraint from a residence, workplace, school, or day care, or prohibiting the person from knowingly coming within, or knowingly remaining within, a specified distance of a location, or a violation of any provision for which the foreign protection order specifically indicates that a violation will be a crime; or

(c) The person is eighteen years or older and within the preceding four hours has assaulted a family or household member as defined in RCW **10.99.020** and the officer believes: (i) A felonious assault has occurred; (ii) an assault has occurred which has resulted in bodily injury to the victim, whether the injury is observable by the responding officer or not; or (iii) that any physical action has occurred which was intended to cause another person reasonably to fear imminent serious bodily injury or death. Bodily injury means physical pain, illness, or an impairment of physical condition. When the officer has probable cause to believe that family or household members have assaulted each other, the officer is not required to arrest both persons. The officer shall arrest the person whom the officer believes to be the primary physical aggressor. In making this determination, the officer shall make every reasonable effort to consider: (A) The intent to protect victims of domestic violence under RCW **10.99.010**; (B) the comparative extent of injuries inflicted or serious threats creating fear of physical injury; and (C) the history of domestic violence of each person involved, including whether the conduct was part of an ongoing pattern of abuse.

(3) Any police officer having probable cause to believe that a person has committed or is committing a violation of any of the following traffic laws shall have the authority to arrest the person:

(a) RCW **46.52.010**, relating to duty on striking an unattended car or other property;

(b) RCW **46.52.020**, relating to duty in case of injury to or death of a person or damage to an attended vehicle;

(c) RCW **46.61.500** or **46.61.530**, relating to reckless driving or racing of vehicles;

(d) RCW **46.61.502** or **46.61.504**, relating to persons under the influence of intoxicating liquor or drugs;

(e) RCW **46.61.503** or **46.25.110**, relating to persons having alcohol or THC in their system;

(f) RCW **46.20.342**, relating to driving a motor vehicle while operator's license is suspended or revoked;

(g) RCW **46.61.5249**, relating to operating a motor vehicle in a negligent manner.

(4) A law enforcement officer investigating at the scene of a motor vehicle accident may arrest the driver of a motor vehicle involved in the accident if the officer has probable cause to believe that the driver has committed in connection with the accident a violation of any traffic law or regulation.

(5)(a) A law enforcement officer investigating at the scene of a motor vessel accident may arrest the operator of a motor vessel involved in the accident if the officer has probable cause to believe that the operator has committed, in connection with the accident, a criminal violation of chapter **79A.60** RCW.

(b) A law enforcement officer investigating at the scene of a motor vessel accident may issue a citation for an infraction to the operator of a motor vessel involved in the accident if the officer has probable cause to believe that the operator has committed, in connection with the accident, a violation of any boating safety law of chapter **79A.60** RCW.

(6) Any police officer having probable cause to believe that a person has committed or is committing a violation of RCW **79A.60.040** shall have the authority to arrest the person.

(7) An officer may act upon the request of a law enforcement officer in whose presence a traffic infraction was committed, to stop, detain, arrest, or issue a notice of traffic infraction to the driver who is believed to have committed the infraction. The request by the witnessing officer shall give an officer the authority to take appropriate action under the laws of the state of Washington.

(8) Any police officer having probable cause to believe that a person has committed or is committing any act of indecent exposure, as defined in RCW **9A.88.010**, may arrest the person.

(9) A police officer may arrest and take into custody, pending release on bail, personal recognizance, or court order, a person without a warrant when the officer has probable cause to believe that an order has been issued of which the person has knowledge under chapter **10.14**RCW and the person has violated the terms of that order.

(10) Any police officer having probable cause to believe that a person has, within twenty-four hours of the alleged violation, committed a violation of RCW **9A.50.020** may arrest such person.

(11) A police officer having probable cause to believe that a person illegally possesses or illegally has possessed a firearm or other dangerous weapon on private or public elementary or secondary school premises shall have the authority to arrest the person.

For purposes of this subsection, the term "firearm" has the meaning defined in RCW **9.41.010** and the term "dangerous weapon" has the meaning defined in RCW **9.41.250** and **9.41.280**(1) (c) through (e).

(12) A law enforcement officer having probable cause to believe that a person has committed a violation under *RCW **77.15.160**(4) may issue a citation for an infraction to the person in connection with the violation.

(13) A law enforcement officer having probable cause to believe that a person has committed a criminal violation under RCW **77.15.809** or**77.15.811** may arrest the person in connection with the violation.

(14) Except as specifically provided in subsections (2), (3), (4), and (7) of this section, nothing in this section extends or otherwise affects the powers of arrest prescribed in Title **46** RCW.

(15) No police officer may be held criminally or civilly liable for making an arrest pursuant to subsection (2) or (9) of this section if the police officer acts in good faith and without malice.

(16)(a) Except as provided in (b) of this subsection, a police officer shall arrest and keep in custody, until release by a judicial officer on bail, personal recognizance, or court order, a person without a warrant when the officer has probable cause to believe that the person has violated RCW **46.61.502** or **46.61.504** or an equivalent local ordinance and the police officer: (i) Has knowledge that the person has a prior offense as defined in RCW **46.61.5055** within ten years; or (ii) has knowledge, based on a review of the information available to the officer at the time of arrest, that the person is charged with or is awaiting arraignment for an offense that would qualify as a prior offense as defined in RCW**46.61.5055** if it were a conviction.

(b) A police officer is not required to keep in custody a person under (a) of this subsection if the person requires immediate medical attention and is admitted to a hospital.

[**2017 c 336 § 3; 2017 c 223 § 1.** Prior: **2016 c 203 § 9; 2016 c 113 § 1;** prior: **2014 c 202 § 307; 2014 c 100 § 2; 2014 c 5 § 1; 2013 2nd sp.s. c 35 § 22;** prior: **2013 c 278 § 4; 2013 c 84 § 32; 2010 c 274 § 201; 2006 c 138 § 23; 2000 c 119 § 4; 1999 c 184 § 14; 1997 c 66 § 10; 1996 c 248 § 4;** prior:**1995 c 246 § 20; 1995 c 184 § 1; 1995 c 93 § 1;** prior: **1993 c 209 § 1; 1993 c 128 § 5; 1988 c 190 § 1;** prior: **1987 c 280 § 20; 1987 c 277 § 2; 1987 c 154 § 1; 1987 c 66 § 1;** prior: **1985 c 303 § 9; 1985 c 267 § 3; 1984 c 263 § 19; 1981 c 106 § 1; 1980 c 148 § 8; 1979 ex.s. c 28 § 1; 1969 ex.s. c 198 § 1.**]
NOTES:

Reviser's note: *(1) RCW **77.15.160** was amended by 2017 3rd sp.s. c 8 § 42, changing subsection (4) to subsection (5), effective January 1, 2018.

(2) This section was amended by 2017 c 223 § 1 and by 2017 c 336 § 3, each without reference to the other. Both amendments are incorporated in the publication of this section under RCW **1.12.025**(2). For rule of construction, see RCW **1.12.025**(1).

Finding—2017 c 336: See note following RCW **9.96.060**.

Findings—2014 c 202: See note following RCW **77.135.010**.

Intent—2010 c 274: "The legislature intends to improve the lives of persons who suffer from the adverse effects of domestic violence and to require reasonable, coordinated measures to prevent domestic violence from occurring. The legislature intends to give law enforcement and the courts better tools to identify violent perpetrators of domestic violence and hold them accountable. The legislature intends to: Increase the safety afforded to individuals who seek protection of public and private agencies involved in domestic violence prevention; improve the ability of agencies to address the needs of victims and their children and the delivery of services; upgrade the quality of treatment programs; and enhance the ability of the justice system to respond quickly and fairly to domestic violence. In order to improve the lives of persons who have, or may suffer, the effects of domestic violence the legislature intends to achieve more uniformity in the decision-making processes at public and private agencies that address domestic violence by reducing inconsistencies and duplications allowing domestic violence victims to achieve safety and stability in their lives." [**2010 c 274 § 101.**]

Short title—2006 c 138: See RCW **7.90.900**.

Application—2000 c 119: See note following RCW **26.50.021**.

Short title—1999 c 184: See RCW **26.52.900**.

Severability—1995 c 246: See note following RCW **26.50.010**.

Effective date—1995 c 184: "This act shall take effect January 1, 1996. Prior to that date, law enforcement agencies, prosecuting authorities, and local governments are encouraged to develop and adopt arrest and charging guidelines regarding criminal trespass." [**1995 c 184 § 2.**]

Effective date—1993 c 128: See RCW **9A.50.902**.

Effective date—1984 c 263: See RCW **26.50.901**.

Arrest procedure involving traffic violations: Chapter **46.64** RCW.

Domestic violence, peace officers—Immunity: RCW **26.50.140**.

Uniform Controlled Substances Act: Chapter **69.50** RCW.

10.31.110

Arrest—Individuals with mental disorders.

(1) When a police officer has reasonable cause to believe that the individual has committed acts constituting a nonfelony crime that is not a serious offense as identified in RCW **10.77.092** and the individual is known by history or consultation with the behavioral health organization to suffer from a mental disorder, the arresting officer may:

(a) Take the individual to a crisis stabilization unit as defined in *RCW **71.05.020**(6). Individuals delivered to a crisis stabilization unit pursuant to this section may be held by the facility for a period of up to twelve hours. The individual must be examined by a mental health professional within three hours of arrival;

(b) Take the individual to a triage facility as defined in RCW **71.05.020**. An individual delivered to a triage facility which has elected to operate as an involuntary facility may be held up to a period of twelve hours. The individual must be examined by a mental health professional within three hours of arrival;

(c) Refer the individual to a mental health professional for evaluation for initial detention and proceeding under chapter **71.05** RCW; or

(d) Release the individual upon agreement to voluntary participation in outpatient treatment.

(2) If the individual is released to the community, the mental health provider shall inform the arresting officer of the release within a reasonable period of time after the release if the arresting officer has specifically requested notification and provided contact information to the provider.

(3) In deciding whether to refer the individual to treatment under this section, the police officer shall be guided by standards mutually agreed upon with the prosecuting authority, which address, at a minimum, the length, seriousness, and recency of the known criminal history of the individual, the mental health history of the individual, where available, and the circumstances surrounding the commission of the alleged offense.

(4) Any agreement to participate in treatment shall not require individuals to stipulate to any of the alleged facts regarding the criminal activity as a prerequisite to participation in a mental health treatment alternative. The agreement is inadmissible in any criminal or civil proceeding. The agreement does not create immunity from prosecution for the alleged criminal activity.

(5) If an individual violates such agreement and the mental health treatment alternative is no longer appropriate:

(a) The mental health provider shall inform the referring law enforcement agency of the violation; and

(b) The original charges may be filed or referred to the prosecutor, as appropriate, and the matter may proceed accordingly.

(6) The police officer is immune from liability for any good faith conduct under this section.

[**2014 c 225 § 57.** Prior: **2011 c 305 § 7; 2011 c 148 § 3; 2007 c 375 § 2.**]

NOTES:

*Reviser's note: RCW **71.05.020** was amended by 2016 sp.s. c 29 § 204, changing subsection (6) to subsection (10), effective April 1, 2018.

Effective date—2014 c 225: See note following RCW **71.24.016**.

Findings—2011 c 305: See note following RCW **74.09.295**.

Certification of triage facilities—Effective date—2011 c 148: See notes following RCW **71.05.020**.

Findings—Purpose—2007 c 375: "The legislature finds that *RCW **10.77.090** contains laws relating to three discrete subjects. Therefore, one purpose of this act is to reorganize some of those laws by creating new sections in the Revised Code of Washington that clarify and identify these discrete subjects.

The legislature further finds that there are disproportionate numbers of individuals with mental illness in jail. The needs of individuals with mental illness and the public safety needs of society at large are better served when individuals with mental illness are provided an opportunity to obtain treatment and support." [**2007 c 375 § 1.**]

*Reviser's note: RCW **10.77.090** was repealed by **2007 c 375 § 17.** For later enactment, see RCW **10.77.084**, **10.77.086**, and **10.77.088**.

Construction—2007 c 375: "Nothing in this act shall be construed to alter or diminish a prosecutor's inherent authority to divert or pursue the prosecution of criminal offenders." [**2007 c 375 § 16.**]

Severability—2007 c 375: "If any provision of this act or its application to any person or circumstance is held invalid, the remainder of the act or the application of the provision to other persons or circumstances is not affected." [**2007 c 375 § 18.**]

10.31.120

Chemical dependency arrests—Treatment—Pilot program. (Expires July 31, 2019.)

(1) A pilot program is established in Snohomish county for the purpose of studying the effect of chemical dependency diversions as described in this section.

(2) When a police officer has reasonable cause to believe that the individual:

(a) Has committed acts constituting a nonfelony crime that is not a serious offense as identified in RCW **9.41.010**;

(b) Has not committed a possible violation of laws relating to driving or being in physical control of a vehicle while under the influence of intoxicating liquor or any drug under chapter **46.20** RCW; and

(c) Is known by history or consultation with staff designated by the county to suffer from a chemical dependency, as defined in *RCW**70.96A.020**, the arresting officer may:

(i) Take the individual to an approved chemical dependency treatment provider for treatment. The individual must be examined by a chemical dependency treatment provider within three hours of arrival;

(ii) Take the individual to an emergency medical service customarily used for incapacitated persons, if no approved treatment program is readily available. The individual must be examined by a chemical dependency treatment provider within three hours of arrival;

(iii) Refer the individual to a chemical dependency professional for initial detention and proceeding under **chapter **70.96A** RCW; or

(iv) Release the individual upon agreement to voluntary participation in outpatient treatment.

(3) If the individual is released to the community, the chemical dependency [treatment] provider shall inform the arresting officer of the release within a reasonable period of time after the release if the arresting officer has specifically requested notification and provided contact information to the provider.

(4) In deciding whether to refer the individual to treatment under this section, the police officer shall be guided by standards mutually agreed upon with the prosecuting

authority, which address, at a minimum, the length, seriousness, and recency of the known criminal history of the individual, the mental health and substance abuse history of the individual, where available, and the circumstances surrounding the commission of the alleged offense.

(5) The police officer shall submit a written report to the prosecuting attorney within ten days.

(6) Any agreement to participate in treatment shall not require individuals to stipulate to any of the alleged facts regarding the criminal activity as a prerequisite to participation in a chemical dependency treatment alternative. The agreement is inadmissible in any criminal or civil proceeding. The agreement does not create immunity from prosecution for the alleged criminal activity.

(7) If an individual violates such agreement and the chemical dependency treatment alternative is no longer appropriate, the chemical dependency [treatment] provider shall inform the referring law enforcement agency of the violation.

(8) Nothing in this section may be construed as barring the referral of charges to the prosecuting attorney, or the filing of criminal charges by the prosecuting attorney.

(9) The police officer, staff designated by the county, or treatment facility personnel are immune from liability for any good faith conduct under this section.

[**2014 c 128 § 2.**]

NOTES:

Reviser's note: *(1) RCW **70.96A.020** was repealed by 2016 sp.s. c 29 § 301, effective April 1, 2018.

(2) Chapter **70.96A RCW was repealed and/or recodified in its entirety pursuant to 2016 sp.s. c 29 §§ 301, effective April 1, 2018, 601, and 701.

Pilot program evaluation—2014 c 128: "Snohomish county shall evaluate the effects of the pilot program as provided in section 2 of this act. Snohomish county shall submit a report to the legislature consistent with RCW **43.01.036**. The report must summarize the effectiveness of the pilot program and include: How often the chemical dependency diversion was used, the kind of treatment the person engaged in, how often treatment was completed, the number of prosecutions, any cost savings to the county or state, any cost shifting from the county or state onto other systems, and the recidivism rate of offenders involved in the pilot program. The report may include any recommendations to the legislature to improve the effectiveness of the pilot program. The report is due July 1, 2015, and every other year until July 1, 2019." [**2014 c 128 § 3.**]

    Expiration date—2014 c 128 §§ 2 and 3: "Sections 2 and 3 of this act expire July 31, 2019." [**2014 c 128 § 6.**]

    Finding—2014 c 128: "The legislature finds that the large number of individuals involved in the juvenile justice and criminal justice systems with substance abuse challenges is of significant concern. Access to effective treatment is critical to the successful treatment of individuals in the early stages of their contact with the juvenile justice and criminal justice systems. Such access may prevent further involvement in the systems. The effective use of substance abuse treatment options can result not only in significant cost savings for the juvenile justice and criminal justice systems, but can benefit the lives of individuals who face substance abuse challenges." [**2014 c 128 § 1.**]

Chapter 10.34 RCW FUGITIVES OF THIS STATE

NOTES:

Escape: Chapter **9A.76** RCW.

Extradition and fresh pursuit: Chapter **10.88** RCW.

Return of parole violators from another state: RCW **9.95.280** through **9.95.300**.

10.34.010
Officer may arrest defendant in any county.

If any person against whom a warrant may be issued for an alleged offense, committed in any county, shall either before or after the issuing of such warrant, escape from, or be out of the county, the sheriff or other officer to whom such warrant may be directed, may pursue and apprehend the party charged, in any county in this state, and for that purpose may command aid, and exercise the same authority as in his or her own county.

[**2010 c 8 § 1033;** Code 1881 § 1922; **1873 p 394 § 220; 1854 p 107 § 28;** RRS § 1950.]

10.34.020
Escape—Retaking prisoner—Authority.

If a person arrested escape or be rescued, the person from whose custody he or she made his or her escape, or was rescued, may immediately pursue and retake him or her at any time, and within any place in the state. To retake the person escaping or rescued, the person pursuing has the same power to command assistance as given in cases of arrest.

[**2010 c 8 § 1034;** Code 1881 § 1032; **1873 p 229 § 212; 1854 p 114 § 76;** RRS § 2085.]

10.34.030
Escape—Retaking in foreign state—Extradition agents.

The governor may appoint agents to make a demand upon the executive authority of any state or territory for the surrender of any fugitive from justice, or any other person charged with a felony or any other crime in this state. Whenever an application shall be made to the governor for the appointment of an agent he or she may require the official submitting the same to provide whatever information is necessary prior to approval of the application.

[**2010 c 8 § 1035; 1993 c 442 § 1; 1967 c 91 § 2; 1891 c 28 § 98;** Code 1881 § 971; **1873 p 217 § 157; 1854 p 102 § 5;** RRS § 2241.]

NOTES:

Effective date—1993 c 442: "This act is necessary for the immediate preservation of the public peace, health, or safety, or support of the state government and its existing public institutions, and shall take effect July 1, 1993." [**1993 c 442 § 2.**]

Chapter 10.37 RCW ACCUSATIONS AND THEIR REQUISITES

NOTES:

Rules of court: Rights of dependents—CrR 3.1 through 3.6.
Ownership of property, proof of: RCW **10.58.060**.

10.37.010
Pleadings required in criminal proceedings.

No pleading other than an indictment, information or complaint shall be required on the part of the state in any criminal proceedings in any court of the state, and when such pleading is in the manner and form as provided by law the defendant shall be required to plead thereto as prescribed by law without any further action or proceedings of any kind on the part of the state.

[**1925 ex.s. c 150 § 3;** RRS § 2050-1. FORMER PARTS OF SECTION: (i) **1927 c 103 § 1;** Code 1881 § 764; RRS § 2023, now codified as RCW**10.37.015**. (ii) **1909 c 87 § 1; 1891 c 117 § 1; 1890 p 100 § 1;** RRS § 2024, now codified as RCW **10.37.026**. (iii) **1891 c 28 § 19;** Code 1881 § 1003;**1873 p 224 § 186; 1869 p 240 § 181;** RRS § 2054, now codified as RCW **10.37.025**.]

10.37.015
Charge by information or indictment—Exceptions.

(1) No person shall be held to answer in any court for an alleged crime or offense, unless upon an information filed by the prosecuting attorney, or upon an indictment by a grand jury, except in cases of misdemeanor or gross misdemeanor before a district or municipal judge, or before a court martial, except as provided in subsection (2) of this section.

(2) Violations of RCW **46.20.342**(1)(c)(iv) may be required by the prosecuting attorney to be referred to his or her office for consideration of filing an information or for entry into a precharge diversion program.
[**2011 c 46 § 1; 1987 c 202 § 167; 1927 c 103 § 1;** Code 1881 § 764; RRS § 2023. Formerly RCW **10.37.010**, part.]
NOTES:
    Intent—1987 c 202: See note following RCW **2.04.190**.

10.37.040
Indictment—Form.

The indictment may be substantially in the following form:

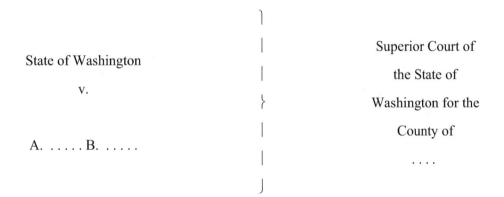

State of Washington	}	Superior Court of
v.		the State of
		Washington for the
		County of
A. . . . . B.		. . . .

A. B. is accused by the grand jury of the . . . ., by this indictment, of the crime of [here insert the name of the crime, if it have one, such as treason, murder, arson, manslaughter, or the like; or if it be a crime having no general name, such as libel, assault and battery, and the like, insert a brief description of it as given by law], committed as follows:

The said A. B. on the . . . . day of . . . . . ., (year) . . . ., in the county of . . . . . ., aforesaid, [here set forth the act charged as a crime.]

Dated at . . . . . ., in the county aforesaid, the . . . . day of . . . . . ., A.D. (year) . . . .

(Signed) C. D., Prosecuting Attorney.

(Indorsed) A true bill.

(Signed) E. F., Foreperson of the Grand Jury.

[**2016 c 202 § 5; 2010 c 8 § 1036; 1891 c 28 § 21;** Code 1881 § 1005; **1873 p 225 § 188; 1869 p 240 § 183;** RRS § 2056.]

10.37.050

Indictment or information—Sufficiency.

The indictment or information is sufficient if it can be understood therefrom—

(1) That it is entitled in a court having authority to receive it;

(2) That it was found by a grand jury or prosecuting attorney of the county in which the court was held;

(3) That the defendant is named, or if his or her name cannot be discovered, that he or she is described by a fictitious name or by reference to a unique genetic sequence of deoxyribonucleic acid, with the statement that his or her real name is unknown;

(4) That the crime was committed within the jurisdiction of the court, except where, as provided by law, the act, though done without the county in which the court is held, is triable therein;

(5) That the crime was committed at some time previous to the finding of the indictment or filing of the information, and within the time limited by law for the commencement of an action therefor;

(6) That the act or omission charged as the crime is clearly and distinctly set forth in ordinary and concise language, without repetition, and in such a manner as to enable a person of common understanding to know what is intended;

(7) The act or omission charged as the crime is stated with such a degree of certainty as to enable the court to pronounce judgment upon a conviction according to the right of the case.

[**2010 c 8 § 1037; 2000 c 92 § 3; 1891 c 28 § 29;** Code 1881 § 1014; **1873 p 226 § 197; 1869 p 242 § 192;** RRS § 2065. FORMER PARTS OF SECTION: (i) **1891 c 28 § 20;** Code 1881 § 1004; **1873 p 224 § 187; 1869 p 240 § 182;** RRS § 2055, now codified as RCW **10.37.052**. (ii) **1891 c 28 § 22;** Code 1881 § 1006; **1873 p 225 § 189; 1854 p 112 § 61; 1869 p 241 § 184;** RRS § 2057, now codified as RCW **10.37.054**. (iii) **1891 c 28 § 30;**Code 1881 § 1015; **1873 p 227 § 198; 1869 p 242 § 193;** RRS § 2066, now codified as RCW **10.37.056**.]

NOTES:

    Intent—**2000 c 92:** See note following RCW **10.73.170**.

10.37.052

Indictment or information—Requisites.

The indictment or information must contain—

(1) The title of the action, specifying the name of the court to which the indictment or information is presented and the names of the parties;

(2) A statement of the acts constituting the offense, in ordinary and concise language, without repetition, and in such manner as to enable a person of common understanding to know what is intended.

[**1891 c 28 § 20;** Code 1881 § 1004; **1873 p 224 § 187; 1869 p 240 § 182;** RRS § 2055. Formerly RCW **10.37.050**, part.]

10.37.054

Indictment or information—Certainty.

The indictment or information must be direct and certain as it regards:

(1) The party charged;

(2) The crime charged; and

(3) The particular circumstances of the crime charged, when they are necessary to constitute a complete crime.

[**1891 c 28 § 22;** Code 1881 § 1006; **1873 p 225 § 189; 1869 p 241 § 184; 1854 p 112 § 61;** RRS § 2057. Formerly RCW **10.37.050**, part.]

10.37.056

Indictment or information—Certain defects or imperfections deemed immaterial.

No indictment or information is insufficient, nor can the trial, judgment or other proceedings thereon be affected, by reason of any of the following matters, which were formerly deemed defects or imperfections:

(1) For want of an allegation of the time or place of any material fact, when the time and place have been once stated;

(2) For the omission of any of the following allegations, namely: "With force and arms," "contrary to the form of the statute or the statutes," or "against the peace and dignity of the state;"

(3) For the omission to allege that the grand jury was impaneled, sworn, or charged;

(4) For any surplusage or repugnant allegation or for any repetition, when there is sufficient matter alleged to indicate clearly the offense and the person charged; nor

(5) For any other matter which was formerly deemed a defect or imperfection, but which does not tend to the prejudice of the substantial rights of the defendant upon the merits.

[**1891 c 28 § 30;** Code 1881 § 1015; **1873 p 227 § 198; 1869 p 242 § 193;** RRS § 2066. Formerly RCW **10.37.050**, part.]

NOTES:

Ownership of property, proof of: RCW **10.58.060**.

10.37.060

Indictment or information—Separation into counts—Consolidation.

When there are several charges against any person, or persons, for the same act or transaction, or for two or more acts or transactions connected together, or for two or more acts or transactions of the same class of crimes or offenses, which may be properly joined, instead of having several indictments or informations the whole may be joined in one indictment, or information, in separate counts; and, if two or more indictments are found, or two or more informations filed, in such cases, the court may order such indictments or informations to be consolidated.

[**1925 ex.s. c 109 § 1; 1891 c 28 § 24;** Code 1881 § 1008; **1873 p 225 § 191; 1869 p 241 § 186;** RRS § 2059.]

10.37.070

Animals—Description of.

When the crime involves the taking of or injury to an animal the indictment or information is sufficiently certain in that respect if it describes the animal by the common name of its class.

[**1891 c 28 § 26;** Code 1881 § 1011; **1873 p 226 § 194; 1869 p 241 § 189;** RRS § 2062.]

NOTES:

Crimes relating to animals: Chapter **9.08** RCW.

Larceny: Chapter **9A.56** RCW.

10.37.080

Forgery—Description of instrument.

When an instrument which is the subject of an indictment or information for forgery has been destroyed or withheld by the act or procurement of the defendant, and the fact of the destruction or withholding is alleged in the indictment or information, and established on the trial, the misdescription of the instrument is immaterial.

[**1891 c 28 § 35;** Code 1881 § 1020; **1873 p 227 § 203; 1854 p 113 § 68;** RRS § 2071.]

NOTES:

Forgery: Chapter **9A.60** RCW.

10.37.090

Injury to person or intention concerning.

When the crime involves the commission of, or an attempt to commit a private injury, and is described with sufficient certainty in other respects to identify the act, an erroneous allegation as to the person injured or intended to be injured is not material. [Code 1881 § 1010; **1873 p 226 § 193; 1869 p 241 § 188;** RRS § 2061.]

10.37.100

Judgment, how pleaded.

In pleading a judgment or other determination of or proceeding before a court or officer of special jurisdiction, it is not necessary to state in the indictment or information the facts conferring jurisdiction; but the judgment, determination or proceeding may be stated to have been duly given or made. The facts conferring jurisdiction, however, must be established on the trial. [**1891 c 28 § 32;** Code 1881 § 1017; **1873 p 227 § 200; 1869 p 242 § 195; 1854 p 112 § 65;** RRS § 2068.]

10.37.110

Larceny or embezzlement—Specification.

In an indictment or information for larceny or embezzlement of money, bank notes, certificates of stock, or valuable securities, or for a conspiracy to cheat or defraud a person of any such property, it is sufficient to allege the larceny or embezzlement, or the conspiracy to cheat and defraud, to be of money, bank notes, certificates of stock, or valuable securities, without specifying the coin, number, denomination or kind thereof. [**1891 c 28 § 38;** Code 1881 § 1023; RRS § 2074.]

NOTES:

Larceny: Chapter **9A.56** RCW.

Ownership of property, proof of: RCW **10.58.060**.

10.37.130

Obscene literature—Description.

An indictment or information for exhibiting, publishing, passing, selling, or offering to sell, or having in possession with such intent, any lewd or obscene book, pamphlet, picture, print, card, paper, or writing, need not set forth any portion of the language used or figures shown upon such book, pamphlet, picture, print, card, paper, or writing, but it is sufficient to state generally the fact of the lewdness or obscenity thereof.

[**1891 c 28 § 39;** Code 1881 § 1024; RRS § 2075.]

NOTES:

Obscenity: Chapter **9.68** RCW.

10.37.140

Perjury—Subornation of perjury—Description of matter.

In an indictment or information for perjury, or subornation of perjury, it is sufficient to set forth the substance of the controversy or matter in respect to which the crime was committed, and in what court or before whom the oath alleged to be false was taken, and that the court or person before whom it was taken had authority to administer it, with proper allegations of the falsity of the matter on which the perjury is assigned; but the indictment or information need not set forth the pleadings, record or proceedings with which the oath is connected, nor the commission or authority of the court or person before whom the perjury was committed.

[**1891 c 28 § 36;** Code 1881 § 1021; **1873 p 228 § 204; 1869 p 243 § 199; 1854 p 112 § 67;** RRS § 2072.]

NOTES:

Perjury: Chapter **9A.72** RCW.

10.37.150

Presumptions of law need not be stated.

Neither presumptions of law nor matters of which judicial notice is taken need be stated in an indictment or information.

[**1891 c 28 § 31;** Code 1881 § 1016; **1873 p 227 § 199; 1869 p 242 § 194;** RRS § 2067.]

10.37.160
Statute—Exact words need not be used.

Words used in a statute to define a crime need not be strictly pursued in the indictment or information, but other words conveying the same meaning may be used.

[**1891 c 28 § 28;** Code 1881 § 1013; **1873 p 226 § 196; 1869 p 241 § 191;** RRS § 2064.]

10.37.170
Statute, private—Description.

In pleading a private statute, or right derived therefrom, it is sufficient to refer, in the indictment or information, to the statute by its title and the day of its passage, and the court must thereupon take judicial notice thereof.

[**1891 c 28 § 33;** Code 1881 § 1018; **1873 p 227 § 201; 1869 p 243 § 196; 1854 p 112 § 66;** RRS § 2069.]

10.37.190
Words and phrases—How used.

The words used in an indictment or information must be construed in their usual acceptation, in common language, except words and phrases defined by law, which are to be construed according to their legal meaning.

[**1891 c 28 § 27;** Code 1881 § 1012; **1873 p 227 § 195; 1869 p 241 § 190;** RRS § 2063.]

Chapter 10.40 RCW ARRAIGNMENT

NOTES:

Rules of court: Arraignment—CrR 4.1.

10.40.050
Entry and use of true name.

If he or she alleges that another name is his or her true name it must be entered in the minutes of the court, and the subsequent proceedings on the indictment or information may be had against him or her by that name, referring also to the name by which he or she is indicted or informed against.

[**2010 c 8 § 1038; 1891 c 28 § 49;** Code 1881 § 1065; **1873 p 232 § 227; 1854 p 116 § 91;** RRS § 2097.]

NOTES:

Action on discovery of true name: RCW **10.46.060**.

10.40.060
Pleading to arraignment.

In answer to the arraignment, the defendant may move to set aside the indictment or information, or he or she may demur or plead to it, and is entitled to one day after arraignment in which to answer thereto if he or she demands it.

[**2010 c 8 § 1039; 1891 c 28 § 50;** Code 1881 § 1045; RRS § 2098.]

10.40.070
Motion to set aside indictment.

The motion to set aside the indictment can be made by the defendant on one or more of the following grounds, and must be sustained:

(1) When any person, other than the grand jurors, was present before the grand jury when the question was taken upon the finding of the indictment, or when any person, other than the grand jurors, was present before the grand jury during the investigation of the charge, except as required or permitted by law;

(2) If the grand jury were not selected, drawn, summoned, impaneled, or sworn as prescribed by law.

[**1983 c 3 § 12; 1957 c 10 § 1;** Code 1881 § 1046; RRS § 2099. FORMER PART OF SECTION: Code 1881 § 1047; RRS § 2100, now codified as RCW**10.40.075**.]

10.40.075

Motion to set aside indictment—Grounds not allowed, when.

The ground of the motion to set aside the indictment mentioned in the fourth subdivision of RCW **10.40.070** is not allowed to a defendant who has been held to answer before indictment.

[Code 1881 § 1047; RRS § 2100. Formerly RCW **10.40.070**, part.]

10.40.090

Sustaining motion—Effect of.

An order to set aside the indictment or information as provided in this chapter shall be no bar to a future prosecution for the same offense.

[**1891 c 28 § 54;** Code 1881 § 1050; RRS § 2104.]

10.40.100

Overruling motion—Pleading over.

If the motion to set aside the indictment [or information] be denied, the defendant must immediately answer the indictment or information, either by demurring or pleading thereto.

[**1891 c 28 § 52;** Code 1881 § 1048; RRS § 2102.]

10.40.110

Demurrer to indictment or information.

The defendant may demur to the indictment or information when it appears upon its face either—

(1) That it does not substantially conform to the requirements of this code;

(2) [That] more than one crime is charged;

(3) That the facts charged do not constitute a crime;

(4) That the indictment or information contains any matter which, if true, would constitute a defense or other legal bar to the action.

[**1891 c 28 § 55;** Code 1881 § 1051; RRS § 2105.]

10.40.120

Sustaining demurrer—When final.

If the demurrer is sustained because the indictment or information contains matter which is a legal defense or bar to the action, the judgment shall be final, and the defendant must be discharged.

[**1891 c 28 § 56;** Code 1881 § 1052; RRS § 2106. FORMER PART OF SECTION: **1891 c 28 § 61;** Code 1881 § 1060; RRS § 2114, now codified as RCW**10.40.125**.]

10.40.125

Sustaining demurrer, etc.—When not final.

The judgment for the defendant on a demurrer to the indictment or information, except where it is otherwise provided, or for an objection taken at the trial to its form or substance, or for variance between the indictment or information and the proof, shall not bar another prosecution for the same offense.

[**1891 c 28 § 61;** Code 1881 § 1060; RRS § 2114. Formerly RCW **10.40.120**, part.]

10.40.140
Overruling demurrer—Pleading over.

If the demurrer is overruled the defendant has a right to put in a plea. If he or she fails to do so, judgment may be rendered against him or her on the demurrer, and, if necessary, a jury may be impaneled to inquire and ascertain the degree of the offense.

[**2010 c 8 § 1040;** Code 1881 § 1053; RRS § 2107.]

10.40.170
Plea of guilty.

The plea of guilty can only be put in by the defendant himself or herself in open court.

[**2010 c 8 § 1041;** Code 1881 § 1056; RRS § 2110. FORMER PART OF SECTION: Code 1881 § 1057; RRS § 2111, now codified as RCW **10.40.175.**]

10.40.180
Plea of not guilty.

The plea of not guilty is a denial of every material allegation in the indictment or information; and all matters of fact may be given in evidence under it, except a former conviction or acquittal.

[**1891 c 28 § 59;** Code 1881 § 1058; RRS § 2112.]

10.40.190
Refusal to answer.

If the defendant fail or refuse to answer the indictment or information by demurrer or plea, a plea of not guilty must be entered by the court.

[**1891 c 28 § 62;** Code 1881 § 1061; **1873 p 232 § 224; 1854 p 116 § 88;** RRS § 2115.]

10.40.200
Deportation of aliens upon conviction—Advisement—Legislative intent.

(1) The legislature finds and declares that in many instances involving an individual who is not a citizen of the United States charged with an offense punishable as a crime under state law, a plea of guilty is entered without the defendant knowing that a conviction of such offense is grounds for deportation, exclusion from admission to the United States, or denial of naturalization pursuant to the laws of the United States. Therefore, it is the intent of the legislature in enacting this section to promote fairness to such accused individuals by requiring in such cases that acceptance of a guilty plea be preceded by an appropriate warning of the special consequences for such a defendant which may result from the plea. It is further the intent of the legislature that at the time of the plea no defendant be required to disclose his or her legal status to the court.

(2) Prior to acceptance of a plea of guilty to any offense punishable as a crime under state law, except offenses designated as infractions under state law, the court shall determine that the defendant has been advised of the following potential consequences of conviction for a defendant who is not a citizen of the United States: Deportation, exclusion from admission to the United States, or denial of naturalization pursuant to the laws of the United States. A defendant signing a guilty plea statement containing the advisement required by this subsection shall be presumed to have received the required advisement. If, after September 1, 1983, the defendant has not been advised as required by this section and the defendant shows that conviction of the offense to which the defendant pleaded guilty may have the consequences for the defendant of deportation, exclusion from admission to the United States, or denial of naturalization pursuant to the laws of the United States, the court, on defendant's motion, shall vacate the judgment and permit the defendant to withdraw the plea of guilty and enter a plea of not guilty. Absent a written acknowledgment by the defendant of the advisement required by this subsection, the defendant shall be presumed not to have received the required advisement.

(3) With respect to pleas accepted prior to September 1, 1983, it is not the intent of the legislature that a defendant's failure to receive the advisement required by subsection (2) of this section should require the vacation of judgment and withdrawal of the plea or constitute grounds for finding a prior conviction invalid.

[**1983 c 199 § 1.**]

NOTES:

Notice to courts—Rules—Forms: "The administrative office of the courts shall notify all courts of the requirements contained in RCW**10.40.200**. The judicial council shall recommend to the supreme court appropriate court rules to ensure compliance with the requirements of RCW **10.40.200**. Until court rules are promulgated, the administrative office of the courts shall develop and distribute forms necessary for the courts to comply with RCW **10.40.200**." [**2005 c 282 § 21; 1983 c 199 § 2.**]

Effective date—1983 c 199 § 1: "Section 1 of this act shall take effect on September 1, 1983." [**1983 c 199 § 3.**]

Chapter 10.43 RCW FORMER ACQUITTAL OR CONVICTION

NOTES:

Discharge of codefendant as bar to further prosecution: RCW **10.46.110**.

Double jeopardy: State Constitution Art. 1 § 9.

10.43.020
Offense embraces lower degree and included offenses.

When the defendant has been convicted or acquitted upon an indictment or information of an offense consisting of different degrees, the conviction or acquittal shall be a bar to another indictment or information for the offense charged in the former, or for any lower degree of that offense, or for an offense necessarily included therein.

[**1891 c 28 § 74**; Code 1881 § 1096; **1873 p 238 § 257; 1854 p 120 § 121**; RRS § 2166.]

NOTES:

Bar as to prosecution for same crime in another degree, or attempt: RCW **10.43.050**.

10.43.030
Conviction or acquittal in other county.

Whenever, upon the trial of any person for a crime, it shall appear that the defendant has already been acquitted or convicted upon the merits, of the same crime, in a court having jurisdiction of such offense in another county of this state, such former acquittal or conviction is a sufficient defense.

[**1909 c 249 § 20**; RRS § 2272.]

10.43.040
Foreign conviction or acquittal.

Whenever, upon the trial of any person for a crime, it appears that the offense was committed in another state or country, under such circumstances that the courts of this state had jurisdiction thereof, and that the defendant has already been acquitted or convicted upon the merits, in a judicial proceeding conducted under the criminal laws of such state or country, founded upon the act or omission with respect to which he or she is upon trial, such former acquittal or conviction is a sufficient defense. Nothing in this section affects or prevents a prosecution in a court of this state of any person who has received administrative or nonjudicial punishment, civilian or military, in another state or country based upon the same act or omission.

[**2010 c 8 § 1042; 1999 c 141 § 1; 1909 c 249 § 19**; RRS § 2271.]

10.43.050
Acquittal, when a bar.

No order of dismissal or directed verdict of not guilty on the ground of a variance between the indictment or information and the proof, or on the ground of any defect in such indictment or information, shall bar another prosecution for the same offense. Whenever a defendant shall be acquitted or convicted upon an indictment or information charging a crime consisting of different degrees, he or she cannot be proceeded against or tried for the same crime in another degree, nor for an attempt to commit such crime, or any degree thereof.

[**2010 c 8 § 1043; 1909 c 249 § 64;** Code 1881 § 769; RRS § 2316.]

NOTES:

Offense embraces lower degree and included offenses: RCW **10.43.020**.

Ownership of property—Proof of: RCW **10.58.060**.

Chapter 10.46 RCW SUPERIOR COURT TRIAL

NOTES:

Criminal rules for superior court: **Rules of court:** Superior Court Criminal Rules (CrR).

Superior court rules: State Constitution Art. 4 § 24.

10.46.020
Trial docket.

The clerk shall, in preparing the docket of criminal cases, enumerate the indictments and informations pending according to the date of their filing, specifying opposite to the title of each action whether it be for a felony or misdemeanor, and whether the defendant be in custody or on bail; and shall, in like manner, enter therein all indictments and informations on which issues of fact are joined, all cases brought to the court on change of venue from other counties, and all cases pending upon appeal from inferior courts.

[**1891 c 28 § 65;** Code 1881 § 1044; **1873 p 231 § 222; 1854 p 115 § 86;** RRS § 2134.]

10.46.060
True name inserted in proceedings.

When a defendant is designated in the indictment or information by a fictitious or erroneous name, and in any stage of the proceedings his or her true name is discovered, it may be inserted in the subsequent proceedings, referring to the fact of his or her being indicted or informed against by the name mentioned in the indictment or information.

[**2010 c 8 § 1044; 1891 c 28 § 23;** Code 1881 § 1007; **1873 p 225 § 190; 1869 p 241 § 185;** RRS § 2058.]

NOTES:

True name: RCW **10.40.050**.

10.46.070
Conduct of trial—Generally.

The court shall decide all questions of law which shall arise in the course of the trial, and the trial shall be conducted in the same manner as in civil actions.

[**1891 c 28 § 70;** Code 1881 § 1088; **1873 p 237 § 249; 1854 p 119 § 111;** RRS § 2158. FORMER PART OF SECTION: 1891 c 28 § 66, part; Code 1881 § 1078; **1873 p 236 § 239; 1854 p 118 § 101;** RRS § 2137, part, now codified as RCW **10.49.020**.]

NOTES:

Rules of court: This section superseded, in part, by CrR 6. See comment preceding CrR 6.1.

10.46.080
Continuances.

A continuance may be granted in any case on the ground of the absence of evidence on the motion of the defendant supported by affidavit showing the materiality of the evidence expected to be obtained, and that due diligence has been used to procure it; and also the name and place of residence of the witness or witnesses; and the substance of the evidence expected to be obtained, and if the prosecuting attorney admit that such evidence would be given, and that it be considered as actually given on the trial or offered and overruled as improper the continuance shall not be granted. [Code 1881 § 1077; **1877 p 206 § 7;** RRS § 2135.]

10.46.085
Continuances not permitted in certain cases.

When a defendant is charged with a crime which constitutes a violation of RCW **9A.64.020** or chapter **9.68**, 9.68A, or **9A.44** RCW, and the alleged victim of the crime is a person under the age of eighteen years, neither the defendant nor the prosecuting attorney may agree to extend the originally scheduled trial date unless the court within its discretion finds that there are substantial and compelling reasons for a continuance of the trial date and that the benefit of the postponement outweighs the detriment to the victim. The court may consider the testimony of lay witnesses and of expert witnesses, if available, regarding the impact of the continuance on the victim. [**1989 c 332 § 7.**]

NOTES:

   Finding—1989 c 332: "The legislature finds that treatment of the emotional problems of child sexual abuse victims may be impaired by lengthy delay in trial of the accused and the resulting delay in testimony of the child victim. The trauma of the abusive incident is likely to be exacerbated by requiring testimony from a victim who has substantially completed therapy and is forced to relive the incident. The legislature finds that it is necessary to prevent, to the extent reasonably possible, lengthy and unnecessary delays in trial of a person charged with abuse of a minor." [**1989 c 332 § 6.**]

10.46.110

Discharging defendant to give evidence.

When two or more persons are included in one prosecution, the court may, at any time before the defendant has gone into his or her defense, direct any defendant to be discharged, that he or she may be a witness for the state. A defendant may also, when there is not sufficient evidence to put him or her on his or her defense, at any time before the evidence is closed, be discharged by the court, for the purpose of giving evidence for a codefendant. The order of discharge is a bar to another prosecution for the same offense.

[**2010 c 8 § 1045;** Code 1881 § 1092; **1873 p 237 § 253; 1854 p 120 § 117;** RRS § 2162.]

NOTES:

Conviction or acquittal—Several defendants: RCW **10.61.035**.

10.46.190

Liability of convicted person for costs—Jury fee.

*** CHANGE IN 2018 *** (SEE **1783-S2.SL**) ***

Every person convicted of a crime or held to bail to keep the peace shall be liable to all the costs of the proceedings against him or her, including, when tried by a jury in the superior court or before a committing magistrate, a jury fee as provided for in civil actions for which judgment shall be rendered and collected. The jury fee, when collected for a case tried by the superior court, shall be paid to the clerk and applied as the jury fee in civil cases is applied.

[**2005 c 457 § 12; 1977 ex.s. c 248 § 1; 1977 ex.s. c 53 § 1; 1961 c 304 § 8;** Code 1881 § 2105; **1869 p 418 § 3;** RRS § 2227.]

NOTES:

Intent—2005 c 457: See note following RCW **43.08.250**.

Disposition of fines and costs: Chapter **10.82** RCW.

Jury

fees: RCW **4.44.110**, **36.18.020**.

in district court: RCW **10.04.050**.

10.46.200

Costs allowed to acquitted or discharged defendant.

No prisoner or person under recognizance who shall be acquitted by verdict or discharged because no indictment is found against him or her, or for want of prosecution, shall be liable for any costs or fees of any officer or for any charge of subsistence while he or she was in custody, but in every such case the fees of the defendant's witnesses, and of the officers for services rendered at the request of the defendant; and charges for subsistence of the defendant while in custody shall be taxed and paid as other costs and charges in such cases.
[**2010 c 8 § 1046;** Code 1881 § 1168; **1877 p 207 § 10; 1854 p 129 § 177;** RRS § 2236.]

10.46.210

Taxation of costs on acquittal or discharge—Generally—Frivolous complaints.

When any person shall be brought before a court or other committing magistrate of any county, city or town in this state, having jurisdiction of the alleged offense, charged with the commission of a crime or misdemeanor, and such complaint upon examination shall appear to be unfounded, no costs shall be payable by such acquitted party, but the same shall be chargeable to the county, city or town for or in which the said complaint is triable, but if the court or other magistrate trying said charge, shall decide the complaint was frivolous or malicious, the judgment or verdict shall also designate who is the complainant, and may adjudge that said complainant pay the costs. In such cases a judgment shall thereupon be entered for the costs against said complainant, who shall stand committed until such costs be paid or discharged by due process of law.

[**1987 c 202 § 168;** Code 1881 § 2103; **1869 p 418 § 1;** RRS § 2225.]

NOTES:

> **Intent—1987 c 202:** See note following RCW **2.04.190**.

10.46.220
Cost bills in felony cases—Certification.

In all convictions for felony, whether capital or punishable by imprisonment in the penitentiary, the clerk of the superior court shall forthwith, after sentence, tax the costs in the case. The cost bill shall be made out in triplicate, and be examined by the prosecuting attorney of the county in which the trial was had. After which the judge of the superior court shall allow and approve such bill or so much thereof, as is allowable by law. The clerk of the superior court shall thereupon, under his or her hand, and under the seal of the court, certify said triplicate cost bills, and shall file one with the papers of cause, and shall transmit one to the administrator for the courts and one to the county auditor of the county in which said felony was committed.

[**2010 c 8 § 1047; 1979 c 129 § 1; 1883 p 35 § 1;** Code 1881 § 2106; RRS § 2228.]

10.46.230
Cost bills in felony cases—Payment.

Upon the receipt of the cost bill, as provided for in the preceding section, the county auditor shall draw warrants for the amounts due each person, as certified in said cost bill, which warrants shall be paid as other county warrants are paid. On receipt of the certified copy of said cost bill, the administrator for the courts shall examine and audit said bill and allow the payment by the state of statutorily required witness fees in cases where conviction of a felony is obtained and the defendant is sentenced to pay a fine or is given a prison sentence even if the sentence is deferred or suspended. Payment shall be allowed by the administrator for the courts in such cases even when the conviction is subsequently reversed or if a new trial is granted.

[**1979 c 129 § 2; 1883 p 35 § 1;** Code 1881 § 2107; **1873 p 250 § 316;** RRS § 2229.]

Chapter 10.52 RCW WITNESSES—

GENERALLY

NOTES:

Discharging defendant to give evidence: RCW **10.46.110**.

Salaried public officers shall not receive additional compensation as witness on behalf of employer, and in certain other cases: RCW **42.16.020**.

Witnesses: **Rules of court:** ER 610, CrR 6.12, CrRLJ 6.12.

10.52.040

Compelling witness to attend and testify—Accused as witness.

Witnesses may be compelled to attend and testify before the grand jury; and witnesses on behalf of the state, or of the defendant, in a criminal prosecution, may be compelled to attend and testify in open court, if they have been subpoenaed, without their fees being first paid or tendered, unless otherwise provided by law; the court may, upon the motion of the prosecuting attorney or defense counsel, recognize witnesses, with or without sureties, to attend and testify at any hearing or trial in any criminal prosecution in any court of this state, or before the grand jury. In default of such recognizance, or in the event that surety is required and has not been obtained, the court shall require the appearance of the witness before the court and shall appoint counsel for the witness if he is indigent and then shall determine that the testimony of the witness would be material to either the prosecution or the defendant and that the witness would not attend the trial of the matter unless detained and, therefore, the court may direct that such witness shall be detained in the custody of the sheriff until the hearing or trial in which the witness is to testify: PROVIDED, That each witness detained for failure to obtain surety shall be paid, in addition to witness fees for actual appearance in court, for each day of his detention a sum equal to the daily jury fee paid to a juror serving in a superior court; and each witness in breach of recognizance and who is detained therefor shall be paid, in addition to witness fees for actual appearance in court, the sum of one dollar for each day of his detention. Any such witness shall be provided food and lodging while so detained. Any person accused of any crime in this state, by indictment, information, or otherwise, may, in the examination or trial of the cause, offer himself, or herself, as a witness in his or her own behalf, and shall be allowed to testify as other witnesses in such case, and when accused shall so testify, he or she shall be subject to all the rules of law relating to cross-examination of other witnesses: PROVIDED, That nothing in this code shall be construed to compel such accused person to offer himself or herself as a witness in such case.

[**1984 c 76 § 17; 1969 ex.s. c 143 § 1; 1915 c 83 § 1; 1891 c 28 § 69;** Code 1881 § 1067; **1873 p 233 § 229; 1871 p 105 § 2; 1854 p 116 § 93;** RRS § 2148. Formerly RCW **10.52.040, 10.52.050, 10.52.070,** and **10.52.080.**]

NOTES:

Rules of court: See CrR 6.13, 6.14.

Rights of accused persons: State Constitution Art. 1 §§ 9, 22 (Amendment 10).

10.52.060
Confrontation of witnesses.

Every person accused of crime shall have the right to meet the witnesses produced against him or her face to face: PROVIDED, That whenever any witness whose deposition shall have been taken pursuant to law by a magistrate, in the presence of the defendant and his or her counsel, shall be absent, and cannot be found when required to testify upon any trial or hearing, so much of such deposition as the court shall deem admissible and competent shall be admitted and read as evidence in such case.

[**2010 c 8 § 1048; 1909 c 249 § 54;** RRS § 2306. Prior: Code 1881 § 765; **1873 p 180 § 2; 1869 p 198 § 2; 1859 p 104 § 2.**]

NOTES:

Reviser's note: Caption for 1909 c 249 § 54 reads as follows: "SEC. 54. WITNESSES."

Rights of accused persons: State Constitution Art. 1 § 22 (Amendment 10).

10.52.090
Incriminating testimony not to be used.

In every case where it is provided in *this act that a witness shall not be excused from giving testimony tending to criminate himself or herself, no person shall be excused from testifying or producing any papers or documents on the ground that his or her testimony may tend to criminate or subject him or her to a penalty or forfeiture; but he or she shall not be prosecuted or subjected to a penalty or forfeiture for or on account of any action, matter or thing concerning which he or she shall so testify, except for perjury or offering false evidence committed in such testimony.

[2010 c 8 § 1049; 1909 c 249 § 39; RRS § 2291.]

NOTES:

Rules of court: Ordering immunity from prosecution—Incriminating testimony not to be used—CrR 6.14.

*Reviser's note: For meaning of "this act," see note following RCW **9.01.120**.

Bribery or corrupt solicitation: State Constitution Art. 2 § 30.

Rights of accused persons: State Constitution Art. 1 §§ 9, 22 (Amendment 10).

Witness not excused from giving testimony tending to incriminate himself in crimes concerning bribery: RCW **9.18.080**.

10.52.100
Identity of child victims of sexual assault not to be disclosed.

Child victims of sexual assault who are under the age of eighteen, have a right not to have disclosed to the public or press at any court proceeding involved in the prosecution of the sexual assault, the child victim's name, address, location, photographs, and in cases in which the child victim is a relative or stepchild of the alleged perpetrator, identification of the relationship between the child and the alleged perpetrator. The court shall ensure that information identifying the child victim is not disclosed to the press or the public and that in the event of any improper disclosure the court shall make all necessary orders to restrict further dissemination of identifying information improperly obtained. Court proceedings include but are not limited to pretrial hearings, trial, sentencing, and appellate proceedings. The court shall also order that any portion of any court records, transcripts, or recordings of court proceedings that contain information identifying the child victim shall be sealed and not open to public inspection unless those identifying portions are deleted from the documents or tapes.

[**1992 c 188 § 9.**]

NOTES:

Reviser's note: As to the constitutionality of this section, see Allied Daily Newspapers v. Eikenberry, 121 Wn.2d 205, 848 P.2d 1258 (1993).

Findings—Intent—Severability—1992 c 188: See notes following RCW **7.69A.020**.

Chapter 10.55 RCW WITNESSES OUTSIDE THE STATE (UNIFORM ACT)

10.55.010
Definitions.

"Witness" as used in this chapter shall include a person whose testimony is desired in any proceeding or investigation by a grand jury or in a criminal action, prosecution or proceeding.

The word "state" shall include any territory of the United States and the District of Columbia.

The word "summons" shall include a subpoena, order or other notice requiring the appearance of a witness.

[**1943 c 218 § 1;** Rem. Supp. 1943 § 2150-1.]

10.55.020
Summoning witness in this state to testify in another state.

If a judge of a court of record in any state which by its laws has made provision for commanding persons within that state to attend and testify in this state certified under the seal of such court that there is a criminal prosecution pending in such court, or that a grand jury investigation has commenced or is about to commence, that a person being within this state is a material witness in such prosecution, or grand jury investigation, and that his or her presence will be required for a specified number of days, upon presentation of such certificate to any judge of a court of record in the county in which such person is, such judge shall fix a time and place for a hearing, and shall make an order directing the witness to appear at a time and place certain for the hearing.

If at a hearing the judge determines that the witness is material and necessary, that it will not cause undue hardship to the witness to be compelled to attend and testify in the prosecution or a grand jury investigation in the other state, and that the laws of the state in which the prosecution is pending, or grand jury investigation has commenced or is about to commence, will give to him or her protection from arrest and the service of civil and criminal process, he or she shall issue a summons, with a copy of the certificate attached, directing the witness to attend and testify in the court where the prosecution is pending, or where a grand jury investigation has commenced or is about to commence and of any other state through which the witness may be required to travel by ordinary course of travel, at a time and place specified in the certificate. In any such hearing the certificate shall be prima facie evidence of all the facts stated therein.

If said certificate recommends that the witness be taken into immediate custody and delivered to an officer of the requesting state to assure his or her attendance in the requesting state, such judge may, in lieu of notification of the hearing, direct that such witness be forthwith brought before him or her for said hearing; and the judge at the hearing being satisfied of the desirability of such custody and delivery, for which determination the certificate shall be prima facie proof of such desirability may, in lieu of issuing subpoena or summons, order that said witness be forthwith taken into custody and delivered to an officer of the requesting state.

If the witness, who is summoned as above provided, after being paid or tendered by some properly authorized person the sum of ten cents a mile for each mile by the ordinary traveled route to and from the court where the prosecution is pending and five dollars for each day, that he or she is required to travel and attend as a witness, fails without good cause to attend and testify as directed in the summons, he or she shall be punished in the manner provided for the punishment of any witness who disobeys a summons issued from a court of record in this state.

[**2010 c 8 § 1050; 1943 c 218 § 2;** Rem. Supp. 1943 § 2150-2. Formerly RCW **10.55.020, 10.55.030, 10.55.040,** and **10.55.050.**]

10.55.060
Witness from another state summoned to testify in this state.

If any person in any state, which by its laws has made provision for commanding persons within its borders to attend and testify in criminal prosecutions, or grand jury investigations commenced or about to commence, in this state, is a material witness either for the prosecution or for the defense, in a criminal action pending in a court of record in this state, or in a grand jury investigation which has commenced or is about to commence, a judge of such court may issue a certificate under the seal of the court stating these facts and specifying the number of days the witness will be required. Said certificate may include a recommendation that the witness be taken into immediate custody and delivered to an officer of this state to assure his or her attendance in this state. This certificate shall be presented to a judge of a court of record in the county in which the witness is found.

If the witness is summoned to attend and testify in this state he or she shall be tendered the sum of ten cents a mile for each mile by the ordinary traveled route to and from the court where the prosecution is pending and five dollars for each day that he or she is required to travel and attend as a witness. A witness who has appeared in accordance with the provisions of the summons shall not be required to remain within this state a longer period of time than the period mentioned in the certificate, unless otherwise ordered by the court. If such witness, after coming into this state, fails without good cause to attend and testify as directed in the summons, he or she shall be punished in the manner provided for the punishment of any witness who disobeys a summons issued from a court of record in this state.

[**2010 c 8 § 1051; 1943 c 218 § 3;** Rem. Supp. 1943 § 2150-3. Formerly RCW **10.55.060, 10.55.070, 10.55.080,** and **10.55.090.**]

10.55.100
Exemption of witness from arrest and service of process.

If a person comes into this state in obedience to a summons directing him or her to attend and testify in this state he or she shall not while in this state pursuant to such summons be subject to arrest or the service of process, civil or criminal, in connection with matters which arose before his or her entrance into this state under the summons.

If a person passes through this state while going to another state in obedience to a summons to attend and testify in that state or while returning therefrom, he or she shall not while so passing through this state be subject to arrest or the service of process, civil or criminal, in connection with matters which arose before his or her entrance into this state under the summons.

[**2010 c 8 § 1052; 1943 c 218 § 4;** Rem. Supp. 1943 § 2150-4.]

10.55.110
Uniformity of interpretation.

This chapter shall be so interpreted and construed as to effectuate its general purpose to make uniform the law of the states which enact it.

[**1943 c 218 § 5;** Rem. Supp. 1943 § 2150-5.]

10.55.120
Short title.

This chapter may be cited as "Uniform Act to Secure the Attendance of Witnesses from Without a State in Criminal Proceedings."

[**1943 c 218 § 6;** Rem. Supp. 1943 § 2150-6.]

Chapter 10.58 RCW EVIDENCE

NOTES:

Evidence

generally: Title **5** RCW.

material to homicide, search and seizure: RCW **10.79.015**.

10.58.010
Rules—Generally.

The rules of evidence in civil actions, so far as practicable, shall be applied to criminal prosecutions.

[Code 1881 § 1071; **1873 p 234 § 233; 1854 p 117 § 97**; RRS § 2152.]

10.58.020
Presumption of innocence—Conviction of lowest degree, when.

Every person charged with the commission of a crime shall be presumed innocent until the contrary is proved by competent evidence beyond a reasonable doubt; and when an offense has been proved against him or her, and there exists a reasonable doubt as to which of two or more degrees he or she is guilty, he or she shall be convicted only of the lowest.

[**2010 c 8 § 1053; 1909 c 249 § 56; 1891 c 28 § 91;** Code 1881 § 767; **1854 p 76 § 3;** RRS § 2308. Formerly RCW **10.58.020** and **10.61.020**.]

NOTES:

Conviction of attempts or lesser or included crimes: RCW **10.61.003**, **10.61.006**, **10.61.010**.

10.58.030

Confession as evidence.

The confession of a defendant made under inducement, with all the circumstances, may be given as evidence against him or her, except when made under the influence of fear produced by threats; but a confession made under inducement is not sufficient to warrant a conviction without corroborating testimony.

[**2010 c 8 § 1054;** Code 1881 § 1070; **1873 p 234 § 232; 1854 p 117 § 96;** RRS § 2151.]

10.58.035

Statement of defendant—Admissibility.

(1) In criminal and juvenile offense proceedings where independent proof of the corpus delicti is absent, and the alleged victim of the crime is dead or incompetent to testify, a lawfully obtained and otherwise admissible confession, admission, or other statement of the defendant shall be admissible into evidence if there is substantial independent evidence that would tend to establish the trustworthiness of the confession, admission, or other statement of the defendant.

(2) In determining whether there is substantial independent evidence that the confession, admission, or other statement of the defendant is trustworthy, the court shall consider, but is not limited to:

(a) Whether there is any evidence corroborating or contradicting the facts set out in the statement, including the elements of the offense;

(b) The character of the witness reporting the statement and the number of witnesses to the statement;

(c) Whether a record of the statement was made and the timing of the making of the record in relation to the making of the statement; and/or

(d) The relationship between the witness and the defendant.

(3) Where the court finds that the confession, admission, or other statement of the defendant is sufficiently trustworthy to be admitted, the court shall issue a written order setting forth the rationale for admission.

(4) Nothing in this section may be construed to prevent the defendant from arguing to the jury or judge in a bench trial that the statement is not trustworthy or that the evidence is otherwise insufficient to convict.
[**2003 c 179 § 1.**]

10.58.038
Polygraph examinations—Victims of alleged sex offenses.

A law enforcement officer, prosecuting attorney, or other government official may not ask or require a victim of an alleged sex offense to submit to a polygraph examination or other truth telling device as a condition for proceeding with the investigation of the offense. The refusal of a victim to submit to a polygraph examination or other truth telling device shall not by itself prevent the investigation, charging, or prosecution of the offense. For the purposes of this section, "sex offense" is any offense under chapter **9A.44** RCW.
[**2007 c 202 § 1.**]

10.58.040
Intent to defraud.

Whenever an intent to defraud shall be made an element of an offense, it shall be sufficient if an intent appears to defraud any person, association or body politic or corporate whatsoever.
[**1909 c 249 § 40;** RRS § 2292.]

10.58.060
Ownership—Proof of.

In the prosecution of any offense committed upon, or in relation to, or in any way affecting any real estate, or any offense committed in stealing, embezzling, destroying, injuring, or fraudulently receiving or concealing any money, goods, or other personal estate, it shall be sufficient, and shall not be deemed a variance, if it be proved on trial that at the time when such offense was committed, either the actual or constructive possession, or the general or special property in the whole, or any part of such real or personal estate, was in the person or community alleged in the indictment or other accusation to be the owner thereof.

[Code 1881 § 963; **1854 p 99 § 133**; RRS § 2156.]

NOTES:

Indictment or information, certain defects or imperfections deemed immaterial:
RCW **10.37.056**.

10.58.080
View of place of crime permissible.

The court may order a view by any jury impaneled to try a criminal case.

[Code 1881 § 1090; **1873 p 237 § 251; 1854 p 120 § 115**; RRS § 2160.]

10.58.090
Sex Offenses—Admissibility.

(1) In a criminal action in which the defendant is accused of a sex offense, evidence of the defendant's commission of another sex offense or sex offenses is admissible, notwithstanding Evidence Rule 404(b), if the evidence is not inadmissible pursuant to Evidence Rule 403.

(2) In a case in which the state intends to offer evidence under this rule, the attorney for the state shall disclose the evidence to the defendant, including statements of witnesses or a summary of the substance of any testimony that is expected to be offered, at least fifteen days before the scheduled date of trial or at such later time as the court may allow for good cause.

(3) This section shall not be construed to limit the admission or consideration of evidence under any other evidence rule.

(4) For purposes of this section, "sex offense" means:

(a) Any offense defined as a sex offense by RCW **9.94A.030**;

(b) Any violation under RCW **9A.44.096** (sexual misconduct with a minor in the second degree); and

(c) Any violation under RCW **9.68A.090** (communication with a minor for immoral purposes).

(5) For purposes of this section, uncharged conduct is included in the definition of "sex offense."

(6) When evaluating whether evidence of the defendant's commission of another sexual offense or offenses should be excluded pursuant to Evidence Rule 403, the trial judge shall consider the following factors:

(a) The similarity of the prior acts to the acts charged;

(b) The closeness in time of the prior acts to the acts charged;

(c) The frequency of the prior acts;

(d) The presence or lack of intervening circumstances;

(e) The necessity of the evidence beyond the testimonies already offered at trial;

(f) Whether the prior act was a criminal conviction;

(g) Whether the probative value is substantially outweighed by the danger of unfair prejudice, confusion of the issues, or misleading the jury, or by considerations of undue delay, waste of time, or needless presentation of cumulative evidence; and

(h) Other facts and circumstances.

[**2008 c 90 § 2.**]

NOTES:

Purpose—Exception to evidence rule—2008 c 90: "In Washington, the legislature and the courts share the responsibility for enacting rules of evidence. The court's authority for enacting rules of evidence arises from a statutory delegation of that responsibility to the court and from Article IV, section 1 of the state Constitution. State v. Fields, 85 Wn.2d 126, 129, 530 P.2d 284 (1975).

The legislature's authority for enacting rules of evidence arises from the Washington supreme court's prior classification of such rules as substantive law. See State v. Sears, 4 Wn.2d 200, 215, 103 P.2d 337 (1940) (the legislature has the power to enact laws which create rules of evidence); State v. Pavelich, 153 Wash. 379, 279 P. 1102 (1929) ("rules of evidence are substantiative law").

The legislature adopts this exception to Evidence Rule 404(b) to ensure that juries receive the necessary evidence to reach a just and fair verdict." [**2008 c 90 § 1.**]

Application—2008 c 90 § 2: "Section 2 of this act applies to any case that is tried on or after its adoption." [**2008 c 90 § 3.**]

Reviser's note: Section 2, chapter 90, Laws of 2008 was approved by the legislature on March 20, 2008, with an effective date of June 12, 2008.

Chapter 10.61 RCW VERDICTS

NOTES:

Rules of court: Verdicts—CrR 6.16.

Former acquittal or conviction—Offense embraces other degrees and included offenses: RCW **10.43.020**, **10.43.050**.

10.61.003
Degree offenses—Inferior degree—Attempt.

Upon an indictment or information for an offense consisting of different degrees, the jury may find the defendant not guilty of the degree charged in the indictment or information, and guilty of any degree inferior thereto, or of an attempt to commit the offense.

[**1891 c 28 § 75;** Code 1881 § 1097; **1854 p 120 § 122;** RRS § 2167. Formerly RCW **10.61.010**, part.] [SLC-RO-11]

NOTES:

Where doubt as to degree, conviction of lowest: RCW **10.58.020**.

10.61.006

Other cases—Included offenses.

In all other cases the defendant may be found guilty of an offense the commission of which is necessarily included within that with which he or she is charged in the indictment or information.

[**2010 c 8 § 1055; 1891 c 28 § 76;** Code 1881 § 1098; **1854 p 120 § 123;** RRS § 2168. Formerly RCW **10.61.010**, part.] [SLC-RO-11]

10.61.010

Conviction of lesser crime.

Upon the trial of an indictment or information, the defendant may be convicted of the crime charged therein, or of a lesser degree of the same crime, or of an attempt to commit the crime so charged, or of an attempt to commit a lesser degree of the same crime. Whenever the jury shall find a verdict of guilty against a person so charged, they shall in their verdict specify the degree or attempt of which the accused is guilty.

[**1909 c 249 § 11;** RRS § 2263. FORMER PARTS OF SECTION: (i) **1891 c 28 § 75;** Code 1881 § 1097; **1854 p 120 § 122;** RRS § 2167, now codified as RCW **10.61.003**. (ii) **1891 c 28 § 76;** Code 1881 § 1098; **1854 p 120 § 123;** RRS § 2168, now codified as RCW **10.61.006**.] [SLC-RO-11]

10.61.035

Conviction or acquittal—Several defendants.

Upon an indictment or information against several defendants any one or more may be convicted or acquitted.

[**1891 c 28 § 37;** Code 1881 § 1022; **1873 p 228 § 205; 1869 p 243 § 200;** RRS § 2073. Formerly RCW **10.61.030**, part.]

NOTES:

Rules of court: This section superseded in part by CrR 6.16. See comment after CrR 6.16.

Discharging defendant to give evidence: RCW **10.46.110**.

10.61.060
Reconsideration of verdict.

When there is a verdict of conviction in which it appears to the court that the jury have mistaken the law, the court may explain the reason for that opinion, and direct the jury to reconsider the verdict; and if after such reconsideration they return the same verdict it must be entered, but it shall be good cause for new trial. When there is a verdict of acquittal the court cannot require the jury to reconsider it.

[**1891 c 28 § 78;** Code 1881 § 1100; **1873 p 239 § 261; 1854 p 121 § 125;** RRS § 2170.]

Chapter 10.64 RCW JUDGMENTS AND SENTENCES

NOTES:

Rules of court: Judgments and sentencing—CrR 7.1 through 7.4.

Assessments required of other convicted persons

offender supervision: RCW **9.94A.780**.

parolees: RCW **72.04A.120**.

Excessive bail or fines, cruel punishment prohibited: State Constitution Art. 1 § 14.

10.64.015
Judgment to include costs—Exception.

*** CHANGE IN 2018 *** (SEE **1783-S2.SL**) ***

When the defendant is found guilty, the court shall render judgment accordingly, and the defendant shall be liable for all costs, unless the court or jury trying the cause expressly find otherwise.

[Code 1881 § 1104; **1873 p 241 § 272; 1854 p 121 § 129;** RRS § 2187. Formerly RCW **10.64.010**, part.]

NOTES:

Requiring defendant to pay costs—Procedure: RCW **10.01.160**, **10.01.170**, chapter **10.82** RCW.

10.64.025
Detention of defendant.

(1) A defendant who has been found guilty of a felony and is awaiting sentencing shall be detained unless the court finds by clear and convincing evidence that the defendant is not likely to flee or to pose a danger to the safety of any other person or the community if released. Any bail bond that was posted on behalf of a defendant shall, upon the defendant's conviction, be exonerated.

(2) A defendant who has been found guilty of one of the following offenses shall be detained pending sentencing: Rape in the first or second degree (RCW **9A.44.040** and **9A.44.050**); rape of a child in the first, second, or third degree (RCW **9A.44.073**, **9A.44.076**, and **9A.44.079**); child molestation in the first, second, or third degree (RCW **9A.44.083**, **9A.44.086**, and **9A.44.089**); sexual misconduct with a minor in the first or second degree (RCW **9A.44.093** and **9A.44.096**); indecent liberties (RCW **9A.44.100**); incest (RCW **9A.64.020**); luring (RCW **9A.40.090**); human trafficking in the first or second degree (RCW **9A.40.100**); promoting commercial sexual abuse of a minor (RCW **9.68A.101**); any class A or B felony that is a sexually motivated offense as defined in RCW **9.94A.030**; a felony violation of RCW **9.68A.090**; or any offense that is, under chapter **9A.28** RCW, a criminal attempt, solicitation, or conspiracy to commit one of those offenses.

[**2011 c 111 § 4; 1996 c 275 § 10; 1989 c 276 § 2.**]

NOTES:

10.64.027

Conditions of release.

In order to minimize the trauma to the victim, the court may attach conditions on release of a defendant under RCW **10.64.025** regarding the whereabouts of the defendant, contact with the victim, or other conditions.

[**1989 c 276 § 5.**]

NOTES:

10.64.060

Form of sentence to penitentiary.

In every case where imprisonment in the penitentiary is awarded against any convict, the form of the sentence shall be, that he or she be punished by confinement at hard labor; and he or she may also be sentenced to solitary imprisonment for such term as the court shall direct, not exceeding twenty days at any one time; and in the execution of such punishment the solitary shall precede the punishment by hard labor, unless the court shall otherwise order.

[**2010 c 8 § 1056;** Code 1881 § 1127; **1873 p 243 § 285; 1854 p 124 § 149;** RRS § 2208.]

NOTES:

Indeterminate sentences: Chapter **9.95** RCW.

Sentencing, 1981 act: Chapter **9.94A** RCW.

10.64.070

Recognizance to maintain good behavior or keep the peace.

Every court before whom any person shall be convicted upon an indictment or information for an offense not punishable with death or imprisonment in the penitentiary may, in addition to the punishment prescribed by law, require such person to recognize with sufficient sureties in a reasonable sum to keep the peace, or to be of good behavior, or both, for any term not exceeding one year, and to stand committed until he or she shall so recognize.

[**2010 c 8 § 1057; 1891 c 28 § 83;** Code 1881 § 1121; **1873 p 242 § 279; 1854 p 123 § 143;** RRS § 2202. FORMER PART OF SECTION: Code 1881 § 1122; **1873 p 242 § 280; 1854 p 123 § 144;** RRS § 2203, now codified as RCW **10.64.075.**]

10.64.075
Breach of recognizance conditions.

In case of the breach of the conditions of any such recognizance, the same proceedings shall be had that are by law prescribed in relation to recognizances to keep the peace.

[Code 1881 § 1122; **1873 p 242 § 280; 1854 p 123 § 144;** RRS § 2203. Formerly RCW **10.64.070,** part.]

10.64.080
Judgments a lien on realty.

Judgments for fines in all criminal actions rendered, are, and may be made liens upon the real estate of the defendant in the same manner, and with like effect as judgments in civil actions.

[Code 1881 § 1111; RRS § 2188.]

10.64.100
Final record—What to contain.

The clerk of the court shall make a final record of all the proceedings in a criminal prosecution within six months after the same shall have been decided, which shall contain a copy of the minutes of the challenge to the panel of the grand jury, the indictment or information, journal entries, pleadings, minutes of challenges to panel of petit jurors, judgment, orders, or decision, and bill of exceptions.

[**1891 c 28 § 85;** Code 1881 § 1134; **1873 p 245 § 292; 1854 p 125 § 156;** RRS § 2224.]

10.64.110
Fingerprint of defendant in felony convictions.

Following June 15, 1977, there shall be affixed to the original of every judgment and sentence of a felony conviction in every court in this state and every order adjudicating a juvenile to be a delinquent based upon conduct which would be a felony if committed by an adult, a fingerprint of the defendant or juvenile who is the subject of the order. When requested by the clerk of the court, the actual affixing of fingerprints shall be done by a representative of the office of the county sheriff.

The clerk of the court shall attest that the fingerprints appearing on the judgment in sentence, order of adjudication of delinquency, or docket, is that of the individual who is the subject of the judgment or conviction, order, or docket entry.

[**1977 ex.s. c 259 § 1.**]

10.64.120
Referral assessments—Probation department oversight committee.

(1) Every judge of a court of limited jurisdiction shall have the authority to levy upon a person a monthly assessment not to exceed one hundred dollars for services provided whenever the person is referred by the court to the misdemeanant probation department for evaluation or supervision services. The assessment may also be made by a judge in superior court when such misdemeanor or gross misdemeanor cases are heard in the superior court.

(2) For the purposes of this section the administrative office of the courts shall define a probation department and adopt rules for the qualifications of probation officers based

on occupational and educational requirements developed by an oversight committee. This oversight committee shall include a representative from the district and municipal court judges' association, the misdemeanant corrections association, the administrative office of the courts, and associations of cities and counties. The oversight committee shall consider qualifications that provide the training and education necessary to (a) conduct presentencing and postsentencing background investigations, including sentencing recommendations to the court regarding jail terms, alternatives to incarceration, and conditions of release; and (b) provide ongoing supervision and assessment of offenders' needs and the risk they pose to the community.

(3) It shall be the responsibility of the probation services office to implement local procedures approved by the court of limited jurisdiction to ensure collection and payment of such fees into the general fund of the city or county treasury.

(4) Revenues raised under this section shall be used to fund programs for probation services and shall be in addition to those funds provided in RCW **3.62.050**.

(5) Assessments and fees levied upon a probationer under this section must be suspended while the probationer is being supervised by another state under RCW **9.94A.745**, the interstate compact for adult offender supervision.
[**2005 c 400 § 7; 2005 c 282 § 22; 1996 c 298 § 6; 1991 c 247 § 3; 1982 c 207 § 4.**]
NOTES:

Reviser's note: This section was amended by 2005 c 282 § 22 and by 2005 c 400 § 7, each without reference to the other. Both amendments are incorporated in the publication of this section under RCW **1.12.025**(2). For rule of construction, see RCW **1.12.025**(1).

Application—Effective date—2005 c 400: See notes following RCW **9.94A.74504**.

10.64.140
Loss of voting rights—Acknowledgment.

(1) When a person is convicted of a felony, the court shall require the defendant to sign a statement acknowledging that:

(a) The defendant's right to vote has been lost due to the felony conviction;

(b) If the defendant is registered to vote, the voter registration will be canceled;

(c) The right to vote is provisionally restored as long as the defendant is not under the authority of the department of corrections;

(d) The defendant must reregister before voting;

(e) The provisional right to vote may be revoked if the defendant fails to comply with all the terms of his or her legal financial obligations or an agreement for the payment of legal financial obligations;

(f) The right to vote may be permanently restored by one of the following for each felony conviction:

(i) A certificate of discharge issued by the sentencing court, as provided in RCW **9.94A.637**;

(ii) A court order issued by the sentencing court restoring the right, as provided in RCW **9.92.066**;

(iii) A final order of discharge issued by the indeterminate sentence review board, as provided in RCW **9.96.050**; or

(iv) A certificate of restoration issued by the governor, as provided in RCW **9.96.020**; and

(g) Voting before the right is restored is a class C felony under RCW **29A.84.660**.

(2) For the purposes of this section, a person is under the authority of the department of corrections if the person is:

(a) Serving a sentence of confinement in the custody of the department of corrections; or

(b) Subject to community custody as defined in RCW **9.94A.030**.
[**2009 c 325 § 5; 2005 c 246 § 1.**]
NOTES:

    Effective date—2005 c 246: "This act takes effect January 1, 2006." [**2005 c 246 § 26.**]

Chapter 10.66 RCW DRUG TRAFFICKERS—

OFF-LIMITS ORDERS

10.66.005
Findings.

The legislature finds that drug abuse is escalating at an alarming rate. New protections need to be established to address this drug crisis which is threatening every stratum of our society. Prohibiting known drug traffickers from frequenting areas for continuous drug activity is one means of addressing this pervasive problem.
[**1989 c 271 § 213.**]

10.66.010
Definitions.

Unless the context clearly requires otherwise, the definitions in this section apply throughout this chapter:

(1) "Applicant" means any person who owns, occupies, or has a substantial interest in property, or who is a neighbor to property which is adversely affected by drug trafficking, including:

(a) A "family or household member" as defined by *RCW **10.99.020**(1), who has a possessory interest in a residence as an owner or tenant, at least as great as a known drug trafficker's interest;

(b) An owner or lessor;

(c) An owner, tenant, or resident who lives or works in a designated PADT area; or

(d) A city or prosecuting attorney for any jurisdiction in this state where drug trafficking is occurring.

(2) "Drug" or "drugs" means a controlled substance as defined in chapter **69.50** RCW or an "imitation controlled substance" as defined in RCW **69.52.020**.

(3) "Known drug trafficker" means any person who has been convicted of a drug offense in this state, another state, or federal court who subsequently has been arrested for a drug offense in this state. For purposes of this definition, "drug offense" means a felony violation of chapter **69.50** or **69.52** RCW or equivalent law in another jurisdiction that involves the manufacture, distribution, or possession with intent to manufacture or distribute, of a controlled substance or imitation controlled substance.

(4) "Off-limits orders" means an order issued by a superior or district court in the state of Washington that enjoins known drug traffickers from entering or remaining in a designated PADT area.

(5) "Protected against drug trafficking area" or "PADT area" means any specifically described area, public or private, contained in an off-limits order. The perimeters of a PADT area shall be defined using street names and numbers and shall include all real property contained therein, where drug sales, possession of drugs, pedestrian or vehicular traffic attendant to drug activity, or other activity associated with drug offenses confirms a pattern associated with drug trafficking. The area may include the full width of streets, alleys and sidewalks on the perimeter, common areas, planting strips, parks and parking areas within the area described using the streets as boundaries.

[**1989 c 271 § 214.**]

NOTES:

　　*Reviser's note: RCW **10.99.020** was amended by 2004 c 18 § 2, changing subsection (1) to subsection (3).

10.66.020
When order may be issued.

A court may enter an off-limits order enjoining a known drug trafficker who has been associated with drug trafficking in an area that the court finds to be a PADT area, from entering or remaining in a designated PADT area for up to one year. This relief may be ordered pursuant to applications for injunctive relief or as part of a criminal proceeding as follows:

(1) In a civil action, including an action brought under this chapter;

(2) In a nuisance abatement action pursuant to chapter **7.43** RCW;

(3) In an eviction action to exclude known drug traffickers or tenants who were evicted for allowing drug trafficking to occur on the premises which were the subject of the eviction action;

(4) As a condition of pretrial release of a known drug trafficker awaiting trial on drug charges. The order shall be in effect until the time of sentencing or dismissal of the criminal charges; or

(5) As a condition of sentencing of any known drug trafficker convicted of a drug offense. The order may include all periods of community placement or community supervision.

[**1989 c 271 § 215.**]

10.66.030
Hearing—Summons.

Upon the filing of an application for an off-limits order under RCW **10.66.020** (1), (2), or (3), the court shall set a hearing fourteen days from the filing of the application, or as soon thereafter as the hearing can be scheduled. If the respondent has not already been served with a summons, the application shall be served on the respondent not less than five court days before the hearing. If timely service cannot be made, the court may set a new hearing date.

[**1989 c 271 § 216.**]

10.66.040
Ex parte temporary order—Hearing—Notice.

Upon filing an application for an off-limits order under this chapter, an applicant may obtain an ex parte temporary off-limits order, with or without notice, only upon a showing that serious or irreparable harm will result to the applicant if the temporary off-limits order is not granted. An ex parte temporary off-limits order shall be effective for a fixed period not to exceed fourteen days, but the court may reissue the order upon a showing of good cause. A hearing on a one-year off-limits order, as provided in this chapter, shall be set for fourteen days from the issuance of the temporary order. The respondent shall be personally served with a copy of the temporary off-limits order along with a copy of the application and notice of the date set for the full hearing. At the hearing, if the court finds that respondent is a known drug trafficker who has engaged in drug trafficking in a particular area, and that the area is associated with a pattern of drug activities, the court shall issue a one-year off-limits order prohibiting the respondent from having any contact with the PADT area. At any time within three months before the expiration of the order, the applicant may apply for a renewal of the order by filing a new petition under this chapter.

[**1989 c 271 § 217.**]

10.66.050
Additional relief—PADT area.

In granting a temporary off-limits order or a one-year off-limits order, the court shall have discretion to grant additional relief as the court considers proper to achieve the purposes of this chapter. The PADT area defined in any off-limits order must be reasonably related to the area or areas impacted by the unlawful drug activity as described by the applicant in any civil action under RCW **10.66.020** (1), (2), or (3). The court in its discretion may allow a respondent, who is the subject of any order issued under RCW **10.66.020** as part of a civil or criminal proceeding, to enter an off-limits area or areas for health or employment reasons, subject to conditions prescribed by the court. Upon request, a certified copy of the order shall be provided to the applicant by the clerk of the court.

[**1999 c 143 § 46; 1989 c 271 § 218.**]

10.66.060
Bond or security.

A temporary off-limits order or a one-year off-limits order may not issue under this chapter except upon the giving of a bond or security by the applicant. The court shall set the bond or security in the amount the court deems proper, but not less than one thousand dollars, for the payment of costs and damages that may be incurred by any party who is found to have been wrongfully restrained or enjoined. A bond or security shall not be required of the state of Washington, municipal corporations, or political subdivisions of the state of Washington.

[**1989 c 271 § 219.**]

10.66.070
Appearance of party.

Nothing in this chapter shall preclude a party from appearing in person or by counsel.

[**1989 c 271 § 220.**]

10.66.080
Notice of order to law enforcement agency.

A copy of an off-limits order granted under this chapter shall be forwarded by the court to the local law enforcement agency with jurisdiction over the PADT area specified in the order on or before the next judicial day following issuance of the order. Upon receipt of the order, the law enforcement agency shall promptly enter it into an appropriate law enforcement information system.

[**1989 c 271 § 221.**]

10.66.090
Penalties.

(1) A person who willfully disobeys an off-limits order issued under this chapter is guilty of a gross misdemeanor.

(2) A person is guilty of a class C felony punishable according to chapter **9A.20** RCW if the person willfully disobeys an off-limits order in violation of the terms of the order and also either:

(a) Enters or remains in a PADT area that is within one thousand feet of any school; or

(b) Is convicted of a second or subsequent violation of this chapter.

[**2003 c 53 § 93; 1989 c 271 § 223.**]

NOTES:

Intent—Effective date—2003 c 53: See notes following RCW **2.48.180**.

10.66.100
Additional penalties.

Any person who willfully disobeys an off-limits order issued under this chapter shall be subject to criminal penalties as provided in this chapter and may also be found in contempt of court and subject to penalties under chapter **7.21** RCW.

[**1999 c 143 § 47; 1989 c 271 § 222.**]

10.66.110
Jurisdiction.

The superior courts shall have jurisdiction of all civil actions and all felony criminal proceedings brought under this chapter. Courts of limited jurisdiction shall have jurisdiction of all misdemeanor and gross misdemeanor criminal actions brought under this chapter.

[**1989 c 271 § 224.**]

10.66.120
Venue.

For the purposes of this chapter, an action may be brought in any county in which any element of the alleged drug trafficking activities occurred.

10.66.130
Modification of order—Notice to law enforcement agency.

Upon application, notice to all parties, and a hearing, the court may modify the terms of an off-limits order. When an order is terminated, modified, or amended before its expiration date, the clerk of the court shall forward, on or before the next judicial day, a true copy of the amended order to the law enforcement agency specified in the order. Upon receipt of an order, the law enforcement agency shall promptly enter it into an appropriate law enforcement information system.

[**1989 c 271 § 226.**]

Chapter 10.70 RCW COMMITMENTS

NOTES:

Execution of death sentence: Chapter **10.95** RCW.

10.70.010
Commitment until fine and costs are paid.

When the defendant is adjudged to pay a fine and costs, the court shall order him or her to be committed to the custody of the sheriff until the fine and costs are paid or secured as provided by law.

[**2010 c 8 § 1058;** Code 1881 § 1119; **1873 p 242 § 277; 1854 p 123 § 141;** RRS § 2200.]

NOTES:

Commitment for failure to pay fine and costs—Execution against defendant's property: RCW **10.82.030**.

Stay of execution for sixty days on recognizance: RCW **10.82.020**, **10.82.025**.

10.70.020
Mittimus upon sentence to imprisonment.

When any person shall be sentenced to be imprisoned in the penitentiary or county jail, the clerk of the court shall, as soon as may be, make out and deliver to the sheriff of the county, or his or her deputy, a transcript from the minutes of the court of such conviction and sentence, duly certified by such clerk, which shall be sufficient authority for such sheriff to execute the sentence, who shall execute it accordingly.
[**2010 c 8 § 1059;** Code 1881 § 1126; **1873 p 243 § 284; 1854 p 124 § 148;** RRS § 2207.]

10.70.140
Aliens committed—Notice to immigration authority.

Whenever any person shall be committed to a state correctional facility, the county jail, or any other state or county institution which is supported wholly or in part by public funds, it shall be the duty of the warden, superintendent, sheriff or other officer in charge of such state or county institution to at once inquire into the nationality of such person, and if it shall appear that such person is an alien, to immediately notify the United States immigration officer in charge of the district in which such penitentiary, reformatory, jail or other institution is located, of the date of and the reasons for such alien commitment, the length of time for which committed, the country of which the person is a citizen, and the date on which and the port at which the person last entered the United States.
[**1992 c 7 § 29; 1925 ex.s. c 169 § 1;** RRS § 2206-1.]

10.70.150
Aliens committed—Copies of clerk's records.

Upon the official request of the United States immigration officer in charge of the territory or district in which is located any court committing any alien to any state or county institution which is supported wholly or in part by public funds, it shall be the duty of the clerk of such court to furnish without charge a certified copy of the complaint, information or indictment and the judgment and sentence and any other record pertaining to the case of the convicted alien.

[**1925 ex.s. c 169 § 2;** RRS § 2206-2.]

Chapter 10.73 RCW CRIMINAL APPEALS

NOTES:

Effect of appellate review by defendant: RCW **9.95.060**, **9.95.062**.

10.73.010
Appeal by defendant.

Appeal by defendant, see Rules of Court.

10.73.040
Bail pending appeal.

In all criminal actions, except capital cases in which the proof of guilt is clear or the presumption great, upon an appeal being taken from a judgment of conviction, the court in which the judgment was rendered, or a judge thereof, must, by an order entered in the journal or filed with the clerk, fix and determine the amount of bail to be required of the appellant; and the appellant shall be committed until a bond to the state of Washington in the sum so fixed be executed on his or her behalf by at least two sureties possessing the qualifications required for sureties on appeal bonds, such bond to be conditioned that the appellant shall appear whenever required, and stand to and abide by the judgment or orders of the appellate court, and any judgment and order of the superior court that may be rendered or made in pursuance thereof. If the appellant be already at large on bail, his or her sureties shall be liable to the amount of their bond, in the same manner and upon the same conditions as if they had executed the bond prescribed by this section; but the court may by order require a new bond in a larger amount or with new sureties, and may commit the appellant until the order be complied with.

[**2010 c 8 § 1060; 1999 c 143 § 48; 1893 c 61 § 31;** RRS § 1747.]

10.73.090
Collateral attack—One year time limit.

(1) No petition or motion for collateral attack on a judgment and sentence in a criminal case may be filed more than one year after the judgment becomes final if the judgment and sentence is valid on its face and was rendered by a court of competent jurisdiction.

(2) For the purposes of this section, "collateral attack" means any form of postconviction relief other than a direct appeal. "Collateral attack" includes, but is not limited to, a personal restraint petition, a habeas corpus petition, a motion to vacate judgment, a motion to withdraw guilty plea, a motion for a new trial, and a motion to arrest judgment.

(3) For the purposes of this section, a judgment becomes final on the last of the following dates:

(a) The date it is filed with the clerk of the trial court;

(b) The date that an appellate court issues its mandate disposing of a timely direct appeal from the conviction; or

(c) The date that the United States Supreme Court denies a timely petition for certiorari to review a decision affirming the conviction on direct appeal. The filing of a motion to reconsider denial of certiorari does not prevent a judgment from becoming final.

[**1989 c 395 § 1.**]

10.73.100

Collateral attack—When one year limit not applicable.

The time limit specified in RCW **10.73.090** does not apply to a petition or motion that is based solely on one or more of the following grounds:

(1) Newly discovered evidence, if the defendant acted with reasonable diligence in discovering the evidence and filing the petition or motion;

(2) The statute that the defendant was convicted of violating was unconstitutional on its face or as applied to the defendant's conduct;

(3) The conviction was barred by double jeopardy under Amendment V of the United States Constitution or Article I, section 9 of the state Constitution;

(4) The defendant pled not guilty and the evidence introduced at trial was insufficient to support the conviction;

(5) The sentence imposed was in excess of the court's jurisdiction; or

(6) There has been a significant change in the law, whether substantive or procedural, which is material to the conviction, sentence, or other order entered in a criminal or civil proceeding instituted by the state or local government, and either the legislature has expressly provided that the change in the law is to be applied retroactively, or a court, in interpreting a change in the law that lacks express legislative intent regarding retroactive application, determines that sufficient reasons exist to require retroactive application of the changed legal standard.

[**1989 c 395 § 2.**]

10.73.110

Collateral attack—One year time limit—Duty of court to advise defendant.

At the time judgment and sentence is pronounced in a criminal case, the court shall advise the defendant of the time limit specified in RCW **10.73.090** and **10.73.100**.

[**1989 c 395 § 4.**]

10.73.120

Collateral attack—One year time limit—Duty of department of corrections to advise.

As soon as practicable after July 23, 1989, the department of corrections shall attempt to advise the following persons of the time limit specified in RCW **10.73.090** and **10.73.100**: Every person who, on July 23, 1989, is serving a term of incarceration, probation, parole, or community supervision pursuant to conviction of a felony.

[**1989 c 395 § 5.**]

10.73.130

Collateral attack—One year time limit—Applicability.

RCW **10.73.090** and **10.73.100** apply only to petitions and motions filed more than one year after July 23, 1989.

[**1989 c 395 § 6.**]

10.73.140

Collateral attack—Subsequent petitions.

If a person has previously filed a petition for personal restraint, the court of appeals will not consider the petition unless the person certifies that he or she has not filed a previous petition on similar grounds, and shows good cause why the petitioner did not raise the new grounds in the previous petition. Upon receipt of a personal restraint petition, the court of appeals shall review the petition and determine whether the person has previously filed a petition or petitions and if so, compare them. If upon review, the court of appeals finds that the petitioner has previously raised the same grounds for review, or that the petitioner has failed to show good cause why the ground was not raised earlier, the court of appeals shall dismiss the petition on its own motion without requiring the state to respond to the petition. Upon receipt of a first or subsequent petition, the court of appeals shall, whenever possible, review the petition and determine if the petition is based on frivolous grounds. If frivolous, the court of appeals shall dismiss the petition on its own motion without first requiring the state to respond to the petition.

[**1989 c 395 § 9.**]

10.73.150
Right to counsel.

Counsel shall be provided at state expense to an adult offender convicted of a crime and to a juvenile offender convicted of an offense when the offender is indigent or indigent and able to contribute as those terms are defined in RCW **10.101.010** and the offender:

(1) Files an appeal as a matter of right;

(2) Responds to an appeal filed as a matter of right or responds to a motion for discretionary review or petition for review filed by the state;

(3) Is under a sentence of death and requests counsel be appointed to file and prosecute a motion or petition for collateral attack as defined in RCW **10.73.090**. Counsel may be provided at public expense to file or prosecute a second or subsequent collateral attack on the same judgment and sentence, if the court determines that the collateral attack is not barred by RCW **10.73.090** or **10.73.140**;

(4) Is not under a sentence of death and requests counsel to prosecute a collateral attack after the chief judge has determined that the issues raised by the petition are not frivolous, in accordance with the procedure contained in rules of appellate procedure 16.11. Counsel shall not be provided at public expense to file or prosecute a second or subsequent collateral attack on the same judgment and sentence;

(5) Responds to a collateral attack filed by the state or responds to or prosecutes an appeal from a collateral attack that was filed by the state;

(6) Prosecutes a motion or petition for review after the supreme court or court of appeals has accepted discretionary review of a decision of a court of limited jurisdiction; or

(7) Prosecutes a motion or petition for review after the supreme court has accepted discretionary review of a court of appeals decision.

[**1995 c 275 § 2.**]

NOTES:

Finding—1995 c 275: "The legislature is aware that the constitutional requirements of equal protection and due process require that counsel be provided for indigent persons and persons who are indigent and able to contribute for the first appeal as a matter of right from a judgment and sentence in a criminal case or a juvenile offender proceeding, and no further. There is no constitutional right to appointment of counsel at public expense to collaterally attack a judgment and sentence in a criminal case or juvenile offender proceeding or to seek discretionary review of a lower appellate court decision.

The legislature finds that it is appropriate to extend the right to counsel at state expense beyond constitutional requirements in certain limited circumstances to persons who are indigent and persons who are indigent and able to contribute as those terms are defined in RCW**10.101.010.**" [**1995 c 275 § 1.**]

Severability—1995 c 275: "If any provision of this act or its application to any person or circumstance is held invalid, the remainder of the act or the application of the provision to other persons or circumstances is not affected." [**1995 c 275 § 5.**]

10.73.160
Court fees and costs.

*** CHANGE IN 2018 *** (SEE **1783-S2.SL**) ***

(1) The court of appeals, supreme court, and superior courts may require an adult offender convicted of an offense to pay appellate costs.

(2) Appellate costs are limited to expenses specifically incurred by the state in prosecuting or defending an appeal or collateral attack from a criminal conviction. Appellate costs shall not include expenditures to maintain and operate government agencies that must be made irrespective of specific violations of the law. Expenses

incurred for producing a verbatim report of proceedings and clerk's papers may be included in costs the court may require a convicted defendant to pay.

(3) Costs, including recoupment of fees for court-appointed counsel, shall be requested in accordance with the procedures contained in Title 14 of the rules of appellate procedure and in Title 9 of the rules for appeal of decisions of courts of limited jurisdiction. An award of costs shall become part of the trial court judgment and sentence.

(4) A defendant who has been sentenced to pay costs and who is not in contumacious default in the payment may at any time petition the court that sentenced the defendant or juvenile offender for remission of the payment of costs or of any unpaid portion. If it appears to the satisfaction of the sentencing court that payment of the amount due will impose manifest hardship on the defendant or the defendant's immediate family, the sentencing court may remit all or part of the amount due in costs, or modify the method of payment under RCW**10.01.170**.

(5) The parents or another person legally obligated to support a juvenile offender who has been ordered to pay appellate costs and who is not in contumacious default in the payment may at any time petition the court that sentenced the juvenile offender for remission of the payment of costs or of any unpaid portion. If it appears to the satisfaction of the sentencing court that payment of the amount due will impose manifest hardship on the parents or another person legally obligated to support a juvenile offender or on their immediate families, the sentencing court may remit all or part of the amount due in costs, or may modify the method of payment.

[**2015 c 265 § 22; 1995 c 275 § 3.**]

NOTES:

> **Finding—Intent—2015 c 265:** See note following RCW **13.50.010**.
>
> **Finding—Severability—1995 c 275:** See notes following RCW **10.73.150**.

10.73.170
DNA testing requests.

(1) A person convicted of a felony in a Washington state court who currently is serving a term of imprisonment may submit to the court that entered the judgment of conviction a verified written motion requesting DNA testing, with a copy of the motion provided to the state office of public defense.

(2) The motion shall:

(a) State that:

(i) The court ruled that DNA testing did not meet acceptable scientific standards; or

(ii) DNA testing technology was not sufficiently developed to test the DNA evidence in the case; or

(iii) The DNA testing now requested would be significantly more accurate than prior DNA testing or would provide significant new information;

(b) Explain why DNA evidence is material to the identity of the perpetrator of, or accomplice to, the crime, or to sentence enhancement; and

(c) Comply with all other procedural requirements established by court rule.

(3) The court shall grant a motion requesting DNA testing under this section if such motion is in the form required by subsection (2) of this section, and the convicted person has shown the likelihood that the DNA evidence would demonstrate innocence on a more probable than not basis.

(4) Upon written request to the court that entered a judgment of conviction, a convicted person who demonstrates that he or she is indigent under RCW **10.101.010** may request appointment of counsel solely to prepare and present a motion under this section, and the court, in its discretion, may grant the request. Such motion for appointment of counsel shall comply with all procedural requirements established by court rule.

(5) DNA testing ordered under this section shall be performed by the Washington state patrol crime laboratory. Contact with victims shall be handled through victim/witness divisions.

(6) Notwithstanding any other provision of law, upon motion of defense counsel or the court's own motion, a sentencing court in a felony case may order the preservation of any biological material that has been secured in connection with a criminal case, or

evidence samples sufficient for testing, in accordance with any court rule adopted for the preservation of evidence. The court must specify the samples to be maintained and the length of time the samples must be preserved.

[**2005 c 5 § 1; 2003 c 100 § 1; 2001 c 301 § 1; 2000 c 92 § 1.**]

NOTES:

Effective date—2005 c 5: "This act is necessary for the immediate preservation of the public peace, health, or safety, or support of the state government and its existing public institutions, and takes effect immediately [March 9, 2005]." [**2005 c 5 § 2.**]

Construction—2001 c 301: "Nothing in this act may be construed to create a new or additional cause of action in any court. Nothing in this act shall be construed to limit any rights offenders might otherwise have to court access under any other statutory or constitutional provision." [**2001 c 301 § 2.**]

Report on DNA testing—2000 c 92: "By December 1, 2001, the office of public defense shall prepare a report detailing the following: (1) The number of postconviction DNA test requests approved by the respective prosecutor; (2) the number of postconviction DNA test requests denied by the respective prosecutor and a summary of the basis for the denials; (3) the number of appeals for postconviction DNA testing approved by the attorney general's office; (4) the number of appeals for postconviction DNA testing denied by the attorney general's office and a summary of the basis for the denials; and (5) a summary of the results of the postconviction DNA tests conducted pursuant to RCW **10.73.170**(2) and (3). The report shall also provide an estimate of the number of persons convicted of crimes where DNA evidence was not admitted because the court ruled DNA testing did not meet acceptable scientific standards or where DNA testing technology was not sufficiently developed to test the DNA evidence in the case." [**2000 c 92 § 2.**]

Intent—2000 c 92: "Nothing in chapter 92, Laws of 2000 is intended to create a legal right or cause of action. Nothing in chapter 92, Laws of 2000 is intended to deny or alter any existing legal right or cause of action. Nothing in chapter 92, Laws of 2000 should be interpreted to deny postconviction DNA testing requests under existing law by convicted and incarcerated persons who were sentenced to confinement for a term less than life or the death penalty." [**2000 c 92 § 4.**]

Chapter 10.77 RCW CRIMINALLY INSANE— PROCEDURES

NOTES:

Rules of court: Cf. CrR 4.2(c).

Individuals with mental illness, commitment: Chapter **71.05** RCW.

Protocols required: RCW **71.05.214**.

10.77.010
Definitions. (Effective until April 1, 2018.)

As used in this chapter:

(1) "Admission" means acceptance based on medical necessity, of a person as a patient.

(2) "Commitment" means the determination by a court that a person should be detained for a period of either evaluation or treatment, or both, in an inpatient or a less-restrictive setting.

(3) "Conditional release" means modification of a court-ordered commitment, which may be revoked upon violation of any of its terms.

(4) A "criminally insane" person means any person who has been acquitted of a crime charged by reason of insanity, and thereupon found to be a substantial danger to other persons or to present a substantial likelihood of committing criminal acts jeopardizing public safety or security unless kept under further control by the court or other persons or institutions.

(5) "Department" means the state department of social and health services.

(6) "Designated mental health professional" has the same meaning as provided in RCW **71.05.020**.

(7) "Detention" or "detain" means the lawful confinement of a person, under the provisions of this chapter, pending evaluation.

(8) "Developmental disabilities professional" means a person who has specialized training and three years of experience in directly treating or working with persons with developmental disabilities and is a psychiatrist or psychologist, or a social worker, and such other developmental disabilities professionals as may be defined by rules adopted by the secretary.

(9) "Developmental disability" means the condition as defined in *RCW **71A.10.020**(4).

(10) "Discharge" means the termination of hospital medical authority. The commitment may remain in place, be terminated, or be amended by court order.

(11) "Furlough" means an authorized leave of absence for a resident of a state institution operated by the department designated for the custody, care, and treatment of the criminally insane, consistent with an order of conditional release from the court under this chapter, without any requirement that the resident be accompanied by, or be in the custody of, any law enforcement or institutional staff, while on such unescorted leave.

(12) "Habilitative services" means those services provided by program personnel to assist persons in acquiring and maintaining life skills and in raising their levels of physical, mental, social, and vocational functioning. Habilitative services include education, training for employment, and therapy. The habilitative process shall be undertaken with recognition of the risk to the public safety presented by the person being assisted as manifested by prior charged criminal conduct.

(13) "History of one or more violent acts" means violent acts committed during: (a) The ten-year period of time prior to the filing of criminal charges; plus (b) the amount of time equal to time spent during the ten-year period in a mental health facility or in confinement as a result of a criminal conviction.

(14) "Immediate family member" means a spouse, child, stepchild, parent, stepparent, grandparent, sibling, or domestic partner.

(15) "Incompetency" means a person lacks the capacity to understand the nature of the proceedings against him or her or to assist in his or her own defense as a result of mental disease or defect.

(16) "Indigent" means any person who is financially unable to obtain counsel or other necessary expert or professional services without causing substantial hardship to the person or his or her family.

(17) "Individualized service plan" means a plan prepared by a developmental disabilities professional with other professionals as a team, for an individual with developmental disabilities, which shall state:

(a) The nature of the person's specific problems, prior charged criminal behavior, and habilitation needs;

(b) The conditions and strategies necessary to achieve the purposes of habilitation;

(c) The intermediate and long-range goals of the habilitation program, with a projected timetable for the attainment;

(d) The rationale for using this plan of habilitation to achieve those intermediate and long-range goals;

(e) The staff responsible for carrying out the plan;

(f) Where relevant in light of past criminal behavior and due consideration for public safety, the criteria for proposed movement to less-restrictive settings, criteria for proposed eventual release, and a projected possible date for release; and

(g) The type of residence immediately anticipated for the person and possible future types of residences.

(18) "Professional person" means:

(a) A psychiatrist licensed as a physician and surgeon in this state who has, in addition, completed three years of graduate training in psychiatry in a program approved by the American medical association or the American osteopathic association and is certified or eligible to be certified by the American board of psychiatry and neurology or the American osteopathic board of neurology and psychiatry;

(b) A psychologist licensed as a psychologist pursuant to chapter **18.83** RCW; or

(c) A social worker with a master's or further advanced degree from a social work educational program accredited and approved as provided in RCW **18.320.010**.

(19) "Registration records" include all the records of the department, behavioral health organizations, treatment facilities, and other persons providing services to the department, county departments, or facilities which identify persons who are receiving or who at any time have received services for mental illness.

(20) "Release" means legal termination of the court-ordered commitment under the provisions of this chapter.

(21) "Secretary" means the secretary of the department of social and health services or his or her designee.

(22) "Treatment" means any currently standardized medical or mental health procedure including medication.

(23) "Treatment records" include registration and all other records concerning persons who are receiving or who at any time have received services for mental illness, which are maintained by the department, by behavioral health organizations and their staffs, and by treatment facilities. Treatment records do not include notes or records maintained for personal use by a person providing treatment services for the department, behavioral health organizations, or a treatment facility if the notes or records are not available to others.

(24) "Violent act" means behavior that: (a)(i) Resulted in; (ii) if completed as intended would have resulted in; or (iii) was threatened to be carried out by a person who had the intent and opportunity to carry out the threat and would have resulted in, homicide, nonfatal injuries, or substantial damage to property; or (b) recklessly creates an immediate risk of serious physical injury to another person. As used in this subsection, "nonfatal injuries" means physical pain or injury, illness, or an impairment of physical condition. "Nonfatal injuries" shall be construed to be consistent with the definition of "bodily injury," as defined in RCW **9A.04.110**.

[<u>2014 c 225 § 58</u>; <u>2011 c 89 § 4</u>; <u>2010 c 262 § 2</u>; <u>2005 c 504 § 106</u>; <u>2004 c 157 §</u> <u>2</u>; <u>2000 c 94 § 12</u>. Prior: <u>1999 c 143 § 49</u>; <u>1999 c 13 § 2</u>; <u>1998 c 297 § 29</u>; <u>1993 c 31 §</u> <u>4</u>; <u>1989 c 420 § 3</u>; <u>1983 c 122 § 1</u>; <u>1974 ex.s. c 198 § 1</u>; <u>1973 1st ex.s. c 117 § 1</u>.]

NOTES:

*Reviser's note: RCW <u>71A.10.020</u> was amended by 2014 c 139 § 2, changing subsection (4) to subsection (5).

Effective date—2014 c 225: See note following RCW <u>71.24.016</u>.

Effective date—2011 c 89: See note following RCW <u>18.320.005</u>.

Findings—2011 c 89: See RCW <u>18.320.005</u>.

Findings—Intent—Severability—Application—Construction—Captions, part headings, subheadings not law—Adoption of rules—Effective dates—2005 c 504: See notes following RCW <u>71.05.027</u>.

Alphabetization—Correction of references—2005 c 504: See note following RCW <u>71.05.020</u>.

Findings—Intent—2004 c 157: "The legislature finds that recent state and federal case law requires clarification of state statutes with regard to competency evaluations and involuntary medication ordered in the context of competency restoration.

The legislature finds that the court in Born v. Thompson, 117 Wn. App. 57 (2003) interpreted the term "nonfatal injuries" in a manner that conflicts with the stated intent of the legislature to: "(1) Clarify that it is the nature of a person's current conduct, current mental condition, history, and likelihood of committing future acts that pose a threat to public safety or himself or herself, rather than simple categorization of offenses, that should determine treatment procedures and level; ... and (3) provide additional opportunities for mental health treatment for persons whose conduct threatens himself or herself or threatens public safety and has led to contact with the criminal justice system" as stated in section 1, chapter 297, Laws of 1998. Consequently, the legislature intends to clarify that it intended "nonfatal injuries" to be interpreted in a manner consistent with the purposes of the competency restoration statutes.

The legislature also finds that the decision in Sell v. United States, ___U.S. ____ (2003), requires a determination whether a particular criminal offense is "serious" in the context of competency restoration and the state's duty to protect the public. The legislature further finds that, in order to adequately protect the public and in order to provide additional opportunities for mental health treatment for persons whose conduct threatens themselves or threatens public safety and has led to contact with the criminal justice system in the state, the determination of those criminal offenses that are "serious" offenses must be made consistently throughout the state. In order to facilitate this consistency, the legislature intends to determine those offenses that are serious in every case as well as the standards by which other offenses may be determined to be serious. The legislature also intends to clarify that a court may, to the extent permitted by federal law and required by the Sell decision, inquire into the civil commitment status of a defendant and may be told, if known." [**2004 c 157 § 1.**]

Severability—2004 c 157: "If any provision of this act or its application to any person or circumstance is held invalid, the remainder of the act or the application of the provision to other persons or circumstances is not affected." [**2004 c 157 § 7.**]

Effective date—2004 c 157: "This act is necessary for the immediate preservation of the public peace, health, or safety, or support of the state government and its existing public institutions, and takes effect immediately [March 26, 2004]." [**2004 c 157 § 8.**]

Purpose—**Construction**—1999 c 13: "The purpose of this act is to make technical nonsubstantive changes to chapters **10.77** and **71.05**RCW. No provision of this act shall be construed as a substantive change in the provisions dealing with persons charged with crimes who are subject to evaluation under chapter **10.77** or **71.05** RCW." [**1999 c 13 § 1.**]

Alphabetization of section—1998 c 297 § 29: "The code reviser shall alphabetize the definitions in RCW **10.77.010** and correct any references." [**1998 c 297 § 51.**]

Effective dates—**Severability**—**Intent**—1998 c 297: See notes following RCW **71.05.010**.

10.77.010

Definitions. (Effective April 1, 2018.)

As used in this chapter:

(1) "Admission" means acceptance based on medical necessity, of a person as a patient.

(2) "Commitment" means the determination by a court that a person should be detained for a period of either evaluation or treatment, or both, in an inpatient or a less-restrictive setting.

(3) "Conditional release" means modification of a court-ordered commitment, which may be revoked upon violation of any of its terms.

(4) A "criminally insane" person means any person who has been acquitted of a crime charged by reason of insanity, and thereupon found to be a substantial danger to other persons or to present a substantial likelihood of committing criminal acts jeopardizing public safety or security unless kept under further control by the court or other persons or institutions.

(5) "Department" means the state department of social and health services.

(6) "Designated crisis responder" has the same meaning as provided in RCW **71.05.020**.

(7) "Detention" or "detain" means the lawful confinement of a person, under the provisions of this chapter, pending evaluation.

(8) "Developmental disabilities professional" means a person who has specialized training and three years of experience in directly treating or working with persons with developmental disabilities and is a psychiatrist or psychologist, or a social worker, and such other developmental disabilities professionals as may be defined by rules adopted by the secretary.

(9) "Developmental disability" means the condition as defined in RCW **71A.10.020**(5).

(10) "Discharge" means the termination of hospital medical authority. The commitment may remain in place, be terminated, or be amended by court order.

(11) "Furlough" means an authorized leave of absence for a resident of a state institution operated by the department designated for the custody, care, and treatment of the criminally insane, consistent with an order of conditional release from the court

under this chapter, without any requirement that the resident be accompanied by, or be in the custody of, any law enforcement or institutional staff, while on such unescorted leave.

(12) "Habilitative services" means those services provided by program personnel to assist persons in acquiring and maintaining life skills and in raising their levels of physical, mental, social, and vocational functioning. Habilitative services include education, training for employment, and therapy. The habilitative process shall be undertaken with recognition of the risk to the public safety presented by the person being assisted as manifested by prior charged criminal conduct.

(13) "History of one or more violent acts" means violent acts committed during: (a) The ten-year period of time prior to the filing of criminal charges; plus (b) the amount of time equal to time spent during the ten-year period in a mental health facility or in confinement as a result of a criminal conviction.

(14) "Immediate family member" means a spouse, child, stepchild, parent, stepparent, grandparent, sibling, or domestic partner.

(15) "Incompetency" means a person lacks the capacity to understand the nature of the proceedings against him or her or to assist in his or her own defense as a result of mental disease or defect.

(16) "Indigent" means any person who is financially unable to obtain counsel or other necessary expert or professional services without causing substantial hardship to the person or his or her family.

(17) "Individualized service plan" means a plan prepared by a developmental disabilities professional with other professionals as a team, for an individual with developmental disabilities, which shall state:

(a) The nature of the person's specific problems, prior charged criminal behavior, and habilitation needs;

(b) The conditions and strategies necessary to achieve the purposes of habilitation;

(c) The intermediate and long-range goals of the habilitation program, with a projected timetable for the attainment;

(d) The rationale for using this plan of habilitation to achieve those intermediate and long-range goals;

(e) The staff responsible for carrying out the plan;

(f) Where relevant in light of past criminal behavior and due consideration for public safety, the criteria for proposed movement to less-restrictive settings, criteria for proposed eventual release, and a projected possible date for release; and

(g) The type of residence immediately anticipated for the person and possible future types of residences.

(18) "Professional person" means:

(a) A psychiatrist licensed as a physician and surgeon in this state who has, in addition, completed three years of graduate training in psychiatry in a program approved by the American medical association or the American osteopathic association and is certified or eligible to be certified by the American board of psychiatry and neurology or the American osteopathic board of neurology and psychiatry;

(b) A psychologist licensed as a psychologist pursuant to chapter **18.83** RCW; or

(c) A social worker with a master's or further advanced degree from a social work educational program accredited and approved as provided in RCW **18.320.010**.

(19) "Registration records" include all the records of the department, behavioral health organizations, treatment facilities, and other persons providing services to the department, county departments, or facilities which identify persons who are receiving or who at any time have received services for mental illness.

(20) "Release" means legal termination of the court-ordered commitment under the provisions of this chapter.

(21) "Secretary" means the secretary of the department of social and health services or his or her designee.

(22) "Treatment" means any currently standardized medical or mental health procedure including medication.

(23) "Treatment records" include registration and all other records concerning persons who are receiving or who at any time have received services for mental illness, which are maintained by the department, by behavioral health organizations and their

staffs, and by treatment facilities. Treatment records do not include notes or records maintained for personal use by a person providing treatment services for the department, behavioral health organizations, or a treatment facility if the notes or records are not available to others.

(24) "Violent act" means behavior that: (a)(i) Resulted in; (ii) if completed as intended would have resulted in; or (iii) was threatened to be carried out by a person who had the intent and opportunity to carry out the threat and would have resulted in, homicide, nonfatal injuries, or substantial damage to property; or (b) recklessly creates an immediate risk of serious physical injury to another person. As used in this subsection, "nonfatal injuries" means physical pain or injury, illness, or an impairment of physical condition. "Nonfatal injuries" shall be construed to be consistent with the definition of "bodily injury," as defined in RCW **9A.04.110**.

[**2016 sp.s. c 29 § 405; 2014 c 225 § 58; 2011 c 89 § 4; 2010 c 262 § 2; 2005 c 504 § 106; 2004 c 157 § 2; 2000 c 94 § 12.** Prior: **1999 c 143 § 49;1999 c 13 § 2; 1998 c 297 § 29; 1993 c 31 § 4; 1989 c 420 § 3; 1983 c 122 § 1; 1974 ex.s. c 198 § 1; 1973 1st ex.s. c 117 § 1.**]

NOTES:

    Effective dates—2016 sp.s. c 29: See note following RCW **71.05.760**.

    Short title—Right of action—2016 sp.s. c 29: See notes following RCW **71.05.010**.

    Effective date—2014 c 225: See note following RCW **71.24.016**.

    Effective date—2011 c 89: See note following RCW **18.320.005**.

    Findings—2011 c 89: See RCW **18.320.005**.

    Findings—Intent—Severability—Application—Construction—Captions, part headings, subheadings not law—Adoption of rules—Effective dates—2005 c 504: See notes following RCW **71.05.027**.

    Alphabetization—Correction of references—2005 c 504: See note following RCW **71.05.020**.

Findings—Intent—2004 c 157: "The legislature finds that recent state and federal case law requires clarification of state statutes with regard to competency evaluations and involuntary medication ordered in the context of competency restoration.

The legislature finds that the court in Born v. Thompson, 117 Wn. App. 57 (2003) interpreted the term "nonfatal injuries" in a manner that conflicts with the stated intent of the legislature to: "(1) Clarify that it is the nature of a person's current conduct, current mental condition, history, and likelihood of committing future acts that pose a threat to public safety or himself or herself, rather than simple categorization of offenses, that should determine treatment procedures and level; ... and (3) provide additional opportunities for mental health treatment for persons whose conduct threatens himself or herself or threatens public safety and has led to contact with the criminal justice system" as stated in section 1, chapter 297, Laws of 1998. Consequently, the legislature intends to clarify that it intended "nonfatal injuries" to be interpreted in a manner consistent with the purposes of the competency restoration statutes.

The legislature also finds that the decision in Sell v. United States, ___U.S.____ (2003), requires a determination whether a particular criminal offense is "serious" in the context of competency restoration and the state's duty to protect the public. The legislature further finds that, in order to adequately protect the public and in order to provide additional opportunities for mental health treatment for persons whose conduct threatens themselves or threatens public safety and has led to contact with the criminal justice system in the state, the determination of those criminal offenses that are "serious" offenses must be made consistently throughout the state. In order to facilitate this consistency, the legislature intends to determine those offenses that are serious in every case as well as the standards by which other offenses may be determined to be serious. The legislature also intends to clarify that a court may, to the extent permitted by federal law and required by the Sell decision, inquire into the civil commitment status of a defendant and may be told, if known." [**2004 c 157 § 1.**]

Severability—2004 c 157: "If any provision of this act or its application to any person or circumstance is held invalid, the remainder of the act or the application of the provision to other persons or circumstances is not affected." [**2004 c 157 § 7.**]

Effective date—2004 c 157: "This act is necessary for the immediate preservation of the public peace, health, or safety, or support of the state government and its existing public institutions, and takes effect immediately [March 26, 2004]." [**2004 c 157 § 8.**]

Purpose—Construction—1999 c 13: "The purpose of this act is to make technical nonsubstantive changes to chapters **10.77** and **71.05**RCW. No provision of this act shall be construed as a substantive change in the provisions dealing with persons charged with crimes who are subject to evaluation under chapter **10.77** or **71.05** RCW." [**1999 c 13 § 1.**]

Alphabetization of section—1998 c 297 § 29: "The code reviser shall alphabetize the definitions in RCW **10.77.010** and correct any references." [**1998 c 297 § 51.**]

Effective dates—Severability—Intent—1998 c 297: See notes following RCW **71.05.010**.

10.77.020
Rights of person under this chapter.

(1) At any and all stages of the proceedings pursuant to this chapter, any person subject to the provisions of this chapter shall be entitled to the assistance of counsel, and if the person is indigent the court shall appoint counsel to assist him or her. A person may waive his or her right to counsel; but such waiver shall only be effective if a court makes a specific finding that he or she is or was competent to so waive. In making such findings, the court shall be guided but not limited by the following standards: Whether the person attempting to waive the assistance of counsel, does so understanding:

(a) The nature of the charges;

(b) The statutory offense included within them;

(c) The range of allowable punishments thereunder;

(d) Possible defenses to the charges and circumstances in mitigation thereof; and

(e) All other facts essential to a broad understanding of the whole matter.

(2) Whenever any person is subjected to an examination pursuant to any provision of this chapter, he or she may retain an expert or professional person to perform an examination in his or her behalf. In the case of a person who is indigent, the court shall upon his or her request assist the person in obtaining an expert or professional person to perform an examination or participate in the hearing on his or her behalf. An expert or professional person obtained by an indigent person pursuant to the provisions of this chapter shall be compensated for his or her services out of funds of the department, in an amount determined by the secretary to be fair and reasonable.

(3) Any time the defendant is being examined by court appointed experts or professional persons pursuant to the provisions of this chapter, the defendant shall be entitled to have his or her attorney present.

(4) In a competency evaluation conducted under this chapter, the defendant may refuse to answer any question if he or she believes his or her answers may tend to incriminate him or her or form links leading to evidence of an incriminating nature.

(5) In a sanity evaluation conducted under this chapter, if a defendant refuses to answer questions or to participate in an examination conducted in response to the defendant's assertion of an insanity defense, the court shall exclude from evidence at trial any testimony or evidence from any expert or professional person obtained or retained by the defendant.
[**2006 c 109 § 1; 1998 c 297 § 30; 1993 c 31 § 5; 1974 ex.s. c 198 § 2; 1973 1st ex.s. c 117 § 2.**]
NOTES:

Application—2006 c 109: "This act applies to all examinations performed on or after June 7, 2006." [**2006 c 109 § 2.**]

Severability—2006 c 109: "If any provision of this act or its application to any person or circumstance is held invalid, the remainder of the act or the application of the provision to other persons or circumstances is not affected." [**2006 c 109 § 3.**]

Effective dates—Severability—Intent—1998 c 297: See notes following RCW **71.05.010**.

10.77.025

Maximum term of commitment or treatment. (Effective until April 1, 2018.)

(1) Whenever any person has been: (a) Committed to a correctional facility or inpatient treatment under any provision of this chapter; or (b) ordered to undergo alternative treatment following his or her acquittal by reason of insanity of a crime charged, such commitment or treatment cannot exceed the maximum possible penal sentence for any offense charged for which the person was committed, or was acquitted by reason of insanity.

(2) Whenever any person committed under any provision of this chapter has not been released within seven days of the maximum possible penal sentence under subsection (1) of this section, and the professional person in charge of the facility believes that the person presents a likelihood of serious harm or is gravely disabled due to a mental disorder, the professional person shall, prior to the expiration of the maximum penal sentence, notify the appropriate *county designated mental health professional of the impending expiration and provide a copy of all relevant information regarding the person, including the likely release date and shall indicate why the person should not be released.

(3) A *county designated mental health professional who receives notice and records under subsection (2) of this section shall, prior to the date of the expiration of the maximum sentence, determine whether to initiate proceedings under chapter **71.05** RCW.

[**2000 c 94 § 13; 1998 c 297 § 31.**]

NOTES:

*Reviser's note: The term "county designated mental health professional" as defined in RCW **10.77.010** was changed to "designated mental health professional" by **2005 c 504 § 106.**

Effective dates—Severability—Intent—1998 c 297: See notes following RCW **71.05.010**.

10.77.025

Maximum term of commitment or treatment. (Effective April 1, 2018.)

(1) Whenever any person has been: (a) Committed to a correctional facility or inpatient treatment under any provision of this chapter; or (b) ordered to undergo alternative treatment following his or her acquittal by reason of insanity of a crime charged, such commitment or treatment cannot exceed the maximum possible penal sentence for any offense charged for which the person was committed, or was acquitted by reason of insanity.

(2) Whenever any person committed under any provision of this chapter has not been released within seven days of the maximum possible penal sentence under subsection (1) of this section, and the professional person in charge of the facility believes that the person presents a likelihood of serious harm or is gravely disabled due to a mental disorder, the professional person shall, prior to the expiration of the maximum penal sentence, notify the appropriate designated crisis responder of the impending expiration and provide a copy of all relevant information regarding the person, including the likely release date and shall indicate why the person should not be released.

(3) A designated crisis responder who receives notice and records under subsection (2) of this section shall, prior to the date of the expiration of the maximum sentence, determine whether to initiate proceedings under chapter **71.05** RCW.
[**2016 sp.s. c 29 § 406; 2000 c 94 § 13; 1998 c 297 § 31.**]
NOTES:

> **Effective dates—2016 sp.s. c 29:** See note following RCW **71.05.760**.

> **Short title—Right of action—2016 sp.s. c 29:** See notes following RCW **71.05.010**.

> **Effective dates—Severability—Intent—1998 c 297:** See notes following RCW **71.05.010**.

10.77.027
Eligible for commitment regardless of cause. (Effective until April 1, 2018.)

When a *county designated mental health professional or a professional person has determined that a person has a mental disorder, and is otherwise committable, the cause of the person's mental disorder shall not make the person ineligible for commitment under chapter **71.05**RCW.

[**2004 c 166 § 3.**]

NOTES:

   *Reviser's note: The term "county designated mental health professional" as defined in RCW **10.77.010** was changed to "designated mental health professional" by **2005 c 504 § 106.**

   Severability—Effective dates—2004 c 166: See notes following RCW **71.05.040**.

10.77.027

Eligible for commitment regardless of cause. (Effective April 1, 2018.)

When a designated crisis responder or a professional person has determined that a person has a mental disorder, and is otherwise committable, the cause of the person's mental disorder shall not make the person ineligible for commitment under chapter **71.05** RCW.

[**2016 sp.s. c 29 § 407; 2004 c 166 § 3.**]

NOTES:

   Effective dates—2016 sp.s. c 29: See note following RCW **71.05.760**.

   Short title—Right of action—2016 sp.s. c 29: See notes following RCW **71.05.010**.

   Severability—Effective dates—2004 c 166: See notes following RCW **71.05.040**.

10.77.030

Establishing insanity as a defense.

(1) Evidence of insanity is not admissible unless the defendant, at the time of arraignment or within ten days thereafter or at such later time as the court may for good cause permit, files a written notice of his or her intent to rely on such a defense.

(2) Insanity is a defense which the defendant must establish by a preponderance of the evidence.

(3) No condition of mind proximately induced by the voluntary act of a person charged with a crime shall constitute insanity.

[**1998 c 297 § 32; 1974 ex.s. c 198 § 3; 1973 1st ex.s. c 117 § 3.**]

NOTES:

Effective dates—Severability—Intent—1998 c 297: See notes following RCW **71.05.010**.

10.77.040

Instructions to jury on special verdict.

Whenever the issue of insanity is submitted to the jury, the court shall instruct the jury to return a special verdict in substantially the following form:

		answer yes or no
1.	Did the defendant commit the act charged?	. . . . .
2.	If your answer to number 1 is yes, do you acquit him or her because of insanity existing at the time of the act charged?	. . . . .
3.	If your answer to number 2 is yes, is the defendant a substantial danger to other persons unless kept under further control by the court or other persons or institutions?	. . . . .
4.	If your answer to number 2 is yes, does the defendant present a substantial likelihood of committing criminal acts jeopardizing public safety or security unless kept under further control by the court or other persons or institutions?	. . . . .
5.	If your answers to either number 3 or number 4 is yes, is it in the best interests of the defendant and others that the defendant be placed in treatment that is less	. . . . .

restrictive than detention in a state mental hospital?

[**1998 c 297 § 33; 1974 ex.s. c 198 § 4; 1973 1st ex.s. c 117 § 4.**]

NOTES:

Effective dates—Severability—Intent—1998 c 297: See notes following RCW **71.05.010**.

10.77.050

Mental incapacity as bar to proceedings.

No incompetent person shall be tried, convicted, or sentenced for the commission of an offense so long as such incapacity continues.

[**1974 ex.s. c 198 § 5; 1973 1st ex.s. c 117 § 5.**]

10.77.060

Plea of not guilty due to insanity—Doubt as to competency—Evaluation—Bail—Report. (Effective until April 1, 2018.)

(1)(a) Whenever a defendant has pleaded not guilty by reason of insanity, or there is reason to doubt his or her competency, the court on its own motion or on the motion of any party shall either appoint or request the secretary to designate a qualified expert or professional person, who shall be approved by the prosecuting attorney, to evaluate and report upon the mental condition of the defendant.

(b) The signed order of the court shall serve as authority for the evaluator to be given access to all records held by any mental health, medical, educational, or correctional facility that relate to the present or past mental, emotional, or physical condition of the defendant. If the court is advised by any party that the defendant may have a developmental disability, the evaluation must be performed by a developmental disabilities professional.

(c) The evaluator shall assess the defendant in a jail, detention facility, in the community, or in court to determine whether a period of inpatient commitment will be necessary to complete an accurate evaluation. If inpatient commitment is needed, the signed order of the court shall serve as authority for the evaluator to request the jail or detention facility to transport the defendant to a hospital or secure mental health facility for a period of commitment not to exceed fifteen days from the time of admission to the facility. Otherwise, the evaluator shall complete the evaluation.

(d) The court may commit the defendant for evaluation to a hospital or secure mental health facility without an assessment if: (i) The defendant is charged with murder in the first or second degree; (ii) the court finds that it is more likely than not that an evaluation in the jail will be inadequate to complete an accurate evaluation; or (iii) the court finds that an evaluation outside the jail setting is necessary for the health, safety, or welfare of the defendant. The court shall not order an initial inpatient evaluation for any purpose other than a competency evaluation.

(e) The order shall indicate whether, in the event the defendant is committed to a hospital or secure mental health facility for evaluation, all parties agree to waive the presence of the defendant or to the defendant's remote participation at a subsequent competency hearing or presentation of an agreed order if the recommendation of the evaluator is for continuation of the stay of criminal proceedings, or if the opinion of the evaluator is that the defendant remains incompetent and there is no remaining restoration period, and the hearing is held prior to the expiration of the authorized commitment period.

(f) When a defendant is ordered to be committed for inpatient evaluation under this subsection (1), the court may delay granting bail until the defendant has been evaluated for competency or sanity and appears before the court. Following the evaluation, in determining bail the court shall consider: (i) Recommendations of the evaluator regarding the defendant's competency, sanity, or diminished capacity; (ii) whether the defendant has a recent history of one or more violent acts; (iii) whether the defendant has previously been acquitted by reason of insanity or found incompetent; (iv) whether it is reasonably likely the defendant will fail to appear for a future court hearing; and (v) whether the defendant is a threat to public safety.

(2) The court may direct that a qualified expert or professional person retained by or appointed for the defendant be permitted to witness the evaluation authorized by subsection (1) of this section, and that the defendant shall have access to all information obtained by the court appointed experts or professional persons. The defendant's expert or professional person shall have the right to file his or her own report following the guidelines of subsection (3) of this section. If the defendant is indigent, the court shall upon the request of the defendant assist him or her in obtaining an expert or professional person.

(3) The report of the evaluation shall include the following:

(a) A description of the nature of the evaluation;

(b) A diagnosis or description of the current mental status of the defendant;

(c) If the defendant suffers from a mental disease or defect, or has a developmental disability, an opinion as to competency;

(d) If the defendant has indicated his or her intention to rely on the defense of insanity pursuant to RCW **10.77.030**, and an evaluation and report by an expert or professional person has been provided concluding that the defendant was criminally insane at the time of the alleged offense, an opinion as to the defendant's sanity at the time of the act, and an opinion as to whether the defendant presents a substantial danger to other persons, or presents a substantial likelihood of committing criminal acts jeopardizing public safety or security, unless kept under further control by the court or other persons or institutions, provided that no opinion shall be rendered under this subsection (3)(d) unless the evaluator or court determines that the defendant is competent to stand trial;

(e) When directed by the court, if an evaluation and report by an expert or professional person has been provided concluding that the defendant lacked the capacity at the time of the offense to form the mental state necessary to commit the charged offense, an opinion as to the capacity of the defendant to have a particular state of mind which is an element of the offense charged;

(f) An opinion as to whether the defendant should be evaluated by a designated mental health professional under chapter **71.05** RCW.

(4) The secretary may execute such agreements as appropriate and necessary to implement this section and may choose to designate more than one evaluator.

[**2012 c 256 § 3; 2004 c 9 § 1; 2000 c 74 § 1; 1998 c 297 § 34; 1989 c 420 § 4; 1974 ex.s. c 198 § 6; 1973 1st ex.s. c 117 § 6.**]

NOTES:

Purpose—Effective date—2012 c 256: See notes following RCW **10.77.068**.

Severability—2000 c 74: "If any provision of this act or its application to any person or circumstance is held invalid, the remainder of the act or the application of the provision to other persons or circumstances is not affected." [**2000 c 74 § 8.**]

Effective dates—Severability—Intent—1998 c 297: See notes following RCW **71.05.010**.

10.77.060

Plea of not guilty due to insanity—Doubt as to competency—Evaluation—Bail—Report. (Effective April 1, 2018.)

(1)(a) Whenever a defendant has pleaded not guilty by reason of insanity, or there is reason to doubt his or her competency, the court on its own motion or on the motion of any party shall either appoint or request the secretary to designate a qualified expert or professional person, who shall be approved by the prosecuting attorney, to evaluate and report upon the mental condition of the defendant.

(b) The signed order of the court shall serve as authority for the evaluator to be given access to all records held by any mental health, medical, educational, or correctional facility that relate to the present or past mental, emotional, or physical condition of the defendant. If the court is advised by any party that the defendant may have a developmental disability, the evaluation must be performed by a developmental disabilities professional.

(c) The evaluator shall assess the defendant in a jail, detention facility, in the community, or in court to determine whether a period of inpatient commitment will be necessary to complete an accurate evaluation. If inpatient commitment is needed, the signed order of the court shall serve as authority for the evaluator to request the jail or detention facility to transport the defendant to a hospital or secure mental health facility for a period of commitment not to exceed fifteen days from the time of admission to the facility. Otherwise, the evaluator shall complete the evaluation.

(d) The court may commit the defendant for evaluation to a hospital or secure mental health facility without an assessment if: (i) The defendant is charged with murder in the first or second degree; (ii) the court finds that it is more likely than not that an evaluation in the jail will be inadequate to complete an accurate evaluation; or (iii) the court finds that an evaluation outside the jail setting is necessary for the health, safety, or welfare of the defendant. The court shall not order an initial inpatient evaluation for any purpose other than a competency evaluation.

(e) The order shall indicate whether, in the event the defendant is committed to a hospital or secure mental health facility for evaluation, all parties agree to waive the presence of the defendant or to the defendant's remote participation at a subsequent competency hearing or presentation of an agreed order if the recommendation of the evaluator is for continuation of the stay of criminal proceedings, or if the opinion of the evaluator is that the defendant remains incompetent and there is no remaining restoration period, and the hearing is held prior to the expiration of the authorized commitment period.

(f) When a defendant is ordered to be committed for inpatient evaluation under this subsection (1), the court may delay granting bail until the defendant has been evaluated for competency or sanity and appears before the court. Following the evaluation, in determining bail the court shall consider: (i) Recommendations of the evaluator regarding the defendant's competency, sanity, or diminished capacity; (ii) whether the defendant has a recent history of one or more violent acts; (iii) whether the defendant has previously been acquitted by reason of insanity or found incompetent; (iv) whether it is reasonably likely the defendant will fail to appear for a future court hearing; and (v) whether the defendant is a threat to public safety.

(2) The court may direct that a qualified expert or professional person retained by or appointed for the defendant be permitted to witness the evaluation authorized by

subsection (1) of this section, and that the defendant shall have access to all information obtained by the court appointed experts or professional persons. The defendant's expert or professional person shall have the right to file his or her own report following the guidelines of subsection (3) of this section. If the defendant is indigent, the court shall upon the request of the defendant assist him or her in obtaining an expert or professional person.

(3) The report of the evaluation shall include the following:

(a) A description of the nature of the evaluation;

(b) A diagnosis or description of the current mental status of the defendant;

(c) If the defendant suffers from a mental disease or defect, or has a developmental disability, an opinion as to competency;

(d) If the defendant has indicated his or her intention to rely on the defense of insanity pursuant to RCW **10.77.030**, and an evaluation and report by an expert or professional person has been provided concluding that the defendant was criminally insane at the time of the alleged offense, an opinion as to the defendant's sanity at the time of the act, and an opinion as to whether the defendant presents a substantial danger to other persons, or presents a substantial likelihood of committing criminal acts jeopardizing public safety or security, unless kept under further control by the court or other persons or institutions, provided that no opinion shall be rendered under this subsection (3)(d) unless the evaluator or court determines that the defendant is competent to stand trial;

(e) When directed by the court, if an evaluation and report by an expert or professional person has been provided concluding that the defendant lacked the capacity at the time of the offense to form the mental state necessary to commit the charged offense, an opinion as to the capacity of the defendant to have a particular state of mind which is an element of the offense charged;

(f) An opinion as to whether the defendant should be evaluated by a designated crisis responder under chapter **71.05** RCW.

(4) The secretary may execute such agreements as appropriate and necessary to implement this section and may choose to designate more than one evaluator.

[2016 sp.s. c 29 § 408; 2012 c 256 § 3; 2004 c 9 § 1; 2000 c 74 § 1; 1998 c 297 § 34; 1989 c 420 § 4; 1974 ex.s. c 198 § 6; 1973 1st ex.s. c 117 § 6.]

NOTES:

Effective dates—2016 sp.s. c 29: See note following RCW 71.05.760.

Short title—Right of action—2016 sp.s. c 29: See notes following RCW 71.05.010.

Purpose—Effective date—2012 c 256: See notes following RCW 10.77.068.

Severability—2000 c 74: "If any provision of this act or its application to any person or circumstance is held invalid, the remainder of the act or the application of the provision to other persons or circumstances is not affected." [2000 c 74 § 8.]

Effective dates—Severability—Intent—1998 c 297: See notes following RCW 71.05.010.

10.77.065

Mental condition evaluations—Reports and recommendations required—Discharge of defendant when determined competent to stand trial. (Effective until April 1, 2018.)

(1)(a)(i) The expert conducting the evaluation shall provide his or her report and recommendation to the court in which the criminal proceeding is pending. For a competency evaluation of a defendant who is released from custody, if the evaluation cannot be completed within twenty-one days due to a lack of cooperation by the defendant, the evaluator shall notify the court that he or she is unable to complete the evaluation because of such lack of cooperation.

(ii) A copy of the report and recommendation shall be provided to the designated mental health professional, the prosecuting attorney, the defense attorney, and the professional person at the local correctional facility where the defendant is being held, or if there is no professional person, to the person designated under (a)(iv) of this subsection. Upon request, the evaluator shall also provide copies of any source documents relevant to the evaluation to the designated mental health professional.

(iii) Any facility providing inpatient services related to competency shall discharge the defendant as soon as the facility determines that the defendant is competent to stand trial. Discharge shall not be postponed during the writing and distribution of the evaluation report. Distribution of an evaluation report by a facility providing inpatient services shall ordinarily be accomplished within two working days or less following the final evaluation of the defendant. If the defendant is discharged to the custody of a local correctional facility, the local correctional facility must continue the medication regimen prescribed by the facility, when clinically appropriate, unless the defendant refuses to cooperate with medication and an involuntary medication order by the court has not been entered.

(iv) If there is no professional person at the local correctional facility, the local correctional facility shall designate a professional person as defined in RCW **71.05.020** or, in cooperation with the behavioral health organization, a professional person at the behavioral health organization to receive the report and recommendation.

(v) Upon commencement of a defendant's evaluation in the local correctional facility, the local correctional facility must notify the evaluator of the name of the professional person, or person designated under (a)(iv) of this subsection, to receive the report and recommendation.

(b) If the evaluator concludes, under RCW **10.77.060**(3)(f), the person should be evaluated by a designated mental health professional under chapter **71.05** RCW, the court shall order such evaluation be conducted prior to release from confinement when the person is acquitted or convicted and sentenced to confinement for twenty-four months or less, or when charges are dismissed pursuant to a finding of incompetent to stand trial.

(2) The designated mental health professional shall provide written notification within twenty-four hours of the results of the determination whether to commence proceedings under chapter **71.05** RCW. The notification shall be provided to the persons identified in subsection (1)(a) of this section.

(3) The prosecuting attorney shall provide a copy of the results of any proceedings commenced by the designated mental health professional under subsection (2) of this section to the secretary.

(4) A facility conducting a civil commitment evaluation under RCW **10.77.086**(4) or **10.77.088**(1)(c)(ii) that makes a determination to release the person instead of filing a civil commitment petition must provide written notice to the prosecutor and defense attorney at least twenty-four hours prior to release. The notice may be given by electronic mail, facsimile, or other means reasonably likely to communicate the information immediately.

(5) The fact of admission and all information and records compiled, obtained, or maintained in the course of providing services under this chapter may also be disclosed to the courts solely to prevent the entry of any evaluation or treatment order that is inconsistent with any order entered under chapter **71.05** RCW.

[**2015 1st sp.s. c 7 § 16.** Prior: **2014 c 225 § 59; 2014 c 10 § 3; 2013 c 214 § 1; 2012 c 256 § 4; 2008 c 213 § 1; 2000 c 74 § 2; 1998 c 297 § 35.**]

NOTES:

    Finding—2015 1st sp.s. c 7: See note following RCW **10.77.075**.

    Effective dates—2015 1st sp.s. c 7: See note following RCW **10.77.073**.

    Effective date—2014 c 225: See note following RCW **71.24.016**.

    Finding—2014 c 10: See note following RCW **10.77.092**.

    Purpose—**Effective date**—2012 c 256: See notes following RCW **10.77.068**.

    Severability—2000 c 74: See note following RCW **10.77.060**.

    Effective dates—**Severability**—**Intent**—1998 c 297: See notes following RCW **71.05.010**.

10.77.065

Mental condition evaluations—Reports and recommendations required—Discharge of defendant when determined competent to stand trial. (Effective April 1, 2018.)

(1)(a)(i) The expert conducting the evaluation shall provide his or her report and recommendation to the court in which the criminal proceeding is pending. For a competency evaluation of a defendant who is released from custody, if the evaluation cannot be completed within twenty-one days due to a lack of cooperation by the defendant, the evaluator shall notify the court that he or she is unable to complete the evaluation because of such lack of cooperation.

(ii) A copy of the report and recommendation shall be provided to the designated crisis responder, the prosecuting attorney, the defense attorney, and the professional person at the local correctional facility where the defendant is being held, or if there is no professional person, to the person designated under (a)(iv) of this subsection. Upon request, the evaluator shall also provide copies of any source documents relevant to the evaluation to the designated crisis responder.

(iii) Any facility providing inpatient services related to competency shall discharge the defendant as soon as the facility determines that the defendant is competent to stand trial. Discharge shall not be postponed during the writing and distribution of the evaluation report. Distribution of an evaluation report by a facility providing inpatient services shall ordinarily be accomplished within two working days or less following the final evaluation of the defendant. If the defendant is discharged to the custody of a local correctional facility, the local correctional facility must continue the medication regimen prescribed by the facility, when clinically appropriate, unless the defendant refuses to cooperate with medication and an involuntary medication order by the court has not been entered.

(iv) If there is no professional person at the local correctional facility, the local correctional facility shall designate a professional person as defined in RCW **71.05.020** or, in cooperation with the behavioral health organization, a professional person at the behavioral health organization to receive the report and recommendation.

(v) Upon commencement of a defendant's evaluation in the local correctional facility, the local correctional facility must notify the evaluator of the name of the professional person, or person designated under (a)(iv) of this subsection, to receive the report and recommendation.

(b) If the evaluator concludes, under RCW **10.77.060**(3)(f), the person should be evaluated by a designated crisis responder under chapter**71.05** RCW, the court shall order such evaluation be conducted prior to release from confinement when the person is acquitted or convicted and sentenced to confinement for twenty-four months or less, or when charges are dismissed pursuant to a finding of incompetent to stand trial.

(2) The designated crisis responder shall provide written notification within twenty-four hours of the results of the determination whether to commence proceedings under chapter **71.05** RCW. The notification shall be provided to the persons identified in subsection (1)(a) of this section.

(3) The prosecuting attorney shall provide a copy of the results of any proceedings commenced by the designated crisis responder under subsection (2) of this section to the secretary.

(4) A facility conducting a civil commitment evaluation under RCW **10.77.086**(4) or **10.77.088**(1)(c)(ii) that makes a determination to release the person instead of filing a civil commitment petition must provide written notice to the prosecutor and defense attorney at least twenty-four hours prior to release. The notice may be given by email, facsimile, or other means reasonably likely to communicate the information immediately.

(5) The fact of admission and all information and records compiled, obtained, or maintained in the course of providing services under this chapter may also be disclosed to the courts solely to prevent the entry of any evaluation or treatment order that is inconsistent with any order entered under chapter **71.05** RCW.

[**2016 sp.s. c 29 § 409; 2015 1st sp.s. c 7 § 16.** Prior: **2014 c 225 § 59; 2014 c 10 § 3; 2013 c 214 § 1; 2012 c 256 § 4; 2008 c 213 § 1; 2000 c 74 § 2;1998 c 297 § 35.**]

NOTES:

Effective dates—2016 sp.s. c 29: See note following RCW **71.05.760**.

Short title—Right of action—2016 sp.s. c 29: See notes following RCW **71.05.010**.

Finding—2015 1st sp.s. c 7: See note following RCW **10.77.075**.

Effective dates—2015 1st sp.s. c 7: See note following RCW **10.77.073**.

Effective date—2014 c 225: See note following RCW **71.24.016**.

Finding—2014 c 10: See note following RCW **10.77.092**.

Purpose—Effective date—2012 c 256: See notes following RCW **10.77.068**.

Severability—2000 c 74: See note following RCW **10.77.060**.

Effective dates—Severability—Intent—1998 c 297: See notes following RCW **71.05.010**.

10.77.068

Competency to stand trial, admissions for inpatient restoration services—Performance targets and maximum time limits—Duties of the department—Report—New entitlement or cause of action not created—No basis for contempt or motion to dismiss.

(1)(a) The legislature establishes the following performance targets and maximum time limits for the timeliness of the completion of accurate and reliable evaluations of competency to stand trial and admissions for inpatient restoration services related to competency to proceed or stand trial for adult criminal defendants. The legislature recognizes that these targets may not be achievable in all cases without compromise to the quality of competency evaluation and restoration services, but intends for the department to manage, allocate, and request appropriations for resources in order to meet these targets whenever possible without sacrificing the accuracy and quality of competency evaluations and restorations, and to otherwise make sustainable improvements and track performance related to the timeliness of competency services:

(i) For a state hospital to extend an offer of admission to a defendant in pretrial custody for legally authorized evaluation services related to competency, or to extend an offer of admission for legally authorized services following dismissal of charges based on incompetence to proceed or stand trial:

(A) A performance target of seven days or less; and

(B) A maximum time limit of fourteen days;

(ii) For a state hospital to extend an offer of admission to a defendant in pretrial custody for legally authorized inpatient restoration treatment related to competency:

(A) A performance target of seven days or less; and

(B) A maximum time limit of fourteen days;

(iii) For completion of a competency evaluation in jail and distribution of the evaluation report for a defendant in pretrial custody:

(A) A performance target of seven days or less; and

(B) A maximum time limit of fourteen days, plus an additional seven-day extension if needed for clinical reasons to complete the evaluation at the determination of the department;

(iv) For completion of a competency evaluation in the community and distribution of the evaluation report for a defendant who is released from custody and makes a reasonable effort to cooperate with the evaluation, a performance target of twenty-one days or less.

(b) The time periods measured in these performance targets and maximum time limits shall run from the date on which the state hospital receives the court referral and charging documents, discovery, police reports, the names and addresses of the attorneys for the defendant and state or county, the name of the judge ordering the evaluation, information about the alleged crime, and criminal history information related to the defendant. The maximum time limits in (a) of this subsection shall be phased in over a one-year period beginning July 1, 2015, in a manner that results in measurable incremental progress toward meeting the time limits over the course of the year.

(c) It shall be a defense to an allegation that the department has exceeded the maximum time limits for completion of competency services described in (a) of this subsection if the department can demonstrate by a preponderance of the evidence that the reason for exceeding the maximum time limits was outside of the department's control including, but not limited to, the following circumstances:

(i) Despite a timely request, the department has not received necessary medical clearance information regarding the current medical status of a defendant in pretrial custody for the purposes of admission to a state hospital;

(ii) The individual circumstances of the defendant make accurate completion of an evaluation of competency to proceed or stand trial dependent upon review of mental health, substance use disorder, or medical history information which is in the custody of a third party and cannot be immediately obtained by the department. Completion of a competency evaluation shall not be postponed for procurement of mental health, substance use disorder, or medical history information which is merely supplementary to the competency determination;

(iii) Completion of the referral is frustrated by lack of availability or participation by counsel, jail or court personnel, interpreters, or the defendant;

(iv) The department does not have access to appropriate private space to conduct a competency evaluation for a defendant in pretrial custody;

(v) The defendant asserts legal rights that result in a delay in the provision of competency services; or

(vi) An unusual spike in the receipt of evaluation referrals or in the number of defendants requiring restoration services has occurred, causing temporary delays until the unexpected excess demand for competency services can be resolved.

(2) The department shall:

(a) Develop, document, and implement procedures to monitor the clinical status of defendants admitted to a state hospital for competency services that allow the state hospital to accomplish early discharge for defendants for whom clinical objectives have been achieved or may be achieved before expiration of the commitment period;

(b) Investigate the extent to which patients admitted to a state hospital under this chapter overstay time periods authorized by law and take reasonable steps to limit the time of commitment to authorized periods; and

(c) Establish written standards for the productivity of forensic evaluators and utilize these standards to internally review the performance of forensic evaluators.

(3) Following any quarter in which a state hospital has failed to meet one or more of the performance targets or maximum time limits in subsection (1) of this section after full implementation of the performance target or maximum time limit, the department shall report to the executive and the legislature the extent of this deviation and describe any corrective action being taken to improve performance. This report must be made publicly available. An average may be used to determine timeliness under this subsection.

(4) Beginning December 1, 2013, the department shall report annually to the legislature and the executive on the timeliness of services related to competency to proceed or stand trial and the timeliness with which court referrals accompanied by charging documents, discovery, and criminal history information are provided to the department relative to the signature date of the court order. The report must be in a form that is accessible to the public and that breaks down performance by county.

(5) This section does not create any new entitlement or cause of action related to the timeliness of competency evaluations or admission for inpatient restoration services related to competency to proceed or stand trial, nor can it form the basis for contempt sanctions under chapter **7.21** RCW or a motion to dismiss criminal charges.

[**2015 c 5 § 1; 2012 c 256 § 2.**]

NOTES:

Purpose—2012 c 256: "The purpose of this act is to sustainably improve the timeliness of services related to competency to stand trial by setting performance expectations, establishing new mechanisms for accountability, and enacting reforms to ensure that forensic resources are expended in an efficient and clinically appropriate manner without diminishing the quality of competency services, and to reduce the time defendants with mental illness spend in jail awaiting evaluation and restoration of competency." [**2012 c 256 § 1.**]

Effective date—2012 c 256: "This act is necessary for the immediate preservation of the public peace, health, or safety, or support of the state government and its existing public institutions, and takes effect May 1, 2012." [**2012 c 256 § 14.**]

10.77.070

Examination rights of defendant's expert or professional person.

When the defendant wishes to be examined by a qualified expert or professional person of his or her own choice such examiner shall be permitted to have reasonable access to the defendant for the purpose of such examination, as well as to all relevant medical and psychological records and reports.

[**1998 c 297 § 36; 1973 1st ex.s. c 117 § 7.**]

NOTES:

Effective dates—Severability—Intent—1998 c 297: See notes following RCW **71.05.010**.

10.77.073

Competency to stand trial—Evaluation—Appointment of qualified expert or professional person. (Expires June 30, 2019.)

(1) The department shall reimburse a county for the cost of appointing a qualified expert or professional person under RCW **10.77.060**(1)(a) subject to subsections (2) through (4) of this section if, at the time of a referral for an evaluation of competency to stand trial in a jail for an in-custody defendant, the department: (a) During the most recent quarter, did not perform at least one-third of the number of jail-based competency evaluations for in-custody defendants as were performed by qualified experts or professional persons appointed by the court in the referring county; or (b) did not meet the performance target for timely completion of competency evaluations under RCW **10.77.068**(1)(a)(iii) during the most recent quarter in fifty percent of cases submitted by the referring county, as documented in the most recent quarterly report under RCW **10.77.068**(3) or confirmed by records maintained by the department.

(2) Appointment of a qualified expert or professional person under this section must be from a list of qualified experts or professional persons assembled with participation by representatives of the prosecuting attorney and the defense bar of the county. The qualified expert or professional person shall complete an evaluation and report that includes the components specified in RCW **10.77.060**(3).

(3) The county shall provide a copy of the evaluation report to the applicable state hospital upon referral of the defendant for admission to the state hospital. The county shall:

(a) In consultation with the department, develop and maintain critical data elements, including data on the timeliness of competency evaluations completed under this section; and

(b) Share this data with the department upon the department's request.

(4) A qualified expert or professional person appointed by a court under this section must be compensated for competency evaluations in an amount that will encourage in-depth evaluation reports. Subject to the availability of amounts appropriated for this specific purpose, the department shall reimburse the county in an amount determined by the department to be fair and reasonable with the county paying any excess costs. The amount of reimbursement established by the department must at least meet the equivalent amount for evaluations conducted by the department.

(5) Nothing in this section precludes either party from objecting to the appointment of an evaluator on the basis that an inpatient evaluation is appropriate under RCW **10.77.060**(1)(d).

(6) This section expires June 30, 2019.

[**2015 1st sp.s. c 7 § 7; 2013 c 284 § 1.**]

NOTES:

Effective dates—2015 1st sp.s. c 7: "(1) Section 7 of this act is necessary for the immediate preservation of the public peace, health, or safety, or support of the state government and its existing public institutions, and takes effect immediately [June 10, 2015].

(2) Sections 1 through 6 and 8 through 15 of this act are necessary for the immediate preservation of the public peace, health, or safety, or support of the state government and its existing public institutions, and take effect July 1, 2015.

(3) Section 16 of this act takes effect April 1, 2016." [**2015 1st sp.s. c 7 § 19.**]

Finding—2015 1st sp.s. c 7: See note following RCW **10.77.075**.

Data gathering and report—2013 c 284: "Within current resources, the office of the state human resources director shall gather market salary data related to psychologists and psychiatrists employed by the department of social and health services and department of corrections and report to the governor and relevant committees of the legislature by June 30, 2013." [**2013 c 284 § 2.**]

Effective date—2013 c 284: "Section 2 of this act is necessary for the immediate preservation of the public peace, health, or safety, or support of the state government and its existing public institutions, and takes effect immediately [May 16, 2013]." [**2013 c 284 § 3.**]

10.77.075

Competency evaluation or competency restoration treatment—Court order.

Within twenty-four hours of the signing of a court order requesting the secretary to provide a competency evaluation or competency restoration treatment:

(1) The clerk of the court shall provide the court order and the charging documents, including the request for bail and certification of probable cause, to the state hospital. If the order is for competency restoration treatment and the competency evaluation was provided by a qualified expert or professional person who was not designated by the secretary, the clerk shall also provide the state hospital with a copy of all previous court orders related to competency or criminal insanity and a copy of any of the evaluation reports;

(2) The prosecuting attorney shall provide the discovery packet, including a statement of the defendant's criminal history, to the state hospital; and

(3) If the court order requires transportation of the defendant to a state hospital, the jail administrator shall provide the defendant's medical clearance information to the state hospital admission staff.

[**2015 1st sp.s. c 7 § 2.**]

NOTES:

Finding—2015 1st sp.s. c 7: "(1) The legislature finds that there are currently no alternatives to competency restoration provided in the state hospitals. Subject to the availability of amounts appropriated for this specific purpose, the legislature encourages the department of social and health services to develop, on a phased-in basis, alternative locations and increased access to competency restoration services under chapter **10.77** RCW for individuals who do not require inpatient psychiatric hospitalization level services.

(2) The department of social and health services shall work with counties and the court to develop a screening process to determine which individuals are safe to receive competency restoration treatment outside the state hospitals." [**2015 1st sp.s. c 7 § 1.**]

Effective dates—2015 1st sp.s. c 7: See note following RCW **10.77.073**.

10.77.078

Competency evaluation or restoration services—Offer of admission—City or county jail to transport defendant.

(1) A city or county jail shall transport a defendant to a state hospital or other secure facility designated by the department within one day of receipt of an offer of admission of the defendant for competency evaluation or restoration services.

(2) City and county jails must cooperate with competency evaluators and the department to arrange for competency evaluators to have reasonable, timely, and appropriate access to defendants for the purpose of performing evaluations under this chapter to accommodate the seven-day performance target for completing competency evaluations for defendants in custody.

[**2015 1st sp.s. c 7 § 3.**]

NOTES:

    Finding—2015 1st sp.s. c 7: See note following RCW **10.77.075**.

    Effective dates—2015 1st sp.s. c 7: See note following RCW **10.77.073**.

10.77.079

Competency to stand trial—Continuation of competency process, dismissal of charges—Exceptions.

(1) If the issue of competency to stand trial is raised by the court or a party under RCW **10.77.060**, the prosecutor may continue with the competency process or dismiss the charges without prejudice and refer the defendant for assessment by a mental health professional, chemical dependency professional, or developmental disabilities professional to determine the appropriate service needs for the defendant.

(2) This section does not apply to defendants with a current charge or prior conviction for a violent offense or sex offense as defined in RCW **9.94A.030**, or a violation of RCW **9A.36.031**(1) (d), (f), or (h).

[**2015 1st sp.s. c 7 § 9.**]

NOTES:

> **Finding**—2015 1st sp.s. c 7: See note following RCW **10.77.075**.
>
> **Effective dates**—2015 1st sp.s. c 7: See note following RCW **10.77.073**.

10.77.080

Motion for acquittal on grounds of insanity—Hearing—Findings.

The defendant may move the court for a judgment of acquittal on the grounds of insanity: PROVIDED, That a defendant so acquitted may not later contest the validity of his or her detention on the grounds that he or she did not commit the acts charged. At the hearing upon the motion the defendant shall have the burden of proving by a preponderance of the evidence that he or she was insane at the time of the offense or offenses with which he or she is charged. If the court finds that the defendant should be acquitted by reason of insanity, it shall enter specific findings in substantially the same form as set forth in RCW **10.77.040**. If the motion is denied, the question may be submitted to the trier of fact in the same manner as other issues of fact.

[**1998 c 297 § 37; 1974 ex.s. c 198 § 7; 1973 1st ex.s. c 117 § 8.**]

NOTES:

> **Effective dates**—**Severability**—**Intent**—1998 c 297: See notes following RCW **71.05.010**.

10.77.084

Stay of proceedings—Treatment—Restoration of competency—Commitment—Other procedures. (Effective until April 1, 2018).

(1)(a) If at any time during the pendency of an action and prior to judgment the court finds, following a report as provided in RCW **10.77.060**, a defendant is incompetent, the court shall order the proceedings against the defendant be stayed except as provided in subsection (4) of this section.

(b) The court may order a defendant who has been found to be incompetent to undergo competency restoration treatment at a facility designated by the department if the defendant is eligible under RCW **10.77.086** or **10.77.088**. At the end of each competency restoration period or at any time a professional person determines competency has been, or is unlikely to be, restored, the defendant shall be returned to court for a hearing, except that if the opinion of the professional person is that the defendant remains incompetent and the hearing is held before the expiration of the current competency restoration period, the parties may agree to waive the defendant's presence, to remote participation by the defendant at a hearing, or to presentation of an agreed order in lieu of a hearing. The facility shall promptly notify the court and all parties of the date on which the competency restoration period commences and expires so that a timely hearing date may be scheduled.

(c) If, following notice and hearing or entry of an agreed order under (b) of this subsection, the court finds that competency has been restored, the court shall lift the stay entered under (a) of this subsection. If the court finds that competency has not been restored, the court shall dismiss the proceedings without prejudice, except that the court may order a further period of competency restoration treatment if it finds that further treatment within the time limits established by RCW **10.77.086** or **10.77.088** is likely to restore competency, and a further period of treatment is allowed under RCW **10.77.086** or **10.77.088**.

(d) If at any time during the proceeding the court finds, following notice and hearing, a defendant is not likely to regain competency, the court shall dismiss the proceedings without prejudice and refer the defendant for civil commitment evaluation or proceedings if appropriate under RCW **10.77.065**, **10.77.086**, or **10.77.088**.

(2) If the defendant is referred for evaluation by a designated mental health professional under this chapter, the designated mental health professional shall provide prompt written notification of the results of the evaluation and whether the person was detained. The notification shall be provided to the court in which the criminal action was

pending, the prosecutor, the defense attorney in the criminal action, and the facility that evaluated the defendant for competency.

(3) The fact that the defendant is unfit to proceed does not preclude any pretrial proceedings which do not require the personal participation of the defendant.

(4) A defendant receiving medication for either physical or mental problems shall not be prohibited from standing trial, if the medication either enables the defendant to understand the proceedings against him or her and to assist in his or her own defense, or does not disable him or her from so understanding and assisting in his or her own defense.

(5) At or before the conclusion of any commitment period provided for by this section, the facility providing evaluation and treatment shall provide to the court a written report of evaluation which meets the requirements of RCW **10.77.060**(3). For defendants charged with a felony, the report following the second competency restoration period or first competency restoration period if the defendant's incompetence is determined to be solely due to a developmental disability or the evaluator concludes that the defendant is not likely to regain competency must include an assessment of the defendant's future dangerousness which is evidence-based regarding predictive validity.

[**2015 1st sp.s. c 7 § 4; 2012 c 256 § 5; 2007 c 375 § 3.**]

NOTES:

Finding—2015 1st sp.s. c 7: See note following RCW **10.77.075**.

Effective dates—2015 1st sp.s. c 7: See note following RCW **10.77.073**.

Purpose—Effective date—2012 c 256: See notes following RCW **10.77.068**.

Findings—Purpose—Construction—Severability—2007 c 375: See notes following RCW **10.31.110**.

Captions not law—2007 c 375: "Captions used in this act are not any part of the law." [**2007 c 375 § 19.**]

10.77.084

Stay of proceedings—Treatment—Restoration of competency—Commitment—Other procedures. (Effective April 1, 2018.)

(1)(a) If at any time during the pendency of an action and prior to judgment the court finds, following a report as provided in RCW **10.77.060**, a defendant is incompetent, the court shall order the proceedings against the defendant be stayed except as provided in subsection (4) of this section.

(b) The court may order a defendant who has been found to be incompetent to undergo competency restoration treatment at a facility designated by the department if the defendant is eligible under RCW **10.77.086** or **10.77.088**. At the end of each competency restoration period or at any time a professional person determines competency has been, or is unlikely to be, restored, the defendant shall be returned to court for a hearing, except that if the opinion of the professional person is that the defendant remains incompetent and the hearing is held before the expiration of the current competency restoration period, the parties may agree to waive the defendant's presence, to remote participation by the defendant at a hearing, or to presentation of an agreed order in lieu of a hearing. The facility shall promptly notify the court and all parties of the date on which the competency restoration period commences and expires so that a timely hearing date may be scheduled.

(c) If, following notice and hearing or entry of an agreed order under (b) of this subsection, the court finds that competency has been restored, the court shall lift the stay entered under (a) of this subsection. If the court finds that competency has not been restored, the court shall dismiss the proceedings without prejudice, except that the court may order a further period of competency restoration treatment if it finds that further treatment within the time limits established by RCW **10.77.086** or **10.77.088** is likely to restore competency, and a further period of treatment is allowed under RCW **10.77.086** or **10.77.088**.

(d) If at any time during the proceeding the court finds, following notice and hearing, a defendant is not likely to regain competency, the court shall dismiss the proceedings without prejudice and refer the defendant for civil commitment evaluation or proceedings if appropriate under RCW **10.77.065**, **10.77.086**, or **10.77.088**.

(2) If the defendant is referred for evaluation by a designated crisis responder under this chapter, the designated crisis responder shall provide prompt written notification of

the results of the evaluation and whether the person was detained. The notification shall be provided to the court in which the criminal action was pending, the prosecutor, the defense attorney in the criminal action, and the facility that evaluated the defendant for competency.

(3) The fact that the defendant is unfit to proceed does not preclude any pretrial proceedings which do not require the personal participation of the defendant.

(4) A defendant receiving medication for either physical or mental problems shall not be prohibited from standing trial, if the medication either enables the defendant to understand the proceedings against him or her and to assist in his or her own defense, or does not disable him or her from so understanding and assisting in his or her own defense.

(5) At or before the conclusion of any commitment period provided for by this section, the facility providing evaluation and treatment shall provide to the court a written report of evaluation which meets the requirements of RCW **10.77.060**(3). For defendants charged with a felony, the report following the second competency restoration period or first competency restoration period if the defendant's incompetence is determined to be solely due to a developmental disability or the evaluator concludes that the defendant is not likely to regain competency must include an assessment of the defendant's future dangerousness which is evidence-based regarding predictive validity.
[**2016 sp.s. c 29 § 410; 2015 1st sp.s. c 7 § 4; 2012 c 256 § 5; 2007 c 375 § 3.**]
NOTES:

     Effective dates—2016 sp.s. c 29: See note following RCW **71.05.760**.

     Short title—Right of action—2016 sp.s. c 29: See notes following RCW **71.05.010**.

     Finding—2015 1st sp.s. c 7: See note following RCW **10.77.075**.

     Effective dates—2015 1st sp.s. c 7: See note following RCW **10.77.073**.

     Purpose—Effective date—2012 c 256: See notes following RCW **10.77.068**.

     Findings—Purpose—Construction—Severability—2007 c 375: See notes following RCW **10.31.110**.

10.77.0845
Evaluation and determination of individual with developmental disability—Program placement—Admissions, limitation.

(1) A defendant found incompetent by the court under RCW **10.77.084** must be evaluated at the direction of the secretary and a determination made whether the defendant is an individual with a developmental disability. Such evaluation and determination must be accomplished as soon as possible following the court's placement of the defendant in the custody of the secretary.

(2) When appropriate, and subject to available funds, if the defendant is determined to be an individual with a developmental disability, he or she may be placed in a program specifically reserved for the treatment and training of persons with developmental disabilities where the defendant has the right to habilitation according to an individualized service plan specifically developed for the particular needs of the defendant. A copy of the evaluation must be sent to the program.

(a) The program must be separate from programs serving persons involved in any other treatment or habilitation program.

(b) The program must be appropriately secure under the circumstances and must be administered by developmental disabilities professionals who shall direct the habilitation efforts.

(c) The program must provide an environment affording security appropriate with the charged criminal behavior and necessary to protect the public safety.

(3) The department may limit admissions of such persons to this specialized program in order to ensure that expenditures for services do not exceed amounts appropriated by the legislature and allocated by the department for such services.

(4) The department may establish admission priorities in the event that the number of eligible persons exceeds the limits set by the department.

[**2012 c 256 § 7.**]

NOTES:

Purpose—Effective date—2012 c 256: See notes following RCW **10.77.068**.

10.77.086

Commitment—Procedure in felony charge.

(1)(a)(i) If the defendant is charged with a felony and determined to be incompetent, until he or she has regained the competency necessary to understand the proceedings against him or her and assist in his or her own defense, but in any event for a period of no longer than ninety days, the court:

(A) Shall commit the defendant to the custody of the secretary who shall place such defendant in an appropriate facility of the department for evaluation and treatment; or

(B) May alternatively order the defendant to undergo evaluation and treatment at some other facility or provider as determined by the department, or under the guidance and control of a professional person. The facilities or providers may include community mental health providers or other local facilities that contract with the department and are willing and able to provide treatment under this section. During the 2015-2017 fiscal biennium, the department may contract with one or more cities or counties to provide competency restoration services in a city or county jail if the city or county jail is willing and able to serve as a location for competency restoration services and if the secretary determines that there is an emergent need for beds and documents the justification, including a plan to address the emergency. Patients receiving competency restoration services in a city or county jail must be physically separated from other populations at the jail and restoration treatment services must be provided as much as possible within a therapeutic environment.

(ii) The ninety day period for evaluation and treatment under this subsection (1) includes only the time the defendant is actually at the facility and is in addition to reasonable time for transport to or from the facility.

(b) For a defendant whose highest charge is a class C felony, or a class B felony that is not classified as violent under RCW **9.94A.030**, the maximum time allowed for the initial period of commitment for competency restoration is forty-five days. The forty-five day period includes only the time the defendant is actually at the facility and is in addition to reasonable time for transport to or from the facility.

(c) If the court determines or the parties agree that the defendant is unlikely to regain competency, the court may dismiss the charges without prejudice without ordering the defendant to undergo restoration treatment, in which case the court shall order that the defendant be referred for evaluation for civil commitment in the manner provided in subsection (4) of this section.

(2) On or before expiration of the initial period of commitment under subsection (1) of this section the court shall conduct a hearing, at which it shall determine whether or not the defendant is incompetent.

(3) If the court finds by a preponderance of the evidence that a defendant charged with a felony is incompetent, the court shall have the option of extending the order of commitment or alternative treatment for an additional period of ninety days, but the court must at the time of extension set a date for a prompt hearing to determine the defendant's competency before the expiration of the second restoration period. The defendant, the defendant's attorney, or the prosecutor has the right to demand that the hearing be before a jury. No extension shall be ordered for a second or third restoration period as provided in subsection (4) of this section if the defendant's incompetence has been determined by the secretary to be solely the result of a developmental disability which is such that competence is not reasonably likely to be regained during an extension. The ninety-day period includes only the time the defendant is actually at the facility and is in addition to reasonable time for transport to or from the facility.

(4) For persons charged with a felony, at the hearing upon the expiration of the second restoration period or at the end of the first restoration period in the case of a defendant with a developmental disability, if the jury or court finds that the defendant is incompetent, or if the court or jury at any stage finds that the defendant is incompetent and the court determines that the defendant is unlikely to regain competency, the charges shall be dismissed without prejudice, and the court shall order the defendant be committed to a state hospital as defined in RCW **72.23.010** for up to seventy-two hours starting from admission to the facility, excluding Saturdays, Sundays, and holidays, for

evaluation for the purpose of filing a civil commitment petition under chapter **71.05** RCW. The criminal charges shall not be dismissed if the court or jury finds that: (a) The defendant (i) is a substantial danger to other persons; or (ii) presents a substantial likelihood of committing criminal acts jeopardizing public safety or security; and (b) there is a substantial probability that the defendant will regain competency within a reasonable period of time. In the event that the court or jury makes such a finding, the court may extend the period of commitment for up to an additional six months. The six-month period includes only the time the defendant is actually at the facility and is in addition to reasonable time for transport to or from the facility.

[**2015 1st sp.s. c 7 § 5; 2013 c 289 § 2; 2012 c 256 § 6; 2007 c 375 § 4.**]

NOTES:

Finding—2015 1st sp.s. c 7: See note following RCW **10.77.075**.

Effective dates—2015 1st sp.s. c 7: See note following RCW **10.77.073**.

Findings—2013 c 289: "The legislature finds that persons with a mental illness or developmental disability are more likely to be victimized by crime than to be perpetrators of crime. The legislature further finds that there are a small number of individuals who commit repeated violent acts against others while suffering from the effects of a mental illness and/or developmental disability that both contributes to their criminal behaviors and renders them legally incompetent to be held accountable for those behaviors. The legislature further finds that the primary statutory mechanisms designed to protect the public from violent behavior, either criminal commitment to a corrections institution, or long-term commitment as not guilty by reason of insanity, are unavailable due to the legal incompetence of these individuals to stand trial. The legislature further finds that the existing civil system of short-term commitments under the Washington's involuntary treatment act is insufficient to protect the public from these violent acts. Finally, the legislature finds that changes to the involuntary treatment act to account for this small number of individuals is necessary in order to serve Washington's compelling interest in public safety and to provide for the proper care of these individuals." [**2013 c 289 § 1.**]

Purpose—Effective date—2012 c 256: See notes following RCW **10.77.068**.

10.77.088
Placement—Procedure in nonfelony charge. (Effective until April 1, 2018.)

(1)(a) If the defendant is charged with a nonfelony crime which is a serious offense as identified in RCW **10.77.092** and found by the court to be not competent, then the court:

(i) Shall commit the defendant to the custody of the secretary who shall place such defendant in an appropriate facility of the department for evaluation and treatment;

(ii) May alternatively order the defendant to undergo evaluation and treatment at some other facility or provider as determined by the department, or under the guidance and control of a professional person. The facilities or providers may include community mental health providers or other local facilities that contract with the department and are willing and able to provide treatment under this section. During the 2015-2017 fiscal biennium, the department may contract with one or more cities or counties to provide competency restoration services in a city or county jail if the city or county jail is willing and able to serve as a location for competency restoration services and if the secretary determines that there is an emergent need for beds and documents the justification, including a plan to address the emergency. Patients receiving competency restoration services in a city or county jail must be physically separated from other populations at the jail and restoration treatment services must be provided as much as possible within a therapeutic environment. The placement under (a)(i) and (ii) of this subsection shall not exceed fourteen days in addition to any unused time of the evaluation under RCW **10.77.060**. The court shall compute this total period and include its computation in the order. The fourteen-day period plus any unused time of the evaluation under RCW **10.77.060**shall be considered to include only the time the defendant is actually at the facility and shall be in addition to reasonable time for transport to or from the facility;

(iii) May alternatively order that the defendant be placed on conditional release for up to ninety days for mental health treatment and restoration of competency; or

(iv) May order any combination of this subsection.

(b) If the court has determined or the parties agree that the defendant is unlikely to regain competency, the court may dismiss the charges without prejudice without ordering the defendant to undergo restoration treatment, in which case the court shall order that the defendant be referred for evaluation for civil commitment in the manner provided in (c) of this subsection.

(c)(i) If the proceedings are dismissed under RCW **10.77.084** and the defendant was on conditional release at the time of dismissal, the court shall order the designated mental health professional within that county to evaluate the defendant pursuant to chapter **71.05** RCW. The evaluation may be conducted in any location chosen by the professional.

(ii) If the defendant was in custody and not on conditional release at the time of dismissal, the defendant shall be detained and sent to an evaluation and treatment facility for up to seventy-two hours, excluding Saturdays, Sundays, and holidays, for evaluation for purposes of filing a petition under chapter **71.05** RCW. The seventy-two hour period shall commence upon the next nonholiday weekday following the court order and shall run to the end of the last nonholiday weekday within the seventy-two-hour period.

(2) If the defendant is charged with a nonfelony crime that is not a serious offense as defined in RCW **10.77.092**:

The court may stay or dismiss proceedings and detain the defendant for sufficient time to allow the designated mental health professional to evaluate the defendant and consider initial detention proceedings under chapter **71.05** RCW. The court must give notice to all parties at least twenty-four hours before the dismissal of any proceeding under this subsection, and provide an opportunity for a hearing on whether to dismiss the proceedings.

[**2015 1st sp.s. c 7 § 6; 2007 c 375 § 5.**]

NOTES:

Finding—2015 1st sp.s. c 7: See note following RCW **10.77.075**.

Effective dates—2015 1st sp.s. c 7: See note following RCW **10.77.073**.

Findings—Purpose—Construction—Severability—2007 c 375: See notes following RCW **10.31.110**.

Captions not law—2007 c 375: See note following RCW **10.77.084**.

10.77.088

Placement—Procedure in nonfelony charge. (Effective April 1, 2018.)

(1)(a) If the defendant is charged with a nonfelony crime which is a serious offense as identified in RCW **10.77.092** and found by the court to be not competent, then the court:

(i) Shall commit the defendant to the custody of the secretary who shall place such defendant in an appropriate facility of the department for evaluation and treatment;

(ii) May alternatively order the defendant to undergo evaluation and treatment at some other facility or provider as determined by the department, or under the guidance and control of a professional person. The facilities or providers may include community mental health providers or other local facilities that contract with the department and are willing and able to provide treatment under this section. During the 2015-2017 fiscal biennium, the department may contract with one or more cities or counties to provide competency restoration services in a city or county jail if the city or county jail is willing and able to serve as a location for competency restoration services and if the secretary determines that there is an emergent need for beds and documents the justification, including a plan to address the emergency. Patients receiving competency restoration services in a city or county jail must be physically separated from other populations at the jail and restoration treatment services must be provided as much as possible within a therapeutic environment. The placement under (a)(i) and (ii) of this subsection shall not exceed fourteen days in addition to any unused time of the evaluation under RCW **10.77.060**. The court shall compute this total period and include its computation in the order. The fourteen-day period plus any unused time of the evaluation under RCW **10.77.060**shall be considered to include only the time the defendant is actually at the facility and shall be in addition to reasonable time for transport to or from the facility;

(iii) May alternatively order that the defendant be placed on conditional release for up to ninety days for mental health treatment and restoration of competency; or

(iv) May order any combination of this subsection.

(b) If the court has determined or the parties agree that the defendant is unlikely to regain competency, the court may dismiss the charges without prejudice without ordering the defendant to undergo restoration treatment, in which case the court shall order that the defendant be referred for evaluation for civil commitment in the manner provided in (c) of this subsection.

(c)(i) If the proceedings are dismissed under RCW **10.77.084** and the defendant was on conditional release at the time of dismissal, the court shall order the designated crisis responder within that county to evaluate the defendant pursuant to chapter **71.05** RCW. The evaluation may be conducted in any location chosen by the professional.

(ii) If the defendant was in custody and not on conditional release at the time of dismissal, the defendant shall be detained and sent to an evaluation and treatment facility for up to seventy-two hours, excluding Saturdays, Sundays, and holidays, for evaluation for purposes of filing a petition under chapter **71.05** RCW. The seventy-two hour period shall commence upon the next nonholiday weekday following the court order and shall run to the end of the last nonholiday weekday within the seventy-two-hour period.

(2) If the defendant is charged with a nonfelony crime that is not a serious offense as defined in RCW **10.77.092**:

The court may stay or dismiss proceedings and detain the defendant for sufficient time to allow the designated crisis responder to evaluate the defendant and consider initial detention proceedings under chapter **71.05** RCW. The court must give notice to all parties at least twenty-four hours before the dismissal of any proceeding under this subsection, and provide an opportunity for a hearing on whether to dismiss the proceedings.

[**2016 sp.s. c 29 § 411; 2015 1st sp.s. c 7 § 6; 2007 c 375 § 5.**]

NOTES:

    Effective dates—2016 sp.s. c 29: See note following RCW **71.05.760**.

Short title—Right of action—2016 sp.s. c 29: See notes following RCW **71.05.010**.

Finding—2015 1st sp.s. c 7: See note following RCW **10.77.075**.

Effective dates—2015 1st sp.s. c 7: See note following RCW **10.77.073**.

Findings—Purpose—Construction—Severability—2007 c 375: See notes following RCW **10.31.110**.

Captions not law—2007 c 375: See note following RCW **10.77.084**.

10.77.091

Placement—Secure facility—Treatment and rights—Custody—Reports.

(1) If the secretary determines in writing that a person committed to the custody of the secretary for treatment as criminally insane presents an unreasonable safety risk which, based on behavior, clinical history, and facility security is not manageable in a state hospital setting, and the secretary has given consideration to reasonable alternatives that would be effective to manage the behavior, the secretary may place the person in any secure facility operated by the secretary or the secretary of the department of corrections. The secretary's written decision and reasoning must be documented in the patient's medical file. Any person affected by this provision shall receive appropriate mental health treatment governed by a formalized treatment plan targeted at mental health rehabilitation needs and shall be afforded his or her rights under RCW **10.77.140**, **10.77.150**, and **10.77.200**. The secretary of the department of social and health services shall retain legal custody of any person placed under this section and review any placement outside of a department mental health hospital every three months, or sooner if warranted by the person's mental health status, to determine if the placement remains appropriate.

(2) Beginning December 1, 2010, and every six months thereafter, the secretary shall report to the governor and the appropriate committees of the legislature regarding the use of the authority under this section to transfer persons to a secure facility. The report shall include information related to the number of persons who have been placed

in a secure facility operated by the secretary or the secretary of the department of corrections, and the length of time that each such person has been in the secure facility. [**2015 c 253 § 1; 2010 c 263 § 2.**]

NOTES:

    Effective date—2015 1st sp.s. c 7: "Section 1, chapter 253, Laws of 2015 is necessary for the immediate preservation of the public peace, health, or safety, or support of the state government and its existing public institutions, and takes effect June 30, 2015." [**2015 1st sp.s. c 7 § 20.**]

10.77.092
Involuntary medication—Serious offenses.

    (1) For purposes of determining whether a court may authorize involuntary medication for the purpose of competency restoration pursuant to RCW **10.77.084** and for maintaining the level of restoration in the jail following the restoration period, a pending charge involving any one or more of the following crimes is a serious offense per se in the context of competency restoration:

    (a) Any violent offense, sex offense, serious traffic offense, and most serious offense, as those terms are defined in RCW **9.94A.030**;

    (b) Any offense, except nonfelony counterfeiting offenses, included in crimes against persons in RCW **9.94A.411**;

    (c) Any offense contained in chapter **9.41** RCW (firearms and dangerous weapons);

    (d) Any offense listed as domestic violence in RCW **10.99.020**;

    (e) Any offense listed as a harassment offense in chapter **9A.46** RCW;

    (f) Any violation of chapter **69.50** RCW that is a class B felony; or

    (g) Any city or county ordinance or statute that is equivalent to an offense referenced in this subsection.

    (2)(a) In a particular case, a court may determine that a pending charge not otherwise defined as serious by state or federal law or by a city or county ordinance is, nevertheless, a serious offense within the context of competency restoration treatment when the conduct in the charged offense falls within the standards established in (b) of this subsection.

(b) To determine that the particular case is a serious offense within the context of competency restoration, the court must consider the following factors and determine that one or more of the following factors creates a situation in which the offense is serious:

(i) The charge includes an allegation that the defendant actually inflicted bodily or emotional harm on another person or that the defendant created a reasonable apprehension of bodily or emotional harm to another;

(ii) The extent of the impact of the alleged offense on the basic human need for security of the citizens within the jurisdiction;

(iii) The number and nature of related charges pending against the defendant;

(iv) The length of potential confinement if the defendant is convicted; and

(v) The number of potential and actual victims or persons impacted by the defendant's alleged acts.

[**2014 c 10 § 2; 2008 c 213 § 2; 2004 c 157 § 3.**]

NOTES:

Finding—2014 c 10: "The legislature finds that there is currently no clear language authorizing courts to order involuntary medications in order to maintain the level of competency restoration in the jail following a competency restoration period and subsequent discharge from a state hospital. This act specifies that maintenance of competency in jail is a purpose for which the court may order a criminal defendant facing serious charges to be involuntarily medicated." [**2014 c 10 § 1.**]

Findings—Intent—Severability—Effective date—2004 c 157: See notes following RCW **10.77.010**.

10.77.093

Involuntary medication—Civil commitment.

When the court must make a determination whether to order involuntary medications for the purpose of competency restoration or for maintenance of competency, the court shall inquire, and shall be told, and to the extent that the prosecutor or defense attorney is aware, whether the defendant is the subject of a pending civil commitment proceeding or has been ordered into involuntary treatment pursuant to a civil commitment proceeding.

[**2004 c 157 § 4.**]

NOTES:

   Findings—Intent—Severability—Effective date—2004 c 157: See notes following RCW **10.77.010**.

10.77.094
Antipsychotic medication, administration.

(1) A state hospital may administer antipsychotic medication without consent to an individual who is committed under this chapter as criminally insane by following the same procedures applicable to the administration of antipsychotic medication without consent to a civilly committed patient under RCW **71.05.217**, except for the following:

(a) The maximum period during which the court may authorize the administration of medication without consent under a single involuntary medication petition shall be the time remaining on the individual's current order of commitment or one hundred eighty days, whichever is shorter; and

(b) A petition for involuntary medication may be filed in either the superior court of the county that ordered the commitment or the superior court of the county in which the individual is receiving treatment, provided that a copy of any order that is entered must be provided to the superior court of the county that ordered the commitment following the hearing. The superior court of the county of commitment shall retain exclusive jurisdiction over all hearings concerning the release of the patient.

(2) The state has a compelling interest in providing antipsychotic medication to a patient who has been committed as criminally insane when refusal of antipsychotic medication would result in a likelihood of serious harm or substantial deterioration or substantially prolong the length of involuntary commitment and there is no less intrusive course of treatment than medication that is in the best interest of the patient.

[**2012 c 256 § 12.**]

NOTES:

> **Purpose—Effective date—2012 c 256:** See notes following RCW **10.77.068**.

10.77.095
Findings—Developmental disabilities.

The legislature finds that among those persons who endanger the safety of others by committing crimes are a small number of persons with developmental disabilities. While their conduct is not typical of the vast majority of persons with developmental disabilities who are responsible citizens, for their own welfare and for the safety of others the state may need to exercise control over those few dangerous individuals who are developmentally disabled, have been charged with crimes that involve a threat to public safety or security, and have been found either incompetent to stand trial or not guilty by reason of insanity. The legislature finds, however, that the use of civil commitment procedures under chapter **71.05** RCW to effect state control over dangerous developmentally disabled persons has resulted in their commitment to institutions for the mentally ill. The legislature finds that existing programs in mental institutions may be inappropriate for persons who are developmentally disabled because the services provided in mental institutions are oriented to persons with mental illness, a condition not necessarily associated with developmental disabilities. Therefore, the legislature believes that, where appropriate, and subject to available funds, persons with developmental disabilities who have been charged with crimes that involve a threat to public safety or security and have been found incompetent to stand trial or not guilty by reason of insanity should receive state services addressing their needs, that such services must be provided in conformance with an individual habilitation plan, and that their initial treatment should be separate and discrete from treatment for persons involved in any other treatment or habilitation program in a manner consistent with the needs of public safety.

[**1998 c 297 § 28; 1989 c 420 § 1.** Formerly RCW **10.77.005**.]

NOTES:

10.77.097
Records and reports accompany defendant upon transfer.

A copy of relevant records and reports as defined by the department, in consultation with the department of corrections, made pursuant to this chapter, and including relevant information necessary to meet the requirements of RCW **10.77.065**(1) and **10.77.084**, shall accompany the defendant upon transfer to a mental health facility or a correctional institution or facility.

[**2008 c 213 § 3; 2000 c 74 § 4; 1998 c 297 § 47.**]

NOTES:

Severability—2000 c 74: See note following RCW **10.77.060**.

Effective dates—Severability—Intent—1998 c 297: See notes following RCW **71.05.010**.

10.77.100
Experts or professional persons as witnesses.

Subject to the rules of evidence, experts or professional persons who have reported pursuant to this chapter may be called as witnesses at any proceeding held pursuant to this chapter. Both the prosecution and the defendant may summon any other qualified expert or professional persons to testify.

[**1974 ex.s. c 198 § 9; 1973 1st ex.s. c 117 § 10.**]

10.77.110
Acquittal of crime.

(1) If a defendant is acquitted of a crime by reason of insanity, and it is found that he or she is not a substantial danger to other persons, and does not present a substantial likelihood of committing criminal acts jeopardizing public safety or security, unless kept

under further control by the court or other persons or institutions, the court shall direct the defendant's release. If it is found that such defendant is a substantial danger to other persons, or presents a substantial likelihood of committing criminal acts jeopardizing public safety or security, unless kept under further control by the court or other persons or institutions, the court shall order his or her hospitalization, or any appropriate alternative treatment less restrictive than detention in a state mental hospital, pursuant to the terms of this chapter.

(2) If the defendant has been found not guilty by reason of insanity and a substantial danger, or presents a substantial likelihood of committing criminal acts jeopardizing public safety or security, so as to require treatment then the secretary shall immediately cause the defendant to be evaluated to ascertain if the defendant is developmentally disabled. When appropriate, and subject to available funds, the defendant may be committed to a program specifically reserved for the treatment and training of developmentally disabled persons. A person so committed shall receive habilitation services according to an individualized service plan specifically developed to treat the behavior which was the subject of the criminal proceedings. The treatment program shall be administered by developmental disabilities professionals and others trained specifically in the needs of developmentally disabled persons. The treatment program shall provide physical security to a degree consistent with the finding that the defendant is dangerous and may incorporate varying conditions of security and alternative sites when the dangerousness of any particular defendant makes this necessary. The department may limit admissions to this specialized program in order to ensure that expenditures for services do not exceed amounts appropriated by the legislature and allocated by the department for such services. The department may establish admission priorities in the event that the number of eligible persons exceeds the limits set by the department.

(3) If it is found that such defendant is not a substantial danger to other persons, and does not present a substantial likelihood of committing criminal acts jeopardizing public safety or security, but that he or she is in need of control by the court or other persons or institutions, the court shall direct the defendant's conditional release.

[2000 c 94 § 14; 1998 c 297 § 39; 1989 c 420 § 6; 1983 c 25 § 1; 1979 ex.s. c 215 § 4; 1974 ex.s. c 198 § 10; 1973 1st ex.s. c 117 § 11.]

NOTES:

Effective dates—Severability—Intent—1998 c 297: See notes following RCW 71.05.010.

10.77.120

Care and treatment of committed person—Hearings—Release.

(1) The secretary shall provide adequate care and individualized treatment to persons found criminally insane at one or several of the state institutions or facilities under the direction and control of the secretary. In order that the secretary may adequately determine the nature of the mental illness or developmental disability of the person committed as criminally insane, all persons who are committed to the secretary as criminally insane shall be promptly examined by qualified personnel in order to provide a proper evaluation and diagnosis of such individual. The examinations of all persons with developmental disabilities committed under this chapter shall be performed by developmental disabilities professionals. Any person so committed shall not be released from the control of the secretary except by order of a court of competent jurisdiction made after a hearing and judgment of release.

(2) Whenever there is a hearing which the committed person is entitled to attend, the secretary shall send the person in the custody of one or more department employees to the county in which the hearing is to be held at the time the case is called for trial. During the time the person is absent from the facility, the person may be confined in a facility designated by and arranged for by the department, but shall at all times be deemed to be in the custody of the department employee and provided necessary treatment. If the decision of the hearing remits the person to custody, the department employee shall return the person to such institution or facility designated by the secretary. If the state appeals an order of release, such appeal shall operate as a stay, and the person shall remain in custody and be returned to the institution or facility designated by the secretary until a final decision has been rendered in the cause.

[**2010 c 263 § 4; 2000 c 94 § 15; 1989 c 420 § 7; 1974 ex.s. c 198 § 11; 1973 1st ex.s. c 117 § 12.**]

10.77.140
Periodic examinations—Developmentally disabled—Reports—Notice to court.

Each person committed to a hospital or other facility or conditionally released pursuant to this chapter shall have a current examination of his or her mental condition made by one or more experts or professional persons at least once every six months. The person may retain, or if the person is indigent and so requests, the court may appoint a qualified expert or professional person to examine him or her, and such expert or professional person shall have access to all hospital records concerning the person. In the case of a committed or conditionally released person who is developmentally disabled, the expert shall be a developmental disabilities professional. The secretary, upon receipt of the periodic report, shall provide written notice to the court of commitment of compliance with the requirements of this section.

[**1998 c 297 § 40; 1989 c 420 § 8; 1974 ex.s. c 198 § 12; 1973 1st ex.s. c 117 § 14.**]

NOTES:

Effective dates—Severability—Intent—1998 c 297: See notes following RCW **71.05.010**.

10.77.145
Authorization to leave facility where person is confined prohibited—Exceptions—Approval by secretary—Notification to county or city law enforcement agency.

(1) No person committed to the custody of the department for the determination of competency to stand trial under RCW **10.77.060**, the restoration of competency for trial under RCW **10.77.084**, **10.77.086**, or **10.77.088**, or following an acquittal by reason of

insanity shall be authorized to leave the facility where the person is confined, except in the following circumstances:

(a) In accordance with conditional release or furlough authorized by a court;

(b) For necessary medical or legal proceedings not available in the facility where the person is confined;

(c) For visits to the bedside of a member of the person's immediate family who is seriously ill; or

(d) For attendance at the funeral of a member of the person's immediate family.

(2) Unless ordered otherwise by a court, no leave under subsection (1) of this section shall be authorized unless the person who is the subject of the authorization is escorted by a person approved by the secretary. During the authorized leave, the person approved by the secretary must be in visual or auditory contact at all times with the person on authorized leave.

(3) Prior to the authorization of any leave under subsection (1) of this section, the secretary must give notification to any county or city law enforcement agency having jurisdiction in the location of the leave destination.

[**2010 c 262 § 1.**]

10.77.150
Conditional release—Application—Secretary's recommendation—Order—Procedure.

(1) Persons examined pursuant to RCW **10.77.140** may make application to the secretary for conditional release. The secretary shall, after considering the reports of experts or professional persons conducting the examination pursuant to RCW **10.77.140**, forward to the court of the county which ordered the person's commitment the person's application for conditional release as well as the secretary's recommendations concerning the application and any proposed terms and conditions upon which the secretary reasonably believes the person can be conditionally released. Conditional release may also contemplate partial release for work, training, or educational purposes.

(2) In instances in which persons examined pursuant to RCW **10.77.140** have not made application to the secretary for conditional release, but the secretary, after considering the reports of experts or professional persons conducting the examination pursuant to RCW **10.77.140**, reasonably believes the person may be conditionally released, the secretary may submit a recommendation for release to the court of the county that ordered the person's commitment. The secretary's recommendation must include any proposed terms and conditions upon which the secretary reasonably believes the person may be conditionally released. Conditional release may also include partial release for work, training, or educational purposes. Notice of the secretary's recommendation under this subsection must be provided to the person for whom the secretary has made the recommendation for release and to his or her attorney.

(3)(a) The court of the county which ordered the person's commitment, upon receipt of an application or recommendation for conditional release with the secretary's recommendation for conditional release terms and conditions, shall within thirty days schedule a hearing. The court may schedule a hearing on applications recommended for disapproval by the secretary.

(b) The prosecuting attorney shall represent the state at such hearings and shall have the right to have the patient examined by an expert or professional person of the prosecuting attorney's choice. If the committed person is indigent, and he or she so requests, the court shall appoint a qualified expert or professional person to examine the person on his or her behalf.

(c) The issue to be determined at such a hearing is whether or not the person may be released conditionally without substantial danger to other persons, or substantial likelihood of committing criminal acts jeopardizing public safety or security.

(d) The court, after the hearing, shall rule on the secretary's recommendations, and if it disapproves of conditional release, may do so only on the basis of substantial evidence. The court may modify the suggested terms and conditions on which the person is to be conditionally released. Pursuant to the determination of the court after hearing, the committed person shall thereupon be released on such conditions as the court determines to be necessary, or shall be remitted to the custody of the secretary. If the order of conditional release includes a requirement for the committed person to report to a community corrections officer, the order shall also specify that the conditionally released person shall be under the supervision of the secretary of corrections or such person as the secretary of corrections may designate and shall follow explicitly the instructions of the secretary of corrections including reporting as directed to a community corrections officer, remaining within prescribed geographical boundaries, and notifying the community corrections officer prior to making any change in the offender's address or employment. If the order of conditional release includes a requirement for the committed person to report to a community corrections officer, the community corrections officer shall notify the secretary or the secretary's designee, if the person is not in compliance with the court-ordered conditions of release.

(4) If the court determines that receiving regular or periodic medication or other medical treatment shall be a condition of the committed person's release, then the court shall require him or her to report to a physician or other medical or mental health practitioner for the medication or treatment. In addition to submitting any report required by RCW **10.77.160**, the physician or other medical or mental health practitioner shall immediately upon the released person's failure to appear for the medication or treatment or upon a change in mental health condition that renders the patient a potential risk to the public report to the court, to the prosecuting attorney of the county in which the released person was committed, to the secretary, and to the supervising community corrections officer.

(5) Any person, whose application for conditional release has been denied, may reapply after a period of six months from the date of denial.

[**2010 c 263 § 5; 1998 c 297 § 41; 1993 c 31 § 6; 1982 c 112 § 1; 1974 ex.s. c 198 § 13; 1973 1st ex.s. c 117 § 15.**]

NOTES:

Effective dates—Severability—Intent—1998 c 297: See notes following RCW **71.05.010**.

10.77.152

Conditional release—Application—County of origin.

(1) In determining whether to support an application for conditional release on behalf of a person committed as criminally insane which would permit the person to reside outside of a state hospital, the secretary may not support a conditional release application to a location outside the person's county of origin unless it is determined by the secretary that the person's return to his or her county of origin would be inappropriate considering any court-issued protection orders, victim safety concerns, the availability of appropriate treatment, negative influences on the person, or the location of family or other persons or organizations offering support to the person. When the department assists in developing a placement under this section which is outside of the county of origin, and there are two or more options for placement, it shall endeavor to develop the placement in a manner that does not have a disproportionate effect on a single county.

(2) If the committed person is not conditionally released to his or her county of origin, the department shall provide the law and justice council of the county in which the person is conditionally released with a written explanation.

(3) For purposes of this section, the offender's county of origin means the county of the court which ordered the person's commitment.

[**2011 c 94 § 1.**]

10.77.155

Conditional release, furlough—Secretary's recommendation.

No court may, without a hearing, enter an order conditionally releasing or authorizing the furlough of a person committed under this chapter, unless the secretary has recommended the release or furlough. If the secretary has not recommended the release or furlough, a hearing shall be held under RCW **10.77.150**.

[**1994 c 150 § 1.**]

10.77.160
Conditional release—Reports.

When a conditionally released person is required by the terms of his or her conditional release to report to a physician, department of corrections community corrections officer, or medical or mental health practitioner on a regular or periodic basis, the physician, department of corrections community corrections officer, medical or mental health practitioner, or other such person shall monthly, for the first six months after release and semiannually thereafter, or as otherwise directed by the court, submit to the court, the secretary, the institution from which released, and to the prosecuting attorney of the county in which the person was committed, a report stating whether the person is adhering to the terms and conditions of his or her conditional release, and detailing any arrests or criminal charges filed and any significant change in the person's mental health condition or other circumstances.

[2010 c 263 § 6; 1993 c 31 § 7; 1973 1st ex.s. c 117 § 16.]

10.77.163
Furlough—Notice—Temporary restraining order.

(1) Before a person committed under this chapter is permitted temporarily to leave a treatment facility for any period of time without constant accompaniment by facility staff, the superintendent, professional person in charge of a treatment facility, or his or her professional designee shall in writing notify the prosecuting attorney of any county to which the person is released and the prosecuting attorney of the county in which the criminal charges against the committed person were dismissed, of the decision conditionally to release the person. The notice shall be provided at least forty-five days before the anticipated release and shall describe the conditions under which the release is to occur.

(2) In addition to the notice required by subsection (1) of this section, the superintendent of each state institution designated for the custody, care, and treatment of persons committed under this chapter shall notify appropriate law enforcement

agencies through the state patrol communications network of the furloughs of persons committed under RCW **10.77.086** or **10.77.110**. Notification shall be made at least thirty days before the furlough, and shall include the name of the person, the place to which the person has permission to go, and the dates and times during which the person will be on furlough.

(3) Upon receiving notice that a person committed under this chapter is being temporarily released under subsection (1) of this section, the prosecuting attorney may seek a temporary restraining order to prevent the release of the person on the grounds that the person is dangerous to self or others.

(4) The notice requirements contained in this section shall not apply to emergency medical furloughs.

(5) The existence of the notice requirements contained in this section shall not require any extension of the release date in the event the release plan changes after notification.

(6) The notice provisions of this section are in addition to those provided in RCW **10.77.205**.

[**2008 c 213 § 4; 1994 c 129 § 4; 1990 c 3 § 106; 1989 c 420 § 9; 1983 c 122 § 2.**]

NOTES:

> **Findings—Intent—1994 c 129:** See note following RCW **4.24.550**.
>
> **Index, part headings not law—Severability—Effective dates—Application—1990 c 3:** See RCW **18.155.900** through **18.155.902**.

10.77.165

Escape or disappearance—Notification requirements.

(1) In the event of an escape by a person committed under this chapter from a state facility or the disappearance of such a person on conditional release or other authorized absence, the superintendent shall provide notification of the person's escape or disappearance for the public's safety or to assist in the apprehension of the person.

(a) The superintendent shall notify:

(i) State and local law enforcement officers located in the city and county where the person escaped and in the city and county which had jurisdiction of the person on the date of the applicable offense;

(ii) Other appropriate governmental agencies; and

(iii) The person's relatives.

(b) The superintendent shall provide the same notification as required by (a) of this subsection to the following, if such notice has been requested in writing about a specific person committed under this chapter:

(i) The victim of the crime for which the person was convicted or the victim's next of kin if the crime was a homicide;

(ii) Any witnesses who testified against the person in any court proceedings if the person was charged with a violent offense; and

(iii) Any other appropriate persons.

(2) Information regarding victims, next of kin, or witnesses requesting the notice, information regarding any other person specified in writing by the prosecuting attorney to receive the notice, and the notice are confidential and shall not be available to the person committed under this chapter.

(3) The notice provisions of this section are in addition to those provided in RCW **10.77.205**.

[**2011 c 305 § 6; 2010 c 28 § 1; 1993 c 31 § 8; 1990 c 3 § 107; 1989 c 420 § 10; 1983 c 122 § 3.**]

NOTES:

Findings—2011 c 305: See note following RCW **74.09.295**.

Index, part headings not law—Severability—Effective dates—Application—1990 c 3: See RCW **18.155.900** through **18.155.902**.

10.77.170
Payments to conditionally released persons.

As funds are available, the secretary may provide payment to a person conditionally released pursuant to RCW **10.77.150**, consistent with the provisions of RCW **72.02.100** and **72.02.110**, and may adopt rules and regulations to do so. [**1973 1st ex.s. c 117 § 17.**]

10.77.180
Conditional release—Periodic review of case.

Each person conditionally released pursuant to RCW **10.77.150** shall have his or her case reviewed by the court which conditionally released him or her no later than one year after such release and no later than every two years thereafter, such time to be scheduled by the court. Review may occur in a shorter time or more frequently, if the court, in its discretion, on its own motion, or on motion of the person, the secretary of social and health services, the secretary of corrections, medical or mental health practitioner, or the prosecuting attorney, so determines. The sole question to be determined by the court is whether the person shall continue to be conditionally released. The court in making its determination shall be aided by the periodic reports filed pursuant to RCW **10.77.140** and **10.77.160**, and the opinions of the secretary and other experts or professional persons.
[**1998 c 297 § 42; 1993 c 31 § 9; 1974 ex.s. c 198 § 14; 1973 1st ex.s. c 117 § 18.**]
NOTES:

Effective dates—Severability—Intent—1998 c 297: See notes following RCW **71.05.010**.

10.77.190
Conditional release—Revocation or modification of terms—Procedure.

(1) Any person submitting reports pursuant to RCW **10.77.160**, the secretary, or the prosecuting attorney may petition the court to, or the court on its own motion may schedule an immediate hearing for the purpose of modifying the terms of conditional release if the petitioner or the court believes the released person is failing to adhere to

the terms and conditions of his or her conditional release or is in need of additional care and treatment.

(2) If the prosecuting attorney, the secretary of social and health services, the secretary of corrections, or the court, after examining the report filed with them pursuant to RCW **10.77.160**, or based on other information received by them, reasonably believes that a conditionally released person is failing to adhere to the terms and conditions of his or her conditional release the court or secretary of social and health services or the secretary of corrections may order that the conditionally released person be apprehended and taken into custody. The court shall be notified of the apprehension before the close of the next judicial day. The court shall schedule a hearing within thirty days to determine whether or not the person's conditional release should be modified or revoked. Both the prosecuting attorney and the conditionally released person shall have the right to request an immediate mental examination of the conditionally released person. If the conditionally released person is indigent, the court or secretary of social and health services or the secretary of corrections or their designees shall, upon request, assist him or her in obtaining a qualified expert or professional person to conduct the examination.

(3) If the hospital or facility designated to provide outpatient care determines that a conditionally released person presents a threat to public safety, the hospital or facility shall immediately notify the secretary of social and health services or the secretary of corrections or their designees. The secretary shall order that the conditionally released person be apprehended and taken into custody.

(4) The court, upon receiving notification of the apprehension, shall promptly schedule a hearing. The issue to be determined is whether the conditionally released person did or did not adhere to the terms and conditions of his or her release, or whether the person presents a threat to public safety. Pursuant to the determination of the court upon such hearing, the conditionally released person shall either continue to be conditionally released on the same or modified conditions or his or her conditional release shall be revoked and he or she shall be committed subject to release only in accordance with provisions of this chapter.

[2010 c 263 § 7; 1998 c 297 § 43; 1993 c 31 § 10; 1982 c 112 § 2; 1974 ex.s. c 198 § 15; 1973 1st ex.s. c 117 § 19.]

NOTES:

Effective dates—Severability—Intent—1998 c 297: See notes following RCW 71.05.010.

10.77.195
Conditional release—Court approval—Compliance—Secretary to coordinate with designated treatment providers, department of corrections staff, and local law enforcement—Rules.

For persons who have received court approval for conditional release, the secretary or the secretary's designee shall supervise the person's compliance with the court-ordered conditions of release. The level of supervision provided by the secretary shall correspond to the level of the person's public safety risk. In undertaking supervision of persons under this section, the secretary shall coordinate with any treatment providers designated pursuant to RCW 10.77.150(3), any department of corrections staff designated pursuant to RCW 10.77.150(2), and local law enforcement, if appropriate. The secretary shall adopt rules to implement this section.

[2010 c 263 § 9.]

10.77.200
Release—Procedure.

(1) Upon application by the committed or conditionally released person, the secretary shall determine whether or not reasonable grounds exist for release. In making this determination, the secretary may consider the reports filed under RCW 10.77.060, 10.77.110, 10.77.140, and 10.77.160, and other reports and evaluations provided by professionals familiar with the case. If the secretary approves the release he or she then shall authorize the person to petition the court.

(2) In instances in which persons have not made application for release, but the secretary believes, after consideration of the reports filed under RCW **10.77.060**, **10.77.110**, **10.77.140**, and **10.77.160**, and other reports and evaluations provided by professionals familiar with the case, that reasonable grounds exist for release, the secretary may petition the court. If the secretary petitions the court for release under this subsection, notice of the petition must be provided to the person who is the subject of the petition and to his or her attorney.

(3) The petition shall be served upon the court and the prosecuting attorney. The court, upon receipt of the petition for release, shall within forty-five days order a hearing. Continuance of the hearing date shall only be allowed for good cause shown. The prosecuting attorney shall represent the state, and shall have the right to have the person who is the subject of the petition examined by an expert or professional person of the prosecuting attorney's choice. If the secretary is the petitioner, the attorney general shall represent the secretary. If the person who is the subject of the petition is indigent, and the person so requests, the court shall appoint a qualified expert or professional person to examine him or her. If the person who is the subject of the petition has a developmental disability, the examination shall be performed by a developmental disabilities professional. The hearing shall be before a jury if demanded by either the petitioner or the prosecuting attorney. The burden of proof shall be upon the petitioner to show by a preponderance of the evidence that the person who is the subject of the petition no longer presents, as a result of a mental disease or defect, a substantial danger to other persons, or a substantial likelihood of committing criminal acts jeopardizing public safety or security, unless kept under further control by the court or other persons or institutions. If the person who is the subject of the petition will be transferred to a state correctional institution or facility upon release to serve a sentence for any class A felony, the petitioner must show that the person's mental disease or defect is manageable within a state correctional institution or facility, but must not be required to prove that the person does not present either a substantial danger to other persons, or a substantial likelihood of committing criminal acts jeopardizing public safety or security, if released.

(4) For purposes of this section, a person affected by a mental disease or defect in a state of remission is considered to have a mental disease or defect requiring supervision when the disease may, with reasonable medical probability, occasionally become active and, when active, render the person a danger to others. Upon a finding that the person who is the subject of the petition has a mental disease or defect in a state of remission under this subsection, the court may deny release, or place or continue such a person on conditional release.

(5) Nothing contained in this chapter shall prohibit the patient from petitioning the court for release or conditional release from the institution in which he or she is committed. The petition shall be served upon the court, the prosecuting attorney, and the secretary. Upon receipt of such petition, the secretary shall develop a recommendation as provided in subsection (1) of this section and provide the secretary's recommendation to all parties and the court. The issue to be determined on such proceeding is whether the patient, as a result of a mental disease or defect, is a substantial danger to other persons, or presents a substantial likelihood of committing criminal acts jeopardizing public safety or security, unless kept under further control by the court or other persons or institutions.

(6) Nothing contained in this chapter shall prohibit the committed person from petitioning for release by writ of habeas corpus.

[2013 c 289 § 7; 2010 c 263 § 8; 2000 c 94 § 16; 1998 c 297 § 44; 1993 c 31 § 11; 1989 c 420 § 11; 1983 c 25 § 2; 1974 ex.s. c 198 § 16; 1973 1st ex.s. c 117 § 20.]
NOTES:

Findings—2013 c 289: See note following RCW 10.77.086.

Effective dates—Severability—Intent—1998 c 297: See notes following RCW 71.05.010.

10.77.205
Sexual or violent offenders—Notice of release, escape, etc.—Definitions.

(1)(a) At the earliest possible date, and in no event later than thirty days before conditional release, release, authorized furlough pursuant to RCW 10.77.163, or transfer to a less-restrictive facility than a state mental hospital, the superintendent shall send written notice of the conditional release, release, authorized furlough, or transfer of a person who has been found not guilty of a sex, violent, or felony harassment offense by reason of insanity and who is now in the custody of the department pursuant to this chapter, to the following:

(i) The chief of police of the city, if any, in which the person will reside; and

(ii) The sheriff of the county in which the person will reside.

(b) The same notice as required by (a) of this subsection shall be sent to the following, if such notice has been requested in writing about a specific person committed under this chapter:

(i) The victim of the crime for which the person was committed or the victim's next of kin if the crime was a homicide;

(ii) Any witnesses who testified against the person in any court proceedings; and

(iii) Any person specified in writing by the prosecuting attorney.

Information regarding victims, next of kin, or witnesses requesting the notice, information regarding any other person specified in writing by the prosecuting attorney to receive the notice, and the notice are confidential and shall not be available to the person committed under this chapter.

(c) In addition to the notice requirements of (a) and (b) of this subsection, the superintendent shall comply with RCW **10.77.163**.

(d) The thirty-day notice requirement contained in (a) and (b) of this subsection shall not apply to emergency medical furloughs.

(e) The existence of the notice requirements in (a) and (b) of this subsection shall not require any extension of the release date in the event the release plan changes after notification.

(2) If a person who has been found not guilty of a sex, violent, or felony harassment offense by reason of insanity and who is committed under this chapter escapes, the superintendent shall immediately notify, by the most reasonable and expedient means available, the chief of police of the city and the sheriff of the county in which the person resided immediately before the person's arrest. If previously requested, the

superintendent shall also notify the witnesses and the victim, if any, of the crime for which the person was committed or the victim's next of kin if the crime was a homicide. The superintendent shall also notify appropriate persons pursuant to RCW **10.77.165**. If the person is recaptured, the secretary shall send notice to the persons designated in this subsection as soon as possible but in no event later than two working days after the department learns of such recapture.

(3) If the victim, the victim's next of kin, or any witness is under the age of sixteen, the notice required by this section shall be sent to the parents or legal guardian of the child.

(4) The department shall send the notices required by this chapter to the last address provided to the department by the requesting party. The requesting party shall furnish the department with a current address.

(5) For purposes of this section the following terms have the following meanings:

(a) "Violent offense" means a violent offense under RCW **9.94A.030**;

(b) "Sex offense" means a sex offense under RCW **9.94A.030**;

(c) "Next of kin" means a person's spouse, state registered domestic partner, parents, siblings, and children;

(d) "Authorized furlough" means a furlough granted after compliance with RCW **10.77.163**;

(e) "Felony harassment offense" means a crime of harassment as defined in RCW **9A.46.060** that is a felony.

[**2009 c 521 § 27**; **2000 c 94 § 17**; **1994 c 129 § 5**; **1992 c 186 § 8**; **1990 c 3 § 104**.]

NOTES:

       Findings—Intent—1994 c 129: See note following RCW **4.24.550**.

       Severability—1992 c 186: See note following RCW **9A.46.110**.

       Index, part headings not law—Severability—Effective dates—Application— 1990 c 3: See RCW **18.155.900** through **18.155.902**.

10.77.207

Persons acquitted of sex offense due to insanity—Release of information authorized.

In addition to any other information required to be released under this chapter, the department is authorized, pursuant to RCW **4.24.550**, to release relevant information necessary to protect the public concerning a person who was acquitted of a sex offense as defined in RCW**9.94A.030** due to insanity and was subsequently committed to the department pursuant to this chapter.

[**1990 c 3 § 105.**]

NOTES:

Index, part headings not law—Severability—Effective dates—Application—1990 c 3: See RCW **18.155.900** through **18.155.902**.

10.77.210

Right to adequate care and treatment—Records and reports.

(1) Any person involuntarily detained, hospitalized, or committed pursuant to the provisions of this chapter shall have the right to adequate care and individualized treatment. The person who has custody of the patient or is in charge of treatment shall keep records detailing all medical, expert, and professional care and treatment received by a committed person, and shall keep copies of all reports of periodic examinations of the patient that have been filed with the secretary pursuant to this chapter. Except as provided in RCW **10.77.205** and **4.24.550**regarding the release of information concerning insane offenders who are acquitted of sex offenses and subsequently committed pursuant to this chapter, all records and reports made pursuant to this chapter, shall be made available only upon request, to the committed person, to his or her attorney, to his or her personal physician, to the supervising community corrections officer, to the prosecuting attorney, to the court, to the protection and advocacy agency, or other expert or professional persons who, upon proper showing, demonstrates a need for access to such records. All records and reports made pursuant to this chapter

shall also be made available, upon request, to the department of corrections or the indeterminate sentence review board if the person was on parole, probation, or community supervision at the time of detention, hospitalization, or commitment or the person is subsequently convicted for the crime for which he or she was detained, hospitalized, or committed pursuant to this chapter.

(2) All relevant records and reports as defined by the department in rule shall be made available, upon request, to criminal justice agencies as defined in RCW **10.97.030**. [**1998 c 297 § 45; 1993 c 31 § 12; 1990 c 3 § 108; 1989 c 420 § 12; 1983 c 196 § 3; 1973 1st ex.s. c 117 § 21.**]

NOTES:

Effective dates—Severability—Intent—1998 c 297: See notes following RCW **71.05.010**.

Index, part headings not law—Severability—Effective dates—Application—1990 c 3: See RCW **18.155.900** through **18.155.902**.

10.77.2101

Implementation of legislative intent.

In developing rules under RCW **10.77.210**(2), the department shall implement the following legislative intent: Increasing public safety; and making decisions based on a person's current conduct and mental condition rather than the classification of the charges. [**1998 c 297 § 46.**]

NOTES:

Effective dates—Severability—Intent—1998 c 297: See notes following RCW **71.05.010**.

10.77.220

Incarceration in correctional institution or facility prohibited—Exceptions.

No person who is criminally insane confined pursuant to this chapter shall be incarcerated in a state correctional institution or facility. This section does not apply to confinement in a mental health facility located wholly within a correctional institution. Confinement of a person who is criminally insane in a county jail or other local facility while awaiting either placement in a treatment program or a court hearing pursuant to this chapter is permitted for no more than seven days.

[**2015 1st sp.s. c 7 § 8; 1982 c 112 § 3; 1974 ex.s. c 198 § 17; 1973 1st ex.s. c 117 § 22.**]

NOTES:

  Finding—2015 1st sp.s. c 7: See note following RCW **10.77.075**.

  Effective dates—2015 1st sp.s. c 7: See note following RCW **10.77.073**.

10.77.230

Appellate review.

Either party may seek appellate review of the judgment of any hearing held pursuant to the provisions of this chapter.

[**1988 c 202 § 16; 1974 ex.s. c 198 § 18; 1973 1st ex.s. c 117 § 23.**]

NOTES:

Rules of court: Cf. RAP 2.2, 18.22.

  Severability—1988 c 202: See note following RCW **2.24.050**.

10.77.240

Existing rights not affected.

Nothing in this chapter shall prohibit a person presently committed from exercising a right presently available to him or her for obtaining release from confinement, including the right to petition for a writ of habeas corpus.

[**1999 c 13 § 3; 1973 1st ex.s. c 117 § 24.**]

NOTES:

  Purpose—Construction—1999 c 13: See note following RCW **10.77.010**.

10.77.250
Responsibility for costs—Reimbursement.

The department shall be responsible for all costs relating to the evaluation and treatment of persons committed to it pursuant to any provisions of this chapter, and the logistical and supportive services pertaining thereto. Reimbursement may be obtained by the department pursuant to RCW **43.20B.330**.

[**1987 c 75 § 1; 1985 c 245 § 1; 1973 1st ex.s. c 117 § 25.**]

NOTES:

Savings—**1987 c 75:** See RCW **43.20B.900**.

10.77.260
Violent act—Presumptions.

(1) In determining whether a defendant has committed a violent act the court must:

(a) Presume that a past conviction, guilty plea, or finding of not guilty by reason of insanity establishes the elements necessary for the crime charged;

(b) Consider that the elements of a crime may not be sufficient in themselves to establish that the defendant committed a violent act; and

(c) Presume that the facts underlying the elements, if unrebutted, are sufficient to establish that the defendant committed a violent act.

(2) The presumptions in subsection (1) of this section are rebuttable.

(3) In determining the facts underlying the elements of any crime under subsection (1) of this section, the court may consider information including, but not limited to, the following material relating to the crime:

(a) Affidavits or declarations made under penalty of perjury;

(b) Criminal history record information, as defined in chapter **10.97** RCW; and

(c) Its own or certified copies of another court's records such as criminal complaints, certifications of probable cause to detain, dockets, and orders on judgment and sentencing.

NOTES:

Severability—**2000 c 74:** See note following RCW **10.77.060**.

10.77.270

Independent public safety review panel—Members—Secretary to submit recommendation—Access to records—Support, rules—Report.

(1) The secretary shall establish an independent public safety review panel for the purpose of advising the secretary and the courts with respect to persons who have been found not guilty by reason of insanity, or persons committed under the involuntary treatment act where the court has made a special finding under RCW **71.05.280**(3)(b). The panel shall provide advice regarding all recommendations to the secretary, decisions by the secretary, or actions pending in court: (a) For a change in commitment status; (b) to allow furloughs or temporary leaves accompanied by staff; (c) not to seek further commitment terms under RCW **71.05.320**; or (d) to permit movement about the grounds of the treatment facility, with or without the accompaniment of staff.

(2) The members of the public safety review panel shall be appointed by the governor for a renewable term of three years and shall include the following:

(a) A psychiatrist;

(b) A licensed clinical psychologist;

(c) A representative of the department of corrections;

(d) A prosecutor or a representative of a prosecutor's association;

(e) A representative of law enforcement or a law enforcement association;

(f) A consumer and family advocate representative; and

(g) A public defender or a representative of a defender's association.

(3) Thirty days prior to issuing a recommendation for conditional release under RCW **10.77.150** or forty-five days prior to issuing a recommendation for release under RCW **10.77.200**, the secretary shall submit its recommendation with the committed person's application and the department's risk assessment to the public safety review panel. The public safety review panel shall complete an independent assessment of the

public safety risk entailed by the secretary's proposed conditional release recommendation or release recommendation and provide this assessment in writing to the secretary. The public safety review panel may, within funds appropriated for this purpose, request additional evaluations of the committed person. The public safety review panel may indicate whether it is in agreement with the secretary's recommendation, or whether it would issue a different recommendation. The secretary shall provide the panel's assessment when it is received along with any supporting documentation, including all previous reports of evaluations of the committed person in the person's hospital record, to the court, prosecutor in the county that ordered the person's commitment, and counsel for the committed person.

(4) The secretary shall notify the public safety review panel at appropriate intervals concerning any changes in the commitment or custody status of persons found not guilty by reason of insanity, or persons committed under the involuntary treatment act where the court has made a special finding under RCW **71.05.280**(3)(b). The panel shall have access, upon request, to a committed person's complete hospital record, and any other records deemed necessary by the public safety review panel.

(5) The department shall provide administrative and financial support to the public safety review panel. The department, in consultation with the public safety review panel, may adopt rules to implement this section.

(6) By December 1, 2014, the public safety review panel shall report to the appropriate legislative committees the following:

(a) Whether the public safety review panel has observed a change in statewide consistency of evaluations and decisions concerning changes in the commitment status of persons found not guilty by reason of insanity;

(b) Whether the public safety review panel should be given the authority to make release decisions and monitor release conditions;

(c) Whether further changes in the law are necessary to enhance public safety when incompetency prevents operation of the criminal justice system and long-term commitment of the criminally insane; and

(d) Any other issues the public safety review panel deems relevant.

[**2013 c 289 § 3; 2010 c 263 § 1.**]

NOTES:

Findings—**2013 c 289:** See note following RCW **10.77.086**.

10.77.280
Office of forensic mental health services.

(1) In order to prioritize goals of accuracy, prompt service to the court, quality assurance, and integration with other services, an office of forensic mental health services is established within the department of social and health services. The office shall be led by a director on at least the level of deputy assistant secretary within the department who shall, after a reasonable period of transition, have responsibility for the following functions:

(a) Operational control of all forensic evaluation services, including specific budget allocation;

(b) Responsibility for training forensic evaluators;

(c) Development of a system to certify forensic evaluators, and to monitor the quality of forensic evaluation reports;

(d) Liaison with courts, jails, and community mental health programs to ensure proper flow of information, coordinate logistical issues, and solve problems in complex circumstances;

(e) Coordination with state hospitals to identify and develop best practice interventions and curricula for services that are unique to forensic patients;

(f) Promotion of congruence across state hospitals where appropriate, and promotion of interventions that flow smoothly into community interventions;

(g) Coordination with regional support networks, behavioral health organizations, community mental health agencies, and the department of corrections regarding community treatment and monitoring of persons on conditional release;

(h) Oversight of forensic data collection and analysis statewide, and appropriate dissemination of data trends and recommendations; and

(i) Oversight of the development, implementation, and maintenance of community forensic programs and services.

(2) The office of forensic mental health services must have a clearly delineated budget separate from the overall budget for state hospital services.

[**2015 1st sp.s. c 7 § 10.**]

NOTES:

> **Finding—2015 1st sp.s. c 7:** See note following RCW **10.77.075**.
>
> **Effective dates—2015 1st sp.s. c 7:** See note following RCW **10.77.073**.

10.77.290

Secretary to adopt rules—2015 1st sp.s. c 7.

The secretary shall adopt rules as may be necessary to implement chapter 7, Laws of 2015 1st sp. sess.

[**2015 1st sp.s. c 7 § 11.**]

NOTES:

> **Finding—2015 1st sp.s. c 7:** See note following RCW **10.77.075**.
>
> **Effective dates—2015 1st sp.s. c 7:** See note following RCW **10.77.073**.

10.77.940

Equal application of 1989 c 420—Evaluation for developmental disability.

The provisions of chapter 420, Laws of 1989 shall apply equally to persons in the custody of the department on May 13, 1989, who were found by a court to be not guilty by reason of insanity or incompetent to stand trial, or who have been found to have committed acts constituting a felony pursuant to RCW **71.05.280**(3) and present a substantial likelihood of repeating similar acts, and the secretary shall cause such persons to be evaluated to ascertain if such persons are developmentally disabled for placement in a program specifically reserved for the treatment and training of persons with developmental disabilities.

[**1999 c 13 § 4; 1989 c 420 § 17.**]

NOTES:

Purpose—Construction—1999 c 13: See note following RCW **10.77.010**.

10.77.950

Construction—Chapter applicable to state registered domestic partnerships—2009 c 521.

For the purposes of this chapter, the terms spouse, marriage, marital, husband, wife, widow, widower, next of kin, and family shall be interpreted as applying equally to state registered domestic partnerships or individuals in state registered domestic partnerships as well as to marital relationships and married persons, and references to dissolution of marriage shall apply equally to state registered domestic partnerships that have been terminated, dissolved, or invalidated, to the extent that such interpretation does not conflict with federal law. Where necessary to implement chapter 521, Laws of 2009, gender-specific terms such as husband and wife used in any statute, rule, or other law shall be construed to be gender neutral, and applicable to individuals in state registered domestic partnerships.

[**2009 c 521 § 26.**]

Chapter 10.79 RCW SEARCHES AND SEIZURES

NOTES:

Rules of court: Search and seizure—CrR 2.3; CrRLJ 2.3.

Alcoholic beverage control, search and seizure: Chapter **66.32** RCW.

Controlled substances, search and seizure: RCW **69.50.509**.

10.79.015

Other grounds for issuance of search warrant.

Any such magistrate, when satisfied that there is reasonable cause, may also, upon like complaint made on oath, issue search warrant in the following cases, to wit:

(1) To search for and seize any counterfeit or spurious coin, or forged instruments, or tools, machines or materials, prepared or provided for making either of them.

(2) To search for and seize any gaming apparatus used or kept, and to be used in any unlawful gaming house, or in any building, apartment or place, resorted to for the purpose of unlawful gaming.

(3) To search for and seize any evidence material to the investigation or prosecution of any homicide or any felony: PROVIDED, That if the evidence is sought to be secured from any radio or television station or from any regularly published newspaper, magazine or wire service, or from any employee of such station, wire service or publication, the evidence shall be secured only through a subpoena duces tecum unless: (a) There is probable cause to believe that the person or persons in possession of the evidence may be involved in the crime under investigation; or (b) there is probable cause to believe that the evidence sought to be seized will be destroyed or hidden if subpoena duces tecum procedures are followed. As used in this subsection, "person or persons" includes both natural and judicial persons.

(4) To search for and seize any instrument, apparatus or device used to obtain telephone or telegraph service in violation of RCW **9.26A.110**or **9.26A.115**.
[**2003 c 53 § 94; 1980 c 52 § 1; 1972 ex.s. c 75 § 2; 1969 c 83 § 1; 1949 c 86 § 1;** Code 1881 § 986; **1873 p 216 § 154; 1854 p 101 § 2;** Rem. Supp. 1949 § 2238. Formerly RCW **10.79.010**, part.]
NOTES:

Intent—**Effective date**—**2003 c 53:** See notes following RCW **2.48.180**.

10.79.020

To whom directed—Contents.

All such warrants shall be directed to the sheriff of the county, or his or her deputy, or to any constable of the county, commanding such officer to search the house or place where the stolen property or other things for which he or she is required to search are believed to be concealed, which place and property, or things to be searched for shall be designated and described in the warrant, and to bring such stolen property or other things, when found, and the person in whose possession the same shall be found, before the magistrate who shall issue the warrant, or before some other magistrate or court having cognizance of the case.

[**2010 c 8 § 1061;** Code 1881 § 969; **1873 p 216 § 155; 1854 p 101 § 3;** RRS § 2239.]

10.79.035
Issuance of search warrants by magistrates.

(1) Any magistrate as defined by RCW **2.20.010**, when satisfied that there is probable cause, may[,] upon application supported by oath or affirmation, issue a search warrant to search for and seize any: (a) Evidence of a crime; (b) contraband, the fruits of crime, or things otherwise criminally possessed; (c) weapons or other things by means of which a crime has been committed or reasonably appears about to be committed; or (d) person for whose arrest there is probable cause or who is unlawfully restrained.

(2) The application may be provided or transmitted to the magistrate by telephone, email, or any other reliable method.

(3) If the magistrate finds that probable cause for the issuance of a warrant exists, the magistrate must issue a warrant or direct an individual whom the magistrate authorizes to affix the magistrate's signature to a warrant identifying the property or person and naming or describing the person, place, or thing to be searched. The magistrate may communicate permission to affix the magistrate's signature to the warrant by telephone, email, or any other reliable method.

(4) The evidence in support of the finding of probable cause and a record of the magistrate's permission to affix the magistrate's signature to the warrant shall be preserved and shall be filed with the issuing court as required by CrRLJ 2.3 or CrR 2.3.

[**2014 c 93 § 3.**]
NOTES:

Finding—Intent—2014 c 93: See note following RCW **2.20.030**.

10.79.040

Search without warrant unlawful—Penalty.

(1) It shall be unlawful for any police officer or other peace officer to enter and search any private dwelling house or place of residence without the authority of a search warrant issued upon a complaint as by law provided.

(2) Any police officer or other peace officer violating the provisions of this section is guilty of a gross misdemeanor.

[**2010 c 8 § 1062; 2003 c 53 § 95; 1921 c 71 § 1;** RRS § 2240-1. FORMER PART OF SECTION: **1921 c 71 § 2;** RRS § 2240-2, now codified as RCW**10.79.045**.]
NOTES:

Intent—Effective date—2003 c 53: See notes following RCW **2.48.180**.

10.79.050

Restoration of stolen property to owner—Duties of officers.

All property obtained by larceny, robbery or burglary, shall be restored to the owner; and no sale, whether in good faith on the part of the purchaser or not, shall divest the owner of his or her rights to such property; and it shall be the duty of the officer who shall arrest any person charged as principal or accessory in any robbery or larceny, to secure the property alleged to have been stolen, and he or she shall be answerable for the same, and shall annex a schedule thereof to his or her return of the warrant.

[**2010 c 8 § 1063;** Code 1881 § 851; **1873 p 192 § 57; 1854 p 84 § 51;** RRS § 2129.]

10.79.060

Strip, body cavity searches—Legislative intent.

It is the intent of the legislature to establish policies regarding the practice of strip searching persons booked into holding, detention, or local correctional facilities. It is the intent of the legislature to restrict the practice of strip searching and body cavity searching persons booked into holding, detention, or local correctional facilities to those situations where such searches are necessary.

[**1983 1st ex.s. c 42 § 1.**]

NOTES:

      Effective date—**1983 1st ex.s. c 42:** "This act is necessary for the immediate preservation of the public peace, health, and safety, the support of the state government and its existing public institutions, and shall take effect on July 1, 1983." [**1983 1st ex.s. c 42 § 10.**]

      Severability—**1983 1st ex.s. c 42:** "If any provision of this act or its application to any person or circumstance is held invalid, the remainder of the act or the application of the provision to other persons or circumstances is not affected." [**1983 1st ex.s. c 42 § 9.**]

10.79.070
Strip, body cavity searches—Definitions.

Unless the context clearly requires otherwise, the definitions in this section apply throughout RCW **10.79.060** through **10.79.110**.

(1) "Strip search" means having a person remove or arrange some or all of his or her clothing so as to permit an inspection of the genitals, buttocks, anus, or undergarments of the person or breasts of a female person.

(2) "Body cavity search" means the touching or probing of a person's body cavity, whether or not there is actual penetration of the body cavity.

(3) "Body cavity" means the stomach or rectum of a person and the vagina of a female person.

(4) "Law enforcement agency" and "law enforcement officer" include local departments of corrections created pursuant to *RCW**70.48.090**(3) and employees thereof.

[**1983 1st ex.s. c 42 § 2.**]

NOTES:

*Reviser's note: RCW **70.48.090** was amended by 2007 c 13 § 1, changing subsection (3) to subsection (4).

Effective date—Severability—1983 1st ex.s. c 42: See notes following RCW **10.79.060**.

10.79.080
Strip, body cavity searches—Warrant, authorization, report.

(1) No person may be subjected to a body cavity search by or at the direction of a law enforcement agency unless a search warrant is issued pursuant to superior court criminal rules.

(2) No law enforcement officer may seek a warrant for a body cavity search without first obtaining specific authorization for the body cavity search from the ranking shift supervisor of the law enforcement authority. Authorization for the body cavity search may be obtained electronically: PROVIDED, That such electronic authorization shall be reduced to writing by the law enforcement officer seeking the authorization and signed by the ranking supervisor as soon as possible thereafter.

(3) Before any body cavity search is authorized or conducted, a thorough pat-down search, a thorough electronic metal-detector search, and a thorough clothing search, where appropriate, must be used to search for and seize any evidence of a crime, contraband, fruits of crime, things otherwise criminally possessed, weapons, or other things by means of which a crime has been committed or reasonably appears about to be committed. No body cavity search shall be authorized or conducted unless these other methods do not satisfy the safety, security, or evidentiary concerns of the law enforcement agency.

(4) A law enforcement officer requesting a body cavity search shall prepare and sign a report regarding the body cavity search. The report shall include:

(a) A copy of the written authorization required under subsection (2) of this section;

(b) A copy of the warrant and any supporting documents required under subsection (1) of this section;

(c) The name and sex of all persons conducting or observing the search;

(d) The time, date, place, and description of the search; and

(e) A statement of the results of the search and a list of any items removed from the person as a result of the search.

The report shall be retained as part of the law enforcement agency's records.

[**1983 1st ex.s. c 42 § 3.**]

NOTES:

Effective date—Severability—1983 1st ex.s. c 42: See notes following RCW **10.79.060**.

10.79.090

Strip, body cavity searches—Medical care not precluded.

Nothing in RCW **10.79.080** or this section may be construed as precluding or preventing the administration of medical care to persons requiring immediate medical care or requesting medical care.

[**1983 1st ex.s. c 42 § 4.**]

NOTES:

Effective date—Severability—1983 1st ex.s. c 42: See notes following RCW **10.79.060**.

10.79.100

Strip, body cavity searches—Standards for conducting.

(1) Persons conducting a strip search shall not touch the person being searched except as reasonably necessary to effectuate the strip search of the person.

(2) Any body cavity search must be performed under sanitary conditions and conducted by a physician, registered nurse, or physician's assistant, licensed to practice in this state, who is trained in the proper medical process and the potential health problems associated with a body cavity search. No health professional authorized by this subsection to conduct a body cavity search shall be held liable in any civil action if

the search is conducted in a manner that meets the standards and requirements of RCW **4.24.290** and **7.70.040**.

(3) Except as provided in subsection (7) of this section, a strip search or body cavity search, as well as presearch undressing or postsearch dressing, shall occur at a location made private from the observation of persons not physically conducting the search. A strip search or body cavity search shall be performed or observed only by persons of the same sex as the person being searched, except for licensed medical professionals as required by subsection (2) of this section.

(4) Except as provided in subsection (5) of this section, no person may be present or observe during the search unless the person is necessary to conduct the search or to ensure the safety of those persons conducting the search.

(5) Nothing in this section prohibits a person upon whom a body cavity search is to be performed from having a readily available person of his or her choosing present at the time the search is conducted. However, the person chosen shall not be a person being held in custody by a law enforcement agency.

(6) RCW **10.79.080** and this section shall not be interpreted as expanding or diminishing the authority of a law enforcement officer with respect to searches incident to arrest or investigatory stop in public.

(7) A strip search of a person housed in a holding, detention, or local correctional facility to search for and seize a weapon may be conducted at other than a private location if there arises a specific threat to institutional security that reasonably requires such a search or if all persons in the facility are being searched for the discovery of weapons or contraband.

[**1983 1st ex.s. c 42 § 5.**]

NOTES:

Effective date—Severability—1983 1st ex.s. c 42: See notes following RCW **10.79.060**.

10.79.110

Strip, body cavity searches—Actions for damages, injunctive relief.

(1) A person who suffers damage or harm as a result of a violation of RCW **10.79.080**, **10.79.090**, **10.79.100**, or **10.79.130** through **10.79.170**may bring a civil action to recover actual damages sustained by him or her. The court may, in its discretion, award injunctive and declaratory relief as it deems necessary.

(2) RCW **10.79.080**, **10.79.090**, **10.79.100**, and **10.79.130** through **10.79.170** shall not be construed as limiting any constitutional, common law, or statutory right of any person regarding any action for damages or injunctive relief, or as precluding the prosecution under another provision of law of any law enforcement officer or other person who has violated RCW **10.79.080**, **10.79.090**, **10.79.100**, or **10.79.130** through**10.79.170**.

[**1986 c 88 § 7**; **1983 1st ex.s. c 42 § 6.**]

NOTES:

Effective date—Severability—1983 1st ex.s. c 42: See notes following RCW **10.79.060**.

10.79.120

Strip, body cavity searches—Application of RCW 10.79.130 through 10.79.160.

RCW **10.79.130** through **10.79.160** apply to any person in custody at a holding, detention, or local correctional facility, other than a person committed to incarceration by order of a court, regardless of whether an arrest warrant or other court order was issued before the person was arrested or otherwise taken into custody unless the court issuing the warrant has determined that the person shall not be released on personal recognizance, bail, or bond. RCW **10.79.130** through **10.79.160** do not apply to a person held for post-conviction incarceration for a criminal offense. The definitions and remedies provided by RCW **10.79.070** and **10.79.110** apply to RCW **10.79.130** through **10.79.160**.

[**1986 c 88 § 1.**]

10.79.130

Strip, body cavity searches—Warrant required—Exceptions.

(1) No person to whom this section is made applicable by RCW **10.79.120** may be strip searched without a warrant unless:

(a) There is a reasonable suspicion to believe that a strip search is necessary to discover weapons, criminal evidence, contraband, or other thing concealed on the body of the person to be searched, that constitutes a threat to the security of a holding, detention, or local correctional facility;

(b) There is probable cause to believe that a strip search is necessary to discover other criminal evidence concealed on the body of the person to be searched, but not constituting a threat to facility security; or

(c) There is a reasonable suspicion to believe that a strip search is necessary to discover a health condition requiring immediate medical attention.

(2) For the purposes of subsection (1) of this section, a reasonable suspicion is deemed to be present when the person to be searched has been arrested for:

(a) A violent offense as defined in RCW **9.94A.030** or any successor statute;

(b) An offense involving escape, burglary, or the use of a deadly weapon; or

(c) An offense involving possession of a drug or controlled substance under chapter **69.41**, 69.50, or **69.52** RCW or any successor statute.

[**1986 c 88 § 2.**]

10.79.140

Strip, body cavity searches—Uncategorized searches—Determination of reasonable suspicion, probable cause—Less-intrusive alternatives.

(1) A person to whom this section is made applicable by RCW **10.79.120** who has not been arrested for an offense within one of the categories specified in RCW **10.79.130**(2) may nevertheless be strip searched, but only upon an individualized determination of reasonable suspicion or probable cause as provided in this section.

(2) With the exception of those situations in which reasonable suspicion is deemed to be present under RCW **10.79.130**(2), no strip search may be conducted without the specific prior written approval of the jail unit supervisor on duty. Before any strip search is conducted, reasonable efforts must be made to use other less-intrusive means, such as pat-down, electronic metal detector, or clothing searches, to determine whether a weapon, criminal evidence, contraband, or other thing is concealed on the body, or whether a health condition requiring immediate medical attention is present. The determination of whether reasonable suspicion or probable cause exists to conduct a strip search shall be made only after such less-intrusive means have been used and shall be based on a consideration of all information and circumstances known to the officer authorizing the strip search, including but not limited to the following factors:

(a) The nature of the offense for which the person to be searched was arrested;

(b) The prior criminal record of the person to be searched; and

(c) Physically violent behavior of the person to be searched, during or after the arrest.

[**1986 c 88 § 3.**]

10.79.150

Strip, body cavity searches—Written record required, contents—Unnecessary persons prohibited.

(1) A written record of any strip search shall be maintained in the individual file of each person strip searched.

(2) With respect to any strip search conducted under RCW **10.79.140**, the record shall contain the following information:

(a) The name of the supervisor authorizing the strip search;

(b) The specific facts constituting reasonable suspicion to believe that the strip search was necessary;

(c) The name and serial number of the officer conducting the strip search and of all other persons present or observing during any part of the strip search;

(d) The time, date, and place of the strip search; and

(e) Any weapons, criminal evidence, contraband, or other thing, or health condition discovered as a result of the strip search.

(3) With respect to any strip search conducted under RCW **10.79.130**(2), the record shall contain, in addition to the offense or offenses for which the person searched was arrested, the information required by subsection (2)(c), (d), and (e) of this section.

(4) The record may be included or incorporated in existing forms used by the facility, including the booking form required under the Washington Administrative Code. A notation of the name of the person strip searched shall also be entered in the log of daily activities or other chronological record, if any, maintained pursuant to the Washington Administrative Code.

(5) Except at the request of the person to be searched, no person may be present or observe during the strip search unless necessary to conduct the search.

[**1986 c 88 § 4.**]

10.79.160
Strip, body cavity searches—Physical examinations for public health purposes excluded.

Physical examinations conducted by licensed medical professionals solely for public health purposes under separate statutory authority shall not be considered searches for purposes of RCW **10.79.120**, **10.79.130**, and **10.79.140**.

[**1986 c 88 § 5.**]

10.79.170
Strip, body cavity searches—Nonliability when search delayed.

No governmental entity and no employee or contracting agent of a governmental entity shall be liable for injury, death, or damage caused by a person in custody when the injury, death, or damage is caused by or made possible by contraband that would have been discovered sooner but for the delay caused by having to seek a search warrant under RCW **10.79.080** or **10.79.130** through **10.79.160**.

[**1986 c 88 § 6.**]

Chapter 10.82 RCW COLLECTION AND DISPOSITION OF FINES AND COSTS

NOTES:

City, county jail prisoners may be compelled to work: RCW **9.92.130**, **9.92.140**, **36.28.100**.

Defendant liable for costs: RCW **10.64.015**.

Fine and costs—Collection procedure, liability for, commitment for failure to pay, execution: RCW **10.01.160** through **10.01.180**.

Jury fee disposition: RCW **10.46.190**.

Payment of fine and costs in installments: RCW **9.92.070**, **10.01.170**.

10.82.010
Execution for fines and costs.

Upon a judgment for fine and costs, and for all adjudged costs, execution shall be issued against the property of the defendant, and returned in the same manner as in civil actions.

[Code 1881 § 1120; **1873 p 242 § 278; 1854 p 123 § 142;** RRS § 2201.]

NOTES:

Judgments a lien on realty: RCW **10.64.080**.

10.82.020
Stay of execution for sixty days on recognizance.

Every defendant against whom a judgment has been rendered for fine and costs, may stay the execution for the fine assessed and costs for sixty days from the rendition of the judgment, by procuring one or more sufficient sureties, to enter into a recognizance in open court, acknowledging themselves to be bail for such fine and costs.

[Code 1881 § 1123; **1873 p 242 § 281; 1854 p 124 § 145;** RRS § 2204. FORMER PART OF SECTION: Code 1881 § 1124; **1873 p 243 § 282; 1854 p 124 § 146;** RRS § 2205, now codified as RCW **10.82.025**.]

10.82.025

Effect of recognizance—Execution of judgment after sixty days.

Such sureties shall be approved by the clerk, and the entry of the recognizance shall be written immediately following the judgment, and signed by the bail, and shall have the same effect as a judgment, and if the fine or costs be not paid at the expiration of the sixty days, a joint execution shall issue against the defendant and the bail, and an execution against the body of the defendant, who shall be committed to jail, to be released as provided in *this act, in committal for default to pay or secure the fine and costs.

[Code 1881 § 1124; **1873 p 243 § 282; 1854 p 124 § 146;** RRS § 2205. Formerly RCW **10.82.020**, part.]

NOTES:

*Reviser's note: The term "this act" apparently refers to "An act to regulate the practice and pleadings in prosecutions for crimes" first enacted by Laws of 1854, page 100.

10.82.030

Commitment for failure to pay fine and costs—Execution against defendant's property—Reduction by payment, labor, or confinement.

If any person ordered into custody until the fine and costs adjudged against him or her be paid shall not, within five days, pay, or cause the payment of the same to be made, the clerk of the court shall issue a warrant to the sheriff commanding him or her to imprison such defendant in the county jail until the amount of such fine and costs owing are paid. Execution may at any time issue against the property of the defendant for that portion of such fine and costs not reduced by the application of this section. The amount of such fine and costs owing shall be the whole of such fine and costs reduced by the amount of any portion thereof paid, and an amount established by the county legislative authority for every day the defendant performs labor as provided in RCW **10.82.040**, and a lesser amount established by the county legislative authority for every day the defendant does not perform such labor while imprisoned.

[**2010 c 8 § 1064; 1991 c 183 § 1; 1983 c 276 § 2; 1967 c 200 § 4; 1891 c 28 § 84;** 1883 p 38 § 1, part; Code 1881 § 1125; **1873 p 243 § 283; 1854 p 124 § 147;** RRS § 2206. Formerly RCW **10.82.030** and **10.82.050**.]

NOTES:

>   **Severability—1967 c 200:** See note following RCW **9.45.122**.

Commitment until fines and costs are paid: RCW **10.70.010**.

Fine and costs, liability of defendant, collection procedure, contempt, commitment, execution: RCW **10.01.160** through **10.01.180**.

10.82.040

Commitment for failure to pay fine and costs—Reduction of amount by performance of labor.

When a defendant is committed to jail, on failure to pay any fines and costs, he or she shall, under the supervision of the county sheriff and subject to the terms of any ordinances adopted by the county commissioners, be permitted to perform labor to reduce the amount owing of the fine and costs.

[**2010 c 8 § 1065; 1967 c 200 § 5;** 1883 p 38 § 1, part; Code 1881 § 1129; **1877 p 206 § 8; 1873 p 243 § 287; 1854 p 124 § 151;** RRS § 2209, part.]

NOTES:

>   **Severability—1967 c 200:** See note following RCW **9.45.122**.

10.82.070

Disposition of monetary payments.

(1) All sums of money derived from costs, fines, penalties, and forfeitures imposed or collected, in whole or in part, by a superior court for violation of orders of injunction, mandamus and other like writs, for contempt of court, or for breach of the penal laws shall be paid in cash by the person collecting the same, within twenty days after the collection, to the county treasurer of the county in which the same have accrued.

(2) Except as provided in RCW **9A.88.120** and **10.99.080**, the county treasurer shall remit monthly thirty-two percent of the money received under this section except for certain costs to the state treasurer for deposit in the state general fund and shall deposit the remainder as provided by law. "Certain costs" as used in this subsection, means those costs awarded to prevailing parties in civil actions under RCW **4.84.010**or **36.18.040**, or those costs awarded against convicted defendants in criminal actions under RCW **10.01.160**, **10.46.190**, or **36.18.040**, or other similar statutes if such costs are specifically designated as costs by the court and are awarded for the specific reimbursement of costs incurred by the state or county in the prosecution of the case, including the fees of defense counsel. Costs or assessments awarded to dedicated accounts, state or local, are not subject to this state allocation or to RCW **7.68.035**.

(3) All fees, fines, forfeitures and penalties collected or assessed by a district court because of the violation of a state law shall be remitted as provided in chapter **3.62** RCW as now exists or is later amended. All fees, fines, forfeitures, and penalties collected or assessed by a superior court in cases on appeal from a lower court shall be remitted to the municipal or district court from which the cases were appealed.

[2012 c 136 § 6; 2012 c 134 § 8; 2009 c 479 § 13; 2004 c 15 § 6; 1995 c 292 § 3; 1988 c 169 § 5; 1987 c 202 § 169; 1985 c 389 § 7; 1984 c 258 § 313; 1969 ex.s. c 199 § 11; 1967 c 122 § 1; 1965 c 158 § 16; 1919 c 30 § 1; 1909 p 323 § 9; 1897 c 118 § 113; 1895 c 68 § 1; 1890 p 383 § 89; 1886 p 20 § 58; Code 1881 § 3211; 1873 p 421 § 3; RRS § 4940. Formerly codified as RCW 9.01.140.]

NOTES:

Effective date—2009 c 479: See note following RCW **2.56.030**.

Intent—2004 c 15: See note following RCW **10.99.080**.

Intent—1987 c 202: See note following RCW **2.04.190**.

Effective date—1985 c 389: See note following RCW **27.24.070**.

Court Improvement Act of 1984—Effective dates—Severability—Short title—1984 c 258: See notes following RCW **3.30.010**.

Intent—1984 c 258: See note following RCW **3.34.130**.

10.82.080

Unlawful receipt of public assistance—Deduction from subsequent assistance payments—Restitution payments.

(1) When a superior court has, as a condition of the sentence for a person convicted of the unlawful receipt of public assistance, ordered restitution to the state of that overpayment or a portion thereof:

(a) The department of social and health services shall deduct the overpayment from subsequent assistance payments as provided in RCW **43.20B.630**, when the person is receiving public assistance; or

(b) Ordered restitution payments may be made at the direction of the court to the clerk of the appropriate county or directly to the department of social and health services when the person is not receiving public assistance.

(2) However, if payments are received by the county clerk, each payment shall be transmitted to the department of social and health services within forty-five days after receipt by the county.
[**1987 c 75 § 2; 1985 c 245 § 2; 1982 c 201 § 1.**]
NOTES:

Savings—1987 c 75: See RCW **43.20B.900**.

10.82.090

Interest on judgments—Disposition of nonrestitution interest.

(1) Except as provided in subsection (2) of this section, financial obligations imposed in a judgment shall bear interest from the date of the judgment until payment, at the rate applicable to civil judgments. All nonrestitution interest retained by the court shall be split twenty-five percent to the state treasurer for deposit in the state general fund, twenty-five percent to the state treasurer for deposit in the judicial information system account as provided in RCW **2.68.020**, twenty-five percent to the county current expense fund, and twenty-five percent to the county current expense fund to fund local courts.

(2) The court may, on motion by the offender, following the offender's release from total confinement, reduce or waive the interest on legal financial obligations levied as a result of a criminal conviction as follows:

(a) The court shall waive all interest on the portions of the legal financial obligations that are not restitution that accrued during the term of total confinement for the conviction giving rise to the financial obligations, provided the offender shows that the interest creates a hardship for the offender or his or her immediate family;

(b) The court may reduce interest on the restitution portion of the legal financial obligations only if the principal has been paid in full;

(c) The court may otherwise reduce or waive the interest on the portions of the legal financial obligations that are not restitution if the offender shows that he or she has personally made a good faith effort to pay and that the interest accrual is causing a significant hardship. For purposes of this section, "good faith effort" means that the offender has either (i) paid the principal amount in full; or (ii) made at least fifteen monthly payments within an eighteen-month period, excluding any payments mandatorily deducted by the department of corrections;

(d) For purposes of (a) through (c) of this subsection, the court may reduce or waive interest on legal financial obligations only as an incentive for the offender to meet his or her legal financial obligations. The court may grant the motion, establish a payment schedule, and retain jurisdiction over the offender for purposes of reviewing and revising the reduction or waiver of interest.

(3) This section only applies to adult offenders.

[**2015 c 265 § 23; 2011 c 106 § 2; 2009 c 479 § 14; 2004 c 121 § 1; 1995 c 291 § 7; 1989 c 276 § 3.**]

NOTES:

> **Finding—Intent—2015 c 265:** See note following RCW **13.50.010**.

> **Finding—2011 c 106:** "(1) The legislature finds that it is in the interest of the public to promote the reintegration into society of individuals convicted of crimes. Research indicates that legal financial obligations may constitute a significant barrier to successful reintegration. The legislature further recognizes that the accrual of interest on nonrestitution debt during the term of incarceration results in many individuals leaving prison with insurmountable debt. These circumstances make it less likely that restitution will be paid in full and more likely that former offenders and their families will remain in poverty. In order to foster reintegration, this act creates a mechanism for courts to eliminate interest accrued on nonrestitution debt during incarceration and improves incentives for payment of legal financial obligations.

> (2) At the same time, the legislature believes that payment of legal financial obligations is an important part of taking personal responsibility for one's actions. The legislature therefore, supports the efforts of county clerks in taking collection action against those who do not make a good faith effort to pay." [**2011 c 106 § 1.**]

> **Effective date—2009 c 479:** See note following RCW **2.56.030**.

> **Severability—1989 c 276:** See note following RCW **9.95.062**.

Chapter 10.85 RCW REWARDS

NOTES:

Offer of rewards by governor: RCW **43.06.010**(8).

10.85.030
Rewards by counties, cities, towns, port commissions authorized.

The legislative authority of any county in the state, a port commission, or the governing body of a city or town, when in its opinion the public good requires it, is hereby authorized to offer and pay a suitable reward to any person or persons for information leading to:

(a) The arrest of a specified person or persons convicted of or charged with any criminal offense; or

(b) The arrest and conviction of a person or persons committing a specified criminal offense.

In the event of crimes against county, port district, city, or town property, including but not limited to road signs, vehicles, buildings, or any other type of county, port district, city, or town property, the legislative authority of any county, a port commission, or the governing body of a city or town may offer and pay a suitable reward to any person or persons who shall furnish information leading to the arrest and conviction of any person of any offense against this county, port district, city, or town property, including but not limited to those offenses set forth in RCW9A.48.070 through 9A.48.090, whether or not the offense is a felony, gross misdemeanor, or misdemeanor.

[1986 c 185 § 1; 1981 c 211 § 1; 1979 ex.s. c 53 § 1; 1975-'76 2nd ex.s. c 25 § 1; 1886 p 124 § 1; RRS § 2249.]

10.85.040

Conflicting claims.

When more than one claimant applies for the payment of any reward, offered by any county legislative authority, board of commissioners of a port district, or city or town governing body, the county legislative authority, board of commissioners of a port district, or city or town governing body shall determine to whom the same shall be paid, and if to more than one person, in what proportion to each; and their determination shall be final and conclusive.

[1986 c 185 § 2; 1979 ex.s. c 53 § 2; 1886 p 124 § 3; RRS § 2251.]

10.85.050
Payment of rewards.

Whenever any reward has been offered by any county legislative authority, board of commissioners of a port district, or city or town governing body in the state under RCW **10.85.030**, the person or persons providing the information shall be entitled to the reward, and the county legislative authority, board of commissioners of a port district, or city or town governing body which has offered the reward is authorized to draw a warrant or warrants out of any money in the county, port district, or city or town treasury, as appropriate, not otherwise appropriated.

[**1986 c 185 § 3; 1979 ex.s. c 53 § 3; 1886 p 124 § 2;** RRS § 2250.]

Chapter 10.88 RCW UNIFORM CRIMINAL EXTRADITION ACT

NOTES:

Fugitives of this state: Chapter **10.34** RCW.

Interstate compact on juveniles: Chapter **13.24** RCW.

Return of parole violators from another state: RCW **9.95.280** through **9.95.300**.

10.88.200
Definitions.

Where appearing in this chapter, the term "governor" includes any person performing the functions of governor by authority of the law of this state. The term "executive authority" includes the governor, and any person performing the functions of governor in a state other than this state, and the term "state" referring to a state other than this state refers to any other state, or the District of Columbia, or territory organized or unorganized of the United States of America.

[**1971 ex.s. c 46 § 1.**]

NOTES:

   Reviser's note: Throughout this chapter, the phrase "this act" has been changed to "this chapter." This act [1971 ex.s. c 46] consists of this chapter, the 1971 amendment of RCW **26.21.050**, and the repeal of RCW **10.88.010** through **10.88.060**.

10.88.210
Authority of governor.

   Subject to the provisions of this chapter, the provisions of the Constitution of the United States controlling, and any and all acts of congress enacted in pursuance thereof, the governor of this state may in his or her discretion have arrested and delivered up to the executive authority of any other state of the United States any person charged in that state with treason, felony, or other crime, who has fled from justice and is found in this state.

[**2010 c 8 § 1066; 1971 ex.s. c 46 § 2.**]

10.88.220
Demand for extradition—Requirements.

   No demand for the extradition of a person charged with crime in another state shall be recognized by the governor unless in writing alleging, except in cases arising under RCW **10.88.250**, that the accused was present in the demanding state at the time of the commission of the alleged crime, and that thereafter he or she fled from the state, and accompanied by a copy of an indictment found or by information supported by affidavit in the state having jurisdiction of the crime, or by a copy of an affidavit made before a magistrate there, together with a copy of any warrant which was issued thereupon; or by a copy of a judgment of conviction or of a sentence imposed in execution thereof, together with a statement by the executive authority of the demanding state that the person claimed has escaped from confinement or has broken the terms of his or her bail, probation, or parole. The indictment, information, or affidavit made before the magistrate must substantially charge the person demanded with having committed a crime under the law of that state; and the copy of indictment, information, affidavit, judgment of conviction, or sentence must be certified or authenticated by the executive authority making the demand.

[**2010 c 8 § 1067; 1971 ex.s. c 46 § 3.**]

10.88.230
Investigation of demand—Report.

When a demand shall be made upon the governor of this state by the executive authority of another state for the surrender of a person so charged with crime, the governor may call upon the attorney general or any prosecuting officer in this state to investigate or assist in investigating the demand, and to report to him or her the situation and circumstances of the person so demanded, and whether he or she ought to be surrendered.

[**2010 c 8 § 1068; 1971 ex.s. c 46 § 4.**]

10.88.240
Return or surrender of person charged in another state.

When it is desired to have returned to this state a person charged in this state with a crime, and such person is imprisoned or is held under criminal proceedings then pending against him or her in another state, the governor of this state may agree with the executive authority of such other state for the extradition of such person before the conclusion of such proceedings or his or her term of sentence in such other state, upon condition that such person be returned to such other state at the expense of this state as soon as the prosecution in this state is terminated.

The governor of this state may also surrender on demand of the executive authority of any other state any person in this state who is charged in the manner provided in RCW **10.88.410** with having violated the laws of the state whose executive authority is making the demand, even though such person left the demanding state involuntarily.

[**2010 c 8 § 1069;** **1971 ex.s. c 46 § 5.**]

10.88.250
Surrender of person charged with crime committed in state other than demanding state.

The governor of this state may also surrender, on demand of the executive authority of any other state, any person in this state charged in such other state in the manner provided in RCW **10.88.220** with committing an act in this state, or in a third state, intentionally resulting in a crime in the state whose executive authority is making the demand, and the provisions of this chapter not otherwise inconsistent, shall apply to such cases, even though the accused was not in that state at the time of the commission of the crime, and has not fled therefrom.

[**1971 ex.s. c 46 § 6.**]

10.88.260
Warrant of arrest.

If the governor decides that the demand should be complied with, he or she shall sign a warrant of arrest, which shall be sealed with the state seal, and be directed to any peace officer or other person whom he or she may think fit to entrust with the execution thereof. The warrant must substantially recite the facts necessary to the validity of its issuance.

[**2010 c 8 § 1070;** **1971 ex.s. c 46 § 7.**]

10.88.270
Authority of officer or other person under warrant.

Such warrant shall authorize the peace officer or other person to whom directed to arrest the accused at any time and any place where he or she may be found within the state and to command the aid of all peace officers or other persons in the execution of the warrant, and to deliver the accused, subject to the provisions of this chapter to the duly authorized agent of the demanding state.

[**2010 c 8 § 1071**; **1971 ex.s. c 46 § 8.**]

10.88.280
Authority to command assistance.

Every such peace officer or other person empowered to make the arrest, shall have the same authority, in arresting the accused, to command assistance therein, as peace officers have by law in the execution of any criminal process directed to them, with like penalties against those who refuse their assistance.

[**1971 ex.s. c 46 § 9.**]

10.88.290
Rights of person arrested.

No person arrested upon such warrant shall be delivered over to the agent whom the executive authority demanding him or her shall have appointed to receive him or her unless he or she shall first be taken forthwith before a judge of a court of record in this state, who shall inform him or her of the demand made for his or her surrender and of the crime with which he or she is charged, and that he or she has the right to demand and procure legal counsel; and if the prisoner or his or her counsel shall state that he or she or they desire to test the legality of his or her arrest, the judge of such court of record shall fix a reasonable time to be allowed him or her within which to apply for a writ of habeas corpus. When such writ is applied for, notice thereof, and of the time and place of hearing thereon, shall be given to the prosecuting officer of the county in which the arrest is made and in which the accused is in custody, and to the said agent of the demanding state: PROVIDED, That the hearing provided for in this section shall not be available except as may be constitutionally required if a hearing on the legality of arrest has been held pursuant to RCW **10.88.320** or **10.88.330**.

[**2010 c 8 § 1072**; **1971 ex.s. c 46 § 10.**]

10.88.300

Delivery of person in violation of RCW 10.88.290—Penalty.

Any officer who shall deliver to the agent for extradition of the demanding state a person in his or her custody under the governor's warrant, in wilful [willful] disobedience to RCW **10.88.290**, shall be guilty of a gross misdemeanor and, on conviction, shall be imprisoned in the county jail for up to three hundred sixty-four days, or be fined not more than one thousand dollars, or both.

[**2011 c 96 § 14; 2010 c 8 § 1073; 1971 ex.s. c 46 § 11.**]

NOTES:

Findings—Intent—2011 c 96: See note following RCW **9A.20.021**.

10.88.310

Confinement of prisoner.

The officer or persons executing the governor's warrant of arrest, or the agent of the demanding state to whom the prisoner may have been delivered may, when necessary, confine the prisoner in the jail of any county or city through which he or she may pass; and the keeper of such jail must receive and safely keep the prisoner until the officer or person having charge of him or her is ready to proceed on his or her route, such officer or person being chargeable with the expense of keeping.

The officer or agent of a demanding state to whom a prisoner may have been delivered following extradition proceedings in another state, or to whom a prisoner may have been delivered after waiving extradition in such other state, and who is passing through this state with such a prisoner for the purpose of immediately returning such prisoner to the demanding state may, when necessary, confine the prisoner in the jail of any county or city through which he or she may pass; and the keeper of such jail must receive and safely keep the prisoner until the officer or agent having charge of him or her is ready to proceed on his or her route, such officer or agent, however, being chargeable with the expense of keeping: PROVIDED, HOWEVER, That such officer or agent shall produce and show to the keeper of such jail satisfactory written evidence of the fact that he or she is actually transporting such prisoner to the demanding state after a requisition by the executive authority of such demanding state. Such prisoner shall not be entitled to demand a new requisition while in this state.

[**2010 c 8 § 1074; 1971 ex.s. c 46 § 12.**]

10.88.320
Charge or complaint—Warrant of arrest.

Whenever any person within this state shall be charged on the oath of any credible person before any judge or magistrate of this state with the commission of any crime in any other state and, except in cases arising under RCW **10.88.250**, with having fled from justice, or with having been convicted of a crime in that state and having escaped from confinement, or having broken the terms of his or her bail, probation, or parole, or whenever complaint shall have been made before any judge or magistrate in this state setting forth on the affidavit of any credible person in another state that a crime has been committed in such other state and that the accused has been charged in such state with the commission of the crime, and, except in cases arising under RCW **10.88.250**, has fled from justice, or with having been convicted of a crime in that state and having escaped from confinement, or having broken the terms of his or her bail, probation, or parole and is believed to be in this state, the judge or magistrate shall issue a warrant directed to any peace officer commanding him or her to apprehend the person named therein, wherever he or she may be found in this state, and to bring him or her before the same or any other judge, magistrate or court who or which may be available in or convenient of access to the place where the arrest may be made, to answer the charge or complaint and affidavit, and a certified copy of the sworn charge or complaint and affidavit upon which the warrant is issued shall be attached to the warrant.

[**2010 c 8 § 1075; 1971 ex.s. c 46 § 13.**]

10.88.330

Arrest without warrant.

(1) The arrest of a person may be lawfully made also by any peace officer or a private person, without a warrant upon reasonable information that the accused stands charged in the courts of a state with a crime punishable by death or imprisonment for a term exceeding one year, but when so arrested the accused must be taken before a judge or magistrate with all practicable speed and complaint must be made against him or her under oath setting forth the ground for the arrest as in RCW **10.88.320**; and thereafter his or her answer shall be heard as if he or she had been arrested on a warrant.

(2) An officer of the United States customs service or the immigration and naturalization service may, without a warrant, arrest a person if:

(a) The officer is on duty;

(b) One or more of the following situations exists:

(i) The person commits an assault or other crime involving physical harm, defined and punishable under chapter **9A.36** RCW, against the officer or against any other person in the presence of the officer;

(ii) The person commits an assault or related crime while armed, defined and punishable under chapter **9.41** RCW, against the officer or against any other person in the presence of the officer;

(iii) The officer has reasonable cause to believe that a crime as defined in (b)(i) or (ii) of this subsection has been committed and reasonable cause to believe that the person to be arrested has committed it;

(iv) The officer has reasonable cause to believe that a felony has been committed and reasonable cause to believe that the person to be arrested has committed it; or

(v) The officer has received positive information by written, telegraphic, teletypic, telephonic, radio, or other authoritative source that a peace officer holds a warrant for the person's arrest; and

(c) The regional commissioner of customs certifies to the state of Washington that the customs officer has received proper training within the agency to enable that officer to enforce or administer this subsection.

[**2010 c 8 § 1076; 1979 ex.s. c 244 § 16; 1971 ex.s. c 46 § 14.**]
NOTES:

        Effective date—1979 ex.s. c 244: See RCW **9A.44.902**.

10.88.340
Preliminary examination—Commitment.

If from the examination before the judge or magistrate it appears that the person held is the person charged with having committed the crime alleged and, except in cases arising under RCW **10.88.250**, that he or she has fled from justice, the judge or magistrate must, by a warrant reciting the accusation, commit him or her to the county jail for such a time not exceeding thirty days and specified in the warrant, as will enable the arrest of the accused to be made under a warrant of the governor on a requisition of the executive authority of the state having jurisdiction of the offense, unless the accused give bail as provided in RCW **10.88.350**, or until he or she shall be legally discharged.
[**2010 c 8 § 1077; 1971 ex.s. c 46 § 15.**]

10.88.350
Bail.

Unless the offense with which the prisoner is charged is shown to be an offense punishable by death or life imprisonment under the laws of the state in which it was committed, a judge or magistrate in this state may admit the person arrested to bail by bond, with sufficient sureties, and in such sum as he or she deems proper, conditioned for his or her appearance before him or her at a time specified in such a bond, and for his or her surrender, to be arrested upon the warrant of the governor of this state.
[**2010 c 8 § 1078; 1971 ex.s. c 46 § 16.**]

10.88.360

Failure to make timely arrest or demand for extradition.

If the accused is not arrested under warrant of the governor by the expiration of the time specified in the warrant or bond, a judge or magistrate may discharge him or her or may recommit him or her for a further period not to exceed sixty days, or a judge or magistrate judge may again take bail for his or her appearance and surrender, as provided in RCW **10.88.350**, but within a period not to exceed sixty days after the date of such new bond: PROVIDED, That the governor may, except in cases in which the offense is punishable under laws of the demanding state by death or life imprisonment, deny a demand for extradition when such demand is not received by the governor before the expiration of one hundred twenty days from the date of arrest in this state of the alleged fugitive, in the absence of a showing of good cause for such delay.
[**2010 c 8 § 1079; 1971 ex.s. c 46 § 17.**]

10.88.370

Failure to appear—Bond forfeiture—Arrest—Recovery on bond.

If the prisoner is admitted to bail, and fails to appear and surrender himself or herself according to the conditions of his or her bond, the judge, or magistrate by proper order, shall declare the bond forfeited and order his or her immediate arrest without warrant if he or she be within this state. Recovery may be had on such bond in the name of the state as in the case of other bonds given by the accused in criminal proceedings within this state.
[**2010 c 8 § 1080; 1971 ex.s. c 46 § 18.**]

10.88.380

Pending criminal prosecution in this state.

If a criminal prosecution has been instituted against such person under the laws of this state and is still pending the governor, in his or her discretion, either may surrender him or her on demand of the executive authority of another state or hold him or her until he or she has been tried and discharged or convicted and punished in this state.

[**2010 c 8 § 1081**; **1971 ex.s. c 46 § 19.**]

10.88.390
Recall or reissuance of warrant.

The governor may recall his or her warrant of arrest or may issue another warrant whenever he or she deems proper.

[**2010 c 8 § 1082**; **1971 ex.s. c 46 § 20.**]

10.88.400
Demand by governor of this state for extradition—Warrant—Agent.

Whenever the governor of this state shall demand a person charged with crime or with escaping from confinement or breaking the terms of his or her bail, probation, or parole in this state, from the executive authority of any other state, or from the appropriate authority of the District of Columbia authorized to receive such demand under the laws of the United States, he or she shall issue a warrant under the seal of this state, to some agent, commanding him or her to receive the person so charged if delivered to him or her and convey him or her to the proper officer of the county in this state in which the offense was committed.

[**2010 c 8 § 1083**; **1971 ex.s. c 46 § 21.**]

10.88.410
Application for requisition for return of person—Contents—Affidavits—Copies.

(1) When the return to this state of a person charged with crime in this state is required, the prosecuting attorney shall present to the governor his or her written application for a requisition for the return of the person charged, in which application shall be stated the name of the person so charged, the crime charged against him or

her, the approximate time, place, and circumstances of its commission, the state in which he or she is believed to be, including the location of the accused therein at the time the application is made and certifying that, in the opinion of the said prosecuting attorney the ends of justice require the arrest and return of the accused to this state for trial and that the proceeding is not instituted to enforce a private claim.

(2) When the return to this state is required of a person who has been convicted of a crime in this state and has escaped from confinement or broken the terms of his or her bail, probation, or parole, the prosecuting attorney of the county in which the offense was committed, the parole board, or the warden of the institution or sheriff of the county, from which escape was made, shall present to the governor a written application for a requisition for the return of such person, in which application shall be stated the name of the person, the crime of which he or she was convicted, the circumstances of his or her escape from confinement or of the breach of the terms of his or her bail, probation, or parole, the state in which he or she is believed to be, including the location of the person therein at the time application is made.

(3) The application shall be verified by affidavit, shall be executed in duplicate, and shall be accompanied by two certified copies of the indictment returned, or information and affidavit filed, or of the complaint made to the judge or magistrate, stating the offense with which the accused is charged, or of the judgment of conviction or of the sentence. The prosecuting officer, parole board, warden, or sheriff may also attach such further affidavits and other documents in duplicate as he or she shall deem proper to be submitted with such application. One copy of the application, with the action of the governor indicated by endorsement thereon, and one of the certified copies of the indictment, complaint, information, and affidavits, or of the judgment of conviction or of the sentence shall be filed in the office of the secretary of state to remain of record in that office. The other copies of all papers shall be forwarded with the governor's requisition.

[**2010 c 8 § 1084; 1971 ex.s. c 46 § 22.**]

10.88.415
Delivery without governor's warrant.

A law enforcement agency shall deliver a person in custody to the accredited agent or agents of a demanding state without the governor's warrant provided that:

(1) Such person is alleged to have broken the terms of his or her probation, parole, bail, or any other release of the demanding state; and

(2) The law enforcement agency has received from the demanding state an authenticated copy of a prior waiver of extradition signed by such person as a term of his or her probation, parole, bail, or any other release of the demanding state and photographs or fingerprints or other evidence properly identifying the person as the person who signed the waiver.

[2001 c 264 § 6.]

NOTES:

Effective date—2001 c 264: See note following RCW 9A.76.110.

10.88.420
Civil process—Service on extradited person.

A person brought into this state by, or after waiver of, extradition based on a criminal charge shall not be subject to service of personal process in civil actions arising out of the same facts as the criminal proceeding to answer which he or she is being or has been returned, until he or she has been finally convicted in the criminal proceeding, or, if acquitted, until he or she has had reasonable opportunity to return to the state from which he or she was extradited.

[2010 c 8 § 1085; 1971 ex.s. c 46 § 23.]

10.88.430
Waiver of extradition.

Any person arrested in this state charged with having committed any crime in another state or alleged to have escaped from confinement, or broken the terms of his or her bail, probation, or parole may waive the issuance and service of the warrant provided for in RCW **10.88.260**and **10.88.270** and all other procedure incidental to extradition proceedings, by executing or subscribing in the presence of a judge of any court of record within this state a writing which states that he or she consents to return to the demanding state: PROVIDED, HOWEVER, That before such waiver shall be executed or subscribed by such person it shall be the duty of such judge to inform such person of his or her rights to the issuance and service of a warrant of extradition and to obtain a writ of habeas corpus as provided for in RCW **10.88.290**.

If and when such consent has been duly executed it shall forthwith be forwarded to the office of the governor of this state and filed therein. The judge shall direct the officer having such person in custody to deliver forthwith such person to the duly accredited agent or agents of the demanding state, and shall deliver or cause to be delivered to such agent or agents a copy of such consent: PROVIDED, HOWEVER, That nothing in this section shall be deemed to limit the rights of the accused person to return voluntarily and without formality to the demanding state, nor shall this waiver procedure be deemed to be an exclusive procedure or to limit the powers, rights, or duties of the officers of the demanding state or of this state.

[**2010 c 8 § 1086;** **1971 ex.s. c 46 § 24.**]

10.88.440
Rights, powers, privileges or jurisdiction of state not waived.

Nothing in this chapter contained shall be deemed to constitute a waiver by this state of its right, power or privilege to try such demanded person for crime committed within this state, or of its right, power or privilege to regain custody of such person by extradition proceedings or otherwise for the purpose of trial, sentence or punishment for any crime committed within this state, nor shall any proceedings had under this chapter which result in, or fail to result in, extradition be deemed a waiver by this state of any of its rights, privileges or jurisdiction in any way whatsoever.

[**1971 ex.s. c 46 § 25.**]

10.88.450

Trial for other crimes.

After a person has been brought back to this state by, or after waiver of extradition proceedings, he or she may be tried in this state for other crimes which he or she may be charged with having committed here as well as that specified in the requisition for his or her extradition.

[**2010 c 8 § 1087; 1971 ex.s. c 46 § 26.**]

10.88.460

Extradition or surrender of obligor—Uniform interstate family support act.

See chapter **26.21A** RCW.

10.88.900

Construction—1971 ex.s. c 46.

The provisions of this chapter shall be so interpreted and construed as to effectuate its general purposes to make uniform the law of those states which enact it, to the extent which it has been enacted by this state.

[**1971 ex.s. c 46 § 27.**]

10.88.910

Short title.

RCW **10.88.200** through **10.88.450** shall be known and may be cited as the Uniform Criminal Extradition Act.

[**1971 ex.s. c 46 § 28.**]

10.88.920

Effective date—1971 ex.s. c 46.

This act shall become effective on July 1, 1971.

[**1971 ex.s. c 46 § 29.**]

Chapter 10.89 RCW UNIFORM ACT ON FRESH PURSUIT

10.89.010
Authority of foreign peace officer.

Any member of a duly organized state, county or municipal peace unit of another state of the United States who enters this state in fresh pursuit, and continues within this state in such fresh pursuit, of a person in order to arrest the person on the ground that he or she is believed to have committed a felony in such other state or a violation of the laws of such other state relating to driving while intoxicated, driving under the influence of drugs or alcohol, driving while impaired, or reckless driving shall have the same authority to arrest and hold such person in custody as has any member of any duly organized state, county or municipal peace unit of this state, to arrest and hold in custody a person on the ground that he or she is believed to have committed a felony or a violation of the laws of such other state relating to driving while intoxicated, driving under the influence of drugs or alcohol, driving while impaired, or reckless driving in this state.

[**1998 c 205 § 1; 1943 c 261 § 1;** Rem. Supp. 1943 § 2252-1. Formerly RCW **10.88.070.**]

10.89.020
Preliminary examination by magistrate.

If an arrest is made in this state by an officer of another state in accordance with the provisions of RCW **10.89.010**, he or she shall, without unnecessary delay, take the person arrested before a magistrate of the county in which the arrest was made, who shall conduct a hearing for the purpose of determining the lawfulness of the arrest. If the magistrate determines that the arrest was lawful, he or she shall commit the person arrested to await for a reasonable time the issuance of an extradition warrant by the governor of this state. If the magistrate determines that the arrest was unlawful, he or she shall discharge the person arrested.

[**2010 c 8 § 1088; 1943 c 261 § 2;** Rem. Supp. 1943 § 2252-2. Formerly RCW **10.88.080.**]

10.89.030
Construction as to lawfulness of arrest.

RCW **10.89.010** shall not be construed so as to make unlawful any arrest in this state which otherwise would be lawful.

[**1943 c 261 § 3;** Rem. Supp. 1943 § 2252-3. Formerly RCW **10.88.100.**]

10.89.040
"State" includes District of Columbia.

For the purpose of this chapter the word "state" shall include the District of Columbia.

[**1943 c 261 § 4;** Rem. Supp. 1943 § 2252-4. Formerly RCW **10.88.110.**]

10.89.050
"Fresh pursuit" defined.

The term "fresh pursuit" as used in this chapter, shall include fresh pursuit as defined by the common law, and also the pursuit of a person who has committed a felony or who reasonably is suspected of having committed a felony or a violation of such other state relating to driving while intoxicated, driving under the influence of drugs or alcohol, driving while impaired, or reckless driving. It shall also include the pursuit of a person suspected of having committed a supposed felony, or a supposed violation of the laws relating to driving while intoxicated, driving under the influence of drugs or

alcohol, driving while impaired, or reckless driving, though no felony or violation of the laws relating to driving while intoxicated, driving under the influence of drugs or alcohol, driving while impaired, or reckless driving actually has been committed, if there is reasonable ground for believing that a felony or a violation of the laws relating to driving while intoxicated, driving under the influence of drugs or alcohol, driving while impaired, or reckless driving has been committed. Fresh pursuit as used herein shall not necessarily imply instant pursuit, but pursuit without unreasonable delay.
[**1998 c 205 § 2; 1943 c 261 § 5;** Rem. Supp. 1943 § 2252-5. Formerly RCW **10.88.090.**]

10.89.060
Duty to send copies to other states.

Upon the passage and approval by the governor of this chapter, it shall be the duty of the secretary of state, or other officer, to certify a copy of this chapter to the executive department of each of the states of the United States.
[**1943 c 261 § 6;** Rem. Supp. 1943 § 2252-6.]

10.89.080
Short title.

This chapter may be cited as the "Uniform Act on Fresh Pursuit."
[**1943 c 261 § 8;** Rem. Supp. 1943 § 2252-8.]

Chapter 10.91 RCW UNIFORM RENDITION OF ACCUSED PERSONS ACT

10.91.010

Arrest and return of released person charged in another state—Violation of release conditions—Request—Documents—Warrant—Investigation.

(1) If a person who has been charged with crime in another state and released from custody prior to final judgment, including the final disposition of any appeal, is alleged to have violated the terms and conditions of his or her release, and is present in this state, a designated agent of the court, judge, or magistrate which authorized the release may request the issuance of a warrant for the arrest of the person and an order authorizing his or her return to the demanding court, judge, or magistrate. Before the warrant is issued, the designated agent must file with a judicial officer of this state the following documents:

(a) An affidavit stating the name and whereabouts of the person whose removal is sought, the crime with which the person was charged, the time and place of the crime charged, and the status of the proceedings against him or her;

(b) A certified copy of the order or other document specifying the terms and conditions under which the person was released from custody; and

(c) A certified copy of an order of the demanding court, judge, or magistrate stating the manner in which the terms and the conditions of the release have been violated and designating the affiant its agent for seeking removal of the person.

(2) Upon initially determining that the affiant is a designated agent of the demanding court, judge, or magistrate, and that there is a probable cause for believing that the person whose removal is sought has violated the terms or conditions of his or her release, the judicial officer shall issue a warrant to a law enforcement officer of this state for the person's arrest.

(3) The judicial officer shall notify the prosecuting attorney of his or her action and shall direct him or her to investigate the case to ascertain the validity of the affidavits and documents required by subsection (1) of this section and the identity and authority of the affiant.

[**2010 c 8 § 1089; 1971 ex.s. c 17 § 2.**]

10.91.020

Preliminary hearing—Waiver—Conditions of release.

(1) The person whose removal is sought shall be brought before the judicial officer without unnecessary delay upon arrest pursuant to the warrant; whereupon the judicial officer shall set a time and place for hearing, and shall advise the person of his or her right to have the assistance of counsel, to confront the witnesses against him or her, and to produce evidence in his or her own behalf at the hearing.

(2) The person whose removal is sought may at this time in writing waive the hearing and agree to be returned to the demanding court, judge, or magistrate. If a waiver is executed, the judicial officer shall issue an order pursuant to RCW **10.91.030**.

(3) The judicial officer may impose conditions of release authorized by the laws of this state which will reasonably assure the appearance at the hearing of the person whose removal is sought.

[**2010 c 8 § 1090; 1971 ex.s. c 17 § 3.**]

10.91.030

Preliminary hearing—Investigation report—Findings—Order authorizing return.

The prosecuting attorney shall appear at the hearing and report to the judicial officer the results of his or her investigation. If the judicial officer finds that the affiant is a designated agent of the demanding court, judge, or magistrate and that the person whose removal is sought was released from custody by the demanding court, judge, or magistrate, and that the person has violated the terms or conditions of his or her release, the judicial officer shall issue an order authorizing the return of the person to the custody of the demanding court, judge, or magistrate forthwith.

[2010 c 8 § 1091; 1971 ex.s. c 17 § 4.]

10.91.040

"Judicial officer of this state," "judicial officer" defined.

For the purpose of this chapter "judicial officer of this state" and "judicial officer" mean a judge of the superior or district court.

[1987 c 202 § 170; 1971 ex.s. c 17 § 5.]

NOTES:

Intent—1987 c 202: See note following RCW 2.04.190.

10.91.050

Costs.

The costs of the procedures required by this chapter shall be borne by the demanding state, except when the designated agent is not a public official. In any case when the designated agent is not a public official, he or she shall bear the cost of such procedures.

[2010 c 8 § 1092; 1971 ex.s. c 17 § 9.]

10.91.910

Construction—1971 ex.s. c 17.

This chapter shall be so construed as to effectuate its general purpose to make uniform the law of those states which enact it.

[1971 ex.s. c 17 § 7.]

10.91.920

Short title.

This chapter may be cited as the "Uniform Rendition of Accused Persons Act."

Chapter 10.92 RCW TRIBAL POLICE OFFICERS

10.92.010
Definitions.

The definitions in this section apply throughout this chapter unless the context clearly requires otherwise.

(1) "General authority Washington peace officer" means an officer authorized to enforce the criminal and traffic laws of the state of Washington generally.

(2) "Tribal police officer" means any person in the employ of one of the federally recognized sovereign tribal governments, whose traditional lands and territories lie within the borders of the state of Washington, to enforce the criminal laws of that government.

[2008 c 224 § 1.]

NOTES:

Effective date—2008 c 224: "This act takes effect July 1, 2008." [**2008 c 224 §** 4.]

10.92.020
Powers—Authority to act as general authority Washington peace officer—Public liability and property damage insurance—Training requirements—Issuance of citation, notice of infraction, or incident report—Jurisdiction—Civil liability—Sovereign tribal governments— Interlocal agreement.

(1) Tribal police officers under subsection (2) of this section shall be recognized and authorized to act as general authority Washington peace officers. A tribal police officer

recognized and authorized to act as a general authority Washington peace officer under this section has the same powers as any other general authority Washington peace officer to enforce state laws in Washington, including the power to make arrests for violations of state laws.

(2) A tribal police officer may exercise the powers of law enforcement of a general authority Washington peace officer under this section, subject to the following:

(a) The appropriate sovereign tribal nation shall submit to the department of enterprise services proof of public liability and property damage insurance for vehicles operated by the peace officers and police professional liability insurance from a company licensed to sell insurance in the state. For purposes of determining adequacy of insurance liability, the sovereign tribal government must submit with the proof of liability insurance a copy of the interlocal agreement between the sovereign tribal government and the local governments that have shared jurisdiction under this chapter where such an agreement has been reached pursuant to subsection (10) of this section.

(i) Within the thirty days of receipt of the information from the sovereign tribal nation, the department of enterprise services shall either approve or reject the adequacy of insurance, giving consideration to the scope of the interlocal agreement. The adequacy of insurance under this chapter shall be subject to annual review by the department of enterprise services.

(ii) Each policy of insurance issued under this chapter must include a provision that the insurance shall be available to satisfy settlements or judgments arising from the tortious conduct of tribal police officers when acting in the capacity of a general authority Washington peace officer, and that to the extent of policy coverage neither the sovereign tribal nation nor the insurance carrier will raise a defense of sovereign immunity to preclude an action for damages under state or federal law, the determination of fault in a civil action, or the payment of a settlement or judgment arising from the tortious conduct.

(b) The appropriate sovereign tribal nation shall submit to the department of enterprise services proof of training requirements for each tribal police officer. To be authorized as a general authority Washington peace officer, a tribal police officer must successfully complete the requirements set forth under RCW **43.101.157**. Any applicant not meeting the requirements for certification as a tribal police officer may not act as a general authority Washington peace officer under this chapter. The criminal justice training commission shall notify the department of enterprise services if:

(i) A tribal police officer authorized under this chapter as a general authority Washington state peace officer has been decertified pursuant to RCW **43.101.157**; or

(ii) An appropriate sovereign tribal government is otherwise in noncompliance with RCW **43.101.157**.

(3) A copy of any citation or notice of infraction issued, or any incident report taken, by a tribal police officer acting in the capacity of a general authority Washington peace officer as authorized by this chapter must be submitted within three days to the police chief or sheriff within whose jurisdiction the action was taken. Any citation issued under this chapter shall be to a Washington court, except that any citation issued to Indians within the exterior boundaries of an Indian reservation may be cited to a tribal court. Any arrest made or citation issued not in compliance with this chapter is not enforceable.

(4) Any authorization granted under this chapter shall not in any way expand the jurisdiction of any tribal court or other tribal authority.

(5) The authority granted under this chapter shall be coextensive with the exterior boundaries of the reservation, except that an officer commissioned under this section may act as authorized under RCW **10.93.070** beyond the exterior boundaries of the reservation.

(6) For purposes of civil liability under this chapter, a tribal police officer shall not be considered an employee of the state of Washington or any local government except where a state or local government has deputized a tribal police officer as a specially commissioned officer. Neither the state of Washington and its individual employees nor any local government and its individual employees shall be liable for the authorization of tribal police officers under this chapter, nor for the negligence or other misconduct of tribal officers. The authorization of tribal police officers under this chapter shall not be deemed to have been a nondelegable duty of the state of Washington or any local government.

(7) Nothing in this chapter impairs or affects the existing status and sovereignty of those sovereign tribal governments whose traditional lands and territories lie within the borders of the state of Washington as established under the laws of the United States.

(8) Nothing in this chapter limits, impairs, or nullifies the authority of a county sheriff to appoint duly commissioned state or federally certified tribal police officers as deputy sheriffs authorized to enforce the criminal and traffic laws of the state of Washington.

(9) Nothing in this chapter limits, impairs, or otherwise affects the existing authority under state or federal law of state or local law enforcement officers to enforce state law within the exterior boundaries of an Indian reservation or to enter Indian country in fresh pursuit, as defined in RCW **10.93.120**, of a person suspected of violating state law, where the officer would otherwise not have jurisdiction.

(10) An interlocal agreement pursuant to chapter **39.34** RCW is required between the sovereign tribal government and all local government law enforcement agencies that will have shared jurisdiction under this chapter prior to authorization taking effect under this chapter. Nothing in this chapter shall limit, impair, or otherwise affect the implementation of an interlocal agreement completed pursuant to chapter **39.34** RCW by July 1, 2008, between a sovereign tribal government and a local government law enforcement agency for cooperative law enforcement.

(a) Sovereign tribal governments that meet all of the requirements of subsection (2) of this section, but do not have an interlocal agreement pursuant to chapter **39.34** RCW and seek authorization under this chapter, may submit proof of liability insurance and training certification to the department of enterprise services. Upon confirmation of receipt of the information from the department of enterprise services, the sovereign tribal government and the local government law enforcement agencies that will have shared jurisdiction under this chapter have one year to enter into an interlocal agreement pursuant to chapter **39.34** RCW. If the sovereign tribal government and the local government law enforcement agencies that will have shared jurisdiction under this chapter are not able to reach agreement after one year, the sovereign tribal governments and the local government law enforcement agencies shall submit to binding arbitration pursuant to chapter **7.04A** RCW with the American arbitration association or successor agency for purposes of completing an agreement prior to authorization going into effect.

(b) For the purposes of (a) of this subsection, those sovereign tribal government and local government law enforcement agencies that must enter into binding arbitration shall submit to last best offer arbitration. For purposes of accepting a last best offer, the arbitrator must consider other interlocal agreements between sovereign tribal governments and local law enforcement agencies in Washington state, any model policy developed by the Washington association of sheriffs and police chiefs or successor agency, and national best practices.

[**2011 1st sp.s. c 43 § 519; 2008 c 224 § 2.**]

NOTES:

      Effective date—Purpose—2011 1st sp.s. c 43: See notes following RCW **43.19.003**.

      Effective date—2008 c 224: See note following RCW **10.92.010**.

Chapter 10.93 RCW WASHINGTON MUTUAL AID PEACE OFFICERS POWERS ACT

10.93.001
Short title—Legislative intent—Construction.

(1) This chapter may be known and cited as the Washington mutual aid peace officer powers act of 1985.

(2) It is the intent of the legislature that current artificial barriers to mutual aid and cooperative enforcement of the laws among general authority local, state, and federal agencies be modified pursuant to this chapter.

(3) This chapter shall be liberally construed to effectuate the intent of the legislature to modify current restrictions upon the limited territorial and enforcement authority of general authority peace officers and to effectuate mutual aid among agencies.

(4) The modification of territorial and enforcement authority of the various categories of peace officers covered by this chapter shall not create a duty to act in extraterritorial situations beyond any duty which may otherwise be imposed by law or which may be imposed by the primary commissioning agency.

[**1985 c 89 § 1.**]

10.93.020
Definitions.

As used in this chapter, the following terms have the meanings indicated unless the context clearly requires otherwise.

(1) "General authority Washington law enforcement agency" means any agency, department, or division of a municipal corporation, political subdivision, or other unit of local government of this state, and any agency, department, or division of state government, having as its primary function the detection and apprehension of persons committing infractions or violating the traffic or criminal laws in general, as distinguished from a limited authority Washington law enforcement agency, and any other unit of government expressly designated by statute as a general authority Washington law enforcement agency. The Washington state patrol and the department of fish and wildlife are general authority Washington law enforcement agencies.

(2) "Limited authority Washington law enforcement agency" means any agency, political subdivision, or unit of local government of this state, and any agency, department, or division of state government, having as one of its functions the apprehension or detection of persons committing infractions or violating the traffic or criminal laws relating to limited subject areas, including but not limited to, the state departments of natural resources and social and health services, the state gambling commission, the state lottery commission, the state parks and recreation commission, the state utilities and transportation commission, the *state liquor control board, the office of the insurance commissioner, and the state department of corrections.

(3) "General authority Washington peace officer" means any full-time, fully compensated and elected, appointed, or employed officer of a general authority

Washington law enforcement agency who is commissioned to enforce the criminal laws of the state of Washington generally.

(4) "Limited authority Washington peace officer" means any full-time, fully compensated officer of a limited authority Washington law enforcement agency empowered by that agency to detect or apprehend violators of the laws in some or all of the limited subject areas for which that agency is responsible. A limited authority Washington peace officer may be a specially commissioned Washington peace officer if otherwise qualified for such status under this chapter.

(5) "Specially commissioned Washington peace officer", for the purposes of this chapter, means any officer, whether part-time or full-time, compensated or not, commissioned by a general authority Washington law enforcement agency to enforce some or all of the criminal laws of the state of Washington, who does not qualify under this chapter as a general authority Washington peace officer for that commissioning agency, specifically including reserve peace officers, and specially commissioned full-time, fully compensated peace officers duly commissioned by the states of Oregon or Idaho or any such peace officer commissioned by a unit of local government of Oregon or Idaho. A reserve peace officer is an individual who is an officer of a Washington law enforcement agency who does not serve such agency on a full-time basis but who, when called by the agency into active service, is fully commissioned on the same basis as full-time peace officers to enforce the criminal laws of the state.

(6) "Federal peace officer" means any employee or agent of the United States government who has the authority to carry firearms and make warrantless arrests and whose duties involve the enforcement of criminal laws of the United States.

(7) "Agency with primary territorial jurisdiction" means a city or town police agency which has responsibility for police activity within its boundaries; or a county police or sheriff's department which has responsibility with regard to police activity in the unincorporated areas within the county boundaries; or a statutorily authorized port district police agency or four-year state college or university police agency which has responsibility for police activity within the statutorily authorized enforcement boundaries of the port district, state college, or university.

(8) "Primary commissioning agency" means (a) the employing agency in the case of a general authority Washington peace officer, a limited authority Washington peace officer, an Indian tribal peace officer, or a federal peace officer, and (b) the commissioning agency in the case of a specially commissioned Washington peace officer (i) who is performing functions within the course and scope of the special commission and (ii) who is not also a general authority Washington peace officer, a limited authority Washington peace officer, an Indian tribal peace officer, or a federal peace officer.

(9) "Primary function of an agency" means that function to which greater than fifty percent of the agency's resources are allocated.

(10) "Mutual law enforcement assistance" includes, but is not limited to, one or more law enforcement agencies aiding or assisting one or more other such agencies through loans or exchanges of personnel or of material resources, for law enforcement purposes.
[2006 c 284 § 16; 2002 c 128 § 1; 1994 c 264 § 3; 1988 c 36 § 5; 1985 c 89 § 2.]
NOTES:

*Reviser's note: The "state liquor control board" was renamed the "state liquor and cannabis board" by **2015 c 70 § 3.**

Effective date—2006 c 284: See RCW **48.135.901.**

10.93.030
Reporting use of authority under this chapter.

The circumstances surrounding any actual exercise of peace officer authority under this chapter shall be timely reported, after the fact, to the Washington law enforcement agency with primary territorial jurisdiction and shall be subject to any reasonable reporting procedure which may be established by such agency.
[1985 c 89 § 3.]

10.93.040
Liability for exercise of authority.

Any liability or claim of liability which arises out of the exercise or alleged exercise of authority by an officer acting within the course and scope of the officer's duties as a peace officer under this chapter is the responsibility of the primary commissioning agency unless the officer acts under the direction and control of another agency or unless the liability is otherwise allocated under a written agreement between the primary commissioning agency and another agency.

[**1985 c 89 § 4.**]

10.93.050
Supervisory control over peace officers.

All persons exercising peace officer powers under this chapter are subject to supervisory control of and limitations imposed by the primary commissioning agency, but the primary commissioning agency may, by agreement with another agency, temporarily delegate supervision over the peace officer to another agency.

[**1985 c 89 § 5.**]

10.93.060
Privileges and immunities applicable.

All of the privileges and immunities from liability, exemption from laws, ordinances, and rules, all pension, relief, disability, worker's compensation insurance, and other benefits which apply to the activity of officers, agents, or employees of any law enforcement agency when performing their respective functions within the territorial limits of their respective agencies shall apply to them and to their primary commissioning agencies to the same degree and extent while such persons are engaged in the performance of authorized functions and duties under this chapter.

[**1985 c 89 § 6.**]

10.93.070
General authority peace officer—Powers of, circumstances.

In addition to any other powers vested by law, a general authority Washington peace officer who possesses a certificate of basic law enforcement training or a certificate of equivalency or has been exempted from the requirement therefor by the Washington state criminal justice training commission may enforce the traffic or criminal laws of this state throughout the territorial bounds of this state, under the following enumerated circumstances:

(1) Upon the prior written consent of the sheriff or chief of police in whose primary territorial jurisdiction the exercise of the powers occurs;

(2) In response to an emergency involving an immediate threat to human life or property;

(3) In response to a request for assistance pursuant to a mutual law enforcement assistance agreement with the agency of primary territorial jurisdiction or in response to the request of a peace officer with enforcement authority;

(4) When the officer is transporting a prisoner;

(5) When the officer is executing an arrest warrant or search warrant; or

(6) When the officer is in fresh pursuit, as defined in RCW **10.93.120**.

[**1985 c 89 § 7.**]

10.93.080
Limited authority peace officer—No additional powers.

A limited authority Washington peace officer shall have no additional powers by virtue of this chapter but shall be limited to those powers already vested by law or hereafter created by separate enactment.

[**1985 c 89 § 8.**]

10.93.090
Specially commissioned peace officer—Powers of, circumstances.

A specially commissioned Washington peace officer who has successfully completed a course of basic training prescribed or approved for such officers by the

Washington state criminal justice training commission may exercise any authority which the special commission vests in the officer, throughout the territorial bounds of the state, outside of the officer's primary territorial jurisdiction under the following circumstances:

(1) The officer is in fresh pursuit, as defined in RCW **10.93.120**; or

(2) The officer is acting pursuant to mutual law enforcement assistance agreement between the primary commissioning agency and the agency with primary territorial jurisdiction.

[**1985 c 89 § 9.**]

10.93.100
Federal peace officers—No additional powers.

Federal peace officers shall have no additional powers by virtue of this chapter but shall be limited to those powers already vested by law or hereafter created by separate enactment.

[**1985 c 89 § 10.**]

10.93.110
Attorney general—No additional powers.

The attorney general shall have no additional powers by virtue of this chapter but shall be limited to those powers already vested by law or hereafter created by separate enactment.

[**1985 c 89 § 11.**]

10.93.120
Fresh pursuit, arrest.

(1) Any peace officer who has authority under Washington law to make an arrest may proceed in fresh pursuit of a person (a) who is reasonably believed to have committed a violation of traffic or criminal laws, or (b) for whom such officer holds a

warrant of arrest, and such peace officer shall have the authority to arrest and to hold such person in custody anywhere in the state.

(2) The term "fresh pursuit," as used in this chapter, includes, without limitation, fresh pursuit as defined by the common law. Fresh pursuit does not necessarily imply immediate pursuit, but pursuit without unreasonable delay.

[**1985 c 89 § 12.**]

10.93.130
Contracting authority of law enforcement agencies.

Under the interlocal cooperation act, chapter **39.34** RCW, any law enforcement agency referred to by this chapter may contract with any other such agency and may also contract with any law enforcement agency of another state, or such state's political subdivision, to provide mutual law enforcement assistance. The agency with primary territorial jurisdiction may require that officers from participating agencies meet reasonable training or certification standards or other reasonable standards.

[**1985 c 89 § 13.**]

10.93.140
State patrol, fish and wildlife exempted.

This chapter does not limit the scope of jurisdiction and authority of the Washington state patrol and the department of fish and wildlife as otherwise provided by law, and these agencies shall not be bound by the reporting requirements of RCW **10.93.030**.

[**2002 c 128 § 2; 1985 c 89 § 14.**]

10.93.900
Effective date—1985 c 89.

This act shall take effect July 1, 1985.

[**1985 c 89 § 17.**

Chapter 10.95 RCW CAPITAL PUNISHMENT—AGGRAVATED FIRST DEGREE MURDER

NOTES:

Homicide: Chapter **9A.32** RCW.

10.95.010
Court rules.

No rule promulgated by the supreme court of Washington pursuant to RCW **2.04.190** and **2.04.200**, now or in the future, shall be construed to supersede or alter any of the provisions of this chapter.

[**1981 c 138 § 1.**]

10.95.020
Definition.

A person is guilty of aggravated first degree murder, a class A felony, if he or she commits first degree murder as defined by RCW**9A.32.030**(1)(a), as now or hereafter amended, and one or more of the following aggravating circumstances exist:

(1) The victim was a law enforcement officer, corrections officer, or firefighter who was performing his or her official duties at the time of the act resulting in death and the victim was known or reasonably should have been known by the person to be such at the time of the killing;

(2) At the time of the act resulting in the death, the person was serving a term of imprisonment, had escaped, or was on authorized or unauthorized leave in or from a

state facility or program for the incarceration or treatment of persons adjudicated guilty of crimes;

(3) At the time of the act resulting in death, the person was in custody in a county or county-city jail as a consequence of having been adjudicated guilty of a felony;

(4) The person committed the murder pursuant to an agreement that he or she would receive money or any other thing of value for committing the murder;

(5) The person solicited another person to commit the murder and had paid or had agreed to pay money or any other thing of value for committing the murder;

(6) The person committed the murder to obtain or maintain his or her membership or to advance his or her position in the hierarchy of an organization, association, or identifiable group;

(7) The murder was committed during the course of or as a result of a shooting where the discharge of the firearm, as defined in RCW**9.41.010**, is either from a motor vehicle or from the immediate area of a motor vehicle that was used to transport the shooter or the firearm, or both, to the scene of the discharge;

(8) The victim was:

(a) A judge; juror or former juror; prospective, current, or former witness in an adjudicative proceeding; prosecuting attorney; deputy prosecuting attorney; defense attorney; a member of the indeterminate sentence review board; or a probation or parole officer; and

(b) The murder was related to the exercise of official duties performed or to be performed by the victim;

(9) The person committed the murder to conceal the commission of a crime or to protect or conceal the identity of any person committing a crime, including, but specifically not limited to, any attempt to avoid prosecution as a persistent offender as defined in RCW **9.94A.030**;

(10) There was more than one victim and the murders were part of a common scheme or plan or the result of a single act of the person;

(11) The murder was committed in the course of, in furtherance of, or in immediate flight from one of the following crimes:

(a) Robbery in the first or second degree;

(b) Rape in the first or second degree;

(c) Burglary in the first or second degree or residential burglary;

(d) Kidnapping in the first degree; or

(e) Arson in the first degree;

(12) The victim was regularly employed or self-employed as a newsreporter and the murder was committed to obstruct or hinder the investigative, research, or reporting activities of the victim;

(13) At the time the person committed the murder, there existed a court order, issued in this or any other state, which prohibited the person from either contacting the victim, molesting the victim, or disturbing the peace of the victim, and the person had knowledge of the existence of that order;

(14) At the time the person committed the murder, the person and the victim were "family or household members" as that term is defined in *RCW **10.99.020**(1), and the person had previously engaged in a pattern or practice of three or more of the following crimes committed upon the victim within a five-year period, regardless of whether a conviction resulted:

(a) Harassment as defined in RCW **9A.46.020**; or

(b) Any criminal assault.

[**2003 c 53 § 96; 1998 c 305 § 1.** Prior: 1995 c 129 § 17 (Initiative Measure No. 159); **1994 c 121 § 3; 1981 c 138 § 2.**]

NOTES:

> ***Reviser's note:** RCW **10.99.020** was amended by 2004 c 18 § 2, changing subsection (1) to subsection (3).

> > **Intent—Effective date—2003 c 53:** See notes following RCW **2.48.180**.

> > **Findings and intent—Short title—Severability—Captions not law—1995 c 129:** See notes following RCW **9.94A.510**.

10.95.030
Sentences for aggravated first degree murder.

(1) Except as provided in subsections (2) and (3) of this section, any person convicted of the crime of aggravated first degree murder shall be sentenced to life imprisonment without possibility of release or parole. A person sentenced to life imprisonment under this section shall not have that sentence suspended, deferred, or commuted by any judicial officer and the indeterminate sentence review board or its successor may not parole such prisoner nor reduce the period of confinement in any manner whatsoever including but not limited to any sort of good-time calculation. The department of social and health services or its successor or any executive official may not permit such prisoner to participate in any sort of release or furlough program.

(2) If, pursuant to a special sentencing proceeding held under RCW **10.95.050**, the trier of fact finds that there are not sufficient mitigating circumstances to merit leniency, the sentence shall be death. In no case, however, shall a person be sentenced to death if the person had an intellectual disability at the time the crime was committed, under the definition of intellectual disability set forth in (a) of this subsection. A diagnosis of intellectual disability shall be documented by a licensed psychiatrist or licensed psychologist designated by the court, who is an expert in the diagnosis and evaluation of intellectual disabilities. The defense must establish an intellectual disability by a preponderance of the evidence and the court must make a finding as to the existence of an intellectual disability.

(a) "Intellectual disability" means the individual has: (i) Significantly subaverage general intellectual functioning; (ii) existing concurrently with deficits in adaptive behavior; and (iii) both significantly subaverage general intellectual functioning and deficits in adaptive behavior were manifested during the developmental period.

(b) "General intellectual functioning" means the results obtained by assessment with one or more of the individually administered general intelligence tests developed for the purpose of assessing intellectual functioning.

(c) "Significantly subaverage general intellectual functioning" means intelligence quotient seventy or below.

(d) "Adaptive behavior" means the effectiveness or degree with which individuals meet the standards of personal independence and social responsibility expected for his or her age.

(e) "Developmental period" means the period of time between conception and the eighteenth birthday.

(3)(a)(i) Any person convicted of the crime of aggravated first degree murder for an offense committed prior to the person's sixteenth birthday shall be sentenced to a maximum term of life imprisonment and a minimum term of total confinement of twenty-five years.

(ii) Any person convicted of the crime of aggravated first degree murder for an offense committed when the person is at least sixteen years old but less than eighteen years old shall be sentenced to a maximum term of life imprisonment and a minimum term of total confinement of no less than twenty-five years. A minimum term of life may be imposed, in which case the person will be ineligible for parole or early release.

(b) In setting a minimum term, the court must take into account mitigating factors that account for the diminished culpability of youth as provided in Miller v. Alabama, 132 S.Ct. 2455 (2012) including, but not limited to, the age of the individual, the youth's childhood and life experience, the degree of responsibility the youth was capable of exercising, and the youth's chances of becoming rehabilitated.

(c) A person sentenced under this subsection shall serve the sentence in a facility or institution operated, or utilized under contract, by the state. During the minimum term of total confinement, the person shall not be eligible for community custody, earned release time, furlough, home detention, partial confinement, work crew, work release, or any other form of early release authorized under RCW **9.94A.728**, or any other form of authorized leave or absence from the correctional facility while not in the direct custody of a corrections officer. The provisions of this subsection shall not apply: (i) In the case of an offender in need of emergency medical treatment; or (ii) for an extraordinary medical placement when authorized under *RCW **9.94A.728**(3).

(d) Any person sentenced pursuant to this subsection shall be subject to community custody under the supervision of the department of corrections and the authority of the indeterminate sentence review board. As part of any sentence under this subsection, the court shall require the person to comply with any conditions imposed by the board.

(e) No later than five years prior to the expiration of the person's minimum term, the department of corrections shall conduct an assessment of the offender and identify programming and services that would be appropriate to prepare the offender for return to the community. To the extent possible, the department shall make programming available as identified by the assessment.

(f) No later than one hundred eighty days prior to the expiration of the person's minimum term, the department of corrections shall conduct, and the offender shall participate in, an examination of the person, incorporating methodologies that are recognized by experts in the prediction of dangerousness, and including a prediction of the probability that the person will engage in future criminal behavior if released on conditions to be set by the board. The board may consider a person's failure to participate in an evaluation under this subsection in determining whether to release the person. The board shall order the person released, under such affirmative and other conditions as the board determines appropriate, unless the board determines by a preponderance of the evidence that, despite such conditions, it is more likely than not that the person will commit new criminal law violations if released. If the board does not order the person released, the board shall set a new minimum term not to exceed five additional years. The board shall give public safety considerations the highest priority when making all discretionary decisions regarding the ability for release and conditions of release.

(g) In a hearing conducted under (f) of this subsection, the board shall provide opportunities for victims and survivors of victims of any crimes for which the offender has been convicted to present statements as set forth in RCW **7.69.032**. The procedures for victim and survivor of victim input shall be provided by rule. To facilitate victim and survivor of victim involvement, county prosecutor's offices shall ensure that any victim impact statements and known contact information for victims of record and survivors of victims are forwarded as part of the judgment and sentence.

(h) An offender released by the board is subject to the supervision of the department of corrections for a period of time to be determined by the board. The department shall monitor the offender's compliance with conditions of community custody imposed by the court or board and promptly report any violations to the board. Any violation of conditions of community custody established or modified by the board are subject to the provisions of RCW **9.95.425** through **9.95.440**.

(i) An offender released or discharged under this section may be returned to the institution at the discretion of the board if the offender is found to have violated a condition of community custody. The offender is entitled to a hearing pursuant to RCW **9.95.435**. The board shall set a new minimum term of incarceration not to exceed five years.

[**2015 c 134 § 5; 2014 c 130 § 9; 2010 c 94 § 3; 1993 c 479 § 1; 1981 c 138 § 3.**]
NOTES:

   ***Reviser's note:** RCW **9.94A.728** was amended by 2015 c 156 § 1, changing subsection (3) to subsection (1)(c).

   Effective date—2015 c 134: See note following RCW **9.94A.501**.

   Application—Effective date—2014 c 130: See notes following RCW **9.94A.510**.

   Purpose—2010 c 94: See note following RCW **44.04.280**.

10.95.035
Return of persons to sentencing court if sentenced prior to June 1, 2014, under this chapter or any prior law, for a term of life without the possibility of parole for an offense committed prior to eighteenth birthday.

(1) A person, who was sentenced prior to June 1, 2014, under this chapter or any prior law, to a term of life without the possibility of parole for an offense committed prior to their eighteenth birthday, shall be returned to the sentencing court or the sentencing court's successor for sentencing consistent with RCW **10.95.030**. Release and supervision of a person who receives a minimum term of less than life will be governed by RCW **10.95.030**.

(2) The court shall provide an opportunity for victims and survivors of victims of any crimes for which the offender has been convicted to present a statement personally or by representation.

(3) The court's order setting a minimum term is subject to review to the same extent as a minimum term decision by the parole board before July 1, 1986.

(4) A resentencing under this section shall not reopen the defendant's conviction to challenges that would otherwise be barred by RCW**10.73.090**, **10.73.100**, **10.73.140**, or other procedural barriers.

[**2015 c 134 § 7; 2014 c 130 § 11.**]

NOTES:

> **Effective date—2015 c 134:** See note following RCW **9.94A.501**.
>
> **Effective date—2014 c 130:** See note following RCW **9.94A.510**.

10.95.040

Special sentencing proceeding—Notice—Filing—Service.

(1) If a person is charged with aggravated first degree murder as defined by RCW **10.95.020**, the prosecuting attorney shall file written notice of a special sentencing proceeding to determine whether or not the death penalty should be imposed when there is reason to believe that there are not sufficient mitigating circumstances to merit leniency.

(2) The notice of special sentencing proceeding shall be filed and served on the defendant or the defendant's attorney within thirty days after the defendant's arraignment upon the charge of aggravated first degree murder unless the court, for good cause shown, extends or reopens the period for filing and service of the notice. Except with the consent of the prosecuting attorney, during the period in which the prosecuting attorney may file the notice of special sentencing proceeding, the defendant may not tender a plea of guilty to the charge of aggravated first degree murder nor may the court accept a plea of guilty to the charge of aggravated first degree murder or any lesser included offense.

(3) If a notice of special sentencing proceeding is not filed and served as provided in this section, the prosecuting attorney may not request the death penalty.

[**1981 c 138 § 4.**]

10.95.050

Special sentencing proceeding—When held—Jury to decide matters presented—Waiver—Reconvening same jury—Impanelling new jury—Peremptory challenges.

(1) If a defendant is adjudicated guilty of aggravated first degree murder, whether by acceptance of a plea of guilty, by verdict of a jury, or by decision of the trial court sitting without a jury, a special sentencing proceeding shall be held if a notice of special sentencing proceeding was filed and served as provided by RCW **10.95.040**. No sort of plea, admission, or agreement may abrogate the requirement that a special sentencing proceeding be held.

(2) A jury shall decide the matters presented in the special sentencing proceeding unless a jury is waived in the discretion of the court and with the consent of the defendant and the prosecuting attorney.

(3) If the defendant's guilt was determined by a jury verdict, the trial court shall reconvene the same jury to hear the special sentencing proceeding. The proceeding shall commence as soon as practicable after completion of the trial at which the defendant's guilt was determined. If, however, unforeseen circumstances make it impracticable to reconvene the same jury to hear the special sentencing proceeding, the trial court may dismiss that jury and convene a jury pursuant to subsection (4) of this section.

(4) If the defendant's guilt was determined by plea of guilty or by decision of the trial court sitting without a jury, or if a retrial of the special sentencing proceeding is necessary for any reason including but not limited to a mistrial in a previous special sentencing proceeding or as a consequence of a remand from an appellate court, the trial court shall impanel a jury of twelve persons plus whatever alternate jurors the trial court deems necessary. The defense and prosecution shall each be allowed to

peremptorily challenge twelve jurors. If there is more than one defendant, each defendant shall be allowed an additional peremptory challenge and the prosecution shall be allowed a like number of additional challenges. If alternate jurors are selected, the defense and prosecution shall each be allowed one peremptory challenge for each alternate juror to be selected and if there is more than one defendant each defendant shall be allowed an additional peremptory challenge for each alternate juror to be selected and the prosecution shall be allowed a like number of additional challenges. [**1981 c 138 § 5.**]

10.95.060

Special sentencing proceeding—Jury instructions—Opening statements—Evidence—Arguments—Question for jury.

(1) At the commencement of the special sentencing proceeding, the trial court shall instruct the jury as to the nature and purpose of the proceeding and as to the consequences of its decision, as provided in RCW **10.95.030**.

(2) At the special sentencing proceeding both the prosecution and defense shall be allowed to make an opening statement. The prosecution shall first present evidence and then the defense may present evidence. Rebuttal evidence may be presented by each side. Upon conclusion of the evidence, the court shall instruct the jury and then the prosecution and defense shall be permitted to present argument. The prosecution shall open and conclude the argument.

(3) The court shall admit any relevant evidence which it deems to have probative value regardless of its admissibility under the rules of evidence, including hearsay evidence and evidence of the defendant's previous criminal activity regardless of whether the defendant has been charged or convicted as a result of such activity. The defendant shall be accorded a fair opportunity to rebut or offer any hearsay evidence.

In addition to evidence of whether or not there are sufficient mitigating circumstances to merit leniency, if the jury sitting in the special sentencing proceeding has not heard evidence of the aggravated first degree murder of which the defendant stands convicted, both the defense and prosecution may introduce evidence concerning the facts and circumstances of the murder.

(4) Upon conclusion of the evidence and argument at the special sentencing proceeding, the jury shall retire to deliberate upon the following question: "Having in mind the crime of which the defendant has been found guilty, are you convinced beyond a reasonable doubt that there are not sufficient mitigating circumstances to merit leniency?"

In order to return an affirmative answer to the question posed by this subsection, the jury must so find unanimously.

[**1981 c 138 § 6.**]

10.95.070

Special sentencing proceeding—Factors which jury may consider in deciding whether leniency merited.

In deciding the question posed by RCW **10.95.060**(4), the jury, or the court if a jury is waived, may consider any relevant factors, including but not limited to the following:

(1) Whether the defendant has or does not have a significant history, either as a juvenile or an adult, of prior criminal activity;

(2) Whether the murder was committed while the defendant was under the influence of extreme mental disturbance;

(3) Whether the victim consented to the act of murder;

(4) Whether the defendant was an accomplice to a murder committed by another person where the defendant's participation in the murder was relatively minor;

(5) Whether the defendant acted under duress or domination of another person;

(6) Whether, at the time of the murder, the capacity of the defendant to appreciate the wrongfulness of his or her conduct or to conform his or her conduct to the requirements of law was substantially impaired as a result of mental disease or defect. However, a person found to have an intellectual disability under RCW **10.95.030**(2) may in no case be sentenced to death;

(7) Whether the age of the defendant at the time of the crime calls for leniency; and

(8) Whether there is a likelihood that the defendant will pose a danger to others in the future.

[**2010 c 94 § 4; 1993 c 479 § 2; 1981 c 138 § 7.**]

NOTES:

> **Purpose**—2010 c 94: See note following RCW **44.04.280**.

10.95.080

When sentence to death or sentence to life imprisonment shall be imposed.

(1) If a jury answers affirmatively the question posed by RCW **10.95.060**(4), or when a jury is waived as allowed by RCW **10.95.050**(2) and the trial court answers affirmatively the question posed by RCW **10.95.060**(4), the defendant shall be sentenced to death. The trial court may not suspend or defer the execution or imposition of the sentence.

(2) If the jury does not return an affirmative answer to the question posed in RCW **10.95.060**(4), the defendant shall be sentenced to life imprisonment as provided in RCW **10.95.030**(1).

[**1981 c 138 § 8.**]

10.95.090

Sentence if death sentence commuted, held invalid, or if death sentence established by chapter held invalid.

If any sentence of death imposed pursuant to this chapter is commuted by the governor, or held to be invalid by a final judgment of a court after all avenues of appeal have been exhausted by the parties to the action, or if the death penalty established by this chapter is held to be invalid by a final judgment of a court which is binding on all courts in the state, the sentence for aggravated first degree murder if there was an affirmative response to the question posed by RCW **10.95.060**(4) shall be life imprisonment as provided in RCW **10.95.030**(1).

[**1981 c 138 § 9.**]

10.95.100

Mandatory review of death sentence by supreme court—Notice—Transmittal—Contents of notice—Jurisdiction.

Whenever a defendant is sentenced to death, upon entry of the judgment and sentence in the trial court the sentence shall be reviewed on the record by the supreme court of Washington.

Within ten days of the entry of a judgment and sentence imposing the death penalty, the clerk of the trial court shall transmit notice thereof to the clerk of the supreme court of Washington and to the parties. The notice shall include the caption of the case, its cause number, the defendant's name, the crime or crimes of which the defendant was convicted, the sentence imposed, the date of entry of judgment and sentence, and the names and addresses of the attorneys for the parties. The notice shall vest with the supreme court of Washington the jurisdiction to review the sentence of death as provided by this chapter. The failure of the clerk of the trial court to transmit the notice as required shall not prevent the supreme court of Washington from conducting the sentence review as provided by chapter 138, Laws of 1981.

[**1981 c 138 § 10.**]

10.95.110

Verbatim report of trial proceedings—Preparation—Transmittal to supreme court—Clerk's papers—Receipt.

(1) Within ten days after the entry of a judgment and sentence imposing the death penalty, the clerk of the trial court shall cause the preparation of a verbatim report of the trial proceedings to be commenced.

(2) Within five days of the filing and approval of the verbatim report of proceedings, the clerk of the trial court shall transmit such verbatim report of proceedings together with copies of all of the clerk's papers to the clerk of the supreme court of Washington. The clerk of the supreme court of Washington shall forthwith acknowledge receipt of

these documents by providing notice of receipt to the clerk of the trial court, the defendant or his or her attorney, and the prosecuting attorney.

[**1981 c 138 § 11.**]

10.95.120

Information report—Form—Contents—Submission to supreme court, defendant, prosecuting attorney.

In all cases in which a person is convicted of aggravated first degree murder, the trial court shall, within thirty days after the entry of the judgment and sentence, submit a report to the clerk of the supreme court of Washington, to the defendant or his or her attorney, and to the prosecuting attorney which provides the information specified under subsections (1) through (8) of this section. The report shall be in the form of a standard questionnaire prepared and supplied by the supreme court of Washington and shall include the following:

(1) Information about the defendant, including the following:

(a) Name, date of birth, gender, marital status, and race and/or ethnic origin;

(b) Number and ages of children;

(c) Whether his or her parents are living, and date of death where applicable;

(d) Number of children born to his or her parents;

(e) The defendant's educational background, intelligence level, and intelligence quotient;

(f) Whether a psychiatric evaluation was performed, and if so, whether it indicated that the defendant was:

(i) Able to distinguish right from wrong;

(ii) Able to perceive the nature and quality of his or her act; and

(iii) Able to cooperate intelligently with his or her defense;

(g) Any character or behavior disorders found or other pertinent psychiatric or psychological information;

(h) The work record of the defendant;

(i) A list of the defendant's prior convictions including the offense, date, and sentence imposed; and

(j) The length of time the defendant has resided in Washington and the county in which he or she was convicted.

(2) Information about the trial, including:

(a) The defendant's plea;

(b) Whether defendant was represented by counsel;

(c) Whether there was evidence introduced or instructions given as to defenses to aggravated first degree murder, including excusable homicide, justifiable homicide, insanity, duress, entrapment, alibi, intoxication, or other specific defense;

(d) Any other offenses charged against the defendant and tried at the same trial and whether they resulted in conviction;

(e) What aggravating circumstances were alleged against the defendant and which of these circumstances was found to have been applicable; and

(f) Names and charges filed against other defendant(s) if tried jointly and disposition of the charges.

(3) Information concerning the special sentencing proceeding, including:

(a) The date the defendant was convicted and date the special sentencing proceeding commenced;

(b) Whether the jury for the special sentencing proceeding was the same jury that returned the guilty verdict, providing an explanation if it was not;

(c) Whether there was evidence of mitigating circumstances;

(d) Whether there was, in the court's opinion, credible evidence of the mitigating circumstances as provided in RCW **10.95.070**;

(e) The jury's answer to the question posed in RCW **10.95.060**(4);

(f) The sentence imposed.

(4) Information about the victim, including:

(a) Whether he or she was related to the defendant by blood or marriage;

(b) The victim's occupation and whether he or she was an employer or employee of the defendant;

(c) Whether the victim was acquainted with the defendant, and if so, how well;

(d) The length of time the victim resided in Washington and the county;

(e) Whether the victim was the same race and/or ethnic origin as the defendant;

(f) Whether the victim was the same sex as the defendant;

(g) Whether the victim was held hostage during the crime and if so, how long;

(h) The nature and extent of any physical harm or torture inflicted upon the victim prior to death;

(i) The victim's age; and

(j) The type of weapon used in the crime, if any.

(5) Information about the representation of the defendant, including:

(a) Date counsel secured;

(b) Whether counsel was retained or appointed, including the reason for appointment;

(c) The length of time counsel has practiced law and nature of his or her practice; and

(d) Whether the same counsel served at both the trial and special sentencing proceeding, and if not, why not.

(6) General considerations, including:

(a) Whether the race and/or ethnic origin of the defendant, victim, or any witness was an apparent factor at trial;

(b) What percentage of the county population is the same race and/or ethnic origin of the defendant;

(c) Whether members of the defendant's or victim's race and/or ethnic origin were represented on the jury;

(d) Whether there was evidence that such members were systematically excluded from the jury;

(e) Whether the sexual orientation of the defendant, victim, or any witness was a factor in the trial;

(f) Whether any specific instruction was given to the jury to exclude race, ethnic origin, or sexual orientation as an issue;

(g) Whether there was extensive publicity concerning the case in the community;

(h) Whether the jury was instructed to disregard such publicity;

(i) Whether the jury was instructed to avoid any influence of passion, prejudice, or any other arbitrary factor when considering its verdict or its findings in the special sentencing proceeding;

(j) The nature of the evidence resulting in such instruction; and

(k) General comments of the trial judge concerning the appropriateness of the sentence considering the crime, defendant, and other relevant factors.

(7) Information about the chronology of the case, including the date that:

(a) The defendant was arrested;

(b) Trial began;

(c) The verdict was returned;

(d) Post-trial motions were ruled on;

(e) Special sentencing proceeding began;

(f) Sentence was imposed;

(g) Trial judge's report was completed; and

(h) Trial judge's report was filed.

(8) The trial judge shall sign and date the questionnaire when it is completed.

[**1981 c 138 § 12.**]

10.95.130

Questions posed for determination by supreme court in death sentence review—Review in addition to appeal—Consolidation of review and appeal.

(1) The sentence review required by RCW **10.95.100** shall be in addition to any appeal. The sentence review and an appeal shall be consolidated for consideration. The defendant and the prosecuting attorney may submit briefs within the time prescribed by the court and present oral argument to the court.

(2) With regard to the sentence review required by chapter 138, Laws of 1981, the supreme court of Washington shall determine:

(a) Whether there was sufficient evidence to justify the affirmative finding to the question posed by RCW **10.95.060**(4); and

(b) Whether the sentence of death is excessive or disproportionate to the penalty imposed in similar cases, considering both the crime and the defendant. For the purposes of this subsection, "similar cases" means cases reported in the Washington Reports or Washington Appellate Reports since January 1, 1965, in which the judge or jury considered the imposition of capital punishment regardless of whether it was imposed or executed, and cases in which reports have been filed with the supreme court under RCW **10.95.120**;

(c) Whether the sentence of death was brought about through passion or prejudice; and

(d) Whether the defendant had an intellectual disability within the meaning of RCW **10.95.030**(2).

[**2010 c 94 § 5; 1993 c 479 § 3; 1981 c 138 § 13.**]

NOTES:

> **Purpose—2010 c 94:** See note following RCW **44.04.280**.

10.95.140

Invalidation of sentence, remand for resentencing—Affirmation of sentence, remand for execution.

Upon completion of a sentence review:

(1) The supreme court of Washington shall invalidate the sentence of death and remand the case to the trial court for resentencing in accordance with RCW **10.95.090** if:

(a) The court makes a negative determination as to the question posed by RCW **10.95.130**(2)(a); or

(b) The court makes an affirmative determination as to any of the questions posed by RCW **10.95.130**(2) (b), (c), or (d).

(2) The court shall affirm the sentence of death and remand the case to the trial court for execution in accordance with RCW **10.95.160** if:

(a) The court makes an affirmative determination as to the question posed by RCW **10.95.130**(2)(a); and

(b) The court makes a negative determination as to the questions posed by RCW **10.95.130**(2) (b), (c), and (d).

[**1993 c 479 § 4; 1981 c 138 § 14.**]

10.95.150

Time limit for appellate review of death sentence and filing opinion.

In all cases in which a sentence of death has been imposed, the appellate review, if any, and sentence review to or by the supreme court of Washington shall be decided and an opinion on the merits shall be filed within one year of receipt by the clerk of the supreme court of Washington of the verbatim report of proceedings and clerk's papers filed under RCW **10.95.110**. If this time requirement is not met, the chief justice of the supreme court of Washington shall state on the record the extraordinary and compelling circumstances causing the delay and the facts supporting such circumstances. A failure to comply with the time requirements of this subsection shall in no way preclude the ultimate execution of a sentence of death.

[**1988 c 202 § 17; 1981 c 138 § 15.**]

NOTES:

Severability—**1988 c 202:** See note following RCW **2.24.050**.

10.95.160

Death warrant—Issuance—Form—Time for execution of judgment and sentence.

(1) If a death sentence is affirmed and the case remanded to the trial court as provided in RCW **10.95.140**(2), a death warrant shall forthwith be issued by the clerk of the trial court, which shall be signed by a judge of the trial court and attested by the clerk thereof under the seal of the court. The warrant shall be directed to the superintendent of the state penitentiary and shall state the conviction of the person named therein and the judgment and sentence of the court, and shall appoint a day on

which the judgment and sentence of the court shall be executed by the superintendent, which day shall not be less than thirty nor more than ninety days from the date the trial court receives the remand from the supreme court of Washington.

(2) If the date set for execution under subsection (1) of this section is stayed by a court of competent jurisdiction for any reason, the new execution date is automatically set at thirty judicial days after the entry of an order of termination or vacation of the stay by such court unless the court invalidates the conviction, sentence, or remands for further judicial proceedings. The presence of the inmate under sentence of death shall not be required for the court to vacate or terminate the stay according to this section.

[**1990 c 263 § 1; 1981 c 138 § 16.**]

10.95.170
Imprisonment of defendant.

The defendant shall be imprisoned in the state penitentiary within ten days after the trial court enters a judgment and sentence imposing the death penalty and shall be imprisoned both prior to and subsequent to the issuance of the death warrant as provided in RCW **10.95.160**. During such period of imprisonment, the defendant shall be confined in the segregation unit, where the defendant may be confined with other prisoners not under sentence of death, but prisoners under sentence of death shall be assigned to single-person cells.

[**1983 c 255 § 1; 1981 c 138 § 17.**]

NOTES:

Convicted female persons, commitment and procedure as to death sentences:

RCW **72.02.250**.

10.95.180
Death penalty—How executed.

(1) The punishment of death shall be supervised by the superintendent of the penitentiary and shall be inflicted by intravenous injection of a substance or substances

in a lethal quantity sufficient to cause death and until the defendant is dead, or, at the election of the defendant, by hanging by the neck until the defendant is dead. In any case, death shall be pronounced by a licensed physician.

(2) All executions, for both men and women, shall be carried out within the walls of the state penitentiary.

[**1996 c 251 § 1; 1986 c 194 § 1; 1981 c 138 § 18.**]

NOTES:

Severability—**1996 c 251:** "If any provision of this act or its application to any person or circumstance is held invalid, the remainder of the act or the application of the provision to other persons or circumstances is not affected." [**1996 c 251 § 2.**]

10.95.185
Witnesses.

(1) Not less than twenty days prior to a scheduled execution, judicial officers, law enforcement representatives, media representatives, representatives of the families of the victims, and representatives from the family of the defendant who wish to attend and witness the execution, must submit an application to the superintendent. Such application must designate the relationship and reason for wishing to attend.

(2) Not less than fifteen days prior to the scheduled execution, the superintendent shall designate the total number of individuals who will be allowed to attend and witness the planned execution. The superintendent shall determine the number of witnesses that will be allowed in each of the following categories:

(a) No less than five media representatives with consideration to be given to news organizations serving communities affected by the crimes or by the commission of the execution of the defendant.

(b) Judicial officers.

(c) Representatives of the families of the victims.

(d) Representatives from the family of the defendant.

(e) Up to two law enforcement representatives. The chief executive officer of the agency that investigated the crime shall designate the law enforcement representatives.

After the list is composed, the superintendent shall serve this list on all parties who have submitted an application pursuant to this section. The superintendent shall develop and implement procedures to determine the persons within each of the categories listed in this subsection who will be allowed to attend and witness the execution.

(3) Not less than ten days prior to the scheduled execution, the superintendent shall file the witness list with the superior court from which the conviction and death warrant was issued with a petition asking that the court enter an order certifying this list as a final order identifying the witnesses to attend the execution. The final order of the court certifying the witness list shall not be entered less than five days after the filing of the petition.

(4) Unless a show cause petition is filed with the superior court from which the conviction and death warrant was issued within five days of the filing of the superintendent's petition, the superintendent's list, by order of the superior court, becomes final, and no other party has standing to challenge its appropriateness.

(5) In no case may the superintendent or the superior court order or allow more than seventeen individuals other than required staff to witness a planned execution.

(6) All witnesses must adhere to the search and security provisions of the department of corrections' policy regarding the witnessing of an execution.

(7) The superior court from which the conviction and death warrant was issued is the exclusive court for seeking judicial process for the privilege of attending and witnessing an execution.

(8) For purposes of this section:

(a) "Judicial officer" means: (i) The superior court judge who signed the death warrant issued pursuant to RCW **10.95.160** for the execution of the individual, (ii) the current prosecuting attorney or a deputy prosecuting attorney of the county from which the final judgment and sentence and death warrant were issued, and (iii) the most recent attorney of record representing the individual sentenced to death.

(b) "Law enforcement representatives" means those law enforcement officers responsible for investigating the crime for which the defendant was sentenced to death.

(c) "Media representatives" means representatives from news organizations of all forms of media serving the state.

(d) "Representatives of the families of the victims" means representatives from the immediate families of the victim(s) of the individual sentenced to death, including victim advocates of the immediate family members. Victim advocates shall include any person working or volunteering for a recognized victim advocacy group or a prosecutor-based or law enforcement-based agency on behalf of victims or witnesses.

(e) "Representative from the family of the defendant" means a representative from the immediate family of the individual sentenced to death.

(f) "Superintendent" means the superintendent of the Washington state penitentiary.
[**1999 c 332 § 1; 1993 c 463 § 2.**]

NOTES:

Policy—**1993 c 463:** "The legislature declares that, to the extent that the attendance of witnesses can be accommodated without compromising the security or the orderly operation of the Washington state penitentiary, it is the policy of the state of Washington to provide authorized individuals the opportunity to attend and witness the execution of an individual sentenced to death pursuant to chapter **10.95** RCW. Further, it is the policy of the state of Washington to provide for access to the execution to credentialed members of the media." [**1993 c 463 § 1.**]

Severability—**1993 c 463:** "If any provision of this act or its application to any person or circumstance is held invalid, the remainder of the act or the application of the provision to other persons or circumstances is not affected." [**1993 c 463 § 3.**]

10.95.190
Death warrant—Record—Return to trial court.

(1) The superintendent of the state penitentiary shall keep in his or her office as part of the public records a book in which shall be kept a copy of each death warrant together with a complete statement of the superintendent's acts pursuant to such warrants.

(2) Within twenty days after each execution of a sentence of death, the superintendent of the state penitentiary shall return the death warrant to the clerk of the

trial court from which it was issued with the superintendent's return thereon showing all acts and proceedings done by him or her thereunder.

[**1981 c 138 § 19.**]

10.95.200
Proceedings for failure to execute on day named.

Whenever the day appointed for the execution of a defendant shall have passed, from any cause, other than the issuance of a stay by a court of competent jurisdiction, without the execution of such defendant having occurred, the trial court which issued the original death warrant shall issue a new death warrant in accordance with RCW **10.95.160**. The defendant's presence before the court is not required. However, nothing in this section shall be construed as restricting the defendant's right to be represented by counsel in connection with issuance of a new death warrant.

[**1990 c 263 § 2; 1987 c 286 § 1; 1981 c 138 § 20.**]

10.95.901
Construction—Chapter applicable to state registered domestic partnerships—2009 c 521.

For the purposes of this chapter, the terms spouse, marriage, marital, husband, wife, widow, widower, next of kin, and family shall be interpreted as applying equally to state registered domestic partnerships or individuals in state registered domestic partnerships as well as to marital relationships and married persons, and references to dissolution of marriage shall apply equally to state registered domestic partnerships that have been terminated, dissolved, or invalidated, to the extent that such interpretation does not conflict with federal law. Where necessary to implement chapter 521, Laws of 2009, gender-specific terms such as husband and wife used in any statute, rule, or other law shall be construed to be gender neutral, and applicable to individuals in state registered domestic partnerships.

[**2009 c 521 § 28.**]

Chapter 10.96 RCW CRIMINAL PROCESS RECORDS

10.96.005
Findings.

The legislature finds that many businesses, associations, and organizations providing goods and services to the public, conducting other activity in Washington, or otherwise affecting residents of Washington now operate nationally or globally and often maintain their business records in a location outside the state of Washington. The legislature further finds that bringing persons or organizations committing crimes in Washington to justice is a matter of great public interest because crimes have a significant effect on businesses, associations, and other organizations that conduct business in Washington, as well as on Washington citizens. Crimes result in significant harm and losses to persons, businesses, associations, and other organizations victimized, as well as persons not directly victimized when businesses or others more directly affected by the crimes must raise prices to cover crime losses. The ability of law enforcement and the criminal justice system to effectively perform their duties to the public often depends upon law enforcement agencies, prosecutors, and criminal defense attorneys being able to obtain and use records relevant to crimes that affect Washington's citizens, businesses, associations, organizations, and others who provide goods or services, or conduct other activity in Washington. In the course of fulfilling their duties to the public, law enforcement agencies, prosecutors, and criminal defense attorneys must frequently obtain records from these entities, and be able to use the records in court. The ability to obtain and use these records has an impact on Washington citizens because it affects the ability to enforce Washington's criminal laws and affects the deterrence value arising from criminal prosecution. Effectively combating crime requires laws facilitating and requiring that all those who possess records relevant to a criminal investigation comply with the legal process issued in connection with criminal investigations or litigation.

[**2008 c 21 § 1.**]

10.96.010
Definitions.

The definitions in this section apply throughout this chapter unless the context clearly requires otherwise.

(1) "Adverse result" includes one or more of the following possible consequences:

(a) Danger to the life or physical safety of an individual;

(b) A flight from prosecution;

(c) The destruction of, potential loss of, or tampering with evidence;

(d) The intimidation of potential witnesses;

(e) Jeopardy to an investigation or undue delay of a trial.

(2) "Applicant" means a law enforcement officer, prosecuting attorney, deputy or special deputy prosecuting attorney, or defense attorney who is seeking criminal process under RCW **10.96.020**.

(3) "Criminal process" means a search warrant or legal process issued pursuant to RCW **10.79.015** and CrR 2.3; any process issued pursuant to chapter **9.73**, 9A.82, 10.27, or **10.29** RCW; and any other legal process signed by a judge of the superior court and issued in a criminal matter which allows the search for or commands production of records that are in the actual or constructive possession of the recipient, regardless of whether the recipient or the records are physically located within the state.

(4) "Defense attorney" means an attorney of record for a person charged with a crime when the attorney is seeking the issuance of criminal process for the defense of the criminal case.

(5) "Properly served" means delivery by hand or in a manner reasonably allowing for proof of delivery if delivered by United States mail, overnight delivery service, or facsimile to the recipient addressee of criminal process.

(6) "Recipient" means a person, as defined in RCW **9A.04.110**, or a business, as defined in RCW **5.45.010**, that has conducted business or engaged in transactions occurring at least in part in this state upon whom criminal process issued under this chapter is properly served.

[**2008 c 21 § 2.**]

10.96.020
Production of records.

This section shall apply to any criminal process allowing for search of or commanding production of records that are in the actual or constructive possession of a recipient who receives service outside Washington, regardless of whether the recipient or the records are physically located within the state.

(1) When properly served with criminal process issued under this section, the recipient shall provide the applicant all records sought pursuant to the criminal process. The records shall be produced within twenty business days of receipt of the criminal process, unless the process requires earlier production. An applicant may consent to a recipient's request for additional time to comply with the criminal process.

(2) Criminal process issued under this section must contain the following language in bold type on the first page of the document: "This [warrant, subpoena, order] is issued pursuant to RCW [insert citation to this statute]. A response is due within twenty business days of receipt, unless a shorter time is stated herein, or the applicant consents to a recipient's request for additional time to comply."

(3) If the judge finds reason to suspect that failure to produce records within twenty business days would cause an adverse result, the criminal process may require production of records within less than twenty business days. A court may reasonably extend the time required for production of the records upon finding that the recipient has shown good cause for that extension and that an extension of time would not cause an adverse result.

(4) When properly served with criminal process issued under this section, a recipient who seeks to quash the criminal process must seek relief from the court where the

criminal process was issued, within the time originally required for production of records. The court shall hear and decide the motion no later than five court days after the motion is filed. An applicant's consent, under subsection (1) of this section, to a recipient's request for additional time to comply with the criminal process does not extend the date by which a recipient must seek the relief designated in this section.

[2008 c 21 § 3.]

10.96.030
Authenticity of records—Verification—Affidavit, declaration, or certification.

(1) Upon written request from the applicant, or if ordered by the court, the recipient of criminal process shall verify the authenticity of records that it produces by providing an affidavit, declaration, or certification that complies with subsection (2) of this section. The requirements of RCW **5.45.020** regarding business records as evidence may be satisfied by an affidavit, declaration, or certification that complies with subsection (2) of this section, without the need for testimony from the custodian of records, regardless of whether the business records were produced by a foreign or Washington state entity.

(2) To be admissible without testimony from the custodian of records, business records must be accompanied by an affidavit, declaration, or certification by its record custodian or other qualified person that includes contact information for the witness completing the document and attests to the following:

(a) The witness is the custodian of the record or sets forth evidence that the witness is qualified to testify about the record;

(b) The record was made at or near the time of the act, condition, or event set forth in the record by, or from information transmitted by, a person with knowledge of those matters;

(c) The record was made in the regular course of business;

(d) The identity of the record and the mode of its preparation; and

(e) Either that the record is the original or that it is a duplicate that accurately reproduces the original.

(3) A party intending to offer a record into evidence under this section must provide written notice of that intention to all adverse parties, and must make the record and affidavit, declaration, or certification available for inspection sufficiently in advance of their offer into evidence to provide an adverse party with a fair opportunity to challenge them. A motion opposing admission in evidence of the record shall be made and determined by the court before trial and with sufficient time to allow the party offering the record time, if the motion is granted, to produce the custodian of the record or other qualified person at trial, without creating hardship on the party or on the custodian or other qualified person.

(4) Failure by a party to timely file a motion under subsection (4) of this section shall constitute a waiver of objection to admission of the evidence, but the court for good cause shown may grant relief from the waiver. When the court grants relief from the waiver, and thereafter determines the custodian of the record shall appear, a continuance of the trial may be granted to provide the proponent of the record sufficient time to arrange for the necessary witness to appear.

(5) Nothing in this section precludes either party from calling the custodian of record of the record or other witness to testify regarding the record.

[2008 c 21 § 4.]

10.96.040

Service of process issued by or in another state.

A Washington recipient, when served with process that was issued by or in another state that on its face purports to be valid criminal process shall comply with that process as if that process had been issued by a Washington court.

[2008 c 21 § 5.]

10.96.050

Recipients' immunity from liability.

A recipient of criminal process or process under RCW **10.96.010** and **10.96.040**, and any other person that responds to such process is immune from civil and criminal liability for complying with the process, and for any failure to provide notice of any disclosure to the person who is the subject of or identified in the disclosure.

[**2008 c 21 § 6.**]

10.96.060
Issuance of criminal process.

A judge of the superior court may issue any criminal process to any recipient at any address, within or without the state, for any matter over which the court has criminal jurisdiction pursuant to RCW **9A.04.030**. This section does not limit a court's authority to issue warrants or legal process under other provisions of state law.

[**2008 c 21 § 7.**]

Chapter 10.97 RCW WASHINGTON STATE

CRIMINAL RECORDS PRIVACY ACT

NOTES:

Public records: Chapter **42.56** RCW.

Records of community sexual assault program and underserved populations provider not available as part of discovery: RCW **70.125.065**.

10.97.010
Declaration of policy.

The legislature declares that it is the policy of the state of Washington to provide for the completeness, accuracy, confidentiality, and security of criminal history record information and victim, witness, and complainant record information as defined in this chapter.

[**1977 ex.s. c 314 § 1.**]

10.97.020
Short title.

This chapter may be cited as the Washington State Criminal Records Privacy Act.

[**1977 ex.s. c 314 § 2.**]

NOTES:

Reviser's note: The phrase "This 1977 amendatory act" has been changed to "This chapter." This 1977 amendatory act [1977 ex.s. c 314] consists of chapter **10.97** RCW and the amendments of RCW **42.17.310**, **43.43.705**, **43.43.710**, **43.43.730**, and **43.43.810**.

10.97.030
Definitions.

For purposes of this chapter, the definitions of terms in this section shall apply.

(1) "The administration of criminal justice" means performance of any of the following activities: Detection, apprehension, detention, pretrial release, post-trial release, prosecution, adjudication, correctional supervision, or rehabilitation of accused persons or criminal offenders. The term also includes criminal identification activities and the collection, storage, dissemination of criminal history record information, and the compensation of victims of crime.

(2) "Conviction or other disposition adverse to the subject" means any disposition of charges other than: (a) A decision not to prosecute; (b) a dismissal; or (c) acquittal; with the following exceptions, which shall be considered dispositions adverse to the subject: An acquittal due to a finding of not guilty by reason of insanity and a dismissal by reason of incompetency, pursuant to chapter **10.77** RCW; and a dismissal entered after a period of probation, suspension, or deferral of sentence.

(3) "Conviction record" means criminal history record information relating to an incident which has led to a conviction or other disposition adverse to the subject.

(4) "Criminal history record information" means information contained in records collected by criminal justice agencies, other than courts, on individuals, consisting of identifiable descriptions and notations of arrests, detentions, indictments, informations, or other formal criminal charges, and any disposition arising therefrom, including acquittals by reason of insanity, dismissals based on lack of competency, sentences, correctional supervision, and release.

The term includes any issued certificates of restoration of opportunities and any information contained in records maintained by or obtained from criminal justice agencies, other than courts, which records provide individual identification of a person together with any portion of the individual's record of involvement in the criminal justice system as an alleged or convicted offender, except:

(a) Posters, announcements, or lists for identifying or apprehending fugitives or wanted persons;

(b) Original records of entry maintained by criminal justice agencies to the extent that such records are compiled and maintained chronologically and are accessible only on a chronological basis;

(c) Court indices and records of public judicial proceedings, court decisions, and opinions, and information disclosed during public judicial proceedings;

(d) Records of traffic violations which are not punishable by a maximum term of imprisonment of more than ninety days;

(e) Records of any traffic offenses as maintained by the department of licensing for the purpose of regulating the issuance, suspension, revocation, or renewal of drivers' or other operators' licenses and pursuant to RCW **46.52.130**;

(f) Records of any aviation violations or offenses as maintained by the department of transportation for the purpose of regulating pilots or other aviation operators, and pursuant to RCW **47.68.330**;

(g) Announcements of executive clemency;

(h) Intelligence, analytical, or investigative reports and files.

(5) "Criminal justice agency" means: (a) A court; or (b) a government agency which performs the administration of criminal justice pursuant to a statute or executive order and which allocates a substantial part of its annual budget to the administration of criminal justice.

(6) "Disposition" means the formal conclusion of a criminal proceeding at whatever stage it occurs in the criminal justice system.

(7) "Dissemination" means disclosing criminal history record information or disclosing the absence of criminal history record information to any person or agency outside the agency possessing the information, subject to the following exceptions:

(a) When criminal justice agencies jointly participate in the maintenance of a single recordkeeping department as an alternative to maintaining separate records, the furnishing of information by that department to personnel of any participating agency is not a dissemination;

(b) The furnishing of information by any criminal justice agency to another for the purpose of processing a matter through the criminal justice system, such as a police department providing information to a prosecutor for use in preparing a charge, is not a dissemination;

(c) The reporting of an event to a recordkeeping agency for the purpose of maintaining the record is not a dissemination.

(8) "Nonconviction data" consists of all criminal history record information relating to an incident which has not led to a conviction or other disposition adverse to the subject, and for which proceedings are no longer actively pending. There shall be a rebuttable presumption that proceedings are no longer actively pending if more than one year has elapsed since arrest, citation, charge, or service of warrant and no disposition has been entered.

[2016 c 81 § 4; 2012 c 125 § 1; 1999 c 49 § 1; 1998 c 297 § 49; 1990 c 3 § 128; 1979 ex.s. c 36 § 1; 1979 c 158 § 5; 1977 ex.s. c 314 § 3.]

NOTES:

Reviser's note: The definitions in this section have been alphabetized pursuant to RCW **1.08.015**(2)(k).

Finding—Conflict with federal requirements—2016 c 81: See notes following RCW **9.97.010**.

Effective dates—Severability—Intent—1998 c 297: See notes following RCW **71.05.010**.

Index, part headings not law—Severability—Effective dates—Application—1990 c 3: See RCW **18.155.900** through **18.155.902**.

10.97.040
Information required—Exceptions.

No criminal justice agency shall disseminate criminal history record information pertaining to an arrest, detention, indictment, information, or other formal criminal charge made after December 31, 1977, unless the record disseminated states the disposition of such charge to the extent dispositions have been made at the time of the request for the information: PROVIDED, HOWEVER, That if a disposition occurring within ten days immediately preceding the dissemination has not been reported to the agency disseminating the criminal history record information, or if information has been received by the agency within the seventy-two hours immediately preceding the dissemination, that information shall not be required to be included in the dissemination: PROVIDED FURTHER, That when another criminal justice agency requests criminal history record information, the disseminating agency may disseminate specific facts and incidents which are within its direct knowledge without furnishing disposition data as otherwise required by this section, unless the disseminating agency has received such disposition data from either: (1) the state patrol, or (2) the court or other criminal justice agency required to furnish disposition data pursuant to RCW**10.97.045**.

No criminal justice agency shall disseminate criminal history record information which shall include information concerning a felony or gross misdemeanor without first making inquiry of the identification section of the Washington state patrol for the purpose of obtaining the most current and complete information available, unless one or more of the following circumstances exists:

(1) The information to be disseminated is needed for a purpose in the administration of criminal justice for which time is of the essence and the identification section is technically or physically incapable of responding within the required time;

(2) The full information requested and to be disseminated relates to specific facts or incidents which are within the direct knowledge of the agency which disseminates the information;

(3) The full information requested and to be disseminated is contained in a criminal history record information summary received from the identification section by the agency which is to make the dissemination not more than thirty days preceding the dissemination to be made;

(4) The statute, executive order, court rule, or court order pursuant to which the information is to be disseminated refers solely to information in the files of the agency which makes the dissemination;

(5) The information requested and to be disseminated is for the express purpose of research, evaluative, or statistical activities to be based upon information maintained in the files of the agency or agencies from which the information is directly sought; or

(6) A person who is the subject of the record requests the information and the agency complies with the requirements in RCW **10.97.080** as now or hereafter amended.

[**1979 ex.s. c 36 § 2; 1977 ex.s. c 314 § 4.**]

10.97.045

Disposition data to initiating agency and state patrol.

Whenever a court or other criminal justice agency reaches a disposition of a criminal proceeding, the court or other criminal justice agency shall furnish the disposition data to the agency initiating the criminal history record for that charge and to the identification section of the Washington state patrol as required under RCW **43.43.745**.

[**1979 ex.s. c 36 § 6.**]

10.97.050

Restricted, unrestricted information—Records.

(1) Conviction records may be disseminated without restriction.

(2) Any criminal history record information which pertains to an incident that occurred within the last twelve months for which a person is currently being processed by the criminal justice system, including the entire period of correctional supervision extending through final discharge from parole, when applicable, may be disseminated without restriction.

(3) Criminal history record information which includes nonconviction data may be disseminated by a criminal justice agency to another criminal justice agency for any purpose associated with the administration of criminal justice, or in connection with the employment of the subject of the record by a criminal justice or juvenile justice agency. A criminal justice agency may respond to any inquiry from another criminal justice agency without any obligation to ascertain the purpose for which the information is to be used by the agency making the inquiry.

(4) Criminal history record information which includes nonconviction data may be disseminated by a criminal justice agency to implement a statute, ordinance, executive order, or a court rule, decision, or order which expressly refers to records of arrest, charges, or allegations of criminal conduct or other nonconviction data and authorizes or directs that it be available or accessible for a specific purpose.

(5) Criminal history record information which includes nonconviction data may be disseminated to individuals and agencies pursuant to a contract with a criminal justice agency to provide services related to the administration of criminal justice. Such contract must specifically authorize access to criminal history record information, but need not specifically state that access to nonconviction data is included. The agreement must limit the use of the criminal history record information to stated purposes and insure the confidentiality and security of the information consistent with state law and any applicable federal statutes and regulations.

(6) Criminal history record information which includes nonconviction data may be disseminated to individuals and agencies for the express purpose of research,

evaluative, or statistical activities pursuant to an agreement with a criminal justice agency. Such agreement must authorize the access to nonconviction data, limit the use of that information which identifies specific individuals to research, evaluative, or statistical purposes, and contain provisions giving notice to the person or organization to which the records are disseminated that the use of information obtained therefrom and further dissemination of such information are subject to the provisions of this chapter and applicable federal statutes and regulations, which shall be cited with express reference to the penalties provided for a violation thereof.

(7) Every criminal justice agency that maintains and disseminates criminal history record information must maintain information pertaining to every dissemination of criminal history record information except a dissemination to the effect that the agency has no record concerning an individual. Information pertaining to disseminations shall include:

(a) An indication of to whom (agency or person) criminal history record information was disseminated;

(b) The date on which the information was disseminated;

(c) The individual to whom the information relates; and

(d) A brief description of the information disseminated.

The information pertaining to dissemination required to be maintained shall be retained for a period of not less than one year.

(8) In addition to the other provisions in this section allowing dissemination of criminal history record information, RCW **4.24.550** governs dissemination of information concerning offenders who commit sex offenses as defined by RCW **9.94A.030**. Criminal justice agencies, their employees, and officials shall be immune from civil liability for dissemination on criminal history record information concerning sex offenders as provided in RCW **4.24.550**.

[**2012 c 125 § 2; 2005 c 421 § 9; 1990 c 3 § 129; 1977 ex.s. c 314 § 5.**]

NOTES:

Index, part headings not law—Severability—Effective dates—Application—1990 c 3: See RCW **18.155.900** through **18.155.902**.

10.97.060
Deletion of certain information, conditions.

Criminal history record information which consists of nonconviction data only shall be subject to deletion from criminal justice agency files which are available and generally searched for the purpose of responding to inquiries concerning the criminal history of a named or otherwise identified individual when two years or longer have elapsed since the record became nonconviction data as a result of the entry of a disposition favorable to the defendant, or upon the passage of three years from the date of arrest or issuance of a citation or warrant for an offense for which a conviction was not obtained unless the defendant is a fugitive, or the case is under active prosecution according to a current certification made by the prosecuting attorney.

Such criminal history record information consisting of nonconviction data shall be deleted upon the request of the person who is the subject of the record: PROVIDED, HOWEVER, That the criminal justice agency maintaining the data may, at its option, refuse to make the deletion if:

(1) The disposition was a deferred prosecution or similar diversion of the alleged offender;

(2) The person who is the subject of the record has had a prior conviction for a felony or gross misdemeanor;

(3) The individual who is the subject of the record has been arrested for or charged with another crime during the intervening period.

Nothing in this chapter is intended to restrict the authority of any court, through appropriate judicial proceedings, to order the modification or deletion of a record in a particular cause or concerning a particular individual or event.

[**1977 ex.s. c 314 § 6.**]

10.97.070

Disclosure of suspect's identity to victim.

(1) Criminal justice agencies may, in their discretion, disclose to persons who have suffered physical loss, property damage, or injury compensable through civil action, the identity of persons suspected as being responsible for such loss, damage, or injury together with such information as the agency reasonably believes may be of assistance to the victim in obtaining civil redress. Such disclosure may be made without regard to whether the suspected offender is an adult or a juvenile, whether charges have or have not been filed, or a prosecuting authority has declined to file a charge or a charge has been dismissed.

(2) Unless the agency determines release would interfere with an ongoing criminal investigation, in any action brought pursuant to this chapter, criminal justice agencies shall disclose identifying information, including photographs of suspects, if the acts are alleged by the plaintiff or victim to be a violation of RCW **9A.50.020**.

(3) The disclosure by a criminal justice agency of investigative information pursuant to subsection (1) of this section shall not establish a duty to disclose any additional information concerning the same incident or make any subsequent disclosure of investigative information, except to the extent an additional disclosure is compelled by legal process.

[**1993 c 128 § 10; 1977 ex.s. c 314 § 7.**]

NOTES:

Effective date—**1993 c 128:** See RCW **9A.50.902**.

10.97.080

Inspection of information by subject—Challenges and corrections.

All criminal justice agencies shall permit an individual who is, or who believes that he or she may be, the subject of a criminal record maintained by that agency, to appear in person during normal business hours of that criminal justice agency and request to see the criminal history record information held by that agency pertaining to the individual. The individual's right to access and review of criminal history record information shall not extend to data contained in intelligence, investigative, or other related files, and shall not be construed to include any information other than that defined as criminal history record information by this chapter.

Every criminal justice agency shall adopt rules and make available forms to facilitate the inspection and review of criminal history record information by the subjects thereof, which rules may include requirements for identification, the establishment of reasonable periods of time to be allowed an individual to examine the record, and for assistance by an individual's counsel, interpreter, or other appropriate persons.

No person shall be allowed to retain or mechanically reproduce any nonconviction data except for the person who is the subject of the record. Such person may retain a copy of their personal nonconviction data information on file, if the criminal justice agency has verified the identities of those who seek to inspect them. Criminal justice agencies may impose such additional restrictions, including fingerprinting, as are reasonably necessary both to assure the record's security and to verify the identities of those who seek to inspect them. The criminal justice agency may charge a reasonable fee for fingerprinting or providing a copy of the personal nonconviction data information pursuant to this section. The provisions of chapter **42.56** RCW shall not be construed to require or authorize copying of nonconviction data for any other purpose.

The Washington state patrol shall establish rules for the challenge of records which an individual declares to be inaccurate or incomplete, and for the resolution of any disputes between individuals and criminal justice agencies pertaining to the accuracy and completeness of criminal history record information. The Washington state patrol shall also adopt rules for the correction of criminal history record information and the dissemination of corrected information to agencies and persons to whom inaccurate or incomplete information was previously disseminated. Such rules may establish time limitations of not less than ninety days upon the requirement for disseminating corrected information.

[2012 c 125 § 3; 2010 c 8 § 1093; 2005 c 274 § 206; 1979 ex.s. c 36 § 3; 1977 ex.s. c 314 § 8.]

10.97.090
Administration by state patrol.

The Washington state patrol is hereby designated the agency of state government responsible for the administration of the 1977 Washington State Criminal Records Privacy Act. The Washington state patrol may adopt any rules and regulations necessary for the performance of the administrative functions provided for in this chapter.

The Washington state patrol shall have the following specific administrative duties:

(1) To establish by rule and regulation standards for the security of criminal history information systems in order that such systems and the data contained therein be adequately protected from fire, theft, loss, destruction, other physical hazard, or unauthorized access;

(2) To establish by rule and regulation standards for personnel employed by criminal justice of other state and local government agencies in positions with responsibility for maintenance and dissemination of criminal history record information; and

(3) To contract with the Washington state auditor or other public or private agency, organization, or individual to perform audits of criminal history record information systems.

[1979 ex.s. c 36 § 4; 1977 ex.s. c 314 § 9.]

10.97.100
Fees.

Criminal justice agencies shall be authorized to establish and collect reasonable fees for the dissemination of criminal history record information to agencies and persons other than criminal justice agencies.

[1977 ex.s. c 314 § 10.]

10.97.110
Civil remedies—Criminal prosecution not affected.

Any person may maintain an action to enjoin a continuance of any act or acts in violation of any of the provisions of this chapter, and if injured thereby, for the recovery of damages and for the recovery of reasonable attorneys' fees. If, in such action, the court shall find that the defendant is violating or has violated any of the provisions of this chapter, it shall enjoin the defendant from a continuance thereof, and it shall not be necessary that actual damages to the plaintiff be alleged or proved. In addition to such injunctive relief, the plaintiff in said action shall be entitled to recover from the defendant the amount of the actual damages, if any, sustained by him or her if actual damages to the plaintiff are alleged and proved. In any suit brought to enjoin a violation of this chapter, the prevailing party may be awarded reasonable attorneys' fees, including fees incurred upon appeal. Commencement, pendency, or conclusion of a civil action for injunction or damages shall not affect the liability of a person or agency to criminal prosecution for a violation of this chapter.

[2010 c 8 § 1094; 1979 ex.s. c 36 § 5; 1977 ex.s. c 314 § 11.]

10.97.120

Criminal penalties—Civil action not affected.

Violation of the provisions of this chapter shall constitute a misdemeanor, and any person whether as principal, agent, officer, or director for himself or herself or for another person, or for any firm or corporation, public or private, or any municipality who or which shall violate any of the provisions of this chapter shall be guilty of a misdemeanor for each single violation. Any criminal prosecution shall not affect the right of any person to bring a civil action as authorized by this chapter or otherwise authorized by law.

[2010 c 8 § 1095; 1977 ex.s. c 314 § 12.]

10.97.130

Child victims of sexual assaults, identification confidential.

Information identifying child victims under age eighteen who are victims of sexual assaults is confidential and not subject to release to the press or public without the permission of the child victim or the child's legal guardian. Identifying information includes the child victim's name, addresses, location, photographs, and in cases in which the child victim is a relative or stepchild of the alleged perpetrator, identification of the relationship between the child and the alleged perpetrator. Information identifying the child victim of sexual assault may be released to law enforcement, prosecutors, judges, defense attorneys, or private or governmental agencies that provide services to the child victim of sexual assault. Prior to release of any criminal history record information, the releasing agency shall delete any information identifying a child victim of sexual assault from the information except as provided in this section.

[1992 c 188 § 8.]

NOTES:

Findings—Intent—Severability—1992 c 188: See notes following RCW **7.69A.020**.

10.97.140
Construction.

Nothing in RCW **40.14.060** or **40.14.070** or chapter **42.56** RCW precludes dissemination of criminal history record information, including nonconviction data, for the purposes of this chapter.

[**2005 c 274 § 207; 1999 c 326 § 4.**]

Chapter 10.98 RCW CRIMINAL JUSTICE INFORMATION ACT

10.98.010
Purpose.

The purpose of this chapter is to provide a system of reporting and disseminating felony criminal justice information that provides: (1) Timely and accurate criminal histories for filing and sentencing under the sentencing reform act of 1981, (2) identification and tracking of felons, and (3) data for statewide planning and forecasting of the felon population.

[**1984 c 17 § 1.**]

10.98.020
Short title.

This chapter may be known and cited as the criminal justice information act.

[**1984 c 17 § 2.**]

10.98.030
Source of conviction histories.

The Washington state patrol identification, child abuse, and criminal history section as established in *RCW **43.43.700** shall be the primary source of felony conviction histories for filings, plea agreements, and sentencing on felony cases.

[**1999 c 143 § 50; 1984 c 17 § 3.**]

NOTES:

*Reviser's note: RCW **43.43.700** was amended by 2006 c 294 § 1, renaming the "identification, child abuse, and criminal history section" as the "identification and criminal history section."

10.98.040
Definitions.

Unless the context clearly requires otherwise, the definitions in this section apply throughout this chapter.

(1) "Arrest and fingerprint form" means the reporting form prescribed by the *identification, child abuse, and criminal history section to initiate compiling arrest and identification information.

(2) "Chief law enforcement officer" includes the sheriff or director of public safety of a county, the chief of police of a city or town, and chief officers of other law enforcement agencies operating within the state.

(3) "Department" means the department of corrections.

(4) "Disposition" means the conclusion of a criminal proceeding at any stage it occurs in the criminal justice system. Disposition includes but is not limited to temporary or permanent outcomes such as charges dropped by police, charges not filed by the prosecuting attorney, deferred prosecution, defendant absconded, charges filed by the prosecuting attorney pending court findings such as not guilty, dismissed, guilty, or guilty—case appealed to higher court.

(5) "Disposition report" means the reporting form prescribed by the *identification, child abuse, and criminal history section to report the legal procedures taken after completing an arrest and fingerprint form. The disposition report shall include but not be limited to the following types of information:

(a) The type of disposition;

(b) The statutory citation for the arrests;

(c) The sentence structure if the defendant was convicted of a felony;

(d) The state identification number; and

(e) Identification information and other information that is prescribed by the *identification, child abuse, and criminal history section.

(6) "Fingerprints" means the fingerprints taken from arrested or charged persons under the procedures prescribed by the Washington state patrol *identification, child abuse, and criminal history section.

(7) "Prosecuting attorney" means the public or private attorney prosecuting a criminal case.

(8) "Section" refers to the Washington state patrol *section on identification, child abuse, and criminal history.

(9) "Sentence structure" means itemizing the components of the felony sentence. The sentence structure shall include but not be limited to the total or partial confinement sentenced, and whether the sentence is prison or jail, community supervision, fines, restitution, or community restitution.

[2002 c 175 § 18; 1999 c 143 § 51; 1985 c 201 § 1; 1984 c 17 § 4.]

NOTES:

*Reviser's note: The "identification, child abuse, and criminal history section" was renamed the "identification and criminal history section" by **2006 c 294 § 1.**

Effective date—2002 c 175: See note following RCW **7.80.130.**

10.98.050
Officials' duties.

(1) It is the duty of the chief law enforcement officer or the local director of corrections to transmit within seventy-two hours from the time of arrest to the section fingerprints together with other identifying data as may be prescribed by the section, and statutory violations of any person lawfully arrested, fingerprinted, and photographed under RCW **43.43.735**. The disposition report shall be transmitted to the prosecuting attorney, county clerk, or appropriate court of limited jurisdiction, whichever is responsible for transmitting the report to the section under RCW **10.98.010**.

(2) At the preliminary hearing or the arraignment of a felony case, the judge shall ensure that the felony defendants have been fingerprinted and an arrest and fingerprint form transmitted to the section. In cases where fingerprints have not been taken, the judge shall order the chief law enforcement officer of the jurisdiction or the local director of corrections, or, in the case of a juvenile, the juvenile court administrator to initiate an arrest and fingerprint form and transmit it to the section. The disposition report shall be transmitted to the prosecuting attorney.

[**1999 c 49 § 2; 1989 c 6 § 1; 1987 c 450 § 6; 1985 c 201 § 2; 1984 c 17 § 5.**]

10.98.060
Arrest and fingerprint form.

The arrest and fingerprint form shall include but not be limited to the following:

(1) Unique numbers associated with the arrest charges. The unique numbering system may be controlled by the local law enforcement agency, however the section shall approve of the numbering system and maintain a current catalog of approved local numbering systems. The purpose of the unique numbering system is to allow tracking of arrest charges through disposition;

(2) An organization code;

(3) Date of arrest;

(4) Local identification number;

(5) The prescribed fingerprints;

(6) Individual identification information and other information prescribed by the section.

[1984 c 17 § 6.]

10.98.070
National crime information center interstate identification index.

The section shall be the sole recipient of arrest and fingerprint forms described in RCW **10.98.060**, fingerprint forms described in RCW**43.43.760**, and disposition reports for forwarding to the federal bureau of investigation as required for participation in the national crime information center interstate identification index. The section shall comply with national crime information center interstate identification index regulations to maintain availability of out-of-state criminal history information.
[1984 c 17 § 7.]

10.98.080
State identification number, furnishing of.

The section shall promptly furnish a state identification number to the originating agency and to the prosecuting attorney who received a copy of the arrest and fingerprint form. In the case of juvenile felony-like adjudications, the section shall furnish, upon request, the state identification number to the juvenile information section of the administrative office of the courts.
[2005 c 282 § 23; 1985 c 201 § 3; 1984 c 17 § 8.]

10.98.090
Disposition forms—Coding.

(1) In all cases where an arrest and fingerprint form is transmitted to the section, the originating agency shall code the form indicating which agency is initially responsible for reporting the disposition to the section. Coding shall include but not be limited to the prosecuting attorney, superior court, district court, municipal court, or the originating agency.

(2) In the case of a superior court or felony disposition, the county clerk or prosecuting attorney shall promptly transmit the completed disposition information to the section. In a county where the judicial information system or other secure method of electronic transfer of information has been implemented between the court and the section, the county clerk shall electronically provide the disposition information. In the case of a felony conviction in a county without the judicial information system or other secure method of electronic transfer of information between the court and the section, the prosecuting attorney shall attach a copy of the judgment and sentence form to the disposition form transmitted to the section. In the case of a lower court disposition, the district or municipal court administrator shall either promptly transmit the completed disposition form or, in a county where the judicial information system or other secure method of electronic transfer of information has been implemented between the court and the section, electronically provide the disposition information to the section. For all other dispositions the originating agency shall promptly transmit the completed disposition form to the section.

[**1998 c 197 § 1; 1985 c 201 § 4; 1984 c 17 § 9.**]

10.98.100
Compliance audit.

The section shall administer a compliance audit at least once annually for each prosecuting attorney, district and municipal court, and originating agency to ensure that all disposition reports have been received and added to the criminal history record information described in RCW **43.43.705**. The section shall identify criminal history record information for which no disposition report has been received and has been outstanding for one year or longer since the date of arrest. Each open arrest shall be researched for a final disposition by section staff or the criminal justice agency shall be furnished a list of outstanding disposition reports for criminal history record information of persons who were arrested or against whom charges were filed by that agency. Each criminal justice agency shall provide the section with a current disposition report or status within sixty days of receipt of notification of open arrest. Cases pending prosecution shall be considered outstanding dispositions in the compliance audit. The results of compliance audits shall be published annually and distributed to legislative committees dealing with criminal justice issues, the office of financial management, and criminal justice agencies and associations.

[2013 c 62 § 1; 2005 c 282 § 24; 1985 c 201 § 5; 1984 c 17 § 10.]

10.98.110
Tracking felony cases.

(1) The department shall maintain records to track felony cases for convicted felons sentenced either to a term of confinement exceeding one year or ordered under the supervision of the department and felony cases under the jurisdiction of the department pursuant to interstate compact agreements.

(2) Tracking shall begin at the time the department receives a judgment and sentence form from a prosecuting attorney and shall include the collection and updating of felons' criminal records from the time of sentencing through discharge.

(3) The department of corrections shall collect information for tracking felons from its offices and from information provided by county clerks, the Washington state patrol *identification, child abuse, and criminal history section, the office of financial management, and any other public or private agency that provides services to help individuals complete their felony sentences.

[1999 c 143 § 52; 1993 c 31 § 1; 1987 c 462 § 2; 1984 c 17 § 11.]

NOTES:

*Reviser's note: The "identification, child abuse, and criminal history section" was renamed the "identification and criminal history section" by **2006 c 294 § 1.**

Effective dates—1987 c 462: See note following RCW **13.04.116.**

10.98.130
Local jail reports.

Local jails shall report to the office of financial management and that office shall transmit to the department the information on all persons convicted of felonies or incarcerated for noncompliance with a felony sentence who are admitted or released from the jails and shall promptly respond to requests of the department for such data. Information transmitted shall include but not be limited to the state identification number, whether the reason for admission to jail was a felony conviction or noncompliance with a felony sentence, and the dates of the admission and release.

The office of financial management may contract with a state or local governmental agency, or combination thereof, or a private organization for the information collection and transmittal under this section.

[1988 c 152 § 1; 1987 c 462 § 3; 1984 c 17 § 13.]

NOTES:

Effective dates—1987 c 462: See note following RCW **13.04.116**.

10.98.140

Criminal justice forecasting—Sentencing records.

(1) The section, the department, and the office of financial management shall be the primary sources of information for criminal justice forecasting. The information maintained by these agencies shall be complete, accurate, and sufficiently timely to support state criminal justice forecasting.

(2) The caseload forecast council shall keep records on all sentencings above or below the standard range defined by chapter **9.94A** RCW. As a minimum, the records shall include the name of the offender, the crimes for which the offender was sentenced, the name and county of the sentencing judge, and the deviation from the standard range. Such records shall be made available to public officials upon request.

[2011 1st sp.s. c 40 § 32; 1987 c 462 § 4; 1985 c 201 § 6; 1984 c 17 § 14.]

NOTES:

Application—Recalculation of community custody terms—2011 1st sp.s. c 40: See note following RCW **9.94A.501**.

Effective dates—1987 c 462: See note following RCW **13.04.116**.

10.98.150

Status reports on felons.

The section and the department shall provide prompt responses to the requests of law enforcement agencies and jails regarding the status of suspected or convicted felons. Dissemination of individual identities, criminal histories, or the whereabouts of a suspected or convicted felon shall be in accordance with chapter **10.97** RCW, the Washington state criminal records privacy act.

[**1984 c 17 § 15.**]

10.98.160

Procedures, development considerations—Washington integrated justice information board, review and recommendations.

In the development and modification of the procedures, definitions, and reporting capabilities of the section, the department, the office of financial management, and the responsible agencies and persons shall consider the needs of other criminal justice agencies such as the administrative office of the courts, local law enforcement agencies, local jails, the indeterminate sentence review board, the clemency board, prosecuting attorneys, and affected state agencies such as the office of financial management and legislative committees dealing with criminal justice issues. The Washington integrated justice information board shall review and provide recommendations to state justice agencies and the courts for development and modification of the statewide justice information network.

[**2011 1st sp.s. c 40 § 33; 2005 c 282 § 25; 2003 c 104 § 2; 1999 c 143 § 53; 1987 c 462 § 5; 1984 c 17 § 16.**]

NOTES:

      Application—Recalculation of community custody terms—2011 1st sp.s. c 40: See note following RCW **9.94A.501**.

      Effective dates—1987 c 462: See note following RCW **13.04.116**.

Chapter 10.99 RCW DOMESTIC VIOLENCE—

OFFICIAL RESPONSE

NOTES:

Arrest without warrant in domestic violence cases: RCW **10.31.100**(2).

Domestic violence prevention: Chapter **26.50** RCW.

Rape crisis centers: Chapters **70.123** and **70.125** RCW.

Shelters for victims of domestic violence: Chapter **70.123** RCW.

Victims, survivors, and witnesses of crimes: Chapter **7.69** RCW.

10.99.010
Purpose—Intent.

The purpose of this chapter is to recognize the importance of domestic violence as a serious crime against society and to assure the victim of domestic violence the maximum protection from abuse which the law and those who enforce the law can provide. The legislature finds that the existing criminal statutes are adequate to provide protection for victims of domestic violence. However, previous societal attitudes have been reflected in policies and practices of law enforcement agencies and prosecutors which have resulted in differing treatment of crimes occurring between cohabitants and of the same crimes occurring between strangers. Only recently has public perception of the serious consequences of domestic violence to society and to the victims led to the recognition of the necessity for early intervention by law enforcement agencies. It is the intent of the legislature that the official response to cases of domestic violence shall stress the enforcement of the laws to protect the victim and shall communicate the attitude that violent behavior is not excused or tolerated. Furthermore, it is the intent of the legislature that criminal laws be enforced without regard to whether the persons involved are or were married, cohabiting, or involved in a relationship.

10.99.020
Definitions.

Unless the context clearly requires otherwise, the definitions in this section apply throughout this chapter.

(1) "Agency" means a general authority Washington law enforcement agency as defined in RCW **10.93.020**.

(2) "Association" means the Washington association of sheriffs and police chiefs.

(3) "Family or household members" means spouses, former spouses, persons who have a child in common regardless of whether they have been married or have lived together at any time, adult persons related by blood or marriage, adult persons who are presently residing together or who have resided together in the past, persons sixteen years of age or older who are presently residing together or who have resided together in the past and who have or have had a dating relationship, persons sixteen years of age or older with whom a person sixteen years of age or older has or has had a dating relationship, and persons who have a biological or legal parent-child relationship, including stepparents and stepchildren and grandparents and grandchildren.

(4) "Dating relationship" has the same meaning as in RCW **26.50.010**.

(5) "Domestic violence" includes but is not limited to any of the following crimes when committed by one family or household member against another:

(a) Assault in the first degree (RCW **9A.36.011**);

(b) Assault in the second degree (RCW **9A.36.021**);

(c) Assault in the third degree (RCW **9A.36.031**);

(d) Assault in the fourth degree (RCW **9A.36.041**);

(e) Drive-by shooting (RCW **9A.36.045**);

(f) Reckless endangerment (RCW **9A.36.050**);

(g) Coercion (RCW **9A.36.070**);

(h) Burglary in the first degree (RCW **9A.52.020**);

(i) Burglary in the second degree (RCW **9A.52.030**);

(j) Criminal trespass in the first degree (RCW **9A.52.070**);

(k) Criminal trespass in the second degree (RCW **9A.52.080**);

(l) Malicious mischief in the first degree (RCW **9A.48.070**);

(m) Malicious mischief in the second degree (RCW **9A.48.080**);

(n) Malicious mischief in the third degree (RCW **9A.48.090**);

(o) Kidnapping in the first degree (RCW **9A.40.020**);

(p) Kidnapping in the second degree (RCW **9A.40.030**);

(q) Unlawful imprisonment (RCW **9A.40.040**);

(r) Violation of the provisions of a restraining order, no-contact order, or protection order restraining or enjoining the person or restraining the person from going onto the grounds of or entering a residence, workplace, school, or day care, or prohibiting the person from knowingly coming within, or knowingly remaining within, a specified distance of a location (RCW **10.99.040**, **10.99.050**, **26.09.300**, **26.10.220**, **26.26.138**,**26.44.063**, **26.44.150**, **26.5 0.060**, **26.50.070**, **26.50.130**, **26.52.070**, or **74.34.145**);

(s) Rape in the first degree (RCW **9A.44.040**);

(t) Rape in the second degree (RCW **9A.44.050**);

(u) Residential burglary (RCW **9A.52.025**);

(v) Stalking (RCW **9A.46.110**); and

(w) Interference with the reporting of domestic violence (RCW **9A.36.150**).

(6) "Employee" means any person currently employed with an agency.

(7) "Sworn employee" means a general authority Washington peace officer as defined in RCW **10.93.020**, any person appointed under RCW**35.21.333**, and any person appointed or elected to carry out the duties of the sheriff under chapter **36.28** RCW.

(8) "Victim" means a family or household member who has been subjected to domestic violence.

[**2004 c 18 § 2; 2000 c 119 § 5; 1997 c 338 § 53; 1996 c 248 § 5; 1995 c 246 § 21; 1994 c 121 § 4; 1991 c 301 § 3; 1986 c 257 § 8; 1984 c 263 § 20;1979 ex.s. c 105 § 2.**]

NOTES:

Findings—Intent—2004 c 18: "The legislature reaffirms its determination to reduce the incident rate of domestic violence. The legislature finds it is appropriate to help reduce the incident rate of domestic violence by addressing the need for improved coordination and accountability among general authority Washington law enforcement agencies and general authority Washington peace officers when reports of domestic violence are made and the alleged perpetrator is a general authority Washington peace officer. The legislature finds that coordination and accountability will be improved if general authority Washington law enforcement agencies adopt policies that meet statewide minimum requirements for training, reporting, interagency cooperation, investigation, and collaboration with groups serving victims of domestic violence. The legislature intends to provide maximum flexibility to general authority Washington law enforcement agencies, consistent with the purposes of this act, in their efforts to improve coordination and accountability when incidents of domestic violence committed or allegedly committed by general authority Washington peace officers are reported." [**2004 c 18 § 1.**]

Application—2000 c 119: See note following RCW **26.50.021**.

Finding—Evaluation—Report—1997 c 338: See note following RCW **13.40.0357**.

Severability—Effective dates—1997 c 338: See notes following RCW **5.60.060**.

Severability—1995 c 246: See note following RCW **26.50.010**.

Finding—1991 c 301: "The legislature finds that:

The collective costs to the community for domestic violence include the systematic destruction of individuals and their families, lost lives, lost productivity, and increased health care, criminal justice, and social service costs.

Children growing up in violent homes are deeply affected by the violence as it happens and could be the next generation of batterers and victims.

Many communities have made headway in addressing the effects of domestic violence and have devoted energy and resources to stopping this violence. However, the process for breaking the cycle of abuse is lengthy. No single system intervention is enough in itself.

An integrated system has not been adequately funded and structured to assure access to a wide range of services, including those of the law/safety/justice system, human service system, and health care system. These services need to be coordinated and multidisciplinary in approach and address the needs of victims, batterers, and children from violent homes.

Given the lethal nature of domestic violence and its effect on all within its range, the community has a vested interest in the methods used to stop and prevent future violence. Clear standards of quality are needed so that perpetrator treatment programs receiving public funds or court-ordered referrals can be required to comply with these standards.

While incidents of domestic violence are not caused by perpetrator's use of alcohol and illegal substances, substance abuse may be a contributing factor to domestic violence and the injuries and deaths that result from it.

There is a need for consistent training of professionals who deal frequently with domestic violence or are in a position to identify domestic violence and provide support and information.

Much has been learned about effective interventions in domestic violence situations; however, much is not yet known and further study is required to know how to best stop this violence." [**1991 c 301 § 1.**]

Severability—1986 c 257: See note following RCW **9A.56.010**.

Effective date—1986 c 257 §§ 3-10: See note following RCW **9A.04.110**.

Effective date—1984 c 263: See RCW **26.50.901**.

Domestic violence defined under the Domestic Violence Prevention Act: RCW **26.50.010**.

10.99.030
Law enforcement officers—Training, powers, duties—Domestic violence reports.

(1) All training relating to the handling of domestic violence complaints by law enforcement officers shall stress enforcement of criminal laws in domestic situations, availability of community resources, and protection of the victim. Law enforcement agencies and community organizations with expertise in the issue of domestic violence shall cooperate in all aspects of such training.

(2) The criminal justice training commission shall implement by January 1, 1997, a course of instruction for the training of law enforcement officers in Washington in the handling of domestic violence complaints. The basic law enforcement curriculum of the criminal justice training commission shall include at least twenty hours of basic training instruction on the law enforcement response to domestic violence. The course of instruction, the learning and performance objectives, and the standards for the training shall be developed by the commission and focus on enforcing the criminal laws, safety of the victim, and holding the perpetrator accountable for the violence. The curriculum shall include training on the extent and prevalence of domestic violence, the importance of criminal justice intervention, techniques for responding to incidents that minimize the likelihood of officer injury and that promote victim safety, investigation and interviewing skills, evidence gathering and report writing, assistance to and services for victims and children, verification and enforcement of court orders, liability, and any additional provisions that are necessary to carry out the intention of this subsection.

(3) The criminal justice training commission shall develop and update annually an in-service training program to familiarize law enforcement officers with the domestic violence laws. The program shall include techniques for handling incidents of domestic violence that minimize the likelihood of injury to the officer and that promote the safety of all parties. The commission shall make the training program available to all law enforcement agencies in the state.

(4) Development of the training in subsections (2) and (3) of this section shall be conducted in conjunction with agencies having a primary responsibility for serving victims of domestic violence with emergency shelter and other services, and representatives to the statewide organization providing training and education to these organizations and to the general public.

(5) The primary duty of peace officers, when responding to a domestic violence situation, is to enforce the laws allegedly violated and to protect the complaining party.

(6)(a) When a peace officer responds to a domestic violence call and has probable cause to believe that a crime has been committed, the peace officer shall exercise arrest powers with reference to the criteria in RCW **10.31.100**. The officer shall notify the victim of the victim's right to initiate a criminal proceeding in all cases where the officer has not exercised arrest powers or decided to initiate criminal proceedings by citation or otherwise. The parties in such cases shall also be advised of the importance of preserving evidence.

(b) A peace officer responding to a domestic violence call shall take a complete offense report including the officer's disposition of the case.

(7) When a peace officer responds to a domestic violence call, the officer shall advise victims of all reasonable means to prevent further abuse, including advising each person of the availability of a shelter or other services in the community, and giving each person immediate notice of the legal rights and remedies available. The notice shall include handing each person a copy of the following statement:

"IF YOU ARE THE VICTIM OF DOMESTIC VIOLENCE, you can ask the city or county prosecuting attorney to file a criminal complaint. You also have the right to file a petition in superior, district, or municipal court requesting an order for protection from domestic abuse which could include any of the following: (a) An order restraining your abuser from further acts of abuse; (b) an order directing your abuser to leave your household; (c) an order preventing your abuser from entering your residence, school, business, or place of employment; (d) an order awarding you or the other parent custody of or visitation with your minor child or children; and (e) an order restraining your abuser from molesting or interfering with minor children in your custody. The forms you need to obtain a protection order are available in any municipal, district, or superior court. Information about shelters and alternatives to domestic violence is available from a statewide twenty-four-hour toll-free hotline at (include appropriate phone number). The battered women's shelter and other resources in your area are . . . . . (include local information)"

(8) The peace officer may offer, arrange, or facilitate transportation for the victim to a hospital for treatment of injuries or to a place of safety or shelter.

(9) The law enforcement agency shall forward the offense report to the appropriate prosecutor within ten days of making such report if there is probable cause to believe that an offense has been committed, unless the case is under active investigation. Upon receiving the offense report, the prosecuting agency may, in its discretion, choose not to file the information as a domestic violence offense, if the offense was committed against a sibling, parent, stepparent, or grandparent.

(10) Each law enforcement agency shall make as soon as practicable a written record and shall maintain records of all incidents of domestic violence reported to it.

(11) Records kept pursuant to subsections (6) and (10) of this section shall be made identifiable by means of a departmental code for domestic violence.

(12) Commencing January 1, 1994, records of incidents of domestic violence shall be submitted, in accordance with procedures described in this subsection, to the Washington association of sheriffs and police chiefs by all law enforcement agencies. The Washington criminal justice training commission shall amend its contract for collection of statewide crime data with the Washington association of sheriffs and police chiefs:

(a) To include a table, in the annual report of crime in Washington produced by the Washington association of sheriffs and police chiefs pursuant to the contract, showing the total number of actual offenses and the number and percent of the offenses that are domestic violence incidents for the following crimes: (i) Criminal homicide, with subtotals for murder and nonnegligent homicide and manslaughter by negligence; (ii) forcible rape, with subtotals for rape by force and attempted forcible rape; (iii) robbery, with subtotals for firearm, knife or cutting instrument, or other dangerous weapon, and strongarm robbery; (iv) assault, with subtotals for firearm, knife or cutting instrument, other dangerous weapon, hands, feet, aggravated, and other nonaggravated assaults; (v) burglary, with subtotals for forcible entry, nonforcible unlawful entry, and attempted forcible entry; (vi) larceny theft, except motor vehicle theft; (vii) motor vehicle theft, with subtotals for autos, trucks and buses, and other vehicles; (viii) arson; and (ix) violations of the provisions of a protection order or no-contact order restraining the person from going onto the grounds of or entering a residence, workplace, school, or day care, provided that specific appropriations are subsequently made for the collection and compilation of data regarding violations of protection orders or no-contact orders;

(b) To require that the table shall continue to be prepared and contained in the annual report of crime in Washington until that time as comparable or more detailed information about domestic violence incidents is available through the Washington state incident based reporting system and the information is prepared and contained in the annual report of crime in Washington; and

(c) To require that, in consultation with interested persons, the Washington association of sheriffs and police chiefs prepare and disseminate procedures to all law enforcement agencies in the state as to how the agencies shall code and report domestic violence incidents to the Washington association of sheriffs and police chiefs.
[**2016 c 136 § 5; 1996 c 248 § 6; 1995 c 246 § 22; 1993 c 350 § 3; 1984 c 263 § 21; 1981 c 145 § 5; 1979 ex.s. c 105 § 3.**]
NOTES:

> **Severability—1995 c 246:** See note following RCW **26.50.010**.
> **Findings—Severability—1993 c 350:** See notes following RCW **26.50.035**.
> **Effective date—1984 c 263:** See RCW **26.50.901**.

10.99.040
Duties of court—No-contact order.

(1) Because of the serious nature of domestic violence, the court in domestic violence actions:

(a) Shall not dismiss any charge or delay disposition because of concurrent dissolution or other civil proceedings;

(b) Shall not require proof that either party is seeking a dissolution of marriage prior to instigation of criminal proceedings;

(c) Shall waive any requirement that the victim's location be disclosed to any person, other than the attorney of a criminal defendant, upon a showing that there is a possibility of further violence: PROVIDED, That the court may order a criminal defense attorney not to disclose to his or her client the victim's location; and

(d) Shall identify by any reasonable means on docket sheets those criminal actions arising from acts of domestic violence.

(2)(a) Because of the likelihood of repeated violence directed at those who have been victims of domestic violence in the past, when any person charged with or arrested for a crime involving domestic violence is released from custody before arraignment or trial on bail or personal recognizance, the court authorizing the release may prohibit that person from having any contact with the victim. The jurisdiction authorizing the release shall determine whether that person should be prohibited from having any contact with the victim. If there is no outstanding restraining or protective order prohibiting that person from having contact with the victim, the court authorizing release may issue, by telephone, a no-contact order prohibiting the person charged or arrested from having contact with the victim or from knowingly coming within, or knowingly remaining within, a specified distance of a location.

(b) In issuing the order, the court shall consider the provisions of RCW **9.41.800**.

(c) The no-contact order shall also be issued in writing as soon as possible, and shall state that it may be extended as provided in subsection (3) of this section. By January 1, 2011, the administrative office of the courts shall develop a pattern form for all no-contact orders issued under this chapter. A no-contact order issued under this chapter must substantially comply with the pattern form developed by the administrative office of the courts.

(3) At the time of arraignment the court shall determine whether a no-contact order shall be issued or extended. So long as the court finds probable cause, the court may issue or extend a no-contact order even if the defendant fails to appear at arraignment. The no-contact order shall terminate if the defendant is acquitted or the charges are dismissed. If a no-contact order is issued or extended, the court may also include in the conditions of release a requirement that the defendant submit to electronic monitoring as defined in RCW **9.94A.030**. If electronic monitoring is ordered, the court shall specify who shall provide the monitoring services, and the terms under which the monitoring

shall be performed. Upon conviction, the court may require as a condition of the sentence that the defendant reimburse the providing agency for the costs of the electronic monitoring.

(4)(a) Willful violation of a court order issued under subsection (2), (3), or (7) of this section is punishable under RCW **26.50.110**.

(b) The written order releasing the person charged or arrested shall contain the court's directives and shall bear the legend: "Violation of this order is a criminal offense under chapter **26.50** RCW and will subject a violator to arrest; any assault, drive-by shooting, or reckless endangerment that is a violation of this order is a felony. You can be arrested even if any person protected by the order invites or allows you to violate the order's prohibitions. You have the sole responsibility to avoid or refrain from violating the order's provisions. Only the court can change the order."

(c) A certified copy of the order shall be provided to the victim.

(5) If a no-contact order has been issued prior to charging, that order shall expire at arraignment or within seventy-two hours if charges are not filed.

(6) Whenever a no-contact order is issued, modified, or terminated under subsection (2) or (3) of this section, the clerk of the court shall forward a copy of the order on or before the next judicial day to the appropriate law enforcement agency specified in the order. Upon receipt of the copy of the order the law enforcement agency shall enter the order for one year or until the expiration date specified on the order into any computer-based criminal intelligence information system available in this state used by law enforcement agencies to list outstanding warrants. Entry into the computer-based criminal intelligence information system constitutes notice to all law enforcement agencies of the existence of the order. The order is fully enforceable in any jurisdiction in the state. Upon receipt of notice that an order has been terminated under subsection (3) of this section, the law enforcement agency shall remove the order from the computer-based criminal intelligence information system.

(7) All courts shall develop policies and procedures by January 1, 2011, to grant victims a process to modify or rescind a no-contact order issued under this chapter. The

administrative office of the courts shall develop a model policy to assist the courts in implementing the requirements of this subsection.

[**2015 c 287 § 9; 2012 c 223 § 3; 2010 c 274 § 309; 2000 c 119 § 18; 1997 c 338 § 54; 1996 c 248 § 7; 1995 c 246 § 23; 1994 sp.s. c 7 § 449; 1992 c 86 § 2; 1991 c 301 § 4; 1985 c 303 § 10; 1984 c 263 § 22; 1983 c 232 § 7; 1981 c 145 § 6; 1979 ex.s. c 105 § 4.**]

NOTES:

> **Intent—2010 c 274:** See note following RCW **10.31.100**.
>
> **Application—2000 c 119:** See note following RCW **26.50.021**.
>
> **Finding—Evaluation—Report—1997 c 338:** See note following

RCW **13.40.0357**.

> **Severability—Effective dates—1997 c 338:** See notes following RCW **5.60.060**.
>
> **Severability—1995 c 246:** See note following RCW **26.50.010**.
>
> **Finding—Intent—Severability—1994 sp.s. c 7:** See notes following

RCW **43.70.540**.

> **Effective date—1994 sp.s. c 7 §§ 401-410, 413-416, 418-437, and 439-**

460: See note following RCW **9.41.010**.

> **Finding—1991 c 301:** See note following RCW **10.99.020**.
>
> **Effective date—1984 c 263:** See RCW **26.50.901**.
>
> **Severability—1983 c 232:** See note following RCW **9.41.010**.

Child abuse, temporary restraining order: RCW **26.44.063**.

Orders for protection in cases of domestic violence: RCW **26.50.030**, **26.50.070**.

Temporary restraining order: RCW **26.09.060**.

10.99.045

Appearances by defendant—Defendant's history—No-contact order.

(1) A defendant arrested for an offense involving domestic violence as defined by RCW **10.99.020** shall be required to appear in person before a magistrate within one judicial day after the arrest.

(2) A defendant who is charged by citation, complaint, or information with an offense involving domestic violence as defined by RCW**10.99.020** and not arrested shall appear in court for arraignment in person as soon as practicable, but in no event later than fourteen days after the next day on which court is in session following the issuance of the citation or the filing of the complaint or information.

(3)(a) At the time of the appearances provided in subsection (1) or (2) of this section, the court shall determine the necessity of imposing a no-contact order or other conditions of pretrial release according to the procedures established by court rule for a preliminary appearance or an arraignment. The court may include in the order any conditions authorized under RCW **9.41.800** and **10.99.040**.

(b) For the purposes of (a) of this subsection, the prosecutor shall provide for the court's review:

(i) The defendant's criminal history, if any, that occurred in Washington or any other state;

(ii) If available, the defendant's criminal history that occurred in any tribal jurisdiction; and

(iii) The defendant's individual order history.

(c) For the purposes of (b) of this subsection, criminal history includes all previous convictions and orders of deferred prosecution, as reported through the judicial information system or otherwise available to the court or prosecutor, current to within the period specified in (d) of this subsection before the date of the appearance.

(d) The periods applicable to previous convictions and orders of deferred prosecution are:

(i) One working day, in the case of previous actions of courts that fully participate in the state judicial information system; and

(ii) Seven calendar days, in the case of previous actions of courts that do not fully participate in the judicial information system. For the purposes of this subsection, "fully participate" means regularly providing records to and receiving records from the system by electronic means on a daily basis.

(4) Appearances required pursuant to this section are mandatory and cannot be waived.

(5) The no-contact order shall be issued and entered with the appropriate law enforcement agency pursuant to the procedures outlined in RCW **10.99.040** (2) and (6). [**2010 c 274 § 301; 2000 c 119 § 19; 1998 c 55 § 2; 1994 sp.s. c 7 § 450; 1984 c 263 § 23; 1983 c 232 § 8; 1981 c 145 § 7.**]

NOTES:

Intent—2010 c 274: See note following RCW **10.31.100**.

Application—2000 c 119: See note following RCW **26.50.021**.

Finding—Intent—Severability—1994 sp.s. c 7: See notes following RCW **43.70.540**.

Effective date—1994 sp.s. c 7 §§ 401-410, 413-416, 418-437, and 439-460: See note following RCW **9.41.010**.

Effective date—1984 c 263: See RCW **26.50.901**.

Severability—1983 c 232: See note following RCW **9.41.010**.

10.99.050

Victim contact—Restriction, prohibition—Violation, penalties—Written order—Procedures—Notice of change.

(1) When a defendant is found guilty of a crime and a condition of the sentence restricts the defendant's ability to have contact with the victim, such condition shall be recorded and a written certified copy of that order shall be provided to the victim.

(2)(a) Willful violation of a court order issued under this section is punishable under RCW **26.50.110**.

(b) The written order shall contain the court's directives and shall bear the legend: Violation of this order is a criminal offense under chapter **26.50** RCW and will subject a violator to arrest; any assault, drive-by shooting, or reckless endangerment that is a violation of this order is a felony.

(3) Whenever an order prohibiting contact is issued pursuant to this section, the clerk of the court shall forward a copy of the order on or before the next judicial day to

the appropriate law enforcement agency specified in the order. Upon receipt of the copy of the order the law enforcement agency shall enter the order for one year or until the expiration date specified on the order into any computer-based criminal intelligence information system available in this state used by law enforcement agencies to list outstanding warrants. Entry into the computer-based criminal intelligence information system constitutes notice to all law enforcement agencies of the existence of the order. The order is fully enforceable in any jurisdiction in the state.

(4) If an order prohibiting contact issued pursuant to this section is modified or terminated, the clerk of the court shall notify the law enforcement agency specified in the order on or before the next judicial day. Upon receipt of notice that an order has been terminated, the law enforcement agency shall remove the order from any computer-based criminal intelligence system.

[2000 c 119 § 20; 1997 c 338 § 55; 1996 c 248 § 8; 1991 c 301 § 5; 1985 c 303 § 12; 1984 c 263 § 24; 1979 ex.s. c 105 § 5.]

NOTES:

      Application—2000 c 119: See note following RCW **26.50.021**.

      Finding—Evaluation—Report—1997 c 338: See note following RCW **13.40.0357**.

      Severability—Effective dates—1997 c 338: See notes following RCW **5.60.060**.

      Finding—1991 c 301: See note following RCW **10.99.020**.

      Effective date—1984 c 263: See RCW **26.50.901**.

10.99.055
Enforcement of orders.

A peace officer in this state shall enforce an order issued by any court in this state restricting a defendant's ability to have contact with a victim by arresting and taking the defendant into custody, pending release on bail, personal recognizance, or court order, when the officer has probable cause to believe that the defendant has violated the terms of that order.

[1984 c 263 § 25; 1983 c 232 § 9; 1981 c 145 § 8.]

NOTES:

Effective date—1984 c 263: See RCW **26.50.901**.

Severability—1983 c 232: See note following RCW **9.41.010**.

10.99.060

Prosecutor's notice to victim—Description of available procedures.

The public attorney responsible for making the decision whether or not to prosecute shall advise the victim of that decision within five days, and, prior to making that decision shall advise the victim, upon the victim's request, of the status of the case. Notification to the victim that charges will not be filed shall include a description of the procedures available to the victim in that jurisdiction to initiate a criminal proceeding.
[**1979 ex.s. c 105 § 6.**]

10.99.070

Liability of peace officers.

A peace officer shall not be held liable in any civil action for an arrest based on probable cause, enforcement in good faith of a court order, or any other action or omission in good faith under this chapter arising from an alleged incident of domestic violence brought by any party to the incident.
[**1979 ex.s. c 105 § 7.**]

10.99.080

Penalty assessment (as amended by 2015 c 265).

(1) All superior courts, and courts organized under Title **3** or **35** RCW, may impose a penalty assessment not to exceed one hundred dollars on any ((person)) adult offender convicted of a crime involving domestic violence. The assessment shall be in addition to, and shall not supersede, any other penalty, restitution, fines, or costs provided by law.

(2) Revenue from the assessment shall be used solely for the purposes of establishing and funding domestic violence advocacy and domestic violence prevention and prosecution programs in the city or county of the court imposing the assessment. Revenue from the assessment shall not be used for indigent criminal defense. If the city or county does not have domestic violence advocacy or domestic violence prevention and prosecution programs, cities and counties may use the revenue collected from the assessment to contract with recognized community-based domestic violence program providers.

(3) The assessment imposed under this section shall not be subject to any state or local remittance requirements under chapter **3.46**, 3.50, 3.62, 7.68, 10.82, or **35.20** RCW.

(4) For the purposes of this section, "convicted" includes a plea of guilty, a finding of guilt regardless of whether the imposition of the sentence is deferred or any part of the penalty is suspended, or the levying of a fine. For the purposes of this section, "domestic violence" has the same meaning as that term is defined under RCW **10.99.020** and includes violations of equivalent local ordinances.

(5) When determining whether to impose a penalty assessment under this section, judges are encouraged to solicit input from the victim or representatives for the victim in assessing the ability of the convicted offender to pay the penalty, including information regarding current financial obligations, family circumstances, and ongoing restitution.
[**2015 c 265 § 24; 2004 c 15 § 2.**]
NOTES:

   Finding—Intent—2015 c 265: See note following RCW **13.50.010**.

10.99.080

Penalty assessment (as amended by 2015 c 275).

(1) All superior courts, and courts organized under Title **3** or **35** RCW, may impose a penalty of one hundred dollars, plus an additional fifteen dollars on any person convicted of a crime involving domestic violence; in no case shall a penalty assessment ((not to)) exceed one hundred fifteen dollars on any person

convicted of a crime involving domestic violence. The assessment shall be in addition to, and shall not supersede, any other penalty, restitution, fines, or costs provided by law.

(2) Revenue from the:

(a) One hundred dollar assessment shall be used solely for the purposes of establishing and funding domestic violence advocacy and domestic violence prevention and prosecution programs in the city or county of the court imposing the assessment. Such revenue from the assessment shall not be used for indigent criminal defense. If the city or county does not have domestic violence advocacy or domestic violence prevention and prosecution programs, cities and counties may use the revenue collected from the assessment to contract with recognized community-based domestic violence program providers.

(b) Fifteen dollar assessment must be remitted monthly to the state treasury for deposit in the domestic violence prevention account.

(3) The one hundred dollar assessment imposed under this section shall not be subject to any state or local remittance requirements under chapter **3.46**, 3.50, 3.62, 7.68, 10.82, or **35.20** RCW.

(4) For the purposes of this section, "convicted" includes a plea of guilty, a finding of guilt regardless of whether the imposition of the sentence is deferred or any part of the penalty is suspended, or the levying of a fine. For the purposes of this section, "domestic violence" has the same meaning as that term is defined under RCW **10.99.020** and includes violations of equivalent local ordinances.

(5) When determining whether to impose a penalty assessment under this section, judges are encouraged to solicit input from the victim or representatives for the victim in assessing the ability of the convicted offender to pay the penalty, including information regarding current financial obligations, family circumstances, and ongoing restitution.
[**2015 c 275 § 14; 2004 c 15 § 2.**]

NOTES:

Reviser's note: RCW **10.99.080** was amended twice during the 2015 legislative session, each without reference to the other. For rule of construction concerning sections amended more than once during the same legislative session, see RCW **1.12.025**.

Intent—**2004 c 15:** "The legislature recognizes that domestic violence is a growing and more visible public safety problem in Washington state than ever before, and that domestic violence-related incidents have a significant bearing on overall law enforcement and court caseloads. The legislature further recognizes the growing costs associated with domestic violence prevention and advocacy programs established by local governments and by community-based organizations.

It is the legislature's intent to establish a penalty in law that will hold convicted domestic violence offenders accountable while requiring them to pay penalties to offset the costs of domestic violence advocacy and prevention programs. It is the legislature's intent that the penalties imposed against convicted domestic violence offenders under section 2 of this act be used for established domestic violence prevention and prosecution programs. It is the legislature's intent that the revenue from the penalty assessment shall be in addition to existing sources of funding to enhance or help prevent the reduction and elimination of domestic violence prevention and prosecution programs." [**2004 c 15 § 1.**]

10.99.090
Policy adoption and implementation.

(1) By December 1, 2004, the association shall develop a written model policy on domestic violence committed or allegedly committed by sworn employees of agencies. In developing the policy, the association shall convene a work group consisting of representatives from the following entities and professions:

(a) Statewide organizations representing state and local enforcement officers;

(b) A statewide organization providing training and education for agencies having the primary responsibility of serving victims of domestic violence with emergency shelter and other services; and

(c) Any other organization or profession the association determines to be appropriate.

(2) Members of the work group shall serve without compensation.

(3) The model policy shall provide due process for employees and, at a minimum, meet the following standards:

(a) Provide prehire screening procedures reasonably calculated to disclose whether an applicant for a sworn employee position:

(i) Has committed or, based on credible sources, has been accused of committing an act of domestic violence;

(ii) Is currently being investigated for an allegation of child abuse or neglect or has previously been investigated for founded allegations of child abuse or neglect; or

(iii) Is currently or has previously been subject to any order under RCW **26.44.063**, this chapter, chapter **10.14** or **26.50** RCW, or any equivalent order issued by another state or tribal court;

(b) Provide for the mandatory, immediate response to acts or allegations of domestic violence committed or allegedly committed by a sworn employee of an agency;

(c) Provide to a sworn employee, upon the request of the sworn employee or when the sworn employee has been alleged to have committed an act of domestic violence, information on programs under RCW **26.50.150**;

(d) Provide for the mandatory, immediate reporting by employees when an employee becomes aware of an allegation of domestic violence committed or allegedly committed by a sworn employee of the agency employing the sworn employee;

(e) Provide procedures to address reporting by an employee who is the victim of domestic violence committed or allegedly committed by a sworn employee of an agency;

(f) Provide for the mandatory, immediate self-reporting by a sworn employee to his or her employing agency when an agency in any jurisdiction has responded to a domestic violence call in which the sworn employee committed or allegedly committed an act of domestic violence;

(g) Provide for the mandatory, immediate self-reporting by a sworn employee to his or her employing agency if the employee is currently being investigated for an allegation of child abuse or neglect or has previously been investigated for founded allegations of child abuse or neglect, or is currently or has previously been subject to any order under

RCW **26.44.063**, this chapter, chapter **10.14** or **26.50** RCW, or any equivalent order issued by another state or tribal court;

(h) Provide for the performance of prompt separate and impartial administrative and criminal investigations of acts or allegations of domestic violence committed or allegedly committed by a sworn employee of an agency;

(i) Provide for appropriate action to be taken during an administrative or criminal investigation of acts or allegations of domestic violence committed or allegedly committed by a sworn employee of an agency. The policy shall provide procedures to address, in a manner consistent with applicable law and the agency's ability to maintain public safety within its jurisdiction, whether to relieve the sworn employee of agency-issued weapons and other agency-issued property and whether to suspend the sworn employee's power of arrest or other police powers pending resolution of any investigation;

(j) Provide for prompt and appropriate discipline or sanctions when, after an agency investigation, it is determined that a sworn employee has committed an act of domestic violence;

(k) Provide that, when there has been an allegation of domestic violence committed or allegedly committed by a sworn employee, the agency immediately make available to the alleged victim the following information:

(i) The agency's written policy on domestic violence committed or allegedly committed by sworn employees;

(ii) Information, including but not limited to contact information, about public and private nonprofit domestic violence advocates and services; and

(iii) Information regarding relevant confidentiality policies related to the victim's information;

(l) Provide procedures for the timely response, consistent with chapters **42.56** and **10.97** RCW, to an alleged victim's inquiries into the status of the administrative investigation and the procedures the agency will follow in an investigation of domestic violence committed or allegedly committed by a sworn employee;

(m) Provide procedures requiring an agency to immediately notify the employing agency of a sworn employee when the notifying agency becomes aware of acts or allegations of domestic violence committed or allegedly committed by the sworn employee within the jurisdiction of the notifying agency; and

(n) Provide procedures for agencies to access and share domestic violence training within their jurisdiction and with other jurisdictions.

(4) By June 1, 2005, every agency shall adopt and implement a written policy on domestic violence committed or allegedly committed by sworn employees of the agency that meet the minimum standards specified in this section. In lieu of developing its own policy, the agency may adopt the model policy developed by the association under this section. In developing its own policy, or before adopting the model policy, the agency shall consult public and private nonprofit domestic violence advocates and any other organizations and professions the agency finds appropriate.

(5)(a) Except as provided in this section, not later than June 30, 2006, every sworn employee of an agency shall be trained by the agency on the agency's policy required under this section.

(b) Sworn employees hired by an agency on or after March 1, 2006, shall, within six months of beginning employment, be trained by the agency on the agency's policy required under this section.

(6)(a) By June 1, 2005, every agency shall provide a copy of its policy developed under this section to the association and shall provide a statement notifying the association of whether the agency has complied with the training required under this section. The copy and statement shall be provided in electronic format unless the agency is unable to do so. The agency shall provide the association with any revisions to the policy upon adoption.

(b) The association shall maintain a copy of each agency's policy and shall provide to the governor and legislature not later than January 1, 2006, a list of those agencies that have not developed and submitted policies and those agencies that have not stated their compliance with the training required under this section.

(c) The association shall, upon request and within its resources, provide technical assistance to agencies in developing their policies.

[**2005 c 274 § 209; 2004 c 18 § 3.**]

NOTES:

    Findings—Intent—2004 c 18: See note following RCW **10.99.020**.

10.99.100
Sentencing—Factors—Defendant's criminal history.

(1) In sentencing for a crime of domestic violence as defined in this chapter, courts of limited jurisdiction shall consider, among other factors, whether:

(a) The defendant suffered a continuing pattern of coercion, control, or abuse by the victim of the offense and the offense is a response to that coercion, control, or abuse;

(b) The offense was part of an ongoing pattern of psychological, physical, or sexual abuse of a victim or multiple victims manifested by multiple incidents over a prolonged period of time; and

(c) The offense occurred within sight or sound of the victim's or the offender's minor children under the age of eighteen years.

(2)(a) In sentencing for a crime of domestic violence as defined in this chapter, the prosecutor shall provide for the court's review:

(i) The defendant's criminal history, if any, that occurred in Washington or any other state;

(ii) If available, the defendant's prior criminal history that occurred in any tribal jurisdiction; and

(iii) The defendant's individual order history.

(b) For the purposes of (a) of this subsection, criminal history includes all previous convictions and orders of deferred prosecution, as reported through the judicial information system or otherwise available to the court or prosecutor, current to within the period specified in (c) of this subsection before the date of sentencing.

(c) The periods applicable to previous convictions and orders of deferred prosecution are:

(i) One working day, in the case of previous actions of courts that fully participate in the state judicial information system; and

(ii) Seven calendar days, in the case of previous actions of courts that do not fully participate in the judicial information system. For the purposes of this subsection, "fully participate" means regularly providing records to and receiving records from the system by electronic means on a daily basis.

[**2010 c 274 § 404.**]

NOTES:

Intent—2010 c 274: See note following RCW **10.31.100**.

10.99.901

Construction—Chapter applicable to state registered domestic partnerships—2009 c 521.

For the purposes of this chapter, the terms spouse, marriage, marital, husband, wife, widow, widower, next of kin, and family shall be interpreted as applying equally to state registered domestic partnerships or individuals in state registered domestic partnerships as well as to marital relationships and married persons, and references to dissolution of marriage shall apply equally to state registered domestic partnerships that have been terminated, dissolved, or invalidated, to the extent that such interpretation does not conflict with federal law. Where necessary to implement chapter 521, Laws of 2009, gender-specific terms such as husband and wife used in any statute, rule, or other law shall be construed to be gender neutral, and applicable to individuals in state registered domestic partnerships.

[**2009 c 521 § 29.**]

Chapter 10.101 RCW INDIGENT DEFENSE SERVICES

10.101.005
Legislative finding.

The legislature finds that effective legal representation must be provided for indigent persons and persons who are indigent and able to contribute, consistent with the constitutional requirements of fairness, equal protection, and due process in all cases where the right to counsel attaches.

[2005 c 157 § 1; 1989 c 409 § 1.]

10.101.010
Definitions.

The following definitions shall be applied in connection with this chapter:

(1) "Anticipated cost of counsel" means the cost of retaining private counsel for representation on the matter before the court.

(2) "Available funds" means liquid assets and disposable net monthly income calculated after provision is made for bail obligations. For the purpose of determining available funds, the following definitions shall apply:

(a) "Liquid assets" means cash, savings accounts, bank accounts, stocks, bonds, certificates of deposit, equity in real estate, and equity in motor vehicles. A motor vehicle necessary to maintain employment and having a market value not greater than three thousand dollars shall not be considered a liquid asset.

(b) "Income" means salary, wages, interest, dividends, and other earnings which are reportable for federal income tax purposes, and cash payments such as reimbursements received from pensions, annuities, social security, and public assistance programs. It includes any contribution received from any family member or other person who is domiciled in the same residence as the defendant and who is helping to defray the defendant's basic living costs.

(c) "Disposable net monthly income" means the income remaining each month after deducting federal, state, or local income taxes, social security taxes, contributory retirement, union dues, and basic living costs.

(d) "Basic living costs" means the average monthly amount spent by the defendant for reasonable payments toward living costs, such as shelter, food, utilities, health care, transportation, clothing, loan payments, support payments, and court-imposed obligations.

(3) "Indigent" means a person who, at any stage of a court proceeding, is:

(a) Receiving one of the following types of public assistance: Temporary assistance for needy families, aged, blind, or disabled assistance benefits, medical care services under RCW **74.09.035**, pregnant women assistance benefits, poverty-related veterans' benefits, food stamps or food stamp benefits transferred electronically, refugee resettlement benefits, medicaid, or supplemental security income; or

(b) Involuntarily committed to a public mental health facility; or

(c) Receiving an annual income, after taxes, of one hundred twenty-five percent or less of the current federally established poverty level; or

(d) Unable to pay the anticipated cost of counsel for the matter before the court because his or her available funds are insufficient to pay any amount for the retention of counsel.

(4) "Indigent and able to contribute" means a person who, at any stage of a court proceeding, is unable to pay the anticipated cost of counsel for the matter before the court because his or her available funds are less than the anticipated cost of counsel but sufficient for the person to pay a portion of that cost.
[**2011 1st sp.s. c 36 § 12; 2010 1st sp.s. c 8 § 12; 1998 c 79 § 2; 1997 c 59 § 3; 1989 c 409 § 2.**]
NOTES:

Reviser's note: The definitions in this section have been alphabetized pursuant to RCW **1.08.015**(2)(k).

Findings—Intent—2011 1st sp.s. c 36: See RCW **74.62.005**.

Effective date—2011 1st sp.s. c 36: See note following RCW **74.62.005**.

Findings—Intent—Short title—Effective date—2010 1st sp.s. c 8: See notes following RCW **74.04.225**.

10.101.020
Determination of indigency—Provisional appointment—Promissory note.

(1) A determination of indigency shall be made for all persons wishing the appointment of counsel in criminal, juvenile, involuntary commitment, and dependency cases, and any other case where the right to counsel attaches. The court or its designee shall determine whether the person is indigent pursuant to the standards set forth in this chapter.

(2) In making the determination of indigency, the court shall also consider the anticipated length and complexity of the proceedings and the usual and customary charges of an attorney in the community for rendering services, and any other circumstances presented to the court which are relevant to the issue of indigency. The appointment of counsel shall not be denied to the person because the person's friends or relatives, other than a spouse who was not the victim of any offense or offenses allegedly committed by the person, have resources adequate to retain counsel, or because the person has posted or is capable of posting bond.

(3) The determination of indigency shall be made upon the defendant's initial contact with the court or at the earliest time circumstances permit. The court or its designee shall keep a written record of the determination of indigency. Any information given by the accused under this section or sections shall be confidential and shall not be available for use by the prosecution in the pending case.

(4) If a determination of eligibility cannot be made before the time when the first services are to be rendered, the court shall appoint an attorney on a provisional basis. If the court subsequently determines that the person receiving the services is ineligible, the court shall notify the person of the termination of services, subject to court-ordered reinstatement.

(5) All persons determined to be indigent and able to contribute, shall be required to execute a promissory note at the time counsel is appointed. The person shall be informed whether payment shall be made in the form of a lump sum payment or periodic payments. The payment and payment schedule must be set forth in writing. The person receiving the appointment of counsel shall also sign an affidavit swearing under penalty of perjury that all income and assets reported are complete and accurate. In addition, the person must swear in the affidavit to immediately report any change in financial status to the court.

(6) The office or individual charged by the court to make the determination of indigency shall provide a written report and opinion as to indigency on a form prescribed by the office of public defense, based on information obtained from the defendant and subject to verification. The form shall include information necessary to provide a basis for making a determination with respect to indigency as provided by this chapter.

[**1997 c 41 § 5; 1989 c 409 § 3.**]

10.101.030
Standards.

Each county or city under this chapter shall adopt standards for the delivery of public defense services, whether those services are provided by contract, assigned counsel, or a public defender office. Standards shall include the following: Compensation of counsel, duties and responsibilities of counsel, case load limits and types of cases, responsibility for expert witness fees and other costs associated with representation, administrative expenses, support services, reports of attorney activity and vouchers, training, supervision, monitoring and evaluation of attorneys, substitution of attorneys or assignment of contracts, limitations on private practice of contract attorneys, qualifications of attorneys, disposition of client complaints, cause for termination of contract or removal of attorney, and nondiscrimination. The standards endorsed by the Washington state bar association for the provision of public defense services should serve as guidelines to local legislative authorities in adopting standards.

[**2005 c 157 § 2; 1989 c 409 § 4.**]

10.101.040
Selection of defense attorneys.

City attorneys, county prosecutors, and law enforcement officers shall not select the attorneys who will provide indigent defense services.

[**1989 c 409 § 5.**]

10.101.050
Appropriated funds—Application, reports.

The Washington state office of public defense shall disburse appropriated funds to counties and cities for the purpose of improving the quality of public defense services. Counties may apply for up to their pro rata share as set forth in RCW **10.101.060** provided that counties conform to application procedures established by the office of public defense and improve the quality of services for both juveniles and adults. Cities may apply for moneys pursuant to the grant program set forth in RCW **10.101.080**. In order to receive funds, each applying county or city must require that attorneys providing public defense services attend training approved by the office of public defense at least once per calendar year. Each applying county or city shall report the expenditure for all public defense services in the previous calendar year, as well as case statistics for that year, including per attorney caseloads, and shall provide a copy of each current public defense contract to the office of public defense with its application. Each individual or organization that contracts to perform public defense services for a county or city shall report to the county or city hours billed for nonpublic defense legal services in the previous calendar year, including number and types of private cases.

[**2005 c 157 § 3.**]

10.101.060
Appropriated funds—Use requirements.

(1)(a) Subject to the availability of funds appropriated for this purpose, the office of public defense shall disburse to applying counties that meet the requirements of RCW **10.101.050** designated funds under this chapter on a pro rata basis pursuant to the formula set forth in RCW**10.101.070** and shall disburse to eligible cities, funds pursuant to RCW **10.101.080**. Each fiscal year for which it receives state funds under this chapter, a county or city must document to the office of public defense that it is meeting the standards for provision of indigent defense services as endorsed by the Washington state bar association or that the funds received under this chapter have been used to make appreciable demonstrable improvements in the delivery of public defense services, including the following:

(i) Adoption by ordinance of a legal representation plan that addresses the factors in RCW **10.101.030**. The plan must apply to any contract or agency providing indigent defense services for the county or city;

(ii) Requiring attorneys who provide public defense services to attend training under RCW **10.101.050**;

(iii) Requiring attorneys who handle the most serious cases to meet specified qualifications as set forth in the Washington state bar association endorsed standards for public defense services or participate in at least one case consultation per case with office of public defense resource attorneys who are so qualified. The most serious cases include all cases of murder in the first or second degree, persistent offender cases, and class A felonies. This subsection (1)(a)(iii) does not apply to cities receiving funds under RCW **10.101.050** through**10.101.080**;

(iv) Requiring contracts to address the subject of compensation for extraordinary cases;

(v) Identifying funding specifically for the purpose of paying experts (A) for which public defense attorneys may file ex parte motions, or (B) which should be specifically designated within a public defender agency budget;

(vi) Identifying funding specifically for the purpose of paying investigators (A) for which public defense attorneys may file ex parte motions, and (B) which should be specifically designated within a public defender agency budget.

(b) The cost of providing counsel in cases where there is a conflict of interest shall not be borne by the attorney or agency who has the conflict.

(2) The office of public defense shall determine eligibility of counties and cities to receive state funds under this chapter. If a determination is made that a county or city receiving state funds under this chapter did not substantially comply with this section, the office of public defense shall notify the county or city of the failure to comply and unless the county or city contacts the office of public defense and substantially corrects the deficiencies within ninety days after the date of notice, or some other mutually agreed period of time, the county's or city's eligibility to continue receiving funds under this chapter is terminated. If an applying county or city disagrees with the determination of the office of public defense as to the county's or city's eligibility, the county or city may file an appeal with the advisory committee of the office of public defense within thirty days of the eligibility determination. The decision of the advisory committee is final. [**2005 c 157 § 4.**]

10.101.070
County moneys.

The moneys shall be distributed to each county determined to be eligible to receive moneys by the office of public defense as determined under this section. Ninety percent of the funding appropriated shall be designated as "county moneys" and shall be distributed as follows:

(1) Six percent of the county moneys appropriated shall be distributed as a base allocation among the eligible counties. A county's base allocation shall be equal to this six percent divided by the total number of eligible counties.

(2) Ninety-four percent of the county moneys appropriated shall be distributed among the eligible counties as follows:

(a) Fifty percent of this amount shall be distributed on a pro rata basis to each eligible county based upon the population of the county as a percentage of the total population of all eligible counties; and

(b) Fifty percent of this amount shall be distributed on a pro rata basis to each eligible county based upon the annual number of criminal cases filed in the county superior court as a percentage of the total annual number of criminal cases filed in the superior courts of all eligible counties.

(3) Under this section:

(a) The population of the county is the most recent number determined by the office of financial management;

(b) The annual number of criminal cases filed in the county superior court is determined by the most recent annual report of the courts of Washington, as published by the office of the administrator for the courts;

(c) Distributions and eligibility for distributions in the 2005-2007 biennium shall be based on 2004 figures for the annual number of criminal cases that are filed as described under (b) of this subsection. Future distributions shall be based on the most recent figures for the annual number of criminal cases that are filed as described under (b) of this subsection.

[**2005 c 157 § 5.**]

10.101.080
City moneys.

The moneys under RCW **10.101.050** shall be distributed to each city determined to be eligible under this section by the office of public defense. Ten percent of the funding appropriated shall be designated as "city moneys" and distributed as follows:

(1) The office of public defense shall administer a grant program to select the cities eligible to receive city moneys. Incorporated cities may apply for grants. Applying cities must conform to the requirements of RCW **10.101.050** and **10.101.060**.

(2) City moneys shall be distributed in a timely manner to accomplish the goals of the grants.

(3) Criteria for award of grants shall be established by the office of public defense after soliciting input from the association of Washington cities. Award of the grants shall be determined by the office of public defense.

[2007 c 59 § 1; 2005 c 157 § 6.]

10.101.900
Construction—Chapter applicable to state registered domestic partnerships—2009 c 521.

For the purposes of this chapter, the terms spouse, marriage, marital, husband, wife, widow, widower, next of kin, and family shall be interpreted as applying equally to state registered domestic partnerships or individuals in state registered domestic partnerships as well as to marital relationships and married persons, and references to dissolution of marriage shall apply equally to state registered domestic partnerships that have been terminated, dissolved, or invalidated, to the extent that such interpretation does not conflict with federal law. Where necessary to implement chapter 521, Laws of 2009, gender-specific terms such as husband and wife used in any statute, rule, or other law shall be construed to be gender neutral, and applicable to individuals in state registered domestic partnerships.

[2009 c 521 § 30.]

Chapter 10.105 RCW
PROPERTY INVOLVED IN A FELONY
10.105.010
Seizure and forfeiture.

(1) The following are subject to seizure and forfeiture and no property right exists in them: All personal property, including, but not limited to, any item, object, tool, substance, device, weapon, machine, vehicle of any kind, money, security, or negotiable instrument, which has been or was actually employed as an instrumentality in the commission of, or in aiding or abetting in the commission of any felony, or which was furnished or was intended to be furnished by any person in the commission of, as a

result of, or as compensation for the commission of, any felony, or which was acquired in whole or in part with proceeds traceable to the commission of a felony. No property may be forfeited under this section until after there has been a superior court conviction of the owner of the property for the felony in connection with which the property was employed, furnished, or acquired.

A forfeiture of property encumbered by a bona fide security interest is subject to the interest of the secured party if at the time the security interest was created, the secured party neither had knowledge of nor consented to the commission of the felony.

(2) Personal property subject to forfeiture under this chapter may be seized by any law enforcement officer of this state upon process issued by any superior court having jurisdiction over the property. Seizure of personal property without process may be made if:

(a) The seizure is incident to an arrest or a search under a search warrant;

(b) The property subject to seizure has been the subject of a prior judgment in favor of the state in a criminal injunction or forfeiture proceeding;

(c) A law enforcement officer has probable cause to believe that the property is directly dangerous to health or safety; or

(d) The law enforcement officer has probable cause to believe that the property was used or is intended to be used in the commission of a felony.

(3) In the event of seizure pursuant to this section, proceedings for forfeiture shall be deemed commenced by the seizure. The law enforcement agency under whose authority the seizure was made shall cause notice to be served within fifteen days following the seizure on the owner of the property seized and the person in charge thereof and any person having any known right or interest therein, including any community property interest, of the seizure and intended forfeiture of the seized property. The notice of seizure may be served by any method authorized by law or court rule including but not limited to service by certified mail with return receipt requested. Service by mail shall be deemed complete upon mailing within the fifteen day period following the seizure. Notice of seizure in the case of property subject to a security interest that has been perfected by filing a financing statement in accordance with

chapter 62A.9A RCW, or a certificate of title shall be made by service upon the secured party or the secured party's assignee at the address shown on the financing statement or the certificate of title.

(4) If no person notifies the seizing law enforcement agency in writing of the person's claim of ownership or right to possession of items specified in subsection (1) of this section within forty-five days of the seizure, the item seized shall be deemed forfeited.

(5) If a person notifies the seizing law enforcement agency in writing of the person's claim of ownership or right to possession of the seized property within forty-five days of the seizure, the law enforcement agency shall give the person or persons a reasonable opportunity to be heard as to the claim or right. The hearing shall be before the chief law enforcement officer of the seizing agency or the chief law enforcement officer's designee, except where the seizing agency is a state agency as defined in RCW **34.12.020**(4), the hearing shall be before the chief law enforcement officer of the seizing agency or an administrative law judge appointed under chapter **34.12** RCW, except that any person asserting a claim or right may remove the matter to a court of competent jurisdiction. Removal may only be accomplished according to the rules of civil procedure. The person seeking removal of the matter must serve process against the state, county, political subdivision, or municipality that operates the seizing agency, and any other party of interest, in accordance with RCW **4.28.080** or **4.92.020**, within forty-five days after the person seeking removal has notified the seizing law enforcement agency of the person's claim of ownership or right to possession. The court to which the matter is to be removed shall be the district court when the aggregate value of the property is within the jurisdictional limit set forth in RCW **3.66.020**. A hearing before the seizing agency and any appeal therefrom shall be under Title **34** RCW. In a court hearing between two or more claimants to the property involved, the prevailing party shall be entitled to a judgment for costs and reasonable attorney's fees. The burden of producing evidence shall be upon the person claiming to be the lawful owner or the person claiming to have the lawful right to possession of the property. The seizing law enforcement agency shall promptly return the property to the claimant upon a

determination by the administrative law judge or court that the claimant is the present lawful owner or is lawfully entitled to possession of the property.

(6) When property is forfeited under this chapter, after satisfying any court-ordered victim restitution, the seizing law enforcement agency may:

(a) Retain it for official use or upon application by any law enforcement agency of this state release such property to such agency for the exclusive use of enforcing the criminal law;

(b) Sell that which is not required to be destroyed by law and which is not harmful to the public.

(7) By January 31st of each year, each seizing agency shall remit to the state treasurer an amount equal to ten percent of the net proceeds of any property forfeited during the preceding calendar year. Money remitted shall be deposited in the state general fund.

(a) The net proceeds of forfeited property is the value of the forfeitable interest in the property after deducting the cost of satisfying any bona fide security interest to which the property is subject at the time of seizure; and in the case of sold property, after deducting the cost of sale, including reasonable fees or commissions paid to independent selling agents.

(b) The value of sold forfeited property is the sale price. The value of retained forfeited property is the fair market value of the property at the time of seizure, determined when possible by reference to an applicable commonly used index, such as the index used by the department of licensing for valuation of motor vehicles. A seizing agency may use, but need not use, an independent qualified appraiser to determine the value of retained property. If an appraiser is used, the value of the property appraised is net of the cost of the appraisal. The value of destroyed property and retained firearms or illegal property is zero.

(c) Retained property and net proceeds not required to be paid to the state treasurer, or otherwise required to be spent under this section, shall be retained by the seizing law enforcement agency exclusively for the expansion and improvement of law enforcement activity. Money retained under this section may not be used to supplant preexisting funding sources.

[2009 c 479 § 15; 1993 c 288 § 2.]

NOTES:

> **Effective date—2009 c 479:** See note following RCW **2.56.030**.

10.105.900
Application.

This chapter does not apply to property subject to forfeiture under chapter **66.32** RCW,

RCW **69.50.505**, **9.41.098**, **9.46.231**, **9A.82.100**,**9A.83.030**, **7.48.090**, or **77.15.070**.

[2003 c 39 § 6; 1994 c 218 § 18; 1993 c 288 § 1.]

NOTES:

> **Effective date—1994 c 218:** See note following RCW **9.46.010**.

Chapter 10.108 RCW BLUE ALERT SYSTEM

10.108.010
Declaration.

There is currently no system in place in Washington state to expedite the apprehension of violent criminals who seriously injure or kill local, state, or federal law enforcement officers. Other states have adopted blue alert systems to achieve this objective. The legislature declares that it is necessary to create a statewide blue alert system to speed the apprehension of violent criminals who kill or seriously injure local, state, or federal law enforcement officers.

[2012 c 37 § 1.]

10.108.020
Definitions.

The definitions in this section apply throughout this chapter unless the context clearly requires otherwise.

(1) "Blue alert system" means a quick response system designed to issue and coordinate alerts following an attack upon a law enforcement officer.

(2) "Investigating law enforcement agency" means the law enforcement agency that has primary jurisdiction over the area or has been delegated and accepted investigatory responsibility in which a law enforcement officer has been seriously injured or killed.

(3) "Law enforcement agency" means a general [authority Washington] law enforcement agency as defined in RCW **10.93.020** and a limited [authority Washington] law enforcement agency as defined in RCW **10.93.020**. Such agencies shall include, but are not limited to, the following:

(a) The Washington state patrol;

(b) All law enforcement agencies and police departments of any political subdivision of the state; and

(c) The department of corrections.

(4) "Law enforcement officer" includes police officers, the attorney general and the attorney general's deputies, sheriffs and their regular deputies, corrections officers, tribal law enforcement officers, park rangers, state fire marshals, municipal fire marshals, sworn members of the city fire departments, county and district firefighters, and agents of the department of fish and wildlife. "Law enforcement officer" also includes an employee of a federal governmental agency who is authorized by law to engage in or supervise the prevention, detection, investigation, or prosecution of, or the incarceration of any person for, any violation of law, and who has statutory powers of arrest.

(5) "Officer's employing law enforcement agency" means the law enforcement agency by which the officer is employed.

[**2012 c 37 § 2.**]

10.108.030
Blue alert system—Plan—Activation—Termination.

(1) Within existing resources, the Washington state patrol, in partnership with the Washington association of sheriffs and police chiefs, shall develop and implement a plan, commonly known as a blue alert system, consistent with the Amber alert program, endangered missing person advisory plan, and the missing person clearinghouse, for voluntary cooperation between local, state, tribal, and other law enforcement agencies, state government agencies, radio and television stations, and cable and satellite systems to enhance the public's ability to assist in apprehending persons suspected of killing or seriously injuring a law enforcement officer. The blue alert system shall include the following:

(a) Procedures to provide support to the investigating law enforcement agency as a resource for the receipt and dissemination of information regarding the suspect and the suspect's whereabouts and/or method of escape;

(b) The process for reporting the information to designated media outlets in Washington; and

(c) Criteria for the investigating law enforcement agency to determine quickly whether an officer has been seriously injured or killed and a blue alert therefore needs to be requested.

(2) The investigating law enforcement agency may request activation of the blue alert system and notify appropriate participants in the blue alert system, when the investigating law enforcement agency believes that:

(a) A suspect has not been apprehended;

(b) A suspect may be a serious threat to the public;

(c) Sufficient information is available to disseminate to the public that could assist in locating and apprehending the suspect;

(d) Release of the information will not compromise the investigation; and

(e) Criteria to ensure that releasing the victim information is proper, as to avoid improper next of kin notification.

(3) When a blue alert is activated, the investigating law enforcement agency shall provide descriptive information under the criminal justice information act, chapter **10.98** RCW, and the national crime information center system.

(4) The investigating law enforcement agency shall terminate the blue alert with respect to a particular suspect when the suspect is located or the incident is otherwise resolved, or when the investigating law enforcement agency determines that the blue alert system is no longer an effective tool for locating and apprehending the suspect.
[**2012 c 37 § 3.**]

10.108.040
Liability immunity.

No cause of action shall be maintained for civil damages in any court of this state against any radio or television broadcasting station or cable television system, or the employees, officers, directors, managers, or agents of the radio or television broadcasting station or cable television system, based on the broadcast of information supplied by law enforcement officials pursuant to the provisions of this chapter. Nothing in this section shall be construed to limit or restrict in any way any immunity or privilege a radio or television broadcasting station or cable television system may have under statute or common law for broadcasting or otherwise disseminating information.
[**2012 c 37 § 4.**]

Chapter 10.109 RCW USE OF BODY WORN CAMERAS

10.109.010
Policies. (Expires July 1, 2019.)

*** CHANGE IN 2018 *** (SEE **6408.SL**) ***

(1) A law enforcement or corrections agency that deploys body worn cameras must establish policies regarding the use of the cameras. The policies must, at a minimum, address:

(a) When a body worn camera must be activated and deactivated, and when a law enforcement or corrections officer has the discretion to activate and deactivate the body worn camera;

(b) How a law enforcement or corrections officer is to respond to circumstances when it would be reasonably anticipated that a person may be unwilling or less willing to communicate with an officer who is recording the communication with a body worn camera;

(c) How a law enforcement or corrections officer will document when and why a body worn camera was deactivated prior to the conclusion of an interaction with a member of the public while conducting official law enforcement or corrections business;

(d) How, and under what circumstances, a law enforcement or corrections officer is to inform a member of the public that he or she is being recorded, including in situations where the person is a non-English speaker or has limited English proficiency, or where the person is deaf or hard of hearing;

(e) How officers are to be trained on body worn camera usage and how frequently the training is to be reviewed or renewed; and

(f) Security rules to protect data collected and stored from body worn cameras.

(2) A law enforcement or corrections agency that deploys body worn cameras before June 9, 2016, must establish the policies within one hundred twenty days of June 9, 2016. A law enforcement or corrections agency that deploys body worn cameras on or after June 9, 2016, must establish the policies before deploying body worn cameras.

(3) This section expires July 1, 2019.

[**2016 c 163 § 5.**]

NOTES:

> **Finding—Intent—2016 c 163:** See note following RCW **42.56.240**.

10.109.020

Ordinance or resolution—Community involvement process.

For a city or town that is not deploying body worn cameras on June 9, 2016, a legislative authority of a city or town is strongly encouraged to adopt an ordinance or resolution authorizing the use of body worn cameras prior to their use by law enforcement or a corrections agency. Any ordinance or resolution authorizing the use of body worn cameras should identify a community involvement process for providing input into the development of operational policies governing the use of body worn cameras.
[2016 c 163 § 6.]

NOTES:

Finding—Intent—2016 c 163: See note following RCW **42.56.240**.

10.109.030

Limitations on use. (Expires July 1, 2019.)

*** CHANGE IN 2018 *** (SEE **6408.SL**) ***

(1) For state and local agencies, a body worn camera may only be used by officers employed by a general authority Washington law enforcement agency as defined in RCW **10.93.020**, any officer employed by the department of corrections, and personnel for jails as defined in RCW **70.48.020** and detention facilities as defined in RCW **13.40.020**.

(2) This section expires July 1, 2019.
[2016 c 163 § 8.]

NOTES:

Finding—Intent—2016 c 163: See note following RCW **42.56.240**.

10.109.900

Task force—2016 c 163. (Expires June 1, 2019.)

(1) The legislature shall convene a task force with the following voting members to examine the use of body worn cameras by law enforcement and corrections agencies:

(a) One member from each of the two largest caucuses of the senate, appointed by the president of the senate;

(b) One member from each of the two largest caucuses in the house of representatives, appointed by the speaker of the house of representatives;

(c) A representative from the governor's office;

(d) Two representatives from the Washington association of prosecuting attorneys;

(e) A representative from the Washington defender association;

(f) A representative of the Washington association of criminal defense lawyers;

(g) A representative from the American civil liberties union of Washington;

(h) A representative from the Washington association of sheriffs and police chiefs;

(i) Four chief local law enforcement officers, at least two of whom must be from local law enforcement agencies that have deployed body worn cameras, appointed jointly by the president of the senate and the speaker of the house of representatives;

(j) Three law enforcement officers, one representing the council of metropolitan police and sheriffs and two representing the Washington council of police and sheriffs;

(k) Two representatives of local governments responsible for oversight of law enforcement, appointed jointly by the president of the senate and the speaker of the house of representatives;

(l) A representative from the Washington coalition for open government;

(m) A representative of the news media, appointed jointly by the president of the senate and the speaker of the house of representatives;

(n) A representative of victims advocacy groups, appointed jointly by the president of the senate and the speaker of the house of representatives;

(o) Two representatives with experience in interactions between law enforcement and the public, appointed by the Washington state commission on African-American affairs;

(p) Two representatives with experience in interactions between law enforcement and the public, appointed by the Washington state commission on Asian Pacific American affairs;

(q) Two representatives with experience in interactions between law enforcement and the public, appointed by the Washington state commission on Hispanic affairs;

(r) One representative of immigrant or refugee communities, appointed jointly by the president of the senate and the speaker of the house of representatives;

(s) One person with expertise in the technology of retaining and redacting body worn camera recordings, appointed jointly by the president of the senate and the speaker of the house of representatives;

(t) Two representatives of the tribal communities with experience in interactions between law enforcement and the public, appointed jointly by the president of the senate and the speaker of the house of representatives;

(u) A public member, appointed jointly by the president of the senate and the speaker of the house of representatives; and

(v) A representative of the Washington state fraternal order of police.

(2) The task force shall choose two cochairs from among its legislative members.

(3) The task force may request such information, recordings, and other records from agencies as the task force deems appropriate for it to effectuate this section. A participating agency must provide such information, recordings, or records upon request subject to exemptions under chapter **42.56** RCW or any applicable law.

(4) Staff support for the task force shall be provided by the senate committee services and the house of representatives office of program research.

(5) Legislative members of the task force may be reimbursed for travel expenses in accordance with RCW **44.04.120**. Nonlegislative members, except those representing an employer, governmental entity, or other organization, are entitled to be reimbursed for travel expenses as provided in RCW **43.03.050** and **43.03.060**.

(6) The expenses of the task force shall be paid jointly by the senate and the house of representatives. Task force expenditures are subject to approval by the senate

facilities and operations committee and the house executive rules committee, or their successor committees.

(7) The task force shall hold public meetings in locations that include rural and urban communities and communities in the eastern and western parts of the state.

(8) The task force shall specifically consider and report on the use of body worn cameras in health care facilities subject to the health insurance portability and accountability act of 1996, P.L. 104-191, and the uniform health care information act, chapter **70.02** RCW. The task force shall consult with subject matter experts, including, but not limited to, the Washington state hospital association and the Washington state medical association, and any findings or recommendations must be consistent with the obligations of health care facilities under both federal and state law.

(9) The task force shall report its findings and recommendations to the governor and the appropriate committees of the legislature by December 1, 2017. The report must include, but is not limited to, findings and recommendations regarding costs assessed to requesters, policies adopted by agencies, retention and retrieval of data, model policies regarding body worn cameras that at a minimum address the issues identified in RCW **10.109.010**, and the use of body worn cameras for gathering evidence, surveillance, and police accountability. The task force must allow a minority report to be included with the task force report if requested by a member of the task force.

(10) This section expires June 1, 2019.

[**2016 c 163 § 7.**]

NOTES:

   Finding—Intent—2016 c 163: See note following RCW **42.56.240**.

Chapter 10.110 RCW INDIVIDUALS IN CUSTODY—HEALTH CARE SERVICES

10.110.010
Officer defined.

For purposes of this chapter, "officer" means a law enforcement officer, corrections officer, or guard supplied by a law enforcement or corrections agency.

[2015 c 267 § 6.]

10.110.020
Individuals in custody for violent offense or sex offense—Officer to accompany or secure.

Any individual in custody for a violent offense or a sex offense as those terms are defined in RCW **9.94A.030** who is brought by, or accompanied by, an officer to a hospital must continue to be accompanied or otherwise secured by an officer during the time that the individual is receiving care at the hospital. However, this section does not apply to an individual being supervised by the department of corrections if the individual's custody is the result solely of a sanction imposed by the department of corrections, the indeterminate sentence review board, or the court, in response to a violation of conditions.

[2015 c 267 § 1.]

10.110.030
Individuals receiving medical care—Requirements for not being accompanied or secured.

(1) An individual receiving medical care under this section need not continue to be accompanied or otherwise secured if:

(a) The individual's medical care provider so indicates; or

(b) The officer determines, using his or her best judgment, that:

(i) The individual does not present an imminent and significant risk of causing physical harm to themselves or another person;

(ii) There is no longer sufficient evidentiary basis to maintain the individual in custody; or

(iii) In the interest of public safety, the presence of the officer is urgently required at another location and the officer determines, using his or her best judgment and in consultation with his or her supervisor, if available on duty, that the public safety interest outweighs the need to accompany or secure the individual in the hospital.

(2)(a) In the event that a medical care provider determines the individual need not be accompanied or otherwise secured pursuant to subsection (1)(a) of this section, the officer has no ongoing duty to accompany or otherwise secure the individual for the duration of their treatment by the hospital. When a medical care provider indicates that a person need not be accompanied or otherwise secured, the hospital must notify the officer or the officer's designee when the individual is expected to be released by the hospital.

(b) If, after a medical provider indicates that the individual need not be accompanied or otherwise secured pursuant to subsection (1)(a) of this section, the individual demonstrates behavior that presents an imminent and significant risk of causing physical harm to themselves or others and the physical condition of the individual renders the individual capable of causing physical harm to themselves or others, the hospital may request the presence of an officer to guard or otherwise accompany the individual, in which case subsection (1)(a) and (b) of this section still apply.

(3) In the event the officer determines the individual need not be accompanied or otherwise secured pursuant to subsection (1)(b)(i) or (ii) of this section, the officer must notify the medical care provider that the officer is leaving the individual unattended or unsecured, in which case the hospital has no duty to notify the officer when the individual is, or expected to be, released from the hospital.

(4) In the event that the officer is urgently required at another location pursuant to subsection (1)(b)(iii) of this section, the officer must notify the medical care provider or, if an immediate departure is required, other hospital staff member that the officer is leaving the individual unattended or unsecured and make a reasonable effort to ensure a replacement officer or other means of accompanying or securing the individual as soon as reasonably possible under the circumstances. The hospital must notify the officer or the officer's designee if the individual is, or is expected to be, released from the hospital prior to the officer or a replacement officer returning to resume accompanying or otherwise securing the individual.

(5) Except for actions or omissions constituting gross negligence or willful misconduct, the hospital and health care providers as defined in chapter **18.130** RCW are immune from liability, including civil liability, professional conduct sanctions, and administrative actions resulting from the individual not being accompanied or secured.
[**2015 c 267 § 2.**]

10.110.040
Treatment in hospital emergency department.

In a case where an individual accompanied or otherwise secured by an officer pursuant to chapter 267, Laws of 2015 is waiting for treatment in a hospital emergency department, the hospital shall see the patient in as expeditious a manner as possible, while taking into consideration best triage practices and federal and state legal obligations regarding appropriate screening and treatment of patients.
[**2015 c 267 § 3.**]

10.110.050
Civil liability.

The provisions of chapter 267, Laws of 2015 do not constitute a special relationship exception to the public duty doctrine. Officers and their employing departments and agencies and representatives are immune from civil liability arising out of the failure to comply with chapter 267, Laws of 2015, unless it is shown that, in the totality of the circumstances, the officer, employing department, agency, or representative acted with gross negligence or bad faith.

[**2015 c 267 § 4.**]

10.110.060

No changes to standard of care—Restraints on pregnant women or youth.

Nothing in this chapter changes the standards of care with regard to the use of restraints on pregnant women or youth in custody as codified in chapters **70.48** and **72.09** RCW.

[**2015 c 267 § 5.**]

Chapter 10.112 RCW SEXUAL

EXPLOITATION OF CHILDREN

10.112.010
Special inquiry judge process—Subpoena for records.

(1) In a criminal investigation of an offense involving the sexual exploitation of children under chapter **9.68A** RCW, the prosecuting attorney shall use the special inquiry judge process established under chapter **10.27** RCW when the prosecuting attorney determines it is necessary to the investigation to subpoena a provider of electronic communication services or remote computing services to obtain records relevant to the investigation, including, but not limited to, records or information that provide the following subscriber or customer information: (a) Name and address; (b)

local and long distance telephone connection records, or records of session times and durations; (c) length of service and types of service utilized; (d) telephone or instrument number or other subscriber number or identity, including any temporarily assigned network address; and (e) means and source of payment for such service, including any credit card or bank account number.

(2) A provider who receives a subpoena for records as provided under subsection (1) of this section may not disclose the existence of the subpoena to the subscribers or customers whose records or information are requested or released under the subpoena.

(3) For the purposes of this section:

(a) "Electronic communication service" means any service that provides to users the ability to send or receive wire or electronic communications.

(b) "Provider" means a provider of electronic communication services or remote computing services.

(c) "Remote computing service" means the provision to the public of computer storage or processing services by means of an electronic communications system.

[**2017 c 114 § 2.**]

NOTES:

Findings—2017 c 114: "The legislature must continue to act to aid law enforcement in their efforts to prevent the unthinkable acts of sexual abuse of children and the horrendous social and emotional trauma experienced by victims of child pornography by expanding the tools available for law enforcement. The legislature finds that the expansion of the internet and computer-related technologies have led to a dramatic increase in the production and availability of child pornography by simplifying how it can be created, distributed, and collected. Between 2005 and 2009, the national center for missing and exploited children's child victim identification program has seen a four hundred thirty-two percent increase in child pornography films and files submitted for identification of the children depicted. The United States department of justice estimates that pornographers have recorded the abuse of more than one million children in the United States alone. Furthermore, there is a direct correlation between individuals who possess, download, and trade graphic images of child pornography and those who molest children. A well-known study conducted by crimes against children research center for the national center for missing and exploited children concluded that an estimated forty percent of those who possess child pornography have also directly victimized a child and fifteen percent have attempted to entice a child over the internet.

Victims of child pornography often experience severe and lasting harm from the permanent memorialization of the crimes committed against them. Child victims endure depression, withdrawal, anger, and other psychological disorders. Each and every time such an image is viewed, traded, printed, or downloaded, the child in that image is victimized again.

Investigators and prosecutors report serious challenges with combating child pornography because offenders can act anonymously on the internet. Investigators track the trading of child pornography by using internet protocol addresses, which are unique identifiers that each computer is assigned when it accesses the internet. Under federal law, if an internet service provider is presented with a subpoena and an internet protocol address by law enforcement, the provider must turn over the names and addresses of account holders matched to it. Access to such information allows investigators to efficiently evaluate investigative leads and determine whether to request a warrant for a specific internet user. The legislature finds that in investigations of child exploitation, the use of a special inquiry judge is the appropriate process for obtaining subpoenas for the production of records from electronic communications providers under a less than probable cause standard while maintaining judicial oversight." [**2017 c 114 § 1.**]

Made in the USA
San Bernardino, CA
04 June 2019